PUNISHMENT

PUNISHMENT

A *Philosophy & Public Affairs* Reader

Edited by A. JOHN SIMMONS, MARSHALL COHEN, JOSHUA COHEN, and CHARLES R. BEITZ

Contributors

JEFFRIE G. MURPHY
ALAN H. GOLDMAN
WARREN QUINN
C. S. NINO
JEAN HAMPTON
MARTHA C. NUSSBAUM
MICHAEL DAVIS
A. JOHN SIMMONS
DAVID A. CONWAY
JEFFREY H. REIMAN
STEPHEN NATHANSON
ERNEST VAN DEN HAAG

Princeton University Press
Princeton, New Jersey

Library of Congress Cataloging-in-Publication Data

Punishment : a philosophy & public
affairs reader / edited by A. John
Simmons . . . [et al.].
p.   cm. — (Philosophy & public
affairs reader)
Includes bibliographical references.
ISBN 0-691-02956-3 (cl)
ISBN 0-691-02955-5 (pbk)
1. Punishment.   I. Simmons, A.
John, 1950–   .   II. Series.
LCC: 94-19058
K5103.P865   1994
303.3'6—dc20   94-19058
                                  CIP

Princeton University Press
books are printed on acid-free
paper and meet the guidelines
for permanence and durability
of the Committee on Production
Guidelines for Book Longevity
of the Council on Library
Resources
Printed in the United States
of America

The essays in this book appeared originally in
the quarterly journal *Philosophy & Public
Affairs,* published by Princeton University
Press.

Jeffrie G. Murphy, "Marxism and Retribution,"
P&PA 2, no. 3 (Spring 1973), copyright ©
1973 by Princeton University Press; Alan H.
Goldman, "The Paradox of Punishment," *P&PA*
9, no. 1 (Fall 1979), copyright © 1979 by
Princeton University Press; Warren Quinn,
"The Right to Threaten and the Right to
Punish," *P&PA* 14, no. 4 (Fall 1985), copyright
© 1985 by Princeton University Press; C. S.
Nino, "A Consensual Theory of Punishment,"
P&PA 12, no. 4 (Fall 1983), copyright © 1983
by Princeton University Press; Jean Hampton,
"The Moral Education Theory of Punishment,"
P&PA 13, no. 3 (Summer 1984), copyright ©
1984 by Princeton University Press; Martha C.
Nussbaum, "Equity and Mercy," *P&PA* 22, no.
2 (Spring 1993), copyright © 1993 by
Princeton University Press; Michael Davis,
"Harm and Retribution," *P&PA* 15, no. 3
(Summer 1986), copyright © 1986 by
Princeton University Press; A. John Simmons,
"Locke and the Right to Punish," *P&PA* 20, no.
4 (Fall 1991), copyright © 1991 by Princeton
University Press; David A. Conway, "Capital
Punishment and Deterrence: Some
Considerations in Dialogue Form," *P&PA* 3,
no. 4 (Summer 1974), copyright © 1974 by
Princeton University Press; Jeffrey H. Reiman,
"Justice, Civilization, and the Death Penalty:
Answering van den Haag," *P&PA* 14, no. 2
(Spring 1985), copyright © 1985 by Princeton
University Press; Stephen Nathanson, "Does
It Matter if the Death Penalty Is Arbitrarily
Administered?" *P&PA* 14, no. 2 (Spring 1985),
copyright © 1985 by Princeton University
Press; Ernest van den Haag, "Refuting Reiman
and Nathanson," *P&PA* 14, no. 2 (Spring
1985), copyright © 1985 by Princeton
University Press.

CONTENTS

INTRODUCTION

The problem of justifying legal punishment has remained at the heart of legal and social philosophy from the very earliest recorded philosophical texts to the most recent. This focus is not difficult to understand. Punishment is, after all, a practice that has been common to virtually all ordered societies, routinely regarded as essential to social stability. It is also, however, a practice that involves the calculated infliction on others of serious pain or loss, something we regard as morally prohibited under normal circumstances. So while most of us are confident that something like our current practice of punishment *can* be justified, we are especially eager in this case to see the justification actually produced; for here our societies might appear to be employing means (to desirable ends) of questionable legitimacy.

Despite this eagerness, philosophers (and other theorists) have yet to approach any general agreement about how legal punishment is to be justified or about whether various central aspects of our current practices even can be justified. But it remains important that philosophers continue their attempts to illuminate these subjects. This is important not simply because of our deep and natural desire to better understand the foundations of our own societies. It is also important because of the contribution such efforts can make to ongoing public debates about punishment, such as those touched off by highly publicized court cases in the United States during the past twenty-five years—debates about the justifiability of the death penalty and its various forms, about corporal punishment (as in the contemplated surgical castration of rapists), about life sentences without parole for three-time felons, and so on. The editors believe that the essays collected in this volume (all of which appeared previously in the pages of *Philosophy & Public Affairs*) mark a significant advance in our understanding of the justification of legal punishment. The essays offer not only important proposals for the improvement of familiar theories of punishment and compelling arguments against some long-respected positions, but also several powerful and quite original approaches to the whole question of justification.

The essays in Part I of this collection take up the most basic question of how any practice of punishment can be morally justified. The long history of the debate over this question contains many proposed answers, but philosophers commonly divide most of these answers into two great traditions of thought. Classical retributivism (standardly associated with the views of Kant and Hegel) maintains that punishment is justified because it gives wrongdoers what they deserve. When punishments "fit" the crimes for which they are imposed, punishment restores a kind of moral balance or harmony that the crime upset. As a purely "backward-looking" theory, retributivism thus finds the present justification for punishment solely in the nature and extent of the past immorality of the criminal. Classical deterrence theory (which is usually utilitarian in inspiration) holds that punishment is justified by its future good consequences and that kinds and amounts of punishment should be determined by what best facilitates happy social interaction. Since punishing criminals normally deters future criminal activity (both by the punished criminal himself and by others, impressed by the example of his punishment), and since it has as well other good consequences (such as disabling the criminal for a time, possibly rehabilitating him, gratifying injured parties, etc.), punishment is morally justified in those common instances where its good consequences outweigh the harm it does to the criminals.

Deterrence theorists often accuse retributivists of confusing their irrational thirst for vengeance with a rational ground for punishment. Retributivists often accuse deterrence theorists of being committed to punishing for societal benefit those who have a *right* not to be so punished (and so imagine utilitarian "scapegoat punishing" of the innocent or excessive, disproportionate punishing in order to "make a point"). The apparent defects of the classical theories have motivated (especially in this century) a number of "hybrid" or "mixed" theories of punishment, which aim to do justice to the insights of both traditions. Thus, for example, it has been proposed (most famously by H.L.A. Hart) that while the justification of the *practice* of punishment is utilitarian, the justification for the *distribution* of

specific punishments *within* that practice is retributive. Retributivist, deterrence (utilitarian), and hybrid theories of punishment are all explored in
the essays in Part I of this volume; but those essays go on as well to propose
new and different directions toward which those seeking a justification of
punishment might turn.

Jeffrie Murphy opens this section with a discussion of classical retributivism, with special emphasis on the views of Kant and Marx. After
defending certain objections to utilitarian theories, Murphy lays out the
"rational will" component of Kant's retributivism—that punishment and
autonomy are rendered consistent by the fact that each criminal actually
wills that those who commit such crimes be punished. But Murphy supports as well Marx's critique of retributivism as "formally correct" but "materially inadequate" to capitalist societies (societies that are nonreciprocal
and in fact necessitate the crimes they punish). Alan Goldman's essay
directs our attention to a basic "paradox" of punishment that must be dealt
with by any account of the justification of punishment. The force of both
retributivist and utilitarian arguments pushes us naturally, Goldman suggests, in the direction of a hybrid theory. But it seems impossible to satisfy
the demands of both theories in the way hybrid theories aspire to do. Given
the low probability that any particular criminal will actually be caught and
punished, effective deterrence of crime requires that we threaten criminals
with far more severe punishments than would actually "fit" (i.e., would be
equivalent in seriousness to) the crimes they commit. Such excessive
punishment seems at once unjustified (for retributivist reasons) and required (for utilitarian ones).

Warren Quinn's paper defends a development of deterrence theory that
appears to answer the traditional worry that such theories must sanction
violating rights (and using those punished as mere means to social ends).
We should, Quinn argues, think of the right to punish as derivable from the
prior right to *threaten* punishment, this latter right being itself derivable
from our rights of self-protection (which include, he claims, the right to
impose a cost on an offender *after* the offense). Punishment is not here
justified as a simple means to the end of criminal deterrence, as on standard deterrence views. Rather, the goal of deterrence justifies making
defensive threats under our rights of self-protection, rights accepted even
by most retributivists. C. S. Nino also attempts to make more acceptable
the deterrence ("social protection") view, again without giving in to retributivist arguments. We can, he argues, take criminals to have *consented*
to assume their liability to punishment, as long as their crimes are volun-

tary and known to be punishable. Punishment can thus be seen as a measure of social protection that typically does respect the autonomy and rights of those punished. Jean Hampton concludes this part of the collection by defending another theory of punishment that incorporates elements of both retributivist and deterrence theories, the theory she calls "the moral education theory of punishment" (and that she associates with the views of Plato and Hegel). Punishment is now to be seen as an important way of teaching criminals (and others) the moral wrongness of their actions. Such a justification for punishment, Hampton claims, takes seriously the importance of deterrence, and does so without treating those punished as mere means to that end, but also acknowledges that punishment must "fit" the crime (because this fit has special educational value).

The papers in Part II of the collection fall into two groups. The first two papers examine specific problems arising within one of the theories debated in Part I—classical retributivism. The third explores questions about the justifiability of particular aspects of our practice of punishment. Martha Nussbaum's contribution focuses on strict retributive justice and its apparent neglect of the particulars of individual cases. Through an extended discussion of Greek and Roman thought, classic and contemporary novels, and recent legal writings, Nussbaum argues that true justice requires equity, a nonretributive sensitivity to particulars. And this sensitivity, she claims, is closely associated with both literary imagination and the inclination toward leniency in punishing. Michael Davis aims in his article to improve retributivism by replacing the familiar "lex talionis" principle, usually found at the heart of retributivist theories. Davis proposes as a superior alternative his "unfair advantage principle," a principle that he claims makes more sense of our actual legal practices and gives us a more reasonable interpretation of making punishments proportionate to crimes. Crime, on Davis's version of retributivism, is a matter of gaining an unfair advantage over the law-abiding, and the punishment due a criminal is determined by calculating the relative value of that advantage.

John Simmons takes up in his paper another traditional problem in the theory of punishment, that of the right to punish. Here the question concerns justifications for a particular person's or group's being the one that actually imposes the appropriate punishments on wrongdoers. Through a discussion of Locke's theory of punishment, Simmons examines the claims that there is a natural right, shared by all persons, to punish wrongdoers in a state of nature, and that lawful governments in civil society possess a "monopoly" on the use of force. He defends modified Lockean versions of both claims, centered on a forfeiture account of the natural right to punish.

The subject of Part III is the justifiability of one particular kind of punishment—capital punishment. Because of the drastic and irreversible nature of capital punishment, its moral status has been actively debated in legal and political forums in many countries for at least a century and a half. But this debate has been nowhere more heated than in the United States during the past two decades. In 1972, of course, the U.S. Supreme Court ruled (in *Furman* v. *Georgia*) that capital punishment violated the Eighth Amendment ban on "cruel and unusual punishment" (at least as that punishment was then administered in Georgia and Texas). Justice Brennan argued that death-penalty statutes are in principle unconstitutional, for the death penalty (among other things) degrades human dignity, must be inflicted arbitrarily, and is an ineffective deterrent. The Court rejected Brennan's abolitionist position four years later (in *Gregg* v. *Georgia*), ruling that capital punishment is permissible if certain procedural safeguards (largely eroded in the years since 1976) were in place to insure proportionate and nondiscriminatory application. But as the papers in this part of the collection clearly illustrate, claims about degradation, arbitrariness, and deterrence continue to occupy center stage in the capital punishment debate.

In his contribution, David Conway explores what might be called "indirect" arguments for the deterrent value of the death penalty. Their proponents take these arguments to obviate reliance on empirical studies (of the effects the use of capital punishment has on murder rates). But given the still inconclusive nature of such studies, Conway's argument that the indirect strategies in fact fail without empirical support appears to require an answer from defenders of capital punishment. While Jeffrey Reiman agrees with Conway about the failure of the deterrence arguments, he argues for the abolition of the death penalty on quite different grounds. Reiman defends a version of retributivism, like many of the theorists he opposes. But his "proportional retributivism" allows that though death may be a just punishment for murderers, this in no way implies that it is *unjust* for society to impose instead some alternative severe punishment, if it regards this as morally preferable. And since, Reiman claims, refusing to impose on criminals the horrible punishment of death would have a civilizing effect on society, capital punishment ought to be abolished.

Stephen Nathanson's article examines the debate about the alleged arbitrariness of applications of the death penalty. He distinguishes the arbitrariness at issue in unreliable determinations of which criminals are the worst (and which ones thus deserve death) from the arbitrariness involved in allowing decisions about which capital criminals to execute to be guided by legally irrelevant categories, such as race. Since the former determinations tend to be influenced by biases of the latter sort, Nathanson argues, irreversible and unnecessary punishments like the death penalty are unjust. It is perhaps worth noting that shortly after the publication of Nathanson's article, the U.S. Supreme Court appeared to rule against the kind of argument he defends (in its 1987 decision in *McCleskey* v. *Kemp*). The Court maintained that in order to challenge the justice of his sentence, the defense needed to demonstrate racial bias in the particular trial and sentencing of McCleskey (a black man, executed in 1991). Reliable *general* statistics (showing that blacks are executed far more often than whites who commit similar crimes) should not, the Court argued, be taken to bear on the justice of executing any particular black criminal.

In our final selection Ernest van den Haag, a longtime proponent of capital punishment, defends his views against the abolitionists. While his claims are challenged in each of the three preceding papers, van den Haag here directly replies only to Reiman and Nathanson. He defends a more severe retributivism than Reiman's and rejects as circular Reiman's argument from the idea of civilization. Against Nathanson he argues that racially biased selection for execution of a few deserving criminals is no injustice to those executed. The injustice lies rather in the failure to execute the remaining deserving criminals. And in a curiously "Parfitian" turn, van den Haag also defends *timely* execution of the guilty, in order to avoid the possibility of unjustly punishing persons who have changed while in prison, and who may consequently no longer deserve their punishments.

PART I

Justifications of Punishment

JEFFRIE G. MURPHY   Marxism and Retribution

Punishment in general has been defended as a means either of amel-iorating or of intimidating. Now what right have you to punish me for the amelioration or intimidation of others? And besides there is his-tory—there is such a thing as statistics—which prove with the most complete evidence that since Cain the world has been neither intimi-dated nor ameliorated by punishment. Quite the contrary. From the point of view of abstract right, there is only one theory of punishment which recognizes human dignity in the abstract, and that is the theory of Kant, especially in the more rigid formula given to it by Hegel. Hegel says: "Punishment is the right of the criminal. It is an act of his own will. The violation of right has been proclaimed by the criminal as his own right. His crime is the negation of right. Punishment is the negation of this negation, and consequently an affirmation of right, solicited and forced upon the criminal by himself."

There is no doubt something specious in this formula, inasmuch as Hegel, instead of looking upon the criminal as the mere object, the slave of justice, elevates him to the position of a free and self-deter-

An earlier version of this essay was delivered to the Third Annual Colloquium in Philosophy ("The Philosophy of Punishment") at the University of Dayton in October, 1972. I am grateful to the Department of Philosophy at the Univer-sity of Dayton for inviting me to participate and to a number of persons at the Colloquium for the useful discussion on my paper at the time. I am also grateful to Anthony D. Woozley of the University of Virginia and to two of my colleagues, Robert M. Harnish and Francis V. Raab, for helping me to clarify the expression of my views.

*mined being. Looking, however, more closely into the matter, we dis-
cover that German idealism here, as in most other instances, has but
given a transcendental sanction to the rules of existing society. Is it
not a delusion to substitute for the individual with his real motives,
with multifarious social circumstances pressing upon him, the abstraction of "free will"—one among the many qualities of man for man
himself? . . . Is there not a necessity for deeply reflecting upon an
alteration of the system that breeds these crimes, instead of glorifying
the hangman who executes a lot of criminals to make room only for
the supply of new ones?*

Karl Marx, "Capital Punishment,"
New York Daily Tribune, *18 February 1853*[1]

Philosophers have written at great length about the moral problems
involved in punishing the innocent—particularly as these problems
raise obstacles to an acceptance of the moral theory of Utilitarianism.
Punishment of an innocent man in order to bring about good social
consequences is, at the very least, not always clearly wrong on utilitarian principles. This being so, utilitarian principles are then to be
condemned by any morality that may be called Kantian in character.
For punishing an innocent man, in Kantian language, involves using
that man as a mere means or instrument to some social good and is

---

1. In a sense, my paper may be viewed as an elaborate commentary on this
one passage, excerpted from a discussion generally concerned with the efficacy
of capital punishment in eliminating crime. For in this passage, Marx (to the
surprise of many I should think) expresses a certain admiration for the classical
retributive theory of punishment. Also (again surprisingly) he expresses this
admiration in a kind of language he normally avoids—i.e., the moral language
of rights and justice. He then, of course, goes on to reject the applicability of
that theory. But the question that initially perplexed me is the following: what
is the explanation of Marx's ambivalence concerning the retributive theory; why
is he both attracted and repelled by it? (This ambivalence is not shared, for
example, by utilitarians—who feel nothing but repulsion when the retributive
theory is even mentioned.) Now except for some very brief passages in *The Holy
Family*, Marx himself has nothing more to say on the topic of punishment beyond what is contained in this brief *Daily Tribune* article. Thus my essay is in
no sense an exercise in textual scholarship (there are not enough texts) but is
rather an attempt to construct an assessment of punishment, Marxist at least in
spirit, that might account for the ambivalence found in the quoted passage. My
main outside help comes, not from Marx himself, but from the writings of the
Marxist criminologist Willem Bonger.

thus not to treat him as an end in himself, in accord with his dignity or worth as a person.

The Kantian position on the issue of punishing the innocent, and the many ways in which the utilitarian might try to accommodate that position, constitute extremely well-worn ground in contemporary moral and legal philosophy.[2] I do not propose to wear the ground further by adding additional comments on the issue here. What I do want to point out, however, is something which seems to me quite obvious but which philosophical commentators on punishment have almost universally failed to see—namely, that problems of the very same kind and seriousness arise for the utilitarian theory with respect to the punishment of the guilty. For a utilitarian theory of punishment (Bentham's is a paradigm) must involve justifying punishment in terms of its social results—e.g., deterrence, incapacitation, and rehabilitation. And thus even a guilty man is, on this theory, being punished because of the instrumental value the action of punishment will have in the future. He is being used as a means to some future good—e.g., the deterrence of others. Thus those of a Kantian persuasion, who see the importance of worrying about the treatment of persons as mere means, must, it would seem, object just as strenuously to the punishment of the guilty on utilitarian grounds as to the punishment of the innocent. Indeed the former worry, in some respects, seems more serious. For a utilitarian can perhaps refine his theory in such a way that it does not commit him to the punishment of the innocent. However, if he is to approve of punishment at all, he must approve of punishing the guilty in at least some cases. This makes the worry about punishing the guilty formidable indeed, and it is odd that this has gone generally unnoticed.[3] It has generally been assumed that if the utilitarian theory can just avoid entailing the permissibility of punishing the innocent, then all objections of a Kantian character to the theory will have been met. This seems to me simply not to be the case.

2. Many of the leading articles on this topic have been reprinted in *The Philosophy of Punishment*, ed. H. B. Acton (London, 1969). Those papers not included are cited in Acton's excellent bibliography.

3. One writer who has noticed this is Richard Wasserstrom. See his "Why Punish the Guilty?" *Princeton University Magazine* 20 (1964), pp. 14-19.

What the utilitarian theory really cannot capture, I would suggest, is the notion of persons having rights. And it is just this notion that is central to any Kantian outlook on morality. Any Kantian can certainly agree that punishing persons (guilty or innocent) may have either good or bad or indifferent consequences and that insofar as the consequences (whether in a particular case or for an institution) are good, this is something in favor of punishment. But the Kantian will maintain that this consequential outlook, important as it may be, leaves out of consideration entirely that which is most morally crucial —namely, the question of rights. Even if punishment of a person would have good consequences, what gives us (i.e., society) the moral right to inflict it? If we have such a right, what is its origin or derivation? What social circumstances must be present for it to be applicable? What does this right to punish tell us about the status of the person to be punished—e.g., how are we to analyze his rights, the sense in which he must deserve to be punished, his obligations in the matter? It is this family of questions which any Kantian must regard as morally central and which the utilitarian cannot easily accommodate into his theory. And it is surely this aspect of Kant's and Hegel's retributivism, this seeing of rights as basic, which appeals to Marx in the quoted passage. As Marx himself puts it: "What right have you to punish me for the amelioration or intimidation of others?" And he further praises Hegel for seeing that punishment, if justified, must involve respecting the rights of the person to be punished.[4] Thus Marx, like Kant, seems prepared to draw the important distinction between (a) what it would be good to do on grounds of utility and (b) what we have a right to do. Since we do not always have the right to do what it would be good to do, this distinction is of the greatest moral importance; and missing the distinction is the Achilles heel of all forms of Utilitarianism. For consider the following example: A Jehovah's Witness needs a blood

4. Marx normally avoids the language of rights and justice because he regards such language to be corrupted by bourgeois ideology. However, if we think very broadly of what an appeal to rights involves—namely, a protest against unjustified coercion—there is no reason why Marx may not legitimately avail himself on occasion of this way of speaking. For there is surely at least some moral overlap between Marx's protests against exploitation and the evils of a division of labor, for example, and the claims that people have a right not to be used solely for the benefit of others and a right to self-determination.

transfusion in order to live; but, because of his (we can agree absurd) religious belief that such transfusions are against God's commands, he instructs his doctor not to give him one. Here is a case where it would seem to be good or for the best to give the transfusion and yet, at the very least, it is highly doubtful that the doctor has a right to give it. This kind of distinction is elementary, and any theory which misses it is morally degenerate.[5]

To move specifically to the topic of punishment: How exactly does retributivism (of a Kantian or Hegelian variety) respect the rights of persons? Is Marx really correct on this? I believe that he is. I believe that retributivism can be formulated in such a way that it is the only morally defensible theory of punishment. I also believe that arguments, which may be regarded as Marxist at least in spirit, can be formulated which show that social conditions as they obtain in most societies make this form of retributivism largely inapplicable within those societies. As Marx says, in those societies retributivism functions merely to provide a "transcendental sanction" for the status quo. If this is so, then the only morally defensible theory of punishment is largely inapplicable in modern societies. The consequence: modern societies largely lack the moral right to punish.[6] The upshot is that a Kantian moral theory (which in general seems to me correct) and a Marxist analysis of society (which, if properly qualified, also seems to me correct) produces a radical and not merely reformist attack not merely on the scope and manner of punishment in our society but on the institution of punishment itself. Institutions of punishment constitute

5. I do not mean to suggest that under no conceivable circumstances would the doctor be justified in giving the transfusion even though, in one clear sense, he had no right to do it. If, for example, the Jehovah's Witness was a key man whose survival was necessary to prevent the outbreak of a destructive war, we might well regard the transfusion as on the whole justified. However, even in such a case, a morally sensitive man would have to regretfully realize that he was sacrificing an important principle. Such a realization would be impossible (because inconsistent) for a utilitarian, for his theory admits only one principle —namely, do that which on the whole maximizes utility. An occupational disease of utilitarians is a blindness to the possibility of genuine moral dilemmas—i.e., a blindness to the possibility that important moral principles can conflict in ways that are not obviously resolvable by a rational decision procedure.

6. I qualify my thesis by the word "largely" to show at this point my realization, explored in more detail later, that no single theory can account for all criminal behavior.

what Bernard Harrison has called structural injustices[7] and are, in the absence of a major social change, to be resisted by all who take human rights to be morally serious—i.e., regard them as genuine action guides and not merely as rhetorical devices which allow people to morally sanctify institutions which in fact can only be defended on grounds of social expediency.

Stating all of this is one thing and proving it, of course, is another. Whether I can ever do this is doubtful. That I cannot do it in one brief article is certain. I cannot, for example, here defend in detail my belief that a generally Kantian outlook on moral matters is correct.[8] Thus I shall content myself for the present with attempting to render at least plausible two major claims involved in the view that I have outlined thus far: (1) that a retributive theory, in spite of the bad press that it has received, is a morally credible theory of punishment—that it can be, H. L. A. Hart to the contrary,[9] a reasonable general justifying aim of punishment; and (2) that a Marxist analysis of a society can undercut the practical applicability of that theory.

THE RIGHT OF THE STATE TO PUNISH

It is strong evidence of the influence of a utilitarian outlook in moral and legal matters that discussions of punishment no longer involve a consideration of the right of anyone to inflict it. Yet in the eighteenth and nineteenth centuries, this tended to be regarded as the central aspect of the problem meriting philosophical consideration. Kant, Hegel, Bosanquet, Green—all tended to entitle their chapters on punishment along the lines explicitly used by Green: "The Right of the State to Punish."[10] This is not just a matter of terminology but reflects, I think, something of deeper philosophical substance. These theorists, unlike the utilitarian, did not view man as primarily a maximizer of personal satisfactions—a maximizer of individual utilities. They were

7. Bernard Harrison, "Violence and the Rule of Law," in *Violence*, ed. Jerome A. Shaffer (New York, 1971), pp. 139-176.

8. I have made a start toward such a defense in my "The Killing of the Innocent," forthcoming in *The Monist* 57, no. 4 (October 1973).

9. H. L. A. Hart, "Prolegomenon to the Principles of Punishment," from *Punishment and Responsibility* (Oxford, 1968), pp. 1-27.

10. Thomas Hill Green, *Lectures on the Principles of Political Obligation* (1885), (Ann Arbor, 1967), pp. 180-205.

inclined, in various ways, to adopt a different model of man—man as a free or spontaneous creator, man as autonomous. (Marx, it may be noted, is much more in line with this tradition than with the utilitarian outlook.)[11] This being so, these theorists were inclined to view punishment (a certain kind of coercion by the state) as not merely a causal contributor to pain and suffering, but rather as presenting at least a prima facie challenge to the values of autonomy and personal dignity and self-realization—the very values which, in their view, the state existed to nurture. The problem as they saw it, therefore, was that of reconciling punishment as state coercion with the value of individual autonomy. (This is an instance of the more general problem which Robert Paul Wolff has called the central problem of political philosophy—namely, how is individual moral autonomy to be reconciled with legitimate political authority?)[12] This kind of problem, which I am inclined to agree is quite basic, cannot even be formulated intelligibly from a utilitarian perspective. Thus the utilitarian cannot even see the relevance of Marx's charge: Even if punishment has wonderful social consequences, what gives anyone the right to inflict it on me?

Now one fairly typical way in which others acquire rights over us is by our own consent. If a neighbor locks up my liquor cabinet to protect me against my tendencies to drink too heavily, I might well regard this as a presumptuous interference with my own freedom, no matter how good the result intended or accomplished. He had no right to do it and indeed violated my rights in doing it. If, on the other hand, I had asked him to do this or had given my free consent to his suggestion that he do it, the same sort of objection on my part would be quite out of order. I had given him the right to do it, and he had the right to do it. In doing it, he violated no rights of mine—even if, at the time of his doing it, I did not desire or want the action to be performed. Here then we seem to have a case where my autonomy may be regarded as intact even though a desire of mine is thwarted. For there is a sense in which the thwarting of the desire can be imputed to me

11. For an elaboration of this point, see Steven Lukes, "Alienation and Anomie," in *Philosophy, Politics and Society* (Third Series), ed. Peter Laslett and W. G. Runciman (Oxford, 1967), pp. 134-156.

12. Robert Paul Wolff, *In Defense of Anarchism* (New York, 1970).

(my choice or decision) and not to the arbitrary intervention of another.

How does this apply to our problem? The answer, I think, is obvious. What is needed, in order to reconcile my undesired suffering of punishment at the hands of the state with my autonomy (and thus with the state's right to punish me), is a political theory which makes the state's decision to punish me in some sense my own decision. If I have willed my own punishment (consented to it, agreed to it) then—even if at the time I happen not to desire it—it can be said that my autonomy and dignity remain intact. Theories of the General Will and Social Contract theories are two such theories which attempt this reconciliation of autonomy with legitimate state authority (including the right or authority of the state to punish). Since Kant's theory happens to incorporate elements of both, it will be useful to take it for our sample.

MORAL RIGHTS AND THE RETRIBUTIVE THEORY OF PUNISHMENT

To justify government or the state is necessarily to justify at least some coercion.[13] This poses a problem for someone, like Kant, who maintains that human freedom is the ultimate or most sacred moral value. Kant's own attempt to justify the state, expressed in his doctrine of the *moral title* (*Befugnis*),[14] involves an argument that coercion is justified only in so far as it is used to prevent invasions against freedom. Freedom itself is the only value which can be used to limit freedom, for the appeal to any other value (e.g., utility) would under-

13. In this section, I have adapted some of my previously published material: *Kant: The Philosophy of Right* (London, 1970), pp. 109-112 and 140-144; "Three Mistakes About Retributivism," *Analysis* (April 1971): 166-169; and "Kant's Theory of Criminal Punishment," in *Proceedings of the Third International Kant Congress*, ed. Lewis White Beck (Dordrecht, 1972), pp. 434-441. I am perfectly aware that Kant's views on the issues to be considered here are often obscure and inconsistent—e.g., the analysis of "willing one's own punishment" which I shall later quote from Kant occurs in a passage the primary purpose of which is to argue that the idea of "willing one's own punishment" makes no sense! My present objective, however, is not to attempt accurate Kant scholarship. My goal is rather to build upon some remarks of Kant's which I find philosophically suggestive.

14. Immanuel Kant, *The Metaphysical Elements of Justice* (1797), trans. John Ladd (Indianapolis, 1965), pp. 35ff.

mine the ultimate status of the value of freedom. Thus Kant attempts
to establish the claim that some forms of coercion (as opposed to
violence) are morally permissible because, contrary to appearance,
they are really consistent with rational freedom. The argument, in
broad outline, goes in the following way. Coercion may keep people
from doing what they desire or want to do on a particular occasion
and is thus prima facie wrong. However, such coercion can be shown
to be morally justified (and thus not absolutely wrong) if it can be
established that the coercion is such that it could have been rationally
willed even by the person whose desire is interfered with:

> Accordingly, when it is said that a creditor has a right to demand
> from his debtor the payment of a debt, this does not mean that he
> can *persuade* the debtor that his own reason itself obligates him to
> this performance; on the contrary, to say that he has such a right
> means only that the use of coercion to make anyone do this is en-
> tirely compatible with everyone's freedom, *including the freedom
> of the debtor*, in accordance with universal laws.[15]

Like Rousseau, Kant thinks that it is only in a context governed by
social practice (particularly civil government and its Rule of Law)
that this can make sense. Laws may require of a person some action
that he does not desire to perform. This is not a violent invasion of his
freedom, however, if it can be shown that in some antecedent position
of choice (what John Rawls calls "the original position"),[16] he would
have been rational to adopt a Rule of Law (and thus run the risk of
having some of his desires thwarted) rather than some other alternative arrangement like the classical State of Nature. This is, indeed,
the only sense that Kant is able to make of classical Social Contract
theories. Such theories are to be viewed, not as historical fantasies,
but as ideal models of rational decision. For what these theories
actually claim is that the only coercive institutions that are morally
justified are those which a group of rational beings could agree to
adopt in a position of having to pick social institutions to govern their
relations:

15. *Ibid.*, p. 37.
16. John Rawls, "Justice as Fairness," *The Philosophical Review* 67 (1958):
164-194; and *A Theory of Justice* (Cambridge, Mass., 1971), especially pp. 17-22.

The contract, which is called *contractus originarius*, or *pactum sociale* . . . need not be assumed to be a fact, indeed it is not [even possible as such. To suppose that would be like insisting] that before anyone would be bound to respect such a civic constitution, it be proved first of all from history that a people, whose rights and obligations we have entered into as their descendants, had *once upon a time* executed such an act and had left a reliable document or instrument, either orally or in writing, concerning this contract. Instead, this contract is a *mere idea* of reason which has undoubted practical reality; namely, to oblige every legislator to give us laws in such a manner that the laws *could* have originated from the united will of the entire people and to regard every subject in so far as he is a citizen as though he had consented to such [an expression of the general] will. This is the testing stone of the rightness of every publicly-known law, for if a law were such that it was impossible for an entire people to give consent to it (as for example a law that a certain class of subjects, by inheritance, should have the privilege of the *status of lords*), then such a law is unjust. On the other hand, if there is a mere *possibility* that a people might consent to a (certain) law, then it is a duty to consider that the law is just even though at the moment the people might be in such a position or have a point of view that would result in their refusing to give their consent to it if asked.[17]

The problem of organizing a state, however hard it may seem, can be solved even for a race of devils, if only they are intelligent. The problem is: "Given a multiple of rational beings requiring universal laws for their preservation, but each of whom is secretly inclined to exempt himself from them, to establish a constitution in such a way that, although their private intentions conflict, they check each other, with the result that their public conduct is the same as if they had no such intentions."[18]

17. Immanuel Kant, "Concerning the Common Saying: This May be True in Theory but Does Not Apply in Practice (1793)," in *The Philosophy of Kant*, ed. and trans. Carl J. Friedrich (New York, 1949), pp. 421-422.

18. Immanuel Kant, *Perpetual Peace* (1795), trans. Lewis White Beck in the Kant anthology *On History* (Indianapolis 1963), p. 112.

Though Kant's doctrine is superficially similar to Mill's later self-protection principle, the substance is really quite different. For though Kant in some general sense argues that coercion is justified only to prevent harm to others, he understands by "harm" only certain invasions of freedom and not simply disutility. Also, his defense of the principle is not grounded, as is Mill's, on its utility. Rather it is to be regarded as a principle of justice, by which Kant means a principle that rational beings could adopt in a situation of mutual choice:

> The concept [of justice] applies only to the relationship of a will to another person's will, not to his wishes or desires (or even just his needs) which are the concern of acts of benevolence and charity. . . . In applying the concept of justice we take into consideration only the form of the relationship between the wills insofar as they are regarded as free, and whether the action of one of them can be conjoined with the freedom of the other in accordance with universal law. Justice is therefore the aggregate of those conditions under which the will of one person can be conjoined with the will of another in accordance with a universal law of freedom.[19]

How does this bear specifically on punishment? Kant, as everyone knows, defends a strong form of a retributive theory of punishment. He holds that guilt merits, and is a sufficient condition for, the infliction of punishment. And this claim has been universally condemned—particularly by utilitarians—as primitive, unenlightened and barbaric.

But why is it so condemned? Typically, the charge is that infliction of punishment on such grounds is nothing but pointless vengeance. But what is meant by the claim that the infliction is "pointless"? If "pointless" is tacitly being analyzed as "disutilitarian," then the whole question is simply being begged. You cannot refute a retributive theory merely by noting that it is a retributive theory and not a utilitarian theory. This is to confuse redescription with refutation and involves an argument whose circularity is not even complicated enough to be interesting.

19. Immanuel Kant, *The Metaphysical Elements of Justice*, p. 34.

Why, then, might someone claim that guilt merits punishment? Such a claim might be made for either of two very different reasons. (1) Someone (e.g., a Moral Sense theorist) might maintain that the claim is a primitive and unanalyzable proposition that is morally ultimate—that we can just intuit the "fittingness" of guilt and punishment. (2) It might be maintained that the retributivist claim is demanded by a general theory of political obligation which is more plausible than any alternative theory. Such a theory will typically provide a technical analysis of such concepts as crime and punishment and will thus not regard the retributivist claim as an indisputable primitive. It will be argued for as a kind of theorem within the system.

Kant's theory is of the second sort. He does not opt for retributivism as a bit of intuitive moral knowledge. Rather he offers a theory of punishment that is based on his general view that political obligation is to be analyzed, quasi-contractually, in terms of reciprocity. If the law is to remain just, it is important to guarantee that those who disobey it will not gain an unfair advantage over those who do obey voluntarily. It is important that no man profit from his own criminal wrongdoing, and a certain kind of "profit" (i.e., not bearing the burden of self-restraint) is intrinsic to criminal wrongdoing. Criminal punishment, then, has as its object the restoration of a proper balance between benefit and obedience. The criminal himself has no complaint, because he has rationally consented to or willed his own punishment. That is, those very rules which he has broken work, when they are obeyed by others, to his own advantage as a citizen. He would have chosen such rules for himself and others in the original position of choice. And, since he derives and voluntarily accepts benefits from their operation, he owes his own obedience as a debt to his fellow-citizens for their sacrifices in maintaining them. If he chooses not to sacrifice by exercising self-restraint and obedience, this is tantamount to his choosing to sacrifice in another way—namely, by paying the prescribed penalty:

> A transgression of the public law that makes him who commits it unfit to be a citizen is called . . . a crime. . . .
>
> What kind and what degree of punishment does public legal justice adopt as its principle and standard? None other than the principle

of equality (illustrated by the pointer of the scales of justice), that is, the principle of not treating one side more favorably than the other. Accordingly, any undeserved evil that you inflict on someone else among the people is one you do to yourself. If you vilify him, you vilify yourself; if you steal from him, you steal from yourself; if you kill him, you kill yourself. . . .

To say, "I will to be punished if I murder someone" can mean nothing more than, "I submit myself along with everyone else to those laws which, if there are any criminals among the people, will naturally include penal laws."[20]

This analysis of punishment regards it as a debt owed to the law-abiding members of one's community; and, once paid, it allows re-entry into the community of good citizens on equal status.

Now some of the foregoing no doubt sounds implausible or even obscurantist. Since criminals typically desire not to be punished, what can it really mean to say that they have, as rational men, really willed their own punishment? Or that, as Hegel says, they have a right to it? Perhaps a comparison of the traditional retributivist views with those of a contemporary Kantian—John Rawls—will help to make the points clearer.[21] Rawls (like Kant) does not regard the idea of the social contract as an historical fact. It is rather a model of rational decision. Respecting a man's autonomy, at least on one view, is not respecting what he now happens, however uncritically, to desire; rather it is to respect what he desires (or would desire) as a rational man. (On Rawls's view, for example, rational men are said to be unmoved by feelings of envy; and thus it is not regarded as unjust to a person or a violation of his rights, if he is placed in a situation where he will envy another's advantage or position. A rational man

20. *Ibid.*, pp. 99, 101, and 105, in the order quoted.
21. In addition to the works on justice by Rawls previously cited, the reader should consult the following for Rawls's application of his general theory to the problem of political obligation: John Rawls, "Legal Obligation and the Duty of Fair Play," in *Law and Philosophy*, ed. Sidney Hook (New York, 1964), pp. 3-18. This has been reprinted in my anthology *Civil Disobedience and Violence* (Belmont, Cal., 1971), pp. 39-52. For a direct application of a similar theory to the problem of punishment, see Herbert Morris, "Persons and Punishment," *The Monist* 52, no. 4 (October 1968): 475-501.

would object, and thus would never consent to, a practice where another might derive a benefit from a position at his expense. He would not, however, envy the position *simpliciter*, would not regard the position as itself a benefit.) Now on Kant's (and also, I think, on Rawls's) view, a man is genuinely free or autonomous only in so far as he is rational. Thus it is man's rational will that is to be respected.

Now this idea of treating people, not as they in fact say that they want to be treated, but rather in terms of how you think they would, if rational, will to be treated, has obviously dangerous (indeed Fascistic) implications. Surely we want to avoid cramming indignities down the throats of people with the offhand observation that, no matter how much they scream, they are really rationally willing every bit of it. It would be particularly ironic for such arbitrary repression to come under the mask of respecting autonomy. And yet, most of us would agree, the general principle (though subject to abuse) also has important applications—for example, preventing the suicide of a person who, in a state of psychotic depression, wants to kill himself. What we need, then, to make the general view work, is a check on its arbitrary application; and a start toward providing such a check would be in the formulation of a public, objective theory of rationality and rational willing. It is just this, according to both Kant and Rawls, which the social contract theory can provide. On this theory, a man may be said to rationally will X if, and only if, X is called for by a rule that the man would necessarily have adopted in the original position of choice—i.e., in a position of coming together with others to pick rules for the regulation of their mutual affairs. This avoids arbitrariness because, according to Kant and Rawls at any rate, the question of whether such a rule would be picked in such a position is objectively determinable given certain (in their view) noncontroversial assumptions about human nature and rational calculation. Thus I can be said to will my own punishment if, in an antecedent position of choice, I and my fellows would have chosen institutions of punishment as the most rational means of dealing with those who might break the other generally beneficial social rules that had been adopted.

Let us take an analogous example: I may not, in our actual society, desire to treat a certain person fairly—e.g., I may not desire to honor a contract I have made with him because so doing would adversely affect my own self-interest. However, if I am forced to honor the contract by the state, I cannot charge (1) that the state has no right to do this, or (2) that my rights or dignity are being violated by my being coerced into doing it. Indeed, it can be said that I rationally will it since, in the original position, I would have chosen rules of justice (rather than rules of utility) and the principle, "contracts are to be honored," follows from the rules of justice.

Coercion and autonomy are thus reconciled, at least apparently. To use Marx's language, we may say (as Marx did in the quoted passage) that one virtue of the retributive theory, at least as expounded by Kant and Hegel on lines of the General Will and Social Contract theory, is that it manifests at least a formal or abstract respect for rights, dignity, and autonomy. For it at least recognizes the importance of attempting to construe state coercion in such a way that it is a product of each man's rational will. Utilitarian deterrence theory does not even satisfy this formal demand.

The question of primary interest to Marx, of course, is whether this formal respect also involves a material respect; i.e., does the theory have application in concrete fact in the actual social world in which we live? Marx is confident that it does not, and it is to this sort of consideration that I shall now pass.

ALIENATION AND PUNISHMENT

What can the philosopher learn from Marx? This question is a part of a more general question: What can philosophy learn from social science? Philosophers, it may be thought, are concerned to offer a priori theories, theories about how certain concepts are to be analyzed and their application justified. And what can the mundane facts that are the object of behavioral science have to do with exalted theories of this sort?

The answer, I think, is that philosophical theories, though not themselves empirical, often have such a character that their intelligibility depends upon certain empirical presuppositions. For example, our moral language presupposes, as Hart has argued,[22] that we are vulnerable creatures—creatures who can harm and be harmed by each

22. H. L. A. Hart, *The Concept of Law* (Oxford, 1961), pp. 189-195.

other. Also, as I have argued elsewhere,[23] our moral language presupposes that we all share certain psychological characteristics—e.g., sympathy, a sense of justice, and the capacity to feel guilt, shame, regret, and remorse. If these facts were radically different (if, as Hart imagines for example, we all developed crustaceanlike exoskeletons and thus could not harm each other), the old moral language, and the moral theories which employ it, would lack application to the world in which we live. To use a crude example, moral prohibitions against killing presuppose that it is in fact possible for us to kill each other.

Now one of Marx's most important contributions to social philosophy, in my judgment, is simply his insight that philosophical theories are in peril if they are constructed in disregard of the nature of the empirical world to which they are supposed to apply.[24] A theory may be formally correct (i.e., coherent, or true for some possible world) but materially incorrect (i.e., inapplicable to the actual world in which we live). This insight, then, establishes the relevance of empirical research to philosophical theory and is a part, I think, of what Marx meant by "the union of theory and practice." Specifically relevant to the argument I want to develop are the following two related points:

(1) The theories of moral, social, political and legal philosophy presuppose certain empirical propositions about man and society. If these propositions are false, then the theory (even if coherent or formally correct) is materially defective and practically inapplicable. (For example, if persons tempted to engage in criminal conduct do not in fact tend to calculate carefully the consequences of their actions, this renders much of deterrence theory suspect.)

23. Jeffrie G. Murphy, "Moral Death: A Kantian Essay on Psychopathy," *Ethics* 82, no. 4 (July 1972): 284-298.
24. Banal as this point may seem, it could be persuasively argued that all Enlightenment political theory (e.g., that of Hobbes, Locke and Kant) is built upon ignoring it. For example, once we have substantial empirical evidence concerning how democracies really work in fact, how sympathetic can we really be to classical theories for the justification of democracy? For more on this, see C. B. Macpherson, "The Maximization of Democracy," in *Philosophy, Politics and Society* (Third Series), ed. Peter Laslett and W. G. Runciman (Oxford, 1967), pp. 83-103. This article is also relevant to the point raised in note 11 above.

(2) Philosophical theories may put forth as a necessary truth that which is in fact merely an historically conditioned contingency. (For example, Hobbes argued that all men are necessarily selfish and competitive. It is possible, as many Marxists have argued, that Hobbes was really doing nothing more than elevating to the status of a necessary truth the contingent fact that the people around him in the capitalistic society in which he lived were in fact selfish and competitive.)[25]

In outline, then, I want to argue the following: that when Marx challenges the material adequacy of the retributive theory of punishment, he is suggesting (a) that it presupposes a certain view of man and society that is false and (b) that key concepts involved in the support of the theory (e.g., the concept of "rationality" in Social Contract theory) are given analyses which, though they purport to be necessary truths, are in fact mere reflections of certain historical circumstances.

In trying to develop this case, I shall draw primarily upon Willem Bonger's *Criminality and Economic Conditions* (1916), one of the few sustained Marxist analyses of crime and punishment.[26] Though I shall not have time here to qualify my support of Bonger in certain necessary ways, let me make clear that I am perfectly aware that his analysis is not the whole story. (No monolithic theory of anything so diverse as criminal behavior could be the whole story.) However, I am convinced that he has discovered part of the story. And my point is simply that insofar as Bonger's Marxist analysis is correct, then to that same degree is the retributive theory of punishment inapplicable in modern societies. (Let me emphasize again exactly how this objection

25. This point is well developed in C. B. Macpherson, *The Political Theory of Possessive Individualism* (Oxford, 1962). In a sense, this point affects even the formal correctness of a theory. For it demonstrates an empirical source of corruption in the analyses of the very concepts in the theory.

26. The writings of Willem Adriaan Bonger (1876-1940), a Dutch criminologist, have fallen into totally unjustified neglect in recent years. Anticipating contemporary sociological theories of crime, he was insisting that criminal behavior is in the province of normal psychology (though abnormal society) at a time when most other writers were viewing criminality as a symptom of psychopathology. His major works are: *Criminality and Economic Conditions* (Boston, 1916); *An Introduction to Criminology* (London, 1936); and *Race and Crime* (New York, 1943).

to retributivism differs from those traditionally offered. Traditionally, retributivism has been rejected because it conflicts with the moral theory of its opponent, usually a utilitarian. This is not the kind of objection I want to develop. Indeed, with Marx, I have argued that the retributive theory of punishment grows out of the moral theory—Kantianism—which seems to me generally correct. The objection I want to pursue concerns the empirical falsity of the factual presuppositions of the theory. If the empirical presuppositions of the theory are false, this does indeed render its application immoral. But the immorality consists, not in a conflict with some other moral theory, but immorality in terms of a moral theory that is at least close in spirit to the very moral theory which generates retributivism itself—i.e., a theory of justice.)[27]

To return to Bonger. Put bluntly, his theory is as follows. Criminality has two primary sources: (1) need and deprivation on the part of disadvantaged members of society, and (2) motives of greed and selfishness that are generated and reinforced in competitive capitalistic societies. Thus criminality is economically based—either directly in the case of crimes from need, or indirectly in the case of crimes growing out of motives or psychological states that are encouraged and developed in capitalistic society. In Marx's own language, such an economic system alienates men from themselves and from each other. It alienates men from themselves by creating motives and needs that are not "truly human." It alienates men from their fellows by encouraging a kind of competitiveness that forms an obstacle to the development of genuine communities to replace mere social aggregates.[28] And in Bonger's thought, the concept of community is

27. I say "at least in spirit" to avoid begging the controversial question of whether Marx can be said to embrace a theory of justice. Though (as I suggested in note 4) much of Marx's own evaluative rhetoric seems to overlap more traditional appeals to rights and justice (and a total lack of sympathy with anything like Utilitarianism), it must be admitted that he also frequently ridicules at least the terms "rights" and "justice" because of their apparent entrenchment in bourgeois ethics. For an interesting discussion of this issue, see Allen W. Wood, "The Marxian Critique of Justice," *Philosophy & Public Affairs* 1, no. 3 (Spring 1972): 244-282.

28. The importance of community is also, I think, recognized in Gabriel de Tarde's notion of "social similarity" as a condition of criminal responsibility. See his *Penal Philosophy* (Boston, 1912). I have drawn on de Tarde's general account in my "Moral Death: A Kantian Essay on Psychopathy."

central. He argues that moral relations and moral restraint are possible only in genuine communities characterized by bonds of sympathetic identification and mutual aid resting upon a perception of
common humanity. All this he includes under the general rubric of
reciprocity.[29] In the absence of reciprocity in this rich sense, moral
relations among men will break down and criminality will increase.[30]
Within bourgeois society, then, crimes are to be regarded as normal,
and not psychopathological, acts. That is, they grow out of need,
greed, indifference to others, and sometimes even a sense of indig-
nation—all, alas, perfectly typical human motives.

To appreciate the force of Bonger's analysis, it is necessary to read
his books and grasp the richness and detail of the evidence he provides
for his claims. Here I can but quote a few passages at random to give
the reader a tantalizing sample in the hope that he will be encouraged
to read further into Bonger's own text:

> The abnormal element in crime is a social, not a biological, element.
> With the exception of a few special cases, crime lies within the
> boundaries of normal psychology and physiology. . . .

> We clearly see that [the egoistic tendencies of the present economic
> system and of its consequences] are very strong. Because of these
> tendencies the social instinct of man is not greatly developed; they
> have weakened the moral force in man which combats the inclina-
> tion towards egoistic acts, and hence toward the crimes which are
> one form of these acts. . . . Compassion for the misfortunes of

29. By "reciprocity" Bonger intends something which includes, but is much
richer than, a notion of "fair trading or bargaining" that might initially be read
into the term. He also has in mind such things as sympathetic identification
with others and tendencies to provide mutual aid. Thus, for Bonger, reciprocity
and egoism have a strong tendency to conflict. I mention this lest Bonger's
notion of reciprocity be too quickly identified with the more restricted notion
found in, for example, Kant and Rawls.

30. It is interesting how greatly Bonger's analysis differs from classical deterrence theory—e.g., that of Bentham. Bentham, who views men as machines
driven by desires to attain pleasure and avoid pain, tends to regard terror as the
primary restraint against crime. Bonger believes that, at least in a healthy society, moral motives would function as a major restraint against crime. When
an environment that destroys moral motivation is created, even terror (as statistics tend to confirm) will not eradicate crime.

others inevitably becomes blunted, and a great part of morality consequently disappears. . . .

As a consequence of the present environment, man has become very egoistic and hence more *capable of crime*, than if the environment had developed the germs of altruism. . . .

There can be no doubt that one of the factors of criminality among the bourgeoisie is bad [moral] education. . . . The children—speaking of course in a general way—are brought up with the idea that they must succeed, no matter how; the aim of life is presented to them as getting money and shining in the world. . . .

Poverty (taken in the sense of absolute want) kills the social sentiments in man, destroys in fact all relations between men. He who is abandoned by all can no longer have any feeling for those who have left him to his fate. . . .

[Upon perception that the system tends to legalize the egoistic actions of the bourgeoisie and to penalize those of the proletariat], the oppressed resort to means which they would otherwise scorn. As we have seen above, the basis of the social feeling is reciprocity. As soon as this is trodden under foot by the ruling class the social sentiments of the oppressed become weak towards them. . . .[31]

The essence of this theory has been summed up by Austin J. Turk. "Criminal behavior," he says, "is almost entirely attributable to the combination of egoism and an environment in which opportunities are not equitably distributed."[32]

31. *Introduction to Criminology*, pp. 75-76, and *Criminality and Economic Conditions*, pp. 532, 402, 483-484, 436, and 407, in the order quoted. Bonger explicitly attacks Hobbes: "The adherents of [Hobbes's theory] have studied principally men who live under capitalism, or under civilization; their correct conclusion has been that egoism is the predominant characteristic of these men, and they have adopted the simplest explanation of the phenomenon and say that this trait is inborn." If Hobbists can cite Freud for modern support, Bonger can cite Darwin. For, as Darwin had argued in the *Descent of Man*, men would not have survived as a species if they had not initially had considerably greater social sentiments than Hobbes allows them.

32. Austin J. Turk, in the Introduction to his abridged edition of Bonger's *Criminality and Economic Conditions* (Bloomington, 1969), p. 14.

No doubt this claim will strike many as extreme and intemperate—a sample of the old-fashioned Marxist rhetoric that sophisticated intellectuals have outgrown. Those who are inclined to react in this way might consider just one sobering fact: of the 1.3 million criminal offenders handled each day by some agency of the United States correctional system, the vast majority (80 percent on some estimates) are members of the lowest 15-percent income level—that percent which is below the "poverty level" as defined by the Social Security Administration.[33] Unless one wants to embrace the belief that all these people are poor because they are bad, it might be well to reconsider Bonger's suggestion that many of them are "bad" because they are poor.[34] At any rate, let us suppose for purposes of discussion that Bonger's picture of the relation between crime and economic conditions is generally accurate. At what points will this challenge the credentials of the contractarian retributive theory as

33. Statistical data on characteristics of offenders in America are drawn primarily from surveys by the Bureau of Census and the National Council on Crime and Delinquency. While there is of course wide disagreement on how such data are to be interpreted, there is no serious disagreement concerning at least the general accuracy of statistics like the one I have cited. Even government publications openly acknowledge a high correlation between crime and socioeconomic disadvantages: "From arrest records, probation reports, and prison statistics a 'portrait' of the offender emerges that progressively highlights the disadvantaged character of his life. The offender at the end of the road in prison is likely to be a member of the lowest social and economic groups in the country, poorly educated and perhaps unemployed. . . . Material failure, then, in a culture firmly oriented toward material success, is the most common denominator of offenders" (*The Challenge of Crime in a Free Society, A Report by the President's Commission on Law Enforcement and Administration of Justice*, U. S. Government Printing Office, Washington, D.C., 1967, pp. 44 and 160). The Marxist implications of this admission have not gone unnoticed by prisoners. See Samuel Jorden, "Prison Reform: In Whose Interest?" *Criminal Law Bulletin* 7, no. 9 (November 1971): 779-787.

34. There are, of course, other factors which enter into an explanation of this statistic. One of them is the fact that economically disadvantaged guilty persons are more likely to wind up arrested or in prison (and thus be reflected in this statistic) than are economically advantaged guilty persons. Thus economic conditions enter into the explanation, not just of criminal behavior, but of society's response to criminal behavior. For a general discussion on the many ways in which crime and poverty are related, see Patricia M. Wald, "Poverty and Criminal Justice," *Task Force Report: The Courts*, U.S. Government Printing Office, Washington, D.C., 1967, pp. 139-151.

outlined above? I should like to organize my answer to this question around three basic topics:

1. *Rational Choice*. The model of rational choice found in Social Contract theory is egoistic—rational institutions are those that would be agreed to by calculating egoists ("devils" in Kant's more colorful terminology). The obvious question that would be raised by any Marxist is: Why give egoism this special status such that it is built, a priori, into the analysis of the concept of rationality? Is this not simply to regard as necessary that which may be only contingently found in the society around us? Starting from such an analysis, a certain result is inevitable—namely, a transcendental sanction for the status quo. Start with a bourgeois model of rationality and you will, of course, wind up defending a bourgeois theory of consent, a bourgeois theory of justice, and a bourgeois theory of punishment.

Though I cannot explore the point in detail here, it seems to me that this Marxist claim may cause some serious problems for Rawls's well-known theory of justice, a theory which I have already used to unpack some of the evaluative support for the retributive theory of punishment. One cannot help suspecting that there is a certain sterility in Rawls's entire project of providing a rational proof for the preferability of a certain conception of justice over all possible alternative evaluative principles, for the description which he gives of the rational contractors in the original position is such as to guarantee that they will come up with his two principles. This would be acceptable if the analysis of rationality presupposed were intuitively obvious or argued for on independent grounds. But it is not. Why, to take just one example, is a desire for wealth a rational trait whereas envy is not? One cannot help feeling that the desired result dictates the premises.[35]

35. The idea that the principles of justice could be proved as a kind of theorem (Rawls's claim in "Justice as Fairness") seems to be absent, if I understand the work correctly, in Rawls's recent A *Theory of Justice*. In this book, Rawls seems to be content with something less than a decision procedure. He is no longer trying to pull his theory of justice up by its own bootstraps, but now seems concerned simply to *exhibit* a certain elaborate conception of justice in the belief that it will do a good job of systematizing and ordering most of our considered and reflective intuitions about moral matters. To this, of course, the Marxist will want to say something like the following: "The considered and reflective in-

2. *Justice, Benefits, and Community.* The retributive theory claims
to be grounded on justice; but is it just to punish people who act out
of those very motives that society encourages and reinforces? If
Bonger is correct, much criminality is motivated by greed, selfishness,
and indifference to one's fellows; but does not the whole society encourage motives of greed and selfishness ("making it," "getting
ahead"), and does not the competitive nature of the society alienate
men from each other and thereby encourage indifference—even, perhaps, what psychiatrists call psychopathy? The moral problem here
is similar to one that arises with respect to some war crimes. When
you have trained a man to believe that the enemy is not a genuine
human person (but only a gook, or a chink), it does not seem quite
fair to punish the man if, in a war situation, he kills indiscriminately.
For the psychological trait you have conditioned him to have, like
greed, is not one that invites fine moral and legal distinctions. There
is something perverse in applying principles that presuppose a sense of
community in a society which is structured to destroy genuine community.[36]

Related to this is the whole allocation of benefits in contemporary

tuitions current in our society are a product of bourgeois culture, and thus any
theory based upon them begs the question against us and in favor of the status
quo." I am not sure that this charge cannot be answered, but I am sure that it
deserves an answer. Someday Rawls may be remembered, to paraphrase Georg
Lukács's description of Thomas Mann, as the last and greatest philosopher of
bourgeois liberalism. The virtue of this description is that it perceives the limitations of his outlook in a way consistent with acknowledging his indisputable
genius. (None of my remarks here, I should point out, are to be interpreted as
denying that our civilization derived major moral benefits from the tradition
of bourgeois liberalism. Just because the freedoms and procedures we associate
with bourgeois liberalism—speech, press, assembly, due process of law, etc.—are
not the only important freedoms and procedures, we are not to conclude with
some witless radicals that these freedoms are not terribly important and that the
victories of bourgeois revolutions are not worth preserving. My point is much
more modest and noncontroversial—namely, that even bourgeois liberalism requires a critique. It is not self-justifying and, in certain very important respects,
is not justified at all.)

36. Kant has some doubts about punishing bastard infanticide and dueling on
similar grounds. Given the stigma that Kant's society attached to illegitimacy
and the halo that the same society placed around military honor, it did not seem
totally fair to punish those whose criminality in part grew out of such approved
motives. See *Metaphysical Elements of Justice*, pp. 106-107.

society. The retributive theory really presupposes what might be called a "gentlemen's club" picture of the relation between man and society— i.e., men are viewed as being part of a community of shared values and rules. The rules benefit all concerned and, as a kind of debt for the benefits derived, each man owes obedience to the rules. In the absence of such obedience, he deserves punishment in the sense that he owes payment for the benefits. For, as rational man, he can see that the rules benefit everyone (himself included) and that he would have selected them in the original position of choice.

Now this may not be too far off for certain kinds of criminals—e.g., business executives guilty of tax fraud. (Though even here we might regard their motives of greed to be a function of societal reinforcement.) But to think that it applies to the typical criminal, from the poorer classes, is to live in a world of social and political fantasy. Criminals typically are not members of a shared community of values with their jailers; they suffer from what Marx calls alienation. And they certainly would be hard-pressed to name the benefits for which they are supposed to owe obedience. If justice, as both Kant and Rawls suggest, is based on reciprocity, it is hard to see what these persons are supposed to reciprocate for. Bonger addresses this point in a passage quoted earlier (p. 236): "The oppressed resort to means which they would otherwise scorn. . . . The basis of social feelings is reciprocity. As soon as this is trodden under foot by the ruling class, the social sentiments of the oppressed become weak towards them."

3. *Voluntary Acceptance.* Central to the Social Contract idea is the claim that we owe allegiance to the law because the benefits we have derived have been voluntarily accepted. This is one place where our autonomy is supposed to come in. That is, having benefited from the Rule of Law when it was possible to leave, I have in a sense consented to it and to its consequences—even my own punishment if I violate the rules. To see how silly the factual presuppositions of this account are, we can do no better than quote a famous passage from David Hume's essay "Of the Original Contract":

Can we seriously say that a poor peasant or artisan has a free choice to leave his country—when he knows no foreign language or manners, and lives from day to day by the small wages which he acquires? We may as well assert that a man, by remaining in a vessel, freely consents to the dominion of the master, though he was carried on board while asleep, and must leap into the ocean and perish the moment he leaves her.

A banal empirical observation, one may say. But it is through ignoring such banalities that philosophers generate theories which allow them to spread iniquity in the ignorant belief that they are spreading righteousness.

It does, then, seem as if there may be some truth in Marx's claim that the retributive theory, though formally correct, is materially inadequate. At root, the retributive theory fails to acknowledge that criminality is, to a large extent, a phenomenon of economic class. To acknowledge this is to challenge the empirical presupposition of the retributive theory—the presupposition that all men, including criminals, are voluntary participants in a reciprocal system of benefits and that the justice of this arrangement can be derived from some eternal and ahistorical concept of rationality.

THE upshot of all this seems rather upsetting, as indeed it is. How can it be the case that everything we are ordinarily inclined to say about punishment (in terms of utility and retribution) can be quite beside the point? To anyone with ordinary language sympathies (one who is inclined to maintain that what is correct to say is a function of what we do say), this will seem madness. Marx will agree that there is madness, all right, but in his view the madness will lie in what we do say—what we say only because of our massive (and often self-deceiving and self-serving) factual ignorance or indifference to the circumstances of the social world in which we live. Just as our whole way of talking about mental phenomena hardened before we knew any neurophysiology—and this leads us astray, so Marx would argue that our whole way of talking about moral and political phenomena hardened before we knew any of the relevant empirical facts about man and society—and this, too, leads us astray. We all suffer from what might be called the *embourgeoisment* of language, and thus part of any revolution will be a linguistic or conceptual revolution. We have grown accustomed to modifying our language or con-

ceptual structures under the impact of empirical discoveries in phys-
ics. There is no reason why discoveries in sociology, economics, or
psychology could not and should not have the same effect on en-
trenched patterns of thought and speech. It is important to remember,
as Russell remarked, that our language sometimes enshrines the
metaphysics of the Stone Age.

Consider one example: a man has been convicted of armed robbery. On investigation, we learn that he is an impoverished black
whose whole life has been one of frustrating alienation from the pre-
vailing socio-economic structure—no job, no transportation if he could
get a job, substandard education for his children, terrible housing and
inadequate health care for his whole family, condescending-tardy-
inadequate welfare payments, harassment by the police but no real
protection by them against the dangers in his community, and near
total exclusion from the political process. Learning all this, would we
still want to talk—as many do—of his suffering punishment under the
rubric of "paying a debt to society"? Surely not. Debt for what? I do
not, of course, pretend that all criminals can be so described. But I
do think that this is a closer picture of the typical criminal than the
picture that is presupposed in the retributive theory—i.e., the picture
of an evil person who, of his own free will, intentionally acts against
those just rules of society which he knows, as a rational man, benefit
everyone including himself.

But what practical help does all this offer, one may ask. How should
we design our punitive practices in the society in which we now live?
This is the question we want to ask, and it does not seem to help
simply to say that our society is built on deception and inequity. How
can Marx help us with our real practical problem? The answer, I
think, is that he cannot and obviously does not desire to do so. For
Marx would say that we have not focused (as all piecemeal reform
fails to focus) on what is truly the real problem. And this is changing
the basic social relations. Marx is the last person from whom we can
expect advice on how to make our intellectual and moral peace with
bourgeois society. And this is surely his attraction and his value.

What does Bonger offer? He suggests, near the end of his book, that
in a properly designed society all criminality would be a problem "for
the physician rather than the judge." But this surely will not do. The

therapeutic state, where prisons are called hospitals and jailers are called psychiatrists, simply raises again all the old problems about the justification of coercion and its reconciliation with autonomy that we faced in worrying about punishment. The only difference is that our coercive practices are now surrounded with a benevolent rhetoric which makes it even harder to raise the important issues. Thus the move to therapy, in my judgment, is only an illusory solution—alienation remains and the problem of reconciling coercion with autonomy remains unsolved. Indeed, if the alternative is having our personalities involuntarily restructured by some state psychiatrist, we might well want to claim the "right to be punished" that Hegel spoke of.[37]

Perhaps, then, we may really be forced seriously to consider a radical proposal. If we think that institutions of punishment are necessary and desirable, and if we are morally sensitive enough to want to be sure that we have the moral right to punish before we inflict it, then we had better first make sure that we have restructured society in such a way that criminals genuinely do correspond to the only model that will render punishment permissible—i.e., make sure that they are autonomous and that they do benefit in the requisite sense. Of course, if we did this then—if Marx and Bonger are right—crime itself and the need to punish would radically decrease if not disappear entirely.

37. This point is pursued in Herbert Morris, "Persons and Punishment." Bonger did not appreciate that "mental illness," like criminality, may also be a phenomenon of social class. On this, see August B. Hollingshead and Frederick C. Redlich, *Social Class and Mental Illness* (New York, 1958). On the general issue of punishment versus therapy, see my *Punishment and Rehabilitation* (Belmont, Cal., forthcoming 1973).

ALAN H. GOLDMAN   The Paradox of
                          Punishment

The paradox of punishment is that a penal institution somewhat similar to that in use in our society seems from a moral point of view to
be both required and unjustified. Usually such a statement would be a
confused way of saying that the practice is a necessary evil, hence it
is justified, all things considered. But in the case of punishment this
reduction does not appear so simple.

The paradox results from the intuitive plausibility of two theses:
one associated with a retributivist point of view and another associated with a utilitarian justification of the institution of punishment.
Some philosophers have thought that objections to these two theories
of punishment could be overcome by making both retributive and utilitarian criteria necessary for the justification of punishment. Utilitarian
criteria could be used to justify the institution, and retributive to justify
specific acts within it; or utilitarian to justify legislative decisions regarding punishment, and retributive to justify enforcement decisions.[1]
(These distinctions in levels of justification are matters of degree,
since when justifying an institution, one must consider acts within it;
and when justifying legislative decisions, one must consider their applications in the judicial system.) The compromise positions, according to which punishment must be both deserved and beneficial, have
considerable plausibility. But if I am right about the two theses to be

1. For classic statements of these mixed positions, see John Rawls, "Two
Concepts of Rules," *Philosophical Review* 64, no. 1 (1955): 3-32; H.L.A. Hart,
"Prolegomenon to the Principles of Punishment," in *Punishment and Responsi-
bility* (Oxford: Clarendon Press, 1968), pp. 1-13.

assessed here, these criteria may be ultimately inconsistent. If so, then the mixed theory of justification, initially attractive, is at least as problematic as its rivals.

Let us consider the retributivist thesis first, since it is likely to be considered the more controversial. The thesis ultimately concerns the amount of punishment justifiable in particular cases. If we are to justify punishment of particular wrongdoers or lawbreakers, that is, if we are to show why *they* cannot legitimately complain of injustice done to them by the imposition of punishment, we must argue that they have forfeited those rights of which we are depriving them. We must say that by violating the rights of others in their criminal activities, they have lost or forfeited their legitimate demands that others honor all their formerly held rights. It seems clear that this is the only way we could convince criminals themselves that they are not being treated unjustly in being punished.[2] Appeal to the idea that the community benefits from a prisoner's role as an example for others would not be sufficient, in view of the severity of the impositions. Persons normally have rights not to be severely imposed upon in order to benefit others. If we are justifiably to ignore these rights, it could only be when they have been forfeited or alienated. And the only way in which this can be done involuntarily is by violation of the rights of others. Since having rights generally entails having duties to honor the same rights of others, it is plausible that when these duties are not fulfilled, the rights cease to exist.

This partial justification of the right to impose punishment upon wrongdoers is retributive in spirit, but not identical to the classic theories of Kant or Hegel, nor to the well-known contemporary retributivist argument of Morris. I do not claim here that a wrongdoer wills or consents to his own punishment by wronging others; or that he would will his action universally if he were rational; or that he would rationally will consequences for himself similar to those suffered by his victim. No rational person would will any such thing; no wrongdoer would construe his action as a consent, tacit or otherwise, to his own punishment.

2. Compare Herbert Morris, "Persons and Punishment," *The Monist* 52, no. 4 (1968): 475-501.

Nor do I view punishment, as Morris views it, as removing some benefit unfairly enjoyed by the criminal.[3] Morris's analysis in terms of balancing social burdens and benefits throughout society faces insuperable objections as well. There is first the objection that this balancing process, to be fair, would have to take account of relative burdens and benefits over each citizen's lifetime, and consider them in relation to those of every other citizen. Hence appeal to this process might not justify particular impositions of punishment for particular criminal acts. Second, this analysis would have counterintuitive implications regarding amounts of punishment for particular crimes, since crimes against property often bring more benefits to their perpetrators than do more serious crimes against persons (crimes involving violation of more precious rights). If we restrict the burden in question to that of self-restraint, and the benefit to that of enjoyment of rights through the self-restraint of others, we come closer to the justification suggested above. But then talk of an unfair advantage that criminals enjoy over others through their criminal acts is somewhat misleading, as is the suggestion that the purpose of punishment is to restore a balance. Why balance just these burdens and benefits and not others? The partial justification for particular impositions of puinshment suggested above appeals more directly to the plausible claim that a condition of having specific rights is that one honors those rights of others (when one is able to do so). When a person violates rights of others, he involuntarily loses certain of his own rights, and the community acquires the right to impose a punishment, if there is social benefit to be derived from doing so.[4]

While violating the rights of others involves forfeiting rights oneself,[5] it is clear that violating specific rights of others does not entail

3. Morris, "Persons and Punishment," pp. 477-478.

4. This way of viewing criminal desert derives from W. D. Ross, *The Right and the Good* (Oxford: Clarendon Press, 1965), pp. 56-64. My position differs from his in that he sees an insuperable problem in equating amounts of punishment and degrees of wrongdoing, and I do not; and in that he sees no problem in balancing utilitarian and retributive considerations in assigning proper amounts of punishment, and I do. See below.

5. Violation of the rights of others may be only a necessary, but not a sufficient, condition for forfeiture if there are certain inalienable rights. The concept

losing *all* one's own rights. If *A* steals fifty dollars from *B*, this does not give *B* or anyone else, official or not, the right to impose all and any conceivable harms upon *A* in return. Nor does *A* thereby become available for any use to which the community then wants to put him. Just as an innocent person can complain if forced to make severe sacrifices for the benefit of others, so a guilty person may claim that violation of any rights beyond those forfeited or alienated in order to benefit others is an injustice. And if we ask which rights are forfeited in violating rights of others, it is plausible to answer just those rights that one violates (or an equivalent set). One continues to enjoy rights only as long as one respects those rights in others: violation constitutes forfeiture. But one retains those rights which one has continued to respect in others. Since deprivation of those particular rights violated is often impracticable, we are justified in depriving a wrongdoer of some equivalent set, or in inflicting harm equivalent to that which would be suffered in losing those same rights (for example, rights to fifty dollars of one's own and not to suffer the trauma of being a victim of theft). Equivalence here is to be measured in terms of some average or normal preference scale, much like the one used by the utilitarian when comparing and equating utilities and disutilities.

It would be difficult for a wrongdoer to complain of injustice when we treat him in a way equivalent to the way in which he treated his victim, provided that we also have a good (consequentialist) reason for imposing upon him in that way. If he cannot demonstrate a morally relevant difference between himself and his victim, then he cannot claim that he must enjoy all those rights that he was willing to violate. But if we deprive him not only of these or equivalent rights, but of ones far more important, whose loss results in far greater harm, then we begin to look like serious wrongdoers ourselves in multiplying violations of rights. It is at this point that the claim that two wrongs do not make a right begins to apply. A claim of injustice or victimization by the community made by the criminal begins to have merit, although in our anger at his wrongdoing, we are often unwilling to

---

of forfeiture is best explained here in terms of a contract model of rights. See my "Rights, Utilities and Contracts," *Canadian Journal of Phliosophy* 3, supplement (1977): 121-135.

hear it. If a person can be said to deserve only so much punishment and no more, then any excess appears to be as objectionable as an equivalent harm imposed upon an innocent person. In fact the stronger thesis concerning the degree of justified imposition can be viewed as the source of the weaker thesis that the innocent should not be punished at all. The latter is implied as a special case of the former. Philosophers have been far more concerned with the thesis as applied to innocents than with its more general application, perhaps because of a supposed difficulty in judging when punishment is equivalent to crime. When we think in terms of forfeiting those rights one violates, or an equivalent set, there is no special difficulty here. One right or set of rights is equivalent to another for these purposes when an average preference scale registers indifference between the loss of either the one or the other. There are problems facing construction of the proper preference scale—for example, the loss of fifty dollars to which one has a right will mean more to a poor person than to a rich person—but these are problems facing any moral theory concerned with distribution. We also need to adjust our concept of deserved punishment to focus upon intention rather than actual harm, and to allow for excuses. I leave these complications to pursue our main topic.

To this retributivist premise might be raised an objection similar to one sometimes made against utilitarian theories of punishment. It might be claimed that our argument limiting the severity of justified punishments errs in calculating harm to the guilty and that to the innocent on the same scale. But, an objector might hold, the guilty do not deserve equal consideration or equal treatment. What they have forfeited in harming others and in violating others' rights is precisely the right to have their own interests considered equally. Society therefore has the right to impose greater harm upon wrongdoers than that done to innocent victims, if it finds it necessary or beneficial to do so. This counterargument rests upon a confusion. Treatment of wrongdoers equal to or the same as rightful treatment of the innocent would demand no harm or deprivation of rights at all. We are not, as this argument suggests, counting the interests of wrongdoers equally with those of the innocent, since we impose harm upon the former but not upon the latter. The prior wrongdoing of the guilty enables us to harm them without treating them unjustly, but only to the extent of treating them as they treated their victims. If we inflict greater harm than this, we become, like them, violators of rights not forfeited and hence wrongdoers ourselves. Their wrongdoing does not give us the right to do equal wrong, or any wrong, ourselves. It must be remembered also that punishment justly imposed is distinct from compensation owed to victims. Justice may well require wrongdoers to be liable for restoring their victims as far as possible to the level of well-being that they would have attained had no injustice occurred (compensation *is* a matter of restoring a balance or returning to a just status quo, while punishment is not). It requires *in addition* that they be made to suffer harm equivalent to that originally caused to the victims.

To bring out the paradox in the justification of punishment, we need to combine this premise regarding the limits of justly imposed punishments with one at least equally plausible from the utilitarian theory. It states that a political institution involving the administration of punishment by state officials can be justified only in terms of the goal of reducing crime and the harms caused by crime to a tolerable level. The state is not concerned to ensure that all its members receive their just positive and negative deserts in some abstract moral sense. It is concerned neither to proportion burdens to benefits in general, nor even to protect all moral rights. Certainly that someone deserves to be harmed in some way, or that he could not complain of injustice at being harmed in some way, does not in itself entail that the state ought to take it upon itself to harm him. At least one other condition is necessary for the state to be justified in adopting rules calling for such official imposition. The wrongs in question must be so grave that the social costs of official interference do not exceed the benefits in terms of reducing these wrongs. There are, for example, moral wrongs whose detection is so unsure that their official prohibition would involve costs too great to be worthwhile: betrayals of friendship, deceptions in love affairs, and so on. The social benefits from an institution of punishment must outweigh the costs, including the harms imposed, especially when these harms are undeserved (occasional punishment of the innocent and excessive punishments of the guilty). That our penal institution does deter crime is the primary source of its justification and social necessity. The state must seek to deter violations of its distributive rules if it is serious about their adoption, and it must seek to deter serious attacks upon persons; the sanctions which attach to these violations exist primarily for this deterrent effect.

Combining this justification for a social penal institution with the limit upon just impositions so that no one may be deprived of rights he has not forfeited, we derive the mixed theory of punishment advocated by Ross and Hart, and endorsed by other philosophers in recent years.[6] This theory views the social goal of punishment as deterrence, and yet recognizes that we are entitled to pursue this goal only when we restrict deprivation of rights to those forfeited through crime or wrongdoing. In actuality proponents of this theory usually state the limitation only as prohibiting punishment of the innocent. But, as argued above, in terms of the broader principle that no one is to be deprived of rights not forfeited, excessive punishment of the guilty is on a par with punishment of the innocent. Thus for officially imposed punishment to be justified, the person punished must have forfeited those rights of which he is deprived, and the state must be entitled to inflict the harm by appeal to the social benefit of deterrence. (This appeal may involve the need to have a rule calling for punishment of a particular type of wrongdoing and the need to apply the rule consistently.)

The problem is that while the mixed theory can avoid punishment of the innocent, it is doubtful that it can avoid excessive punishment of the guilty if it is to have sufficient deterrent effect to make the social costs worthwhile. In our society the chances of apprehension and punishment for almost every class of crime are well under fifty percent. Given these odds a person pursuing what he considers his maximum prospective benefit may not be deterred by the threat of an imposition of punishment equivalent to the violation of the rights of the potential victim. If threats of sanctions are not sufficient to deter such people, they would probably fail to reduce crime to a tolerable enough level to make the social costs of the penal institution worthwhile. On the other hand, in order to deter crime at all effectively, given reason-

6. See, for example, Michael Lessnoff, "Two justifications of Punishment," *The Philosophical Quarterly* 21, no. 83 (1971): 141-148.

able assumptions about police efficiency at bearable costs, sanctions must be threatened and applied which go far beyond the equivalence relation held to be just. The limitation stipulated in our first premise then, in effect, annuls just and effective pursuit of the social goal stipulated in our second premise. And yet pursuit of this goal seems morally required and impossible without effective punitive threats. Hence the paradox, or, more strictly, the dilemma.

Caught in this dilemma, our society does not limit punishment to deprivation of rights forfeited, that is, rights of others which have been violated by the criminal. Especially in regard to crimes against property, punishments by imprisonment are far more severe, on the average, than the harm caused to victims of these crimes. Probably because such punishment is administered by officials of the state, cloaked in appropriate ritual and vested with authority, most of us systematically ignore its relative severity. If, however, we imagine an apolitical context, in which there is money and property, but no penal institution, would theft of several thousand dollars justify the victim's taking the perpetrator and locking him away in some small room for five to ten years? In our society such deprivation of freedom is a small portion of the harms likely to be suffered in prison as punishment for a felonious crime against property. The disproportion between violated or deprived rights of the victims and those of the criminals in these crimes is obvious.

It might be argued that we could lower penalties to make them equal to harms from crimes and yet still have a deterrent effect, since for most persons, the threat of official sanctions simply adds to internal moral sanctions against harmful or criminal acts. Furthermore, for people who enjoy a decent standard of living without turning to criminal activity, it will not be worth even minimal risk of public exposure to attempt to increase acquisitions by criminal means. For such persons, who are reasonably well-off and have much to lose if apprehended, the moral disapproval of the community might be felt as a more serious harm than an actual prison sentence or fine. The problem with these claims is that they do not apply to the typical criminal in our society, or to the potential criminal whom threats of punishment are intended to deter. We may assume the potential criminal has a fairly desperate economic situation, and therefore, at most, a neutral attitude toward risk. Thus suggestions to the community to sharply lower penalties for property crimes would be taken about as seriously as is epistemological skepticism outside philosophy classrooms and articles. Even suggestions to eliminate the more horrid aspects of prison life that are not officially part of the penalty of imprisonment are met with resistance. I am convinced that punishments, when administered at all, tend to be far more severe than harms suffered in those particular crimes against property for which these punishments are imposed. Yet, while this strikes me as seriously unjust, it does not appear that we can afford at present to lessen the deterrent force of sanctions for potential criminals to the point at which they stand to lose nothing by attempting further crimes. At stake is not only increased harm to innocent victims but our ability to put into effect those distributive rules we consider just. (Assuming that we do consider some such set of rules just, the problem that I am defining will be real.)

Others have noted conflicts between utilitarian criteria for proper amounts of punishment and what is called the retributive proportionality principle.[7] This states that more serious crimes should draw more severe penalties. It fails to match utilitarian criteria in application. This is because utilitarian criteria call for a deterrent threat sufficient to bring crimes of a given class down to a tolerable level; and deterrent threat varies not only with the severity of the punishment threatened but also with such factors as the comparative probability of apprehension and conviction for various types of crime, and the degree to which various crimes are normally preceded by unemotional prudential calculations. Crimes which are more difficult to prosecute call for more severe threats, while threats are wasted for crimes of passion. But these variables are irrelevant to moral rights violated and harm suffered by the victims of the crimes, the sole variables relevant according to retributive criteria of proportionality. The conflict I have noted above is, however, more fundamental, since the absolute limitation

7. Michael Clark, "The Moral Gradation of Punishment," *The Philosophical Quarterly* 21, no. 83 (1971): 132-140; Alan Wertheimer, "Should the Punishment Fit the Crime?" *Social Theory & Practice* 3, no. 4 (1975): 403-423.

upon justified punishment in terms of equivalence to loss of rights violated is more basic than the proportionality principle. It is clear that we require absolute as well as proportionate limits, since without absolute limits all punishments might be too severe or the spread between them might be too great, even if they are arranged in correct order of severity.[8] It is plausible again, therefore, to view the proportionality principle as a particular implication of the absolute limits for various punishments, much as we viewed the prohibition against punishing the innocent. The absolute equivalence limitation, as we may call it, is the fundamental retributive principle; and it is this principle which appears to be fundamentally in conflict with the utilitarian goal of adequate deterrence.[9]

In trying to resolve this conflict, in which it appears that we require a penal institution, that we cannot deter crime if we are just in imposing punishment, and that we should not have a penal institution unless to deter crime, we might inquire first whether we have exhausted the potential justification of punishment as a necessary evil. I have been arguing so far as if the rights of criminals not to suffer excessive punishment through violation of rights not forfeited is opposed merely by utilities on the side of the noncriminal community. Normally rights override collective utilities and disutilities, which may be what made the initial argument so puzzling, if we feel that punishment beyond the equivalence limitation is necessary for purposes of deterrence. But we can view the conflict as one between opposing rights, and see our legitimate goal as the minimization of violations of rights throughout the community. A limit to the severity of punishments that renders their deterrent threats ineffective results in greater disutility to potential victims in the community, and also in avoidable crimes that violate people's rights not to be harmed. Furthermore,

---

8. This is admitted by Wertheimer, "Should the Punishment Fit the Crime?" p. 410. But he fails to say more on this subject, again probably because he views it as impossible to calculate an equivalence between punishment and crime. See also John Kleinig, *Punishment and Desert* (The Hague: Martinus Nijhoff, 1973), pp. 118-119.

9. The one philosopher who notes a possible conflict here is Robert Nozick, in *Anarchy, State, and Utopia* (New York: Basic Books, 1974), pp. 59-63. Nozick does not defend both premises, however.

since presumably more potential criminals are deterred than punished when sanctions are substantial, we minimize violations of rights by applying such sanctions. Thus even if punishments with effective deterrent force are beyond what is deserved by criminals and therefore appear to violate their rights, and even if we do not prefer the interests and rights of the innocent over those of the guilty but oppose them on an equal scale, we are, figuring purely quantitatively, still justified in imposing the more severe penalties. We are justified in doing so until the prima facie violations of criminal rights are no longer exceeded by further deterrence of crimes against others.

Normally when rights are opposed, we adopt exceptive clauses in those we feel must give way, and in this way resolve the conflicts. Often the carving out of an exceptive clause in a right formerly recognized represents recognition of the fact that some must accept sacrifices to prevent harms to others. An exceptive clause is added when the harm to be prevented greatly outweighs the sacrifice involved in losing part of the formerly recognized right. Thus we might say here that criminals have rights not to suffer punishment beyond the equivalence limitation, except when such punishment is necessary to prevent greater or more violations of the rights of innocent people. This would be a more perspicuous way of saying that punishment as we know it is justified as a necessary evil. If punishment beyond the equivalence limitation can be justified in this way, then it is not unjust. If it is not unjust, then we do not treat criminals wrongly by adopting this practice, although we do perhaps treat them regrettably.

Thus an argument similar in form to the utilitarian defense of punishment can be stated within the retributivist's framework of satisfaction of rights. While this may seem a plausible way to avoid the force of our paradox, it unfortunately has serious flaws. The principal problem with this argument is that it misrepresents the way in which conflicts among apparent rights are resolved and exceptive clauses adopted. We do not aggregate rights against one another as we aggregate utilities and disutilities.[10] If I have a right to free speech, for example, it is not canceled according to how many people might be offended by what I want to say on particular occasions. Rights are

10. For expansion on this point, see my "Rights, Utilities and Contracts."

ordered according to their individual importance, not according to how many people occupy opposing sides on particular occasions of application. This is clear in the case of the prohibition against punishing the innocent as well. An innocent person may not be punished in order to prevent many harms to other persons who have rights not to be harmed. It was argued above that excessive punishment of the guilty is on a par with punishment of the innocent: the amount by which punishment of a guilty person exceeds what is just is morally equivalent to that amount of punishment of an innocent person (except for the initial shame of being punished at all). If we do not accept that innocent people may be punished to prevent violations (by rioting vigilantes, in the usual example) of rights of others, then we cannot accept as justification for excessive punishment of the guilty that there tend to be more crimes prevented than excessive punishments imposed when deterrence is effective. One who argued that punishment is justified as a necessary evil would have to advocate punishment of the innocent on the same aggregative grounds.[11]

If we compare the amount of harm from excessive punishment necessary to create effective deterrence from crimes against property to the amount of harm caused by those crimes in single cases (rather than aggregatively), it is far from clear that the latter exceeds the former, especially given the many indignities of life in prison. In cases in which harms from violations of rights taken singly are equal, we normally are not justified in aggregating rights of the greater number against those of the fewer in deciding how to act. This can be illustrated by the story in which the seeker of vengeance takes five hostages and threatens to kill them unless the community executes his lifelong enemy. I take it that the community would not be justified in capitulating to his demand. The moral wrongness of doing so is not reducible solely to the need to discourage future demands of the same type by grudge holders. Capitulation would still be wrong in an isolated case unlikely to recur. Even if we alter the story so that the kidnapper

11. For one who appears to argue in this way, see Gertrude Ezorsky, "Punishment and Excuses," in *Punishment and Human Rights*, ed. Milton Goldinger (Cambridge, Ma.: Schenkman, 1974), pp. 99-115. As she does not distinguish between aggregating and ordering rights individually, it is difficult to tell whether her argument appeals to purely aggregative grounds.

threatens greater harm to each hostage than the harm which he demands be done to his enemy (say he threatens to kill each hostage unless the townspeople cut off his enemy's arm), I am not convinced that they ought to impose the lesser harm to prevent the greater. The difference between causing harm and merely not preventing it may be significant in this example, but the same distinction applies in the case of imposing excessive punishment to prevent crimes against members of the community. If these cases are analogous to each other and to the case in which punishment of the innocent is contemplated, as they appear to me to be, then we cannot justify excessive punishment of criminals in order to prevent deterrable crime.

It might be thought that in the case of the guilty there is a relevant difference which we have not yet considered. Publicizing the penalties attached to each class of crime warns people in advance of the potential consequences of criminal activities. In this way they are able to control their own futures. If they choose to engage in criminal activity, they in a real sense "bring the punishment upon themselves." This is the sense to be made of the claim that criminals have chosen their penalties through their behavior, in contrast to the sense considered earlier: the Kantian claim that wrongdoers somehow will to be punished. That criminals have been warned may be thought to constitute an important difference between their situation, even when excessively punished, and that of innocent victims of crime. When penalties are made public, they can be avoided completely by those who choose not to take the risk of incurring them; whereas innocent victims of crime are helpless to avoid the harms imposed upon them by criminals. This again might be construed as legitimate grounds for society's choosing to protect potential victims at the expense of criminals, who could have avoided any punishment whatsover if they had chosen to act within the law. It might even be said to create a kind of desert for the punishment imposed, much as an advance announcement of a prize or reward creates desert for those who fulfill the conditions stipulated. If positive desert can be created simply through the creation of a rule setting forth conditions for a reward, perhaps this is an element of negative desert as well, if in the latter case one can easily avoid fulfilling the conditions set forth in the rule. In any case, harm to innocent victims may be worse or more objectionable than harm to the guilty, since crimes against the innocent are unexpected and often unavoidable. Hence we can justifiably choose to protect the innocent at the additional expense of the guilty.

Again, however, this argument is flawed and cannot create the distinction we seek. While advance notice of penalties attached to various crimes may be a necessary condition for just imposition of punishment, it is never a sufficient condition justifying the imposition of any punishment that society chooses to inflict, no matter how severe. The case of rules creating positive entitlements to rewards is different. If someone has some benefit to give away, he normally can give it to whomever he chooses without wronging others. He also can create whatever frivolous rules or contests he likes for determining who is to receive his gift or prize. Those who satisfy the criteria in the rules, or those who win the contests, then become entitled to the benefits. (They will not *deserve* the benefits, however, if their qualifying acts are independently morally objectionable.) But in the case of imposing harm, one cannot justify doing so merely by giving adequate warning. My warning you that I will assault you if you say anything I believe to be false does nothing to justify my assaulting you, even if you could avoid it by saying nothing. A society's giving warning that it will cut off the hands of thieves does not justify its doing so. In general, having warned someone that he would be treated unjustly is no justification for then doing so, even if, once warned, he could have avoided the unjust treatment by acting in some way other than the way he acted. The harm imposed must be independently justified. Once we have determined the proper amount of punishment for wrongdoing (I have argued that it is determined by social utility up to the equivalence limitation), adequate warning is normally a further necessary condition for just imposition. That criminals could have avoided punishment by having acted differently is again one reason why we are justified in punishing them at all. It does not justify excessive punishment. As for harm causing less suffering when it is expected, I would think that often the opposite is the case. Even when awaiting expected punishment is not as bad as actually suffering it, it certainly adds to the suffering of being punished. It is true that the resentment against undeserved harm felt by victims of crime adds to their suffering; but then undeserved excessive punishment of the guilty will be resented also. Thus none of the points of the previous paragraph justify excessive punishment of the guilty. Since giving warning to criminals does not reduce the harm imposed upon them to less than the harm suffered by victims, on average in single cases, it does not give us grounds for imposing excessive punishment to prevent crimes.

There remains one final argument to the effect that official punishment which exceeds the equivalence limitation can be justified as the lesser of two evils likely to occur. The worse evil is not only the occurrence of crime beyond what appears to be a tolerable level but also a reign of private vengeance and attacks upon wrongdoers by those without legitimate authority to do so. The evil to be prevented now includes harm to wrongdoers or criminals themselves. When punishment does not at least approximate giving satisfaction to the victims of crime and to those in the community who wish to demonstrate their moral outrage, these individuals will take it upon themselves to exact punishment instead of, or in addition to, that officially imposed. This would be likely to lead to an escalation of private vendettas, substituting reigns of private terror for law and relative tranquility.[12] In order to prevent this escalation, the state is justified in imposing penalties between those which private citizens, and especially innocent victims, would like to see imposed, and those which are deemed independently just because they fall within the equivalence limitation and deprive criminals only of those rights which they have forfeited. Criminals ought not to complain of such penalties, which are, despite appearances, to the benefit of criminals themselves, as opposed to likely alternatives.

The first problem with this final version of the lesser evil argument is that it again has the state imposing unjustified harm in capitulation to threats of greater harm. Thus it too seems to violate the principle to be derived from the hostage example and similar cases. If we think of rights as "side constraints"[13] to the pursuit of legitimate social goals,

12. For a recent statement of the traditional justification of official punishment as preferable to private revenge, see Lisa Perkins, "Suggestion for a Justification of Punishment," *Ethics* 81, no. 1 (1970): 55-61.

13. See Robert Nozick, *Anarchy, State, and Utopia*, pp. 28-29.

we will remain unwilling to accept such justification for their viola-tion. More importantly in this context, if the greater evil to be pre-vented is that of private vengeance; and if we admit that previous arguments do not justify punishment beyond the equivalence limita-tion merely to prevent other types of crime; then society could attack just *this* evil by threatening and applying more severe punishments only against those who seek private revenge against common crimi-nals. This argument in fact would justify greater punishment only of the private punishers, only of those who react in anger to common criminals. Such sanctions could prevent the envisaged escalation of harms without harming the latter group in ways unjustified on other grounds. Once more I am not suggesting this as a serious alternative to our current penal institutions. Certainly once more it would not be taken seriously by officials or by society at large. I am pointing out only that this final argument, like the previous ones, does not appear to justify what we seek to justfiy: imposition of punishments sufficient to reduce crimes to tolerable levels.

Thus we are blocked from grasping that horn of the dilemma which holds punishment beyond the equivalence limitation to be unjust and therefore unjustified. But to grasp the other horn by sharply reducing penalties for many crimes and hence sharply lowering their deterrence effect seems equally or more impalatable. Is there some other alterna-tive? The usually suggested alternative to punishment as we know it —involuntary psychiatric "treatment" of criminals—has been widely criticized in the literature, and little needs to be added on that subject here. When treatment is involuntary, it involves deprivation of rights normally held, rights not to be involuntarily submitted to such treat-ment. This suffices to classify it as punitive in our sense, at least to bring it under the equivalence limitation. While the intent here is not to harm, deprivation of rights and forceful alteration of personality may certainly be felt and legitimately counted as harm. The means employed often involve mental and physical suffering as severe as those involved in the more traditional forms of punishment and are usually added to these more traditional forms, including involuntary confinement, rather than being genuine replacements for them. Thus it is not an alternative that would enable us to resolve our dilemma.

There are, of course, ways of increasing deterrent effects of punishments without increasing their severity. Given the variables affecting deterrence mentioned earlier, one can, for example, increase the force of threats by improving chances of detection. One can add personnel to police forces and remove procedural constraints upon detection, apprehension, and conviction efforts. But there are social costs, not the least of which include possible abuses, convictions of innocent people, and invasions of privacy, which place limits upon the justified pursuit of this course. It has been suggested also in a recent article that penalties ought to be imposed more consistently and automatically, that inconsistent application of punishment resulting from extensive discretionary powers at all levels of enforcement significantly lowers effective deterrence.[14] It is not clear, first, that even fully automatic arrest, prosecution, and sentencing would enable us to reduce penalties to fit within the equivalence limitation and still have effective deterrence against property crimes. Second, the elimination of discretion on the part of enforcement officials undoubtedly would result in more unjust punishments in many cases, punishments which ought not to be imposed at all in the particular circumstances of particular cases. Third, there is the short-term problem of overcrowded courts and prisons, and this would have to be overcome before this suggestion could be at all capable of implementation.

The final, most fundamental, and most promising alternative would be (not surprisingly) to attack the social and economic causes of crime by reducing the great inequalities in our society. I have nothing to say against this, except that the means to accomplish it short of authoritarian political mechanisms have eluded us. But even were we to progressively achieve the egalitarian program and approach a just economic and social distribution, I believe that the moral problem defined here would remain, though perhaps in less acute form. Many would still be tempted to crime, and deterrence seemingly would still be required. It would still be true that genuinely just punishment would not suffice to deter avoidable harm to innocent members of the community, or to enforce genuinely just distributive rules.

14. Alan Wertheimer, "Deterrence and Retribution," *Ethics* 86, no. 3 (1976): 181-199.

WARREN QUINN

The Right to Threaten
and the Right to Punish

Most of us feel certain that punishment is, in many cases, fully justified. But as to the nature of the justification we are perplexed and uncertain. I do not refer here to punishment within the family. Parents are natural educators morally charged with the task of turning their young dependents into civilized adults, and they need, common sense insists, the possibility of punishing to succeed. But civic punishment, in which one adult is made to suffer for his past wrongdoing by other adults who officially represent the community, raises different problems.[1] It is not, of course, that we doubt its utility. Common sense urges, no less here than in the case of family discipline, that some form of civic punishment is necessary for a decent social order. The difficulty lies rather in the question of authority or right. For on the modern liberal view, adult criminals are not dependents of the community, and the community is not assigned the moral task of forming or improving their characters. How then does its right to punish them arise?

The major source of theoretical difficulty here is the fact that the restrictions, confinements, and deprivations of property and life that make up standard civic punishments would, if imposed in nonpenal contexts, be opposed by various important moral rights of liberty, life, and property. If these evils did not come by way of just punishment, a person subjected

I would like to thank Philippa Foot, Miles Morgan, Stephen Munzer, David Sachs, the Editors of *Philosophy & Public Affairs*, and, especially, Rogers Albritton for helpful comments on earlier drafts.

1. I would simply call this kind of punishment "legal" if I were certain that having a code of punishable behavior and designated authorities to punish always, even in very simple societies, adds up to having a legal system. In any case, I shall help myself to the word "crime" for the kind of thing that is properly punished by this type of punishment.

to them could object to his treatment in ways that would have serious moral weight.[2] To understand how civic punishment can be morally justified, therefore, we must first understand why these familiar rights do not stand in its way. There is, it is important to note, a parallel theoretical issue in the case of self-defense. In defending oneself against an unjust attack, one may put the attacker at some risk of being harmed or even killed, a risk that one could not create in most other contexts without violating some of his rights. Here, however, we feel that we can explain why an attacker's objections to such a defense do not count. How could morality first declare that certain aggressions would be serious violations of our rights and then extend to these aggressions an immunity from interference comparable to that which it assigns to innocent actions? But no parallel explanation seems available in the case of punishment. We cannot punish a crime until it is beyond influence.

If criminals fully retained their ordinary rights to liberty, life, and property, these rights would either raise a morally decisive barrier against punishment, in which case it would *violate* them, or they would create an obstacle that a case for punishment could override, in which case it could *justifiably infringe* them. Justified punishment could not, of course, violate rights. But perhaps it could be thought to infringe them. This idea invites us to include proper punishment in the class of actions, such as the expropriation of private property in time of national emergency, in which we regretfully but justifiably encroach upon someone's rights in order to prevent some evil. But, upon reflection, this assimilation appears doubtful.[3] For justified infringement of rights is a special moral circumstance creating special moral demands not present in the case of punishment. When one has harmed someone in the course of justifiably infringing his moral rights, it is always appropriate and sometimes required that one express regret and offer compensation. But when punishment is fully justified, expressing regret seems, at most, morally optional, and making compensation seems definitely out of place. We do not feel that a properly punished criminal is entitled to either.

2. Having a moral right, in the sense I intend throughout this article, is having a moral status in virtue of which one's objecting (or objecting that could be done on one's behalf) to what others might (or might not) do creates at least a prima facie obligation that they refrain from doing (or not doing) it.

3. Herbert Morris expresses such a doubt in "The Status of Rights," *Ethics* 92 (Oct. 1983): 45, and also offers some plausible objections to received conceptions of infringement.

It thus appears that a morally justifiable practice of punishment can neither violate *nor* infringe a criminal's rights. And therefore the central problem for any moral theory that takes both punishment and rights seriously is to show how this can be so despite the fact that in punishing we subject people to treatment that in other contexts would violate or at least infringe their rights. This is not, of course, the only interesting moral question that can be raised about punishment. A particular punishment might be unwise or unkind without violating any rights. But, as a natural working hypothesis, I shall assume that when punishment is *unjustified* because of the evil imposed on the punished person, it is unjustified as a violation of one or another of his rights. In discussing the question of rights, therefore, I shall often speak as if I am discussing the general question of justification. If this assumption should prove false, my argument will bear only on the specific question of the right to punish, that is, the question how punishment can be shown not to violate a punished person's moral rights.

The way I shall set about answering this question differs from the way state-of-nature theorists often proceed. They typically begin by assuming a nonproblematic right of private punishment (or, as I shall say, retaliation) in a state of nature. And from this they infer that the central philosophical problem for the theory of civic punishment is to show how such a right can be preempted by the state.[4] Now, accepting their idea that the right to civic punishment must somehow arise out of a more fundamental right to private retaliation, I agree that this is an important problem. But even in the case of retaliation, there is a more basic question. To give an adequate account of justified retaliation in a state of nature we must be able to explain why an offender's moral rights do not stand in opposition to the evil inflicted upon him. Justified retaliation raises, therefore, the same fundamental question raised by civic punishment. And since it is this question that I wish to answer, I shall avoid altogether the less basic question how a community can rightfully forbid private retaliation and force its members to accept instead the protections of civic punishment. I shall do this by restricting the discussion to communities whose members prefer the protections afforded by their practices of civic punishment to those they could hope to gain by threatening retaliation.[5]

4. The problem that occupies Robert Nozick in Part I of *Anarchy, State and Utopia* (New York: Basic Books, 1974).

5. To further lighten my burden, I shall also limit the discussion to punishment for acts

Before presenting my own account, it may be well to consider briefly how some familiar theories would address the problem of the right to punish. If any of these theories had a fully satisfying account of this right, there would be no need to continue looking. We may begin with consequentialist theories. Act consequentialism justifies an individual act of punishment by direct reference to its results. Among the most useful of these results is strengthening the deterrent effect on others of the ongoing threat. Since this consequence is a conspicuous social benefit, a plausible consequentialism cannot set it aside as irrelevant to the question of justification. Indeed, it is by reference to this kind of benefit that, under this theory, most justified acts of punishment receive the major part of their justification.

In rule consequentialism this kind of benefit enters into the justification of the practice of punishment as a whole and therefore also into the justification of acts of punishment. For a practice, insofar as it can be consequentially justified, includes those events that help constitute its existence, and these constituents must, in the present case, include the particular acts of punishment that would not otherwise occur. These acts are therefore a large part of what is justified when the practice as a whole is justified. And their deterrent effects on others are a large part of what does the justifying. It thus appears that both kinds of consequentialists are ready to justify punishments, at least in part, by reference to their deterrent effects on others. And even in rule consequentialism, the deterrent effects on others of a *particular* act of punishment may, in theory, tip the balance so as to justify the practice that contains it and, therefore, serve to justify the act itself.

To apply consequentialist theory of justification to the question of rights, we seem driven to the following result: Punished persons have no rights that stand against their punishment because, in part, punishing them is so often useful in helping to deter others from committing crimes. But I, for one, find this answer deeply disturbing. There may indeed be situations in which utility decides the presence or absence of moral rights. But to justify punishment in this way is to say that properly punished people lack the relevant rights because, in large part, they make such useful object lessons for others. In no other case, however, do we suppose

---

that clearly violate people's public moral rights, acts such as murder, theft, assault, and fraud.

that ordinary rights to liberty and life fail to apply *because* their application would stand in the way of some socially profitable use of people.[6] Our rights, by their very nature, are kinds of moral properties that resist such attempts to justify incursions upon them. The most that can follow from an appeal to the general utility of using people is that any rights that stand in its way may be justifiably infringed. But it is implausible, as we have seen, to regard punishment as justified infringement.

A deterrent theorist might escape this kind of objection by restricting his appeal to the deterrent effects of punishment on the person who is punished. Punishing in an attempt to make a criminal's future behavior morally acceptable could not naturally be construed as making use of him. And in aiming at the social utility that would result from this improvement rather than at the punished person's edification, punishers would not be liable to the charge of paternalism. The trouble is that such an account restricts the class of cases in which punishment can be justified and thus unreasonably restricts the kinds of liabilities to punishment that can be created. Suppose, for example, that we discover that a certain type of person is psychologically capable of committing only one murder. Such a person need never murder at all, but if he does murder once he will never murder again. If such people could be identified, we could not on this view rightly punish them for murder since we could not justify this punishment as a way of keeping them from committing future murders. And this seems to imply that we could not, except as a bluff, have the threat of punishment for murder stand against them in our penal code. But this implication seems absurd. Surely we might rightly make them liable to punishment in hope of deterring the single murder that each is capable of committing.[7]

We must also consider the family of retributivist theories of punishment. Often, caught up in establishing a supposed duty to punish, retributivists do not directly address the question of right. But when they

6. The military draft in wartime may seem an exception to this claim. But even here it would be odd to argue directly from social need to the conclusion that people have no right not to be forced into military service. Claims about what is *owed* the community in return for alleged benefits received from it are at least implicit in all common-sense justifications of conscription. Moreover, it may be possible to view conscription as a justifiable infringement of liberty rights and to interpret the various forms of preferential treatment accorded to veterans as forms of compensation.

7. This objection, suitably modified, can also be used against other educative and reformist conceptions of punishment.

do, some retributivists invoke the idea of *forfeiture*. The rights that would otherwise have barred us from doing the sorts of thing we do in punishing, for instance, depriving the criminal of liberty or life, have been forfeited by his own behavior. These rights are seen as conditional and, therefore, liable to deteriorate or disappear unless preserved by a certain moral prudence. This conditionality can be seen as a basic feature of the operation of natural moral law that provides an independently intelligible "clearing of the way" for retribution.

The appeal to forfeiture as an independently intelligible moral mechanism is, however, problematic. The proper authorities are entitled to punish Jones, a generally decent young man who has foolishly stolen Smith's car, by depriving him of up to the amount of liberty forfeited in the theft. But suppose that before any such punishment takes place, Smith, for reasons having nothing whatever to do with the theft, kidnaps Jones and deprives him of exactly that amount of liberty. In this situation it is natural to suppose that Smith not only wrongs Jones but specifically violates his right to liberty. Perhaps this is because Jones forfeits his right to the community as a whole and not to Smith in particular. But suppose that the community in which Jones lives has the unjust practice of seizing and confining political dissenters. And suppose that shortly after his crime Jones, who also happens to be a dissenter, is officially seized and, for a time, quarantined to prevent the spread of his political views (views having nothing to do with his theft). Again, we would naturally suppose that Jones's right to liberty had been violated by his community, even if he were confined only for a period that would constitute an acceptable punishment for his theft and were never punished thereafter. But surely all this strongly suggests that the conditionality of Jones's right to liberty (the conditionality invoked by the doctrine of forfeiture) makes essential reference to punishment.[8] Jones has not forfeited his right without qual-

---

8. To deny this would be to adopt a theory of forfeiture according to which Jones's crime has to some extent made him an *outlaw*, someone whose basic moral rights do not stand in the way of a certain amount of ill-treatment whether or not it comes by way of punishment. Someone who held this idea of forefeiture might try to show that it could be restricted in various ways by moral and legal conventions. He might in this way hope to account for the fact that, in our own moral and legal systems, Jones forfeits his conventionally specified liberty right only in that he may be punished. On such a view, forefeiture would be restricted only in some systems of social morality; in other morally acceptable systems outlawry in some degree would be the regular consequence of crime. It is this last suggestion that I find disturbing.

ification, he has forfeited it in that he may be subjected to a certain penalty (presumably the proper penalty for the crime) by certain people (presumably those with the right to punish him). It seems, therefore, that the idea of forfeiture in this kind of case comes to no more than the idea that the criminal's rights do not in fact stand in the way of his being punished. The appeal to forfeiture does not, as it first seemed, provide an explanation of why this is so.[9]

It is sometimes thought that the force of an appeal to forfeiture lies in the moral necessity of reciprocating respect for rights. But it is not clear how this necessity can help explain why the loss of rights arising from nonreciprocation focuses so precisely on punishment. Moreover, such an account is hard pressed in other ways. If respect is treated as an *attitude*, then many people who never steal may have as little respect for property as Jones, who may have uncharacteristically succumbed to an unusually strong temptation.[10] Yet these others do not, in virtue of their attitude, forfeit any rights. If, on the other hand, respect is taken to refer only to actions, then it is not clear what role the idea of reciprocation is to be assigned. Suppose Smith wrongly takes Jones's car at the very same time

9. Forfeiture of the kind we are discussing might be distingushed from forfeiture whose very possibility is created by a contract that both creates a right and specifies the precise ways in which it may be lost. Some philosophers might appeal to forfeiture of the latter kind by construing the right to punish as deriving from a hypothetical social contract that both creates and limits various social rights. On such a picture, our natural disapproval of, for example, murder and assault, would lead us to design our rights in a way that stipulated forfeiture for such acts. And certain other natural desiderata would lead us to specify that this forfeiture be to the community for the specific purpose of punishment. While tempting, this kind of account raises some difficult questions. First, there is the familiar problem of the actual moral force of a hypothetical agreement. Second, it would have to be shown that such a view can make sense of the morally intuitive upper limits on punishment. And this would be difficult, I think, even if the hypothetical contractors were trying to minimize the likelihood of the worst things that can happen to them. For in the design of their future practice they will focus not so much on individual crimes, and how best to deal with them, as on the bearing of alternative possible practices on their lifetime prospects. And since one very bad, but empirically possible, lifetime prospect is to be a *repeated* victim of a certain kind of crime, it may be reasonable to design the practice so as to tolerate, under certain empirically possible situations, Draconian penalties. Finally, this picture of the right to punish seems to give no account of the right of retaliation in a state of nature—a right which, to my mind, not only exists but raises the same basic theoretical problem as does the right to punish.

10. There is also the difficulty of explaining why Jones doesn't lose his rights only for the period in which he remains disrespectful of others' rights. Without such an explanation it will not be clear with what right we punish people who have reformed in the interval between crime and punishment.

that Jones takes his. They apparently reciprocate the same degree of respect for each other's rights. But surely this does not mean that neither may be punished. Crimes may be punishable even though everyone commits about the same number of them.

A retributivist may, however, omit any appeal to forfeiture in his account of the right to punish. He may argue that the special moral character of retribution, its status under justice as something *deserved*, demands that morality make room for it.[11] Morality would, on such a view, be internally inconsistent if it fully extended ordinary rights into penal contexts. Since it is not inconsistent, a person who gets what he deserves cannot object by appealing to any moral right. When retributivism is thus conceived, evaluation of its account of the right to punish must focus on the moral credentials of retribution itself. Since a critical examination of these credentials would take me beyond my present purpose, I shall make only two brief observations. First, it seems clear that retributivism is burdened by a prima facie mystery. The idea that it is just (and, therefore, in some sense morally good) to harm someone's interests simply because he has wrongly harmed someone else's interests is, when considered in the cold light of reason, hard to understand. Second, one may doubt that an appeal to particular moral intuitions can help to dispel the mystery. For while we would often be inclined to assent to the claim that a particular person deserves to suffer for what he has done, the thought behind our inclination may not be adequately expressed in the precise words we accept. Our underlying thought may simply be that the criminal ought to be punished for his crime and that his punishment will be justified not by its effects but by the fact of the crime itself. But this intuition can

11. Some quasi-retributivist conceptions that bring punishment under the heading of rectification also do without forfeiture. Versions of these views can be found in Herbert Morris's "Persons and Punishment," *The Monist* 52, no. 4 (October 1968): 475–501, and in Jeffrie Murphy's *Retribution, Justice and Therapy* (Boston: Reidel, 1979), pp. 73–115 and 223–49. Such accounts, while attractive in many ways, face a number of problems. If punishment is modeled on the payment of a debt or the cancellation of an illicit liberty, it must be explained why the matter cannot be set right, voluntarily, in other ways. Moreover, in clear cases of rectification, there is the possibility of transferring the misappropriated property or power either to its rightful owner or to someone with a better claim to it than the wrongful possessor has. In punishment, however, there is a "taking away" from the criminal without any obvious transfer of what is taken away to anyone else. For some other criticisms of these views see Richard Burgh's "Do the Guilty Deserve Punishment?," *Journal of Philosophy* 79, no. 4 (April 1982): 193–210.

be valid in the nonretributivist account of punishment that I shall now present.

This conception, unlike those we have considered, gives equal attention to two temporally distinct components of the practice of punishment. The first is establishing the real risk of punishment, creating serious *threats* of punishment designed to deter crime. The second is, of course, the actual *punishing* of those who have ignored the threats. According to this conception, the standard theories err in assuming that the right to threaten punishment derives from the anticipation of an independently intelligible right to punish. The central idea of this conception is, in contrast, that the right to make people liable to punishment is the *ground* of our right to punish.[12] Another way to put this claim is to say that according to conventional theories one cannot object to being subject to the threat of punishment because one will not, if one commits the offense, be able to object to being punished, whereas on the present view, it is because one could not object to the threat in the first place that one cannot, later, object to being punished.

To create (or establish) a threat against x, in the quasi-technical sense that I intend in this discussion, is *first, deliberately to create a real risk that x will suffer a certain evil if he does or omits a certain specified action and second, to warn x of the existence of this risk, where by these means x may possibly be deterred from the act or omission.*[13] I mean this quasi-technical use to include the making of ordinary sincere threats.[14] In this most simple case the conditional danger lies in the intention of the threatener to carry out the threat. But in typical practices of punishment the conditional danger derives from an already existing "machinery" of the law. This "machinery" is, in large part, made up of the dispositions of various functionaries to make their assigned contributions to the proc-

12. Thomas Hurka advances this idea in "Rights and Capital Punishment," *Dialogue* 21, no. 4 (December 1982): 649. (But he seems to take it back or at least to modify it on p. 659, where he asserts that punishment, by which I take him to mean punishing, is impermissible unless *it* promotes the social good.) Hurka suggests a view of punishment in many respects like the one I am advancing, but he defends it on p. 650 with what seems to me a very dubious libertarian argument.

13. As I mean it, the warning condition is satisfied where a general risk that applies to x is publicized but x does not, through his own fault, become aware of it and in cases where x knows of the risk independently of any explicit warning that might be given.

14. But mere bluffs and threats in which the threatener hasn't really decided whether he would carry out the threat are excluded.

ess by which guilty persons come to be punished. But I shall also be considering a kind of general threat in which the danger is created by activating artificial devices. To speak of a threat in such a case will further extend the ordinary notion, which normally includes the idea that the threatened evil will come by way of some intentional human action.

When we create threats of punishment we are, according to the theory I wish to develop, justified by our rights of *self-protection*.[15] It is morally legitimate to create these threats because it is morally legitimate to try to protect ourselves in this way against violations of our moral rights. Viewed the other way round, we cannot object to certain deterrent threats of punishment that stand against us because others have a right to try to protect themselves from us by these means. The theory asserts that a practice of punishment is at its moral core a practice of self-protective threats.

I shall try to make this two-stage conception of punishment clearer and more plausible in the course of the discussion. But even from the present sketch one can see that it is in some ways like both standard deterrent and standard retributive theories. Like the former, it refers the justification of punishment to the goal of prevention. But unlike them, it does not try to justify *acts* of punishment as means to that end.[16] Only the prior threats are justified in this way. Like familiar retributive theories, it is backward-looking in its account of the right to punish, but unlike them it invokes no primitive notion of desert. Instead it explains the right to punish by reference to the right to establish the original threat.

This conception raises two different questions. First, whether the right to create the threat of punishment is, as I claim, grounded in a right of self-protection. Second, whether the right to punish is, as I claim, derivative from the right to establish the threat. The first question is not totally

15. In "The Doomsday Machine: Proportionality, Punishment and Prevention," *The Monist* 63, no. 2 (April 1980), Lawrence Alexander distinguishes two different practices within what we call punishment, one of which rests on what I call rights of self-protection.

16. In this respect it may seem to be like the well-known mixed views of punishment put forward by John Rawls in "Two Concepts of Rules," *Philosophical Review* 44 (1955): 3–32, and H.L.A. Hart in "Prolegomenon to the Principles of Punishment" in Hart, *Punishment and Responsibility* (New York: Oxford University Press, 1968). In their rule-consequentialist aspects, however, both these views (if my previous argument was correct) justify acts of punishment, taken collectively, by reference to their collective preventive effects. The crucial distinction in these theories is between whole (practice) and part (act) while in the present theory it is between the earlier threat and the later punishment.

independent of the second, and we therefore need a strategy for resolving all of its independently resolvable parts. The strategy I have chosen is to construct an imaginary practice of threatening in which all threatened evils are to be delivered by fully automatic devices. This twist allows us to examine the moral basis for making threats in abstraction from the question of the specific right to carry them out. The kind of automated practice I will construct is, of course, meant to be *purely self-protective* in its function and moral ground. I shall examine such a practice in Section I, where I shall not presuppose that it is, apart from its automatic character, the moral equivalent of punishment. I shall compare the two practices in Section II, where I shall argue that they are indistinguishable in the distribution of acceptable penalties. I will try to show that, apart from the question of the right to carry out actual punishment, there is nothing in the workings of a justified practice of punishment that prevents us from seeing it as a practice of self-protective threats. I shall confront the final difficulty in Section III, where I shall try to show how the right to punish can derive from the right to create the earlier threat.

I

Let us imagine ourselves existing at some time in the future when, our social structures having been destroyed by earlier upheavals, we come together to form a new community. Being scientifically very advanced, although no more moral or prudent than we were, we are together capable of making fantastically complex devices that can (at least as well as we can) detect wrongdoing in our new community, identify and apprehend those who are responsible, establish their guilt, and subject them to incarcerations (and perhaps other evils) that I shall call mechanical-punishments, or m-punishments for short.[17] Let us further imagine that we have lost whatever taste we once had for retribution and are interested only in protection. The devices attract us, therefore, in their deterrent rather than in their retributive capacities. Furthermore, we are not particularly concerned with the theoretical question whether using the devices for protection would constitute a new form of civic punishment.

17. The antecedents of these devices in the current literature are Lawrence Alexander's Doomsday Machines which differ from our devices in offering only one drastic penalty for any crime, and James Buchanan's automatic enforcing agents in *The Limits of Liberty* (Chicago: University of Chicago Press, 1975), p. 95.

We are prepared, however, to acknowledge that there may be limits within the morality of self-protection that resemble limits on justifiable punishment. And we are therefore glad of the sophistication of the devices, which may not only be programmed to mete out different m-punishments for different crimes, but may also be set, in virtue of their remarkable (but not infallible) ability to determine the state of mind in which someone committed a crime, to withhold m-punishments in kinds of cases that we do not wish to bring under the threats. We are also glad that the devices can be so conservatively programmed that they will never be "fooled" into m-punishing the innocent. For, as it happens, we prefer this form of safety even though it means that the devices may sometimes fail to identify the guilty, a possibility made even more likely by our further wish that they be programmed to "pay" scrupulous attention to civil liberties in their criminal "investigations."[18]

It is not surprising that we are drawn to the prospect of deterring crime by means of the general threats posed by these devices. We are attracted, to be sure, by their efficiency and powers of discrimination (which I am supposing to be at least as great as ours), but we are even more pleased to leave the unpleasant business of enforcement to nonhuman enforcers. For it must be remembered that these automatic devices, while marvelously sophisticated, are not persons responsible for authentic moral choices. Should we choose to use them, their operation would involve only that choice and the choices that determined their design and program. To insure the completeness of this desirable isolation from human control let us also suppose that once the devices have been activated for a certain predetermined period, they cannot then be interfered with. For the choice whether or not to stop or alter them could, at some point, be tantamount to the choice whether or not someone will be m-punished.

The fact that our only choices are initial ones seems to throw new light on the question of our right to protect ourselves by way of threats. Without the devices, an effective system of deterrent threats can exist only if some of us are prepared to make independent choices to carry them out. And these independent acts must, it naturally appears, be justified in one of

18. Throughout this article I shall simply ignore the difficulty of justifying a practice that, like all actual practices, sometimes punishes the innocent. And by imagining devices that are programmed to operate under all the principled constraints that would govern the best human punishers, I hope to avoid any objection to their automatic and artificial character.

the familiar but unsatisfying ways already considered.[19] With the devices,
however, there are no such independent choices. There is instead an
initial choice to establish an ongoing deterrent threat, where it is foreseen
that this will, in all probability, cause m-punishments to occur. In this
situation, our choice to bring about future m-punishments is *derivative*,
an unavoidable consequence of our more basic choice to set up the threat.
That this is so is shown by the fact that we would not choose to create
the threat if we foresaw that m-punishments would occur without protecting us, but that we would choose to create the threat if we foresaw
that it would be so effective that m-punishments would never occur. And
it is morally significant that our choice to bring about m-punishments is,
in this sense, derivative. For derivative choices may sometimes be justified by that which can be said for the basic choices to which they attach.
In our new situation, therefore, we may be able to see how to justify
bringing about m-punishments even if we cannot see how to justify
independent choices to carry out threats that have failed.

This restructuring of the problem would not be available if we were
retributivists using the devices as surrogate retributors. For then each
m-punishment would be a kind of end for us. But our actual end is nothing
other than protection from crime. And it is the threat of m-punishment
rather than m-punishment itself that we call upon this end to justify. It
is important, however, to see that our choice is to create a *real* and not
a deceptive, threat. A deceptive threat may have the advantage of not
leading to any m-punishments, but it will not protect us as well as a real
threat. For some people will have to know of the deception. And, in the
scientifically advanced community we are imagining, others will surely
suspect it. More important, such deception would be morally insupport-
able. It is one thing for a private individual to protect himself by bluffing.
But it is an altogether different thing for civic authorities, acting in their
official capacities, to practice wholesale deception in a matter as vital as
this to each citizen's interest. We therefore have both practical and moral
reasons to create a real threat if we create any.

It does not, however, follow from the fact that our threat is real and
will, therefore, almost certainly lead to m-punishments that our initial
justification must appeal to the anticipated deterrent effects of those m-

19. I shall argue in Section III that this appearance is deceptive, and that the justificatory
structure of an actual punishment system is really like that of a system of m-punishment.

punishments. If such an appeal were necessary, then the future m-punishments themselves, along with the threat of them, would enter our
scheme of justification as means of protection. But the justifiction we
seek makes no such appeal. We see that each m-punishment will occur
as the result of the previous existence of a real threat, and we insist that
each such prior threat be completely justified by reference to the protection that *it* can be expected to create.

To see how this justification works, we may begin by considering the
initial period from the moment of activation up through the occurrence
of the first crime that the devices will subsequently m-punish. We do not
know exactly how long or short this period will be. But we have good
empirical grounds for believing that, given human nature, it cannot be
very long. The activators must therefore ask themselves whether they
would be justified in establishing the threat (with its risk of giving rise
to m-punishments) for any stretch of time that might realistically constitute this initial period even if the deterrent force of the threat were not
to be reinforced by the publicized occurrence of any m-punishment. This
is to insist on a justification for activating the devices for any such stretch
that appeals only to protection that would result from the publicized fact
of activation itself (from the general belief that the devices will work)
and from possible artificial demonstrations of their effectiveness.

If the protection created by these factors alone would justify establishing the threat for any such duration, then the first m-punishment would
clearly be justified, not as a means to later protection, but as an unavoidable empirical consequence of our having enjoyed an earlier protection.[20] And each subsequent m-punishment would presumably be justified in the same manner, by reference to the period of threatening that
preceded it. Of course, there may come a time when the deterrent effects
of publicized m-punishments become essential to the continued justifiability of the ongoing threat. If, fantastically, all m-punishments were
kept secret, some would-be criminals might eventually cease to believe
in the reality of m-punishment. But given that each actual nonsecret m-
punishment is justified by reference to the threat that preceded it, each

20. Speaking of the justification of m-punishments is, of course, shorthand for speaking
of the justification of the original activation insofar as it was foreseeable that they would
result. As already noted, m-punishments are not real actions, and the devices are not real
agents. So, strictly speaking, m-punishments are not the sorts of things that can be morally
justified or unjustified.

may be allowed to contribute its deterrent effects to the case for the continuing threat. For it does so as something already justified quite independently of those effects.

The key to this scheme is the fact that activation for a shorter term never depends for its justification on activation for a longer term. The first, second, third, etc. m-punishments are therefore each justified as empirically unavoidable costs of and not as producers of protection. Each m-punishment is seen as the byproduct of a period to which it does not contribute any deterrence. And it is nothing other than the fact that there is no separate choice to bring about the m-punishments, that our choices are tied together in a single initial choice to activate and create the standing threat, that makes this pattern of justification stand out.

On this conception, everything depends on our initial right to protect ourselves by placing would-be criminals under real threats. This right is akin to, but in some ways different from, the right of self-defense and the right to construct protective barriers. It allows us to make offenses less tempting by attaching to them the real prospect of costs, in this case costs that may, as a matter of the operation of automatic devices, follow crimes. If each member of our imaginary community possessed such a right and exercised it by authorizing that all others in the community be placed under the discipline of the devices not to commit offenses against him, then the activation could, on the present view, be completely justified.

The claim that there is such a right is made plausible by considering other, more familiar, self-protective rights that permit us to create serious risks for wrongdoers. First, we may mount appropriately limited, violent self-defense against attacks on our persons and property. Second, we may erect barriers, such as difficult-to-scale fences, to prevent such attacks. Third, we may arrange that an automatic cost *precede* or *accompany* the violation of some right, a cost that is not designed to frustrate the violation but rather to provide a strong reason not to attempt it. The one-way tire spikes placed at the exits of private parking areas provide a commonplace example. And fourth, we may confine those who have shown in the crimes they have committed that they cannot be controlled by other strategies of self-protection.

The first, second, and fourth of these familiar rights are, most fundamentally, rights to render or try to render someone incapable of committing or consummating some crime or crimes. In defending ourselves, we try to frustrate an offense by disabling the offender.[21] The harm we thereby create may be justified as a means of incapacitating the criminal *or* as an unavoidable side effect of an attempt to block the crime. In erecting very high fences or in confining the incorrigible we attempt to render would-be offenders unable to undertake various offenses. The third right (like the right to which we appeal in activating the devices) has, however, a different strategic character. In attaching costs to crimes, we attempt to prevent an offense by giving the would-be offender reason not to undertake it.[22] But both the basic strategies of incapacitation and threat are designed to protect, and both involve, as we have seen, a connection between the commission of a crime and the possibility of a resulting evil.

Each of these familiar four rights of self-protection has the same wide scope, holding not only within civil society but also in a state of nature. Individuals in a state of nature may defend themselves, set up obstructive barriers, establish automatic costs to accompany violations of their rights, and confine those who are incorrigibly dangerous. I also claim that they have the right to which the activators appeal, the right to use devices that promise costs to follow violations of rights. I cannot, of course, prove this. But reflection on certain features of the other rights of self-protection makes this claim plausible. Consider, for example, the form of self-defense in which the evil that results for the attacker is a side effect rather than a means of defense. The moral acceptability of this form of self-defense shows clearly that the evils created by a legitimate strategy of self-protection need not be justified by reference to *their* effects.

The comparison with the right to create threats of evils to precede or accompany an offense provides even more support. Suppose the best fence that someone in a state of nature can erect to block an attack on his life cannot stop some vigorous and agile enemies. He would then, under this right, be permitted to place dangerous spikes at the top of the fence in order to discourage those who could otherwise scale it. These spikes, like the more familiar ones in parking lots, would not stop a would-

21. Philippa Foot points out to me that one might do this by psychological rather than physical means, by falsely saying, for example, "Your son has been killed."

22. The prospect of a vigorous self-defense may also, of course, give a would-be offender such a reason. But the justification for risking injury to an attacker in defending ourselves does not, I am supposing, arise out of our prior right to create the threat of this injury. If one thinks otherwise, then the justificatory structure I allege to be present in the case of punishment is already present in self-defense.

be offender who is willing to accept any cost, but they would provide most would-be offenders with excellent reasons to hold back. But suppose, to take the story one step further, our defender cannot arrange the spikes so that they offer a threat of injury to someone entering his territory but can arrange them so that they clearly offer a threat of injury to an enemy leaving his territory after an attack. And suppose that the latter arrangement would discourage attacks just as effectively as the former. It would, I submit, be very odd to think that he could have the right to build the first kind of fence but not the second.[23] What morally relevant difference could it make to a would-be wrongdoer that the injury whose prospect is designed to discourage him will come earlier or later? In either case, the injury is not there to stop him if he tries to attack but rather to motivate him not to attack. But building the second kind of fence is nothing more than creating an automatic cost to *follow* an offense. It is, in fact, a very primitive kind of m-retaliating device.

If we do indeed have the self-protective right to create the prospect of such costs, then each of us would, prior to the establishment of a public system of protection, have the right to protect himself by activating a suitably programmed personal m-retaliation device like the public devices that, thanks to our combined resources, we now possess. Of course, even in our imaginary situation we do not have such personal devices, but the fact that we would have the moral right to use them bears directly on our present problem. For each of us may now contribute that private self-protective right to the general authorization to activate the public devices we actually possess. But here a new problem arises. For even if everyone, as I am supposing, prefers protection by the devices to protection by other available means, not everyone is likely to prefer protection by the devices *and* the risk of suffering m-punishments to protection by other means *and* the risk of suffering from the use of those means by others. Some people, whom we may call *rejectors*, will surely fear the increased risk of suffering for their own future crimes more than they welcome the increased protection against the crimes of others. But we may safely

---

23. It would not, in every case, follow from the fact that he could build the second kind of fence instead of the first that he could build a fence that combined the two threats. My view here is that there is a single self-protective right to attach deterrent costs to offenses whether these costs are to precede, accompany, or follow the offense. If this is correct, then it is plausible to think that there must be a common limit to the total costs that can be attached to a given offense. The fence that poses a two-way threat might exceed this limit.

assume that most people, whom we may call *acceptors*, will prefer the practice of m-punishment, all things considered, and would therefore agree to its full implementation.

It is the acceptors who will, in the situation I am imagining, bring about full activation of the devices in a series of partial activations. Their first step will be to activate the devices with a program that places everyone under threat not to violate the rights of any acceptor. In doing this each acceptor will draw on his own right to make private self-protective threats. The acceptors will then proceed to ask each rejector, in turn, to permit them to extend the operation of the devices so that all are placed under threat not to violate *his* rights. Since even the rejectors welcome the increased protection against crime provided by threats of civic m-punishments, each will be willing. For in accepting this offer of protection a (former) rejector incurs no new risk for himself. His risk of being m-punished comes not from his own acceptance but from that by others. Each person's right of self-protection will thus be exercised and everyone will be brought under the discipline of the devices.[24]

It is important to see that this justification for placing rejectors under the threat of m-punishment is not an argument from fairness. It is not that a rejector may be made subject to the threats because he himself wishes to be protected by those same threats as they fall on others. If that were the argument, the rejector could escape the liabilities of the practice by simply withdrawing from its protections. Instead, the situation in a civil society is the same as in a state of nature, where it is clear that one person may make reasonably limited threats of m-retaliation against others quite independently of whether any of them returns the threats. The source of the first person's right to threaten lies in his legitimate interest in safeguarding himself from the possible misconduct of the others rather than in what the others must, in fairness, accept in return for their threats against him. It is for this reason that one cannot gain moral exemption from these threats by renouncing the use of them. (The same thing also holds of self-defense. One does not lose the right to defend onself against a wrongdoer if, strangely, he has renounced the right to defend himself.) So once a rejector sees that, whatever he decides, others

24. While the acceptors would have agreed to the full practice, and so to their own liability to m-punishment, the full practice does not come about by way of any such agreement. As it happens, no one actually agrees to his own full liability to m-punishment. For that liability always arises by way of other people exercising their right of self-protection.

may justifiably subject him to the discipline of the devices, he will see that he has every reason to authorize his own protection.[25]

Our justification for activating the devices is now complete. Because of its special character, it escapes the earlier objections to the familiar deterrent and retributive theories of punishment. It is clear, for instance, that in placing someone under a threat in hope of keeping him from crime, we are not using him. This does not mean, of course, that threatening in the interest of self-protection is never morally objectionable. To threaten someone is to bring a certain kind of force to bear on him (a force that we identify as intimidation when it is not justified), and such force in human affairs is often wrong. But threatening a person so that he will act in certain ways and using him so that others shall act in certain

25. Of course the rejectors might agree among themselves to refuse the protection of the devices and to form instead a partial state of nature within the community, in which their relations with each other would be reciprocally disciplined by threats of retaliation and their relations with acceptors would be governed by their own threats of retaliation and the acceptors' threats of m-punishment. But there are reasons to doubt that any agreement to execute such a limited escape from the devices would be clearly enough in their interest to be stable. One gain from such an agreement would be the reduced risk involved in violating the rights of other rejectors (since retaliation is less sure than m-punishment). One loss would be an increased risk of misplaced retaliation by other rejectors. (Acceptors are less vulnerable to this risk since rejectors know that the devices will punish all improper retaliations.) But the gain is of doubtful importance. For to the extent that the rejectors' choice to forego protection by the devices indicates that they have little to protect, they may be unattractive as targets of criminal opportunity. (While disadvantaged criminal rejectors may, for reasons of convenience, prey largely on other disadvantaged rejectors, they may stand to gain relatively little real advantage from this.) And the loss is significant. For to the extent that the rejectors' choice indicates that they are indifferent to the moral order, the risk of misplaced retaliation by them is indeed frightening. Thus even if the rejectors would prefer no practice of m-punishment at all, they will have reasons to prefer a total practice to a partial practice of the type in question. Moreover, whenever any party to such an agreement broke faith and went over to the acceptors there would probably be, if the above is correct, even more reason for others to follow. (And such defection could not rationally be prevented by threatening reprisal or even by threatening specially dreadful retaliations for any crimes that defectors might commit against the remaining rejectors. For reprisals or improperly severe retaliations against acceptors by rejectors are themselves crimes that the devices will m-punish.) Of course, if the original acceptors could rightly, as I think they might, make it impossible for the rejectors to communicate, for instance, by surprising each of them with a sudden, irrevocable, and required choice, then the rejectors, assuming that an agreement to reject the practice would be in their collective interest, would be in a prisoner's dilemma. For each would see that no matter what the others did, he would be best off choosing more rather than less protection. Assuming that a fully general practice of m-punishment would be socially beneficial overall, this is a case in which a prisoner's dilemma would work for rather than against the community as a whole!

ways involve quite different moral relations to his will. That a threat is designed to make the threatened party behave as he morally should is a fact that gives it, if not full justification, at least some moral support. However, the fact that an injury to someone helps keep others in line is almost nothing in its moral favor. This means that while a right to punish a criminal in order to deter others cannot be basic (but must, when it exists, derive from some more fundamental right), a right to compel potential criminals to respect one's rights could be basic.[26]

Nor is it the case that we must appeal to forfeiture in order to explain our rights of self-protection. In fact, such an appeal would be subject to the earlier objections. We get a better explanation of these rights if we focus on *actions* and the protections that morality may assign to or withhold from them rather than on *agents* and the general rights they may keep or forfeit. Innocent actions that do not menace others are *morally protected*. This protection consists in the fact that we may not in general attempt to prevent them coercively or frustrate them violently. Violations of important moral rights are, on the other hand, *morally exposed*. That is, we may try to prevent or frustrate them by means that would, in other contexts, violate their agents' rights. That morality should withhold some protection from some seriously wrong actions is easily understood. For these are the very acts that, morally speaking, should not take place. And, to draw a final contrast with retributivism, the explanation of why rights must be contoured so as to permit threats, namely, the appeal to the need to protect ourselves from crime, has an obviousness and compelling clarity missing in retributivists' accounts of the right to punish. That morality should expose would-be wrongdoers to threats in order to prevent wrongdoing is easier to understand than that morality should expose actual wrongdoers to retribution.

Before concluding this examination of m-punishment, we must briefly consider the upper limits on the severity of the m-punishment that may justifiably be threatened for a given type of crime.[27] That there are such

26. It will become clear in Section III that I think it *can* be morally permissible to punish someone with the intention of deterring others, so long as the right to punish is independently secured.

27. In "The Doomsday Machine" Alexander claims that we may threaten those who are competent and free with *any* penalty for any violation of our rights. He argues from an alleged lack of constraints on the self-protective right to construct dangerous barriers such as moats and electric fences. But I think there are substantial constraints even here, constraints that may easily be obscured by the fact that these barriers are generally created

limits and that they are a proper part of the morality of self-protection can be seen by looking at other self-protective rights. The moral right to defend our property does not permit us to kill a burglar whom we know intends us no physical harm. Nor may we erect an extremely dangerous barrier to prevent harmless trespassing. These examples show that the morality of self-protection contains its own rough standard of proportionality. While we may attempt to prevent more serious crimes by creating risks of greater evils, some evils are too great for some crimes. This idea of proportionality is *not* tied to the ideas of retribution and desert. No retributivist claims that the right of self-defense is a right of retribution, but no retributivist can plausibly deny that the right of self-defense is governed by some requirement of proportionality.

The theory of these limits is complex and difficult, and I can here make only some general and tentative suggestions. Using self-defense as a guide, it seems that we do not have to justify particular self-protective threats by any hard and fast criterion of expected general utility. Someone defending himself against an attacker is not burdened by the need to justify the degree of danger that his defense creates by reference to its chance of success. He is entitled to defend himself in ways that put his attacker at risk of evils that are intuitively proportionate to the intended offense even if there is very little chance that the defense will succeed. The same is surely true of self-protective threatening. A penalty cannot be ruled out simply because the threat of it creates more danger for potential wrongdoers than protection for potential victims of crime.

It also seems clear that ·self-protective threats are not subject to the

---

to prevent a variety of crimes ranging from relatively minor intrusions to very serious assaults. With such a wide range of protection in mind we tend to allow the barrier to create dangers that might be unacceptable if it were used to prevent only the less serious crimes. Thus it would be more defensible to put a very dangerous electric fence around one's house than around a vacant piece of land from which one wished to discourage poaching. And in the latter case, I think it would be seriously wrong to erect such a fence. One should not be confused here by the fact that we may not be obligated to *remove* a barrier that is no more than appropriately dangerous for typical wrongdoers when we realize that some particular wrongdoer may have a special liability to be hurt by it. That is, after all, a special case. Alexander is scandalized by the thought that we might be able to frustrate or deter a crime but not be morally permitted to do so. One can understand this reaction but nevertheless feel certain that such cases are frequent. It must be remembered, however, that if a wrongdoer has proved himself ready to brave all obstacles that we may properly place in the path of his crimes, we may call upon the right of preventive confinement. But we should not confuse this right with the right to carry out threats.

retributivist's standard of equivalence—that the degree of the threatened evil must equal, or at least not exceed, the degree of the evil created by (or intended in) the offense. For if, in a single self-protective response to a possible crime, we may not create an evil for the would-be wrongdoer exceeding that present or intended in the offense, it is hard to see why the *sum* of our self-protective responses to that crime should not be governed by the same limit. But, intuitively, there is no such overall limit, and its adoption would not seem advisable. Self-protective threats of m-punishments will be our defenses of first resort, serving to keep contemplated offenses from ever eventuating. Their capacity to play this role would be considerably diminished if potential criminals knew that any injury they might receive from a victim's self-defense would reduce their m-punishment. Indeed, such an arrangement would sometimes encourage criminals to persevere when they might otherwise be stopped by fear of a vigorous defense. And in some instances it would mean that criminals could not be penalized at all. Consider, for example, a case in which one breaks the arm of an assailant in an unsuccessful attempt to prevent his breaking one's own arm. It seems absurd to think that we must program the devices to withhold m-punishment in such a case.

It also seems absurd to suppose that strict equivalence sets the limit for any individual self-protective response. We may certainly risk breaking both arms of an assailant to keep him from breaking one of ours. And we may threaten m-punishments that are, by ordinary preference rankings, worse than the evils typically inflicted by the crimes they address.[28] There is, however, one consideration that suggests that the limits on what may be threatened must often be set somewhat lower than the limits on what may be done in self-defense. When a threat is made we cannot be sure that this is our last chance of self-protection. But when we are forced to defend ourselves, it is almost always because our other options have run out.

The aim of self-protection does not, however, provide a carte blanche. Self-defense does not, as I have noted, justify any degree of violence against any attack. And some form of proportionality must surely also be observed in making threats of m-punishment. But it is an important and interesting question just why this should be so. Assuming that a potential

---

28. This is true for serious crimes that because of standard insurance typically result in negligible net loss to the victim and crimes, such as some violations of privacy, that typically result in no harm at all.

criminal does not have to violate our rights, why must we take care not
to threaten him with too much in order to deter him?

Morality, I have claimed, exposes wrongs so that they may be prevented
or frustrated. It therefore designs variances in some of our rights so that
these rights will not interfere with a range of defensive strategies. The
question before us is why our rights do not give way so completely that
any defense or any threat may be directed against any offense. The answer, I think, is that they retain some force in order to protect those
aspects of ourselves and our lives that go beyond any situation in which
we choose to commit a crime. Someone who disregards a serious penal
threat jeopardizes not only himself and his interests as they are then,
but also himself and his interests as they have been and will be. In
imposing limits on the dangers that may be placed in his path, morality
refuses, in effect, to regard him at the time of a criminal choice as a fully
competent disposer of the whole of himself and his life.[29] We may wonder
whether morality would extend this protection to beings who were fully
rational and totally consistent over time. But it is surely appropriate for
us. For human criminals, like the rest of us, have interests and psychological identities that vastly exceed what they can see and defend in a
single part of their lives. Morality requires some respect and protection
for these larger components of a criminal's identity and good even while
it permits us to protect ourselves against him. The result of these conflicting moral pressures is, as one would expect, a compromise.

This compromise naturally results in an upper bound to what may be
threatened for a given crime, a limit that wisely allows more serious m-
punishments to be threatened for more serious crimes. Such a constraint
sets a limit to the worst thing that may happen to a wrongdoer as a direct
effect of the threat against him.[30] A limit of this form can also be defended
from the point of view of the comparative importance of the various rights
involved.[31] If one is trying to protect oneself from having one's pocket

29. This is, in one sense, paternalistic. But not in the way in which paternalism is usually
thought to be objectionable. Objectionable paternalism prohibits people from doing what
they may wish to do on the ground that it may be bad for them, and so causes complaints
from those who are protected. The present constraints, however, raise objections not from
those whom they protect but from those whose protection they limit.

30. By a direct effect I mean one that falls within the direct intention expressed in the
threat. If the threat is a threat of death, then death can be a direct effect. If, however, the
threat is of a certain term of imprisonment, and such imprisonment quite accidentally
happens to cause death, the death is not a direct effect of the threat.

31. See Hurka's "Rights and Capital Punishment," p. 652.

picked one should simply not have the life of the potential pickpocket at one's disposal as material from which to fashion threats. A credible threat of death for such a crime would be a grave moral indignity which even the certainty of deterrence would not diminish.

The ceilings on what may be threatened for different categories of crime must also vary to some extent with several factors other than the seriousness of the offense. First, it is plausible to think that the ceiling may be raised for persons who are especially dangerous, people who have shown themselves ready to commit serious crimes.[32] Second, the ceiling may be raised for crimes that are especially prevalent or are threatening to become so. Here the limit on the threatened evil may be raised generally and not only for people who have demonstrated their particular dangerousness. But this factor should be allowed much less influence than the first. For it is natural to suppose that circumstances largely beyond one's control should not significantly increase one's penal liabilities.[33] Third, the ceiling may be raised for crimes whose detection rates are especially low, at least if this promises a noticeable gain in prevention. But this too would have a limited impact for the reason just mentioned. (This third factor, it should be noted, creates a special theoretical problem that will be important later. In effect, the more severe m-punishments introduced by this consideration are justified only because the guilty are less likely to suffer them. And I believe this means that what is justified in such a case is not the straightforward threat of an m-punishment but the threat of a certain [no doubt vaguely specified] *probability* of receiving an m-punishment. In real practices of punishment the analogous threats are, I shall claim, justified only as threats to *try* to punish.)

II

In imagining our new community and its amazing devices we have, in effect, examined a particular type of protective social practice, the practice

32. Of course, at the moment someone commits a serious crime he is undeniably dangerous. Dangerousness must therefore refer to the general disposition of a person toward the type of crime in question during some fairly long period of time. Taken in this sense, a person may commit a crime without having been dangerous.

33. But to allow this factor to have some influence is not to use the additional jeopardy to a particular potential criminal as a means of deterring others. The additional strength of the threat against him simply addresses the fact that he is a member of the community and that members of the community have, in general, shown an alarming tendency toward the crime in question.

of m-punishment. One of its features, the fact that no persons have to
carry out the threats, clearly distinguishes it from punishment. And the
fact that it is fully grounded in rights of self-protection might appear to
mark another difference. My task in the rest of this article is to show
that neither of these features is incompatible with the thesis that acceptable practices of m-punishment and acceptable practices of punishment have, *au fond*, the same moral nature. In this section I shall address
the second feature, arguing that the penalties of any intuitively justified
practice of punishment would be what we should expect if the moral
point of the practice were self-protection. Some terminology will be helpful here. Let's say that a possible practice of punishment and a possible
practice of m-punishment are *counterparts* if both threaten penalties of
just the same severity for just the same crimes.[34] The thesis that I now
wish to defend is this: Every intuitively justified practice of punishment
has as its counterpart a practice of m-punishment justified by rights of
self-protection, and vice versa. I shall call this the thesis of the functional
moral equivalence of counterpart practices (or, for short, the thesis of
functional equivalence). This thesis is composed of two claims: first, that
exactly the same offenses are properly penalizable in each practice and,
second, that all offenses properly penalizable in both practices are penalizable to exactly the same degree in each.

We may take up the somewhat less difficult question of degree of
penalization first. It is hard to see how punishments or m-punishments
could ever, in being too mild, violate the rights of those who come under
threat of them. Our question therefore becomes whether some properly
penalizable crime might be subject to a justified threat of a certain punishment even though the counterpart threat of an equally severe m-
punishment would be too harsh, or vice versa. Now it seems hard to
imagine that a punishment for a given type of crime might be acceptable
but the counterpart m-punishment too severe. If a crime is serious enough
to be punishable with a severe penalty it must be a very unwelcome
violation of rights and therefore subject, under the right of self-protection,
to the threat of a severe m-punishment.

However, it might seem that justified m-punishments could be *more*
severe than justified punishments for the same crime. For we have seen
that the right of self-protective threatening is not subject to retributory

---

34. I shall also speak of similarly positioned threats and penalties in counterpart practices
as counterpart threats and counterpart penalties.

equivalence as a limit on what may be threatened. But, so far as I can see, our ordinary intuitions about particular punishments reject this limit just as decisively. At least this is true if retributory equivalence is determined by anything like usual preference rankings. Consider, for example, our typical legal penalties for crimes against property. Surely the average person, even the average thief, would prefer to have his car stolen than to be confined for a month or two. And the same disregard for retributory equivalence is present in many common punishments for assault and molestation. Not very many people would prefer spending six months in a typical American jail to receiving a serious beating that left no long-term disability. Yet this sentence would not seem overly harsh as punishment for such a crime.[35]

Alan Goldman, who remarks on these disparities, finds our intuitions in these cases are paradoxical because he holds that a theory of forefeiture is the most plausible account of the right to punish.[36] In rejecting that account, however, the present theory of punishment rejects the paradox. When considered in light of retributive principles, these widely accepted punishments can, it is true, seem absurdly high. But if our intuitions are to provide any kind of useful touchstone we must not ignore them when they operate most independently of theoretical preconception. And I can see nothing in our actual working intuitions about the upper limits on degrees of punishment that is hostile to the idea that punishments may be set as high as m-punishments. Moreover, each of the special factors that can properly influence the severity of self-protective threats seems equally capable of influencing our feelings about punishment. Consider, for example, the higher penalties we often assign to repeat offenses. Past conviction operates here as a criterion of dangerousness with respect to the type of crime in question. It is also true that we sometimes feel justified in threatening somewhat greater punishments for crimes that are especially prevalent in the community as well as for crimes that pose especially difficult problems of detection and conviction.

Having looked briefly at the question of degree, we must turn to the

35. A disproportion between harm done in the commission of a crime and harm received in punishment can hardly be avoided in punishments for attempted but unsuccessful crimes. Here retributory equivalence must refer, I suppose, to the harm intended by the criminal.

36. "The Paradox of Punishment," *Philosophy & Public Affairs* 9, no. 1 (Fall 1979): 42–58.

more difficult question whether counterpart practices would justifiably threaten penalties for just the same offenses. At first, it seems clear that wherever we properly threaten punishment the counterpart threat of an m-punishment would be equally justified on purely self-protective grounds. This is true even for threats against attempted crimes. If we did not bring substantial attempts under threat of m-punishment, would-be criminals would know that they could, without risk, always place themselves in an advantageous position from which to decide whether or not to risk committing penalizable crimes. They could start the project and then decide to abort it if the risk of proceeding seemed too great, or to complete the project (under the favorable terms secured by their preparation) if the risk seemed low. Not to place some attempted crimes under threat of penalty would be very dangerous.37

A more serious challenge to functional equivalence is presented by people who give evidence that they are incited by the prospect of penalties to commit the very crimes to which the penalties attach. It might seem that such people would, if not compulsive or incompetent, be punishable even though it would not be sensible to place them under self-protective threats of m-punishment. In one kind of case (certainly the most familiar), we may know that a person is *sometimes* led toward crime by the prospect of a penalty that usually deters him. It is plausible to think that we may let ordinary general threats of m-punishment stand against such people, even against those particular crimes that they may commit because of the threats. For were we to exempt such crimes, knowledge of the exemption might encourage these people to indulge their more ordinary criminal motives in the hope of seeming to have acted from the

---

37. The punishment of unsuccessful attempts to commit crimes presents theoretical difficulties for more than one conception of punishment. The class of attempted burglaries (whether completed or not) is wider than the class of burglaries (since all burglaries have been attempted but not all attempted burglaries succeed), and therefore we have more to fear from a burglary than from an attempted one. This suggests that the ceiling on the self-protective threat against attempted burglary should be set somewhat lower than the ceiling on the threat against completed burglary. On the way of looking at the matter most congenial to my theory, we do not make any threat specifically directed against attempted *but unsuccessful* burglary, since that class of actions is not particularly dangerous. Rather we make a threat against attempted burglary (whether successful or not) but stipulate that, in cases where an attempt succeeds, the force of the threat is preempted by the force of the threat against actual burglary. As Bentham pointed out, it would be a serious defensive error to make the penalties for attempted crimes as severe as those for completed crimes, since that would eliminate an important incentive to abort crimes under way.

special motive. There seems nothing unjust in increasing our overall protection against someone who is free and able to avoid committing crimes by allowing threats to stand against him on the rare occasions when they do more harm than good. In another (and certainly rarer) kind of case, we may know that a person is so frequently and strongly incited by the prospect of penalties that he would be less dangerous overall were he exempted from the usual threats.[38] We might, of course, be inclined to keep him under them for fear of the effects on others of exempting him. For if we did exempt him, some people who do not suffer from his condition might commit crimes in the hope of appearing to suffer from it. But to refuse for this reason to exempt the known victims of this kind of irrationality would be morally questionable. It would seem to be a matter of using them to gain protection against others.

I am, therefore, inclined to think that such people may not be brought under self-protective threats of m-punishment. And this means that there is, in theory if not in practice, a class of free, but extremely irrational, wrongful acts that may not be m-punished. But how do such offenses stand with regard to punishment? It is not, I think, counterintuitive to judge that the people who commit them are irrational and abnormal in a way that throws doubt on their fitness for inclusion in a genuine practice of punishment. To present them with the prospect of punishment would, in effect, be to *invite* them to commit crimes. A certain kind of retributivist will, of course, disagree with this exemption, finding in this kind of perversely undeterrable crime need for the most stringent, and therefore the most criminally exciting, punishments. But here, I cannot help thinking, retributivism shows itself in a disadvantageous light.

We must now turn to the question whether every m-punishable crime is also punishable. Here different problems arise. The cases that most

38. Note that it might be sensible to place such a person under threat of m-punishment for any criminal act that he can be determined to have committed from more ordinary criminal motives. And if he were sufficiently alert and had enough self-control, these special threats might give us all the protection we could get in the normal case. For the moment that he became aware that he might be about to commit a crime in some perverse reaction to being threatened, he would remember that the special threats do not, then and there, apply to him. The reaction would therefore subside, and he would be brought into a more rational relation to the special threats that stand against him. Substituting these special threats would not make sense, however, if he could not remember their special character or if he could not control his emotional reactions once they had begun. But in that case, he is under such serious psychological handicaps that we may surely doubt that he is fit for punishment.

call for examination are those in which real punishment seems illegitimate despite the fact that an objective violation of rights has occurred.
The question we must ask is whether these cases would also be excluded
from a just self-protective practice of m-punishment. To begin, we may
consider punishment of innocent third parties, for example, punishing
parents for crimes committed by their children. Such a form of punishment is certainly ruled out by ordinary moral intuition. But threatening
third parties might be a very effective means of self-protection. Nevertheless, I think we can see why these threats would be morally illegitimate
considered strictly under rights of self-protection. For whether or not they
succeed in deterring a given crime is not ultimately in the hands of the
party who is in risk of receiving the penalty. And, no matter what the
gain in protection, it is manifestly unjust to threaten to inflict an evil on
someone when it is not up to him to do that which will prevent it.[39]

It is also important to consider cases in which punishing would not be
justified because of the criminal's special mental condition at the time
of the crime. We may first consider the already mentioned case of compulsion.[40] It might seem that there could be no self-protective point to
placing compulsives under threat. But this is incorrect. If genuine com-

39. That this third-party constraint holds properly of the morality of self-protection (and
not just of the morality of retribution) can be seen in the case of self-defense. We can
construct imaginary examples in which a wrongful attack by one person could be physically
frustrated by means of violent reactions directed against another person who is no party to
the attack. Imagine a pair of Siamese twins, A and B, joined so that both will be seriously
injured or die if B is shot but so that B will not die or be seriously injured if only A is shot
(if A is killed B may be surgically separated and saved). Suppose that A assaults you with
the intention to do you grievous bodily harm (dragging the reluctant and vainly struggling
B along). You have a gun, but are physically prevented from aiming it at A. You can,
however, injure or kill A by shooting B. But surely, even though you would be within your
rights to shoot A, the attacker, you cannot shoot the innocent B even to protect your life.
This is not because injury or death is something that B does not deserve. If you were able
to shoot and injure A his injuries would not, I think, be counted by the theory of retribution
as part of his just deserts. These would come only later in his proper punishment. You
may not shoot the innocent B because you are not defending yourself against *him*. This
very fundamental constraint on activities of self-protection is primarily a matter of what
may be in itself intended or done as a means. We must not let it be obscured by overattention
to cases in which self-defense puts nonattackers at risk incidentally. Third-party threats
would, of course, make direct rather than incidental use of a danger that is not in one's
power to prevent.

40. Perhaps compulsion is a matter of degree. If so, then when there is at least some
freedom there may also be room for limited threats and hence for limited penalties. Note
also that threatening certain people might actually enable them to break the grip of what
would otherwise have been their compulsions.

pulsives were excluded, some people who are not true compulsives would be encouraged to commit crimes in the hope of seeming to have been compelled. And since neither we nor the devices can ever be absolutely certain that someone acted wholly by compulsion in committing a crime, even those who give every indication of having been compelled may actually be faking. We therefore have deterrent reasons for refusing to exempt genuine compulsives from our threats. And the thought that we might properly do this is encouraged by a possible analogy with self-defense. We are not obligated to worry about the chance that a defense may be unable to frustrate a crime. Indeed, we are entitled to defend ourselves in ways that can harm an attacker even if we are virtually certain that we cannot succeed because of, say, the attacker's strength. Why then should we worry about the fact that our threats in some cases probably cannot succeed because of someone's compulsion?

The difference is this: Self-defense against an actual criminal is justified as a way of disabling him, while threats are justified as a way of giving a potential criminal reasons. Defending oneself is therefore an activity in which the attacker is simply acted upon. In threatening, however, one assigns a morally essential active role to the threatened party. He is to consider the reasons he is given by the threat and is, if all goes according to plan, to refrain from certain criminal choices at least partly for those reasons. It is one thing to cast someone in this role who (we are certain) will ignore the reasons. But it is quite another to assign the role to someone who cannot be influenced by them. That would be unjust. Nothing like this injustice is present, however, in the case of self-defense that cannot succeed.

The same argument applies, of course, to any mental state in which a person is unable to take account of his reasons for action, for example, hysteria, extreme depression, and a variety of mental illnesses. A related but somewhat different reason applies to people who do harm unwittingly without thereby violating any duty of precaution. Someone who acts in this way is simply not in a position to bring a threat of m-punishment into his deliberation about what he sees himself as doing. Placing such choices under threat of m-punishment would, again, be unjust. It would assign a role to the threatened person that he will be unable to play given what he knows.[41]

41. Acceptable threats to hold someone strictly liable for a type of proscribed action are, I think, best conceived as threats that warn people to take extreme precaution not to do

Suppose, however, the problem that raises the question of punishability is not lack of freedom or relevant factual knowledge. Suppose someone knowingly commits a crime who is free in the sense of being able to engage in and act on his practical deliberations but is unable to understand or appreciate the moral order behind the penal code. Suppose, for example, that we were to discover the existence of a genetic amoralism, a condition that deprives its victim of any moral sensibility or internal moral motivation but does not affect any other cognitive or deliberative faculty. Some genetically amoral people are, we discover, good citizens in whom any antisocial motives are held in check by the nonmoral civilizing motives that affect us all: desire for the esteem of others, fear of disgrace, and especially fear of civic sanctions. Others, perhaps a significant proportion, are criminals. Now, surely we could threaten those genetically amoral people who are free, clearheaded and concerned for their own well-being with m-punishment in an attempt to deter them from crime. But since they are not, in some sense, morally responsible for what they do, could we punish them? Here again I think it is important to consult our moral intuitions in practice rather than when they have passed through the filter of retributive theory. If we do, I think we shall conclude that whether someone is to blame for his own amorality or immorality is, by itself, irrelevant to our actual decisions when and when not to punish him. We routinely punish and, I think, rightly punish sociopathic criminals whom we have absolutely no empirically respectable reason to blame for their conditions. What matters to us is whether

---

the action, even unintentionally. If someone has taken every extreme precaution that can reasonably be required, he may not, on my view, be penalized. The strictness of strict liability cannot properly be strictness in principle. Holding someone subject to threats for forms of behavior that he, through his own fault, does not know to be proscribed is, I think, a special form of strict liability. (Any adult would, of course, have to be mentally defective not to know that the kinds of actions we have been discussing are crimes.) Each of us is, in effect, under threat to take care to learn what is proscribed by the penal code before we act in a manner to which the code may address itself, and the penalty for a failure to take this care, when this leads to the commission of a crime, is the very penalty set for that crime. On this view, when someone is properly penalized for a law of which he was ignorant, the threat with reference to which he is penalized must involve the general (and generally understood) warning to take care to inform oneself about the contents of the penal code. And the evil referred to in this threat is not a penalty, in the usual sense, but rather the prospect of receiving one of a number of different penalties in case the failure to inform oneself leads one to commit one of a number of different crimes. Such threats are special in lacking a full description of the threatened danger. But, since one can always find out the precise character of the danger before one runs afoul of it, they can be fair.

they clearly understood the threats against them and were capable of being deterred by them.[42]

But what about the more extreme case of people who are free in the way we have been considering but whose moral *and* nonmoral sense of reality is not as it should be? Take someone who believes that God tells him to kill as many people as possible. Of course, we sometimes suppose that people who suffer from such massive delusions are in the grip of these delusions in a way that undermines their freedom. But perhaps this is not always true. We must therefore consider possible cases in which people who are disturbed in their thinking but are nevertheless free and able to deliberate, commit crimes. Now we certainly feel that punishment ought to be ruled out in many such cases. And the question is whether the practice of m-punishment would treat these cases in the same way. There is, I think, one reason to think it would. For even if a madman can deliberate, he may not be able to grasp the danger posed by threats of m-punishment; or while he may in some sense grasp the danger, he may be unable to give it proper weight in his deliberation. The rationale for not including such people under threats is therefore the same as that for excluding compulsives. It would be unjust to create dangers for them that they cannot escape or cannot have a reasonable chance of escaping.

But perhaps not all mad criminals are unable to give threats of m-punishment enough weight in their deliberations. Perhaps there are some who retain enough hold on reality to appreciate the full force of the threats. Indeed I suspect that we are confronted with just such crazy but deterrable people in increasing numbers—terrorists and fanatics who act in the name of insane causes but who seem, since they take considerable trouble not to be caught, capable of being influenced by threats. Such people could certainly be placed under threat of m-punishment. But it is equally true, I think, that they may be threatened with punishment properly so called. And I am sure that the thought that they are punishable accords with the ordinary judgments of most of us. It is undeniably true that there is a sense in which such people are often not

---

42. Our own legal systems make knowing right from wrong a condition of punishability in at least certain kinds of cases. But in practice I think that this condition cannot require more than that one be well aware of the contents of the moral code of one's community and the character of its major moral distinctions. And this is a kind of knowledge that genetically amoral and other disturbed persons could fully possess.

to be blamed for what they do. They are not like those of us who commit crimes from familiar and contemptible motives of greed or lust, and they may be no more responsible for their disturbed outlook than genetically amoral persons are responsible for their lack of genuine moral motivation. But there is a sense in which they may be held responsible for the real crimes they commit. For they commit them freely and deliberately in full knowledge that they are under threat designed to deter them. This sense of responsibility is usually enough to satisfy our everyday sense that punishment is in order, and, if I am right, it also ought to be enough for us in theory.

Two observations may help make the thesis of functional moral equivalence more plausible in these cases of mentally disturbed criminals. First, the fact that a disturbed person is at various times deterred by threat of m-punishment does not entail that he is, in the relevant sense, deterrable at the time he commits a particular crime. Justice requires that a threat apply to a criminal choice only if *in making that choice* (or the choices that lead to it) the criminal is able to understand the threat that applies to him, is able to appreciate the threatened penalty as something unwelcome, and is able to avoid the crime. Second, we have imagined that the devices are programmed to mete out m-punishments for any crime that was properly subject to our self-protective threats. But there can be genuinely humane (and therefore moral) reasons not to punish a crime, especially when the offender is mentally disturbed, that do not call into question our right to punish. If we wish to get a fair comparison of the two practices, we must either imagine ourselves as punishing whenever we see ourselves as having a strict moral right to do so or, preferably, we must imagine the devices to be programmed with principles of humanity as further constraints on their operation.

III

The thesis of functional moral equivalence should, to the extent that I have succeeded in making it out, incline us to take seriously the idea that the moral essence of a just practice of punishment and that of its counterpart practice of m-punishment are the same, that both are systems of deterrent threats fully justified by rights of self-protection. But a difficulty remains. For real punishment involves not only creating threats but also carrying them out and therefore raises questions that do not arise in the case of m-punishment. While the dangers to potential wrong-doers may be no greater under a practice of punishment, their realization will require real persons to perform various real actions all of which will clearly stand in need of some kind of moral justification. And it may seem that no appeal to our right to protect ourselves from possible crimes could serve to establish a right to do anything about those crimes once they had become actual. But the problem is, in a way, even worse. For the right to which we appealed when activating the m-punishing devices was the right to attach *automatic* costs to crimes. But in the case of punishment we need to appeal to a right to attach costs that will have to be imposed by human agents. Thus we seem forced back upon a particularly acute version of the difficulty with which we began.

But while it is true that the move from threats of m-punishment to those of punishment generates these new and difficult philosophical problems, it is, in my view, a mistake to assume that only an *independent* account of the right to punish can solve them. For this is to assume that the right to establish the threat of punishment is posterior in the order of explanation to the right to punish. But while very natural, this assumption is, I think, mistaken. In my view, the right to establish the real threat of punishment is the moral *ground* of the right to punish. I shall presently try to defend this hypothesis. But first we should briefly consider how the hypothesis would, when added to our previous results, enable us to reach the conclusion that practices of punishment and m-punishment rest on the same moral foundation.

To say that the right to establish a genuine threat is prior to the right to punish (or that the former right grounds the latter) is to make two claims: first, that the right to set up the threat can be established without first raising the question of the right to punish and, second, that the right to the threat implies the right to punish. According to the first claim, a case that prescinds from any consideration of how one will later be justified in punishing and concentrates exclusively on what is to be said for and against the creation of the real prospect of punishment for crime (that is, the real likelihood that a criminal will be punished) can be sufficient to establish the right to the threat of punishment. If this claim is true, then in our moral deliberations about setting up a practice of punishment we may regard the creation of the threat *as if* it amounted to causally determining our wills so that we would in fact try to punish crimes and would do so without raising any further question of right.[43] But this is to claim that the right to set up the threat of punishment may be treated as if it were the right to threaten that which will come about automatically, that is, as a causal consequence not subject to a certain kind of further moral scrutiny.

The first claim therefore implies that the right to establish threats of m-punishment and the right to establish counterpart threats of punishment are on the same moral footing, that the right to attach automatic costs must generalize into a right to attach costs that are either automatically or personally imposed. For apart from the fact that the threat of punishment is the threat to *do* something (the fact that we are to set aside), the morally relevant structure of the situations in which we establish the counterpart practices is the same. In both there are holders of rights who wish to protect themselves from potential violators of these rights, and in both there is the possibility of creating conditional dangers that will tend to deter crime. And according to the second claim (that the right to the threat implies the right to punish), considerations that suffice to establish our right to the threat of punishment will also suffice to establish the right to punish when the time comes. Since we are now justified in creating the real prospect of punishment we will later be justified in punishing. The thesis of the explanatory priority of the right to create the threat of punishment thus means that a practice of real punishment, both at the time it is established and later, has the same basis in moral rights as its counterpart practice of m-punishment.

But why should we believe that the right to establish the threat is prior? The ultimate plausibility of the hypothesis lies in the fact that it gives a more satisfying account of the right to punish than any alternative. The best defense here, as in the case of other highly theoretical moral claims, is an argument to the best explanation. I shall not, therefore, attempt any kind of proof. There are, however, certain reflections that can make my hypothesis seem dubious (or even incoherent), and it is to some of these that I now turn. One line of thought begins with the way in which establishing real threats of punishment must involve the formation of conditional intentions. In the simplest case an individual threatener must himself form an intention to punish crimes, and in more complex cases

43. That is, not raising any further moral questions about our right to punish kinds of crime that are properly placed under the threats.

various members of a penal establishment must form various intentions that together could be thought of as a collective intention to punish crimes. Once one sees the role of intention in the creation of a threat of punishment, one will be reminded that, in standard cases, the moral justification for forming an intention is dependent upon the justification one anticipates having later for doing the thing intended. And, generalizing on these standard cases, it will seem that the justification for establishing a threat could not be prior to the justification for punishing.

That the justification for forming intentions is usually parasitic on the anticipated justification for the thing intended is not surprising. In the vast majority of cases there is nothing of moral interest to assess in the formation of an intention other than the independent moral character of its object. The typical intention has no morally interesting life of its own. What will bear on people's good or ill, respect or violate their rights, is the action intended and not the coming to intend it. In this respect, however, conditional intentions whose expression is designed to deter or induce future action in others form a very special class. This is all the more true when the insincere expression of these intentions is, as in the case of promises and official public threats, morally questionable. In such cases, morality takes an interest not only in what we ultimately do but also in whether or not we form the intention to do it. Moreover, these intentions are embedded in actions, promises, and threats, that clearly have an impact on the good or ill of ourselves and others and therefore have a striking moral character of their own. The conditional intentions to punish or to contribute to a joint undertaking of punishing contained in the setting up of a practice of punishment are not, therefore, typical. It is not plausible to say of them that they have no moral interest apart from that of their objects.

That this is so can be seen by reflecting on the case of sincere promises to pay for future services. On the view that the justifiability of forming an intention always derives from the independent justifiability of its object, we could be justified in sincerely promising to do something only if we could justifiably do that thing independently of having been justified in making the promise. But this is not always the case. We may be morally permitted to do some things only because we *were* morally permitted to promise to do them. For example, the guardian of a ward and his estate would not, typically, have the moral right to disburse the ward's funds to *give* someone something for services rendered the ward in the absence of any prior agreement, but he surely would have the moral right to *pay* someone for services rendered under an earlier contract justifiably entered into in behalf of the ward's interests. Appeal to the ward's interests here plays a crucial role in accounting for the right to expend the ward's funds. This can be seen by noticing that a promise to pay made by the guardian in the foreknowledge that the services would be rendered *whether or not* there was a prospect of payment might create no moral claim on the ward's funds. If this were so, a plausible explanation of why the guardian may honor a promise made in order to secure the welfare of the ward but may not (with the ward's funds) honor a promise made in indifference or hostility to the interests of the ward is that in the former case, but not in the latter, making the promise was justified in the first place. In such cases the question of primary moral moment arises at the time the promise is made: Can it be justified by the way in which it may be hoped to benefit the ward? And it is important to keep in mind that we are not speaking here of insincere promises. The question is whether the guardian would be justified in making a promise with the full intention to honor it.

The same moral structure is present, I would argue, in the case of threats. What one may sincerely threaten to do in order to avoid certain things is not always determined by what one could do independently of the fact that one had the right to threaten. But suppose it is granted that certain promises and agreements involving the formation of conditional intentions can be independently evaluated in the way indicated. It might, nevertheless, be argued that it is a mistake to think that this can be generalized to the case of threats. For the relevant kind of case arises only when there is a way for the justification of an earlier act to carry forward to a later one. What enables the justification for the guardian's rightful promising to ground the later justification for making payment seems to be the fact that once he has promised, he is *obligated* to pay. Obligation contains permission, and therefore provides a moral medium that can carry an earlier justification forward.

This, in effect, threatens to reduce my view about punishment to absurdity. For, the objection continues, it is absurd to suppose that one could have the right to establish a real threat of punishment but not, *ceteris paribus*, the right to punish. In the case of the guardian's promise the analogous absurdity (that he might have the right to make the promise but not, *ceteris paribus*, the right to honor it) is avoided by the convenient fact that promises create obligations that carry permission forward. But there is no comparable forward-reaching moral mechanism in the case of the threat. For there is no general obligation on the part of penal authorities to punish every crime they have the right to punish. It must be, the objection concludes, that the moral alignment between threat and punishment is due to the priority of the right to punish rather than the priority of the right to threaten. This is, perhaps, the most serious line of objection to my conception. To escape its force, I must be able to explain how a prior right to establish the threat of a given punishment *could* transfer forward to the right to mete it out. *And I must be able to explain this in a way that never presupposes that the right to punish has been secured first.*

I shall now try to construct just such an explanation. It consists in a series of steps that lead from threatening to punishing such that each step not only implies the next but, if I am right, implies it without presupposing it. The steps are these:

(1) At t_1, x cannot object to the fact that we then create a real threat that, if he commits a crime of type C at t_2, we will thereafter try to see to it that he receives a punishment of type P.

(2) At t_1, x cannot object to the fact that, if he commits a crime of type C at t_2, we will thereafter try to see to it that he receives a punishment of type P.

(3) After t_2, x cannot object to the fact that, if he has committed a crime of type C at t_2, we are trying to see to it that he receives a punishment of type P.

(4) After t_2, x cannot object to the fact that, if he has committed a crime of type C at t_2, we are actually seeing to it that he receives a punishment of type P.

(5) At and for some time after t_3, x cannot object to the fact that, if he has committed a crime of type C at t_2, we are subjecting him to a punishment of type P.

(6) If x has committed a crime of type C at t_2, then *at and for some time after t_3*, x cannot object to the fact that we are subjecting him to a punishment of type P.

The steps are to be interpreted as follows: "We" refers to all citizens who authorize members of the penal establishment to fulfill their various functions in the case of x's crime. "Seeing to it that x receives a punishment" refers to the complete performance of all these functions, that is, investigating the crime and apprehending, convicting, and fully punishing x for having done it, all carried out in the name of all the authorizing citizens. And "trying to see to it that x receives a punishment" refers to this collective activity insofar as it is begun but is uncertain of completion despite the best efforts of all concerned. (We can, in the intended sense, be trying to see to it that x receives a punishment in the detective work done before x is identified as the criminal.) T_1 is the time at which the threat is created, t_2 the time at which the crime in question is committed, and t_3 the time at which the punishment begins. And at each step, the kind of objection that x lacks is one whose force would show the presence of some moral right and could, therefore, obligate us to see to it that the objectionable state of affairs did not obtain. I shall speak of a state of affairs to which x cannot, in this sense, object as one that is morally acceptable to him.

(1) is, of course, our starting place. It asserts that at t_1 we have a moral right, so far as x is concerned, to create the threat that we will try to see to his punishment if he commits a certain crime. To make the assertion as plausible as possible, we may suppose that x's mental condition makes him a clear candidate for placement under penal threats and that the threatened punishment is appropriate to the crime. To create this particular threat is to shape the present order of things so as to make the conditional (that we will try to punish x if he commits the relevant crime) probable, and to warn x that this has been done. Often, in creating such a threat, we actually succeed in making the conditional *true*. That is, we succeed in affecting the present order of things so that if the threatened party does commit a future crime, we will, in accordance with our present intentions and plans and only because of those intentions and plans, try to see to his punishment.[44] Suppose that in creating the present threat against x at t_1 we actually succeed in making the relevant conditional true in this sense. Assuming that our sincere threat is a morally appropriate self-protective measure, x cannot at t_1 object to our making this conditional as likely as possible. But then he cannot object that in making it as likely as possible we actually make it true. And if he cannot object

---

44. "Because" here indicates that the attempt to punish would not follow the crime if we had not formed the earlier intentions and plans. It does not, however, express a sense of causality incompatible with human choice. Often we would not in fact make a choice had we not made some earlier one.

to this, he cannot object to the truth of the conditional itself. Moreover, none of these inferences seems to depend on some hidden way in which the implying proposition presupposes the implied proposition. The best explanation of why x cannot at t_1 object to the fact that we will try to see to his later punishment should he commit the crime seems to consist in the fact that he cannot at t_1 object to our creating the self-protective threat that we will do so. (1) therefore implies (2) without presupposing it.

(3) brings the acceptability (unobjectionableness) expressed in (2) forward to a time after the crime has occurred. In both steps the same conditional state of affairs (if x commits the crime at t_2, then after t_2 we try to see to it that he is punished) is said to be morally acceptable to x. In (2), that state of affairs is seen by x from an earlier perspective, and in (3) it is seen by him from a later perspective contemporary with our attempt to punish him.[45] Either step *could*, for all we yet know, be prior in the order of explanation to the other. The earlier acceptability could be derived from the anticipated acceptability of trying to see to x's punishment. Or, as I claim, the latter could be based on the former. In any case, it is certainly tempting to think that one of these steps must explain the other.

But whichever we take to be prior, we have strong reason to reject any suggestion that the two judgments may *differ* in truth value. For if they do come apart in this way, it must be that they express incompatible moral conceptions. Relative to a single morality, a given state of affairs will be morally acceptable to x at all times if it is acceptable to him at any. This is because the notion of having a morally relevant objection that I intend here is *objective*, not a matter of whether x *knows* a good objection but whether there *is*, in principle, one that could be put forward in his behalf. And an objection that could be put forward for x at one time could, in principle, be put forward for him in some form at any other time. If, for example, x can rightly object at t_2 that trying to punish him harms his interests without furthering ours, he could have rightly objected at t_1 that the punishment we then threatened might turn out to be like this. But both we and x then knew that although this unhappy result was a real possibility, it did not provide x with a legitimate objection.[46]

45. (2), therefore, uses the future tense while (3) uses the present tense. But these uses of tense are unessential. Each step could be expressed in a tenseless idiom.
46. The moral structure of our situation here must be distinguished from that of nuclear

Moreover, we should not be mislead by the possibility that new information may arise between t_1 and t_2 that would make the attempt to punish morally objectionable. Even if such a development could not have been predicted in a particular case, provision for it could and, in principle, should have been made. The threat should have been conditionalized so that it would not apply in case the unexpected information did arise. For example, even if we could not have predicted that x would become a kleptomaniac we could and should have restricted our threats against him so that they would not apply in this eventuality. This technique for bringing threats and attempts to punish into moral alignment in no way presupposes the explanatory priority of the one over the other.[47] It is nothing other than an expression of the requirement that (2) and (3) be equivalent. And it is just this required equivalence that explains the possibility of deriving (3) from (2). The important point is that the equivalence holds because the relevant notion of acceptability is governed by a constraint of temporal neutrality and not because an objection to the threat must derive from some prior objection to punishing. This explanation can be understood quite independently of resolving the question which step comes first in the order of explanation.

Let us now consider the inference from (3) to (4). The reference to "trying" in (2) and (3) is, I think, essential if threats of higher penalties can be justified, as I think they can, by reference to unusually low detection rates. In these cases the original threat is acceptable only because we may fail to bring off what we threaten. What x cannot object to at t_1 in these cases is not, in the first instance, the prospect of our actually seeing to it that he receives the specified penalty in full, but rather the prospect of our trying to see to it.[48] This means that we must find a way

---

deterrence. There, in the hope of reducing our chances of being attacked, we threaten to do that which will, among other things, destroy innocent third parties. If such threats could, as some believe, be morally justified, they would be justified despite the good objections of these innocent third parties. Their objections would be overridden by the expectation that the threat will help us avert disaster. Should such a threat fail to deter an attack, our expectation will be proved false and the innocent third parties' objections will remain unopposed by any cogent moral counterargument. The present derivation, resting as it does on the claim that there is *no* good objection to creating the threats, could not even begin in such a case.

47. I have already argued that the morality of self-protective threatening can account for all, or most, intuitively plausible limitations on punishing.

48. I assume here that it would be unintelligible to suppose that a morally unacceptable prospect could be rendered acceptable by lowering the probability of its realization, but that

of bridging the gap between the attempt and the thing attempted. My strategy for this rests on two premises. First, that trying to see to it that x is fully punished is, once the attempt begins to be successful, the very same activity as seeing to it that he is fully punished.[49] And second, that the acceptability of an action or activity under one description entails its acceptability under any other true description. This second premise results directly from the fact that the notion of acceptability contained in my argument is to be understood in an "all things considered" or "*überhaupt*" sense. One has or lacks an objection in this sense to an action (or to a state of affairs containing an action) no matter how the action is described. Seeing to x's punishment will therefore be acceptable to x, all things considered, just in case it is the same activity as trying to see to x's punishment.

My identification of these activities rests on a general claim that trying to do something and actually doing it can be the very same action or activity differently described. I do not claim, of course, that in a protracted but eventually successful attempt to open a door one is from the very start actually opening the door. For such simple actions as this, only the last moment of a successful attempt belongs to the action attempted.[50] But for most activities that include a variety of different actions as parts, actual performance is to be identified with attempted performance from the moment that the attempt begins to succeed. For example, a doctor's attempt to heal someone completely (once it begins to succeed) and his healing that person completely are the same activity. And the same is true, I claim, for a successful attempt to bring someone to full justice and the actual bringing of him to full justice. If our attempt to see to it that x is punished for his crime is, all things considered, acceptable to x, our actually seeing to it must also be acceptable to him.

---

it is fully intelligible that a prospect of someone's attempting something might be acceptable, not because of the low probability that the attempt will occur, but because of the low probability that it will succeed.

49. This is relevant because (1) through (6) can be understood to refer directly to our activities. For example, (3) can be rewritten: "Our *trying* to see to it that x receives a punishment of type P for having committed a crime of type C at t_2 is (after t_2) something to which x cannot object," and (4) can be rewritten: "Our actually *seeing* to it that x receives a punishment of type P. . . ."

50. Even in such a simple case I would deny that a trying can be successful only in virtue of being succeeded by a doing that is no longer a trying. Otherwise there could be no such thing as a trying that succeeds from the very start.

This account of the inference from (3) to (4) is, like that of the inference from (2) to (3), neutral with regard to priorities. Some description of what we are doing in regard to x must, one thinks, be the morally *relevant* one, the one that explains why he cannot object. But when our action is both a trying and a doing, the inference from its acceptability under one description to its acceptability under the other holds whichever description has explanatory priority. That there is no basis for insisting that the acceptability of the doing (the succeeding) must ground the acceptability of the trying can perhaps be seen by drawing an analogy with the logic of permission.[51] You may grant me permission to try to A without granting me explicit permission to A. Indeed, when it is highly unlikely that I can A, permission to try may be all that you are in a logical position to grant. More to the present point, it may be that you are willing and able to grant me permission to try to A if you believe that my chance of succeeding is low, but you would not otherwise be willing or, perhaps, able to grant me permission to A. But if in such a situation you do grant me permission to try to A, there can be no further question about my A-ing having been done with your permission should I succeed. This suggests that it is intelligible to begin with the thought that in certain cases morality grants us a permission to try to see to it that someone receives punishment from which we can *infer* that, should we succeed, we will have acted permissibly.

Thus, both the inferences from (2) to (3) and from (3) to (4) depend on what might be called the logic of the relevant notion of moral acceptability to x and on the fact that the states of affairs judged to be acceptable to x in each pair of statements are, in one way or another, identical. The inference from (4) to (5) is based on the principle that it cannot be acceptable to x that we do a number of things unless, in so acting, it is acceptable to him that we do each of them. The action referred to in (5), punishing x, is a proper part of the activity referred to in (4), seeing to it that x is punished. There is no way in which x could lack an objection to the whole of that activity if he had an objection to this part of it. The acceptability to x of our punishing him is not, however, prior to the acceptability to him of our seeing to it that he is punished. For the latter involves bringing x to trial and convicting him, and x may rightly object to any punishment not embedded within such an acceptable whole.

51. Suggested by Rogers Albritton.

Only the inference from (5) to (6) remains to be considered. Suppose we ascribe to (5) an underlying form in which what x cannot object to is the conditional proposition as a whole. Then the inference to (6) will call upon a modal principle similar to one found in the logic of possibility. That acceptability should be governed by such a principle does not seem odd. For it is very like a form of permissibility, permissibility as seen from the point of view of a person acted upon, and permissibility can be understood as possibility in a normative system. On the other hand, if we ascribe to (5) an underlying form in which under a specified condition (x's committing a crime) x lacks an objection to a nonconditional proposition (that we subject him to a punishment), then the inference to (6) requires nothing but *modus ponens*.

If this account of the relation between these steps is correct, it follows that if a threat of punishment could be fully justified by the rights of self-protection that justify a threat of m-punishment, the force of these rights would carry forward to the act of punishing. If the urgency of self-protection makes moral room for threats it also makes moral room for punishment. But this means that a justified practice of punishment *can* be intelligibly conceived to have the same moral essence as its counterpart practice of m-punishment. It is possible to hold that punishing a criminal for a crime does not violate his rights *because* subjecting him to the threat of punishment for such a crime did not violate his rights in the first place.

I now wish to consider a possible criticism, the reply to which will help bring out an important feature of this conception. The objection is directed against the very idea that the later acceptability of an action can derive from the earlier acceptability of its prospect. It starts with the initially plausible looking assumption that if the explanatory structure I invoke to explain punishment is valid, it should also apply in purely prudential situations. Consider the following fascinating case invented by Gregory Kavka.[52] An eccentric millionaire offers N a fortune to form the intention to drink a toxin that will make him feel rather ill. N would, quite sensibly, be glad to accept such a temporary unpleasantness in order to get the fortune, but that is not what he has been asked to do. He is offered the fortune as a return not for the action itself but for forming the *present* intention to perform it at a later time. And worse, the eccentric millionaire can tell whether N has succeeded in forming

---

52. "The Toxin Puzzle," *Analysis* 43, no. 1 (January 1983): 33–36.

the desired intention by interpreting his brain states, and insists on paying N well before the toxin is to be drunk. Kavka thinks that it is at least very doubtful that in such a bizarre situation the unhappy N *can* rationally form the intention to drink the toxin. For as N thinks ahead to the time of the action, he can see that he will then have a serious reason not to drink the toxin and no reason whatsoever to drink it.[53] And foreseeing that he will be in such a state, he cannot with justification form the intention to drink it.

Kavka's doubt is very plausible. Indeed, I feel convinced that under the terms of the case N cannot rationally form the intention to drink the toxin. But if the case of punishment contains a viable justificatory structure, why isn't it also present here? Why couldn't N simply regard forming the intention to drink the toxin as an item of prior justification that will lend its justification to the later act? Our sense that drinking the toxin would not be rational seems to show that it is at least very doubtful that things can be conceived in this way; and this may suggest that there is something amiss in the very idea of actions being derivatively justified by reference to earlier actions or conditions that refer to them. But this suggestion rests on a false assimilation. The sphere of purely prudential rationality unconstrained by morality has features that rule out the special structure present in punishment. When prudential rationality is at issue, one is not, I think, able to separate the question of an action's justification from the question of the reasons one has for doing it. If one's reasons are good enough the action is prudentially justified; otherwise, it is not. In the toxin case the benefits that attach to forming the intention can provide no reason to do the intended action and thus cannot make it acceptable even in prospect.[54]

This difficulty need *not* arise, however, when the question of justifi-

---

53. N is not allowed to induce false belief in himself or to provide himself with independent moral motivation by, e.g., promising someone to drink the toxin.

54. David Gauthier in his recent paper "Deterrence, Maximization and Rationality," *Ethics* 94, no. 3 (April 1984), presents a view in which, so far as I can see, it would be rational for N to drink the toxin given the benefits that attach to forming the sincere intention to do so. For Gauthier advocates assessing the rationality of individual actions by first assessing the rationality of the largest temporal stretches of activity in which they occur (see p. 488). What he fails to make clear, at least to me, is how an agent who follows this policy is to think of his reasons. Is N at the later time to think that he has a good reason to drink the toxin despite the fact that no good will come of it? And if so, what does this good reason amount to? Or is N to think that this kind of choice can be rational in the absence of any reasons to make it? Neither option seems to me inviting.

cation is moral. For a moral justification need not be a function of one's reasons for acting. I am morally justified in reading your book because I have obtained your permission to do so; but my reason for reading the book is certainly not that I obtained this permission but that I hope thereby to amuse or instruct myself. The moral justification for an act of punishment does not have to lie in the punisher's reasons for punishing. Nor does his justification have to provide him with reasons to punish. Motives that do not in themselves morally justify an action can nevertheless constitute one's real reasons for doing it, and be perfectly acceptable in this role. In the case of punishment, such motives are not hard to find. Among them are those in which the two standard theories try to find its justification, righteous anger, and a desire to maintain the deterrent credibility of the penal institution.[55] Even more conspicuous, at least in complex practices like our own, are those mundane motives that arise from the fact that those who punish are expressly charged and employed to do so. Given that the punisher is in some sense aware of the justification provided by the right to make the earlier threats, he cannot be blamed for acting on reasons provided by any of these motives. And because we, as threateners, can foresee that we, as punishers, will have such reasons for punishing, it can be fully rational of us to form the collective conditional intention to punish.

Other objections could be made to this conception of the moral relation

55. The present theory can therefore accommodate some of the claims of retributivism as an account, not of the right to punish, but of a morally legitimate rationale for exercising part or all of that right. Nothing I have said so far implies that the natural desire to make wrongdoers suffer, given that one had the right to do so, is contrary to moral virtue. And its moral acceptability is suggested by the fact that benevolence does not seem to condemn us in taking some satisfaction in evils that wrongdoers suffer as, e.g., accidental results of their crimes. These natural attitudes must, of course, be held within certain bounds; otherwise they become cruel and vindictive. And perhaps the appropriate limit for *this* part of morality is some version of retributory equivalence. Note that the motive for punishing provided by our righteous anger, like that provided by our prudent desire to preserve the credibility of our penal institution, would not seem to generate the obligation to punish in any particular case. But that obligation might sometimes arise from other considerations. I see no reason, for example, why a penal code might not rightly mandate punishment for certain crimes or why authorities might not rightly promise the general public to punish in certain kinds of case. Moreover, I find myself strongly attracted to the idea that punishment of a crime can express the value society attaches to its victim and to his violated rights, and that not punishing or punishing too little may, in some cases, do the victim or his memory a moral injury. (For a discussion of other things that punishment might express see Joel Feinberg's "The Expressive Function of Punishment," *The Monist* 49, no. 3 [July 1965]: 397–408.)

between threatening and punishing. But here, as in earlier parts of the discussion, limitations of space have forced me to set aside some interesting problems and complications for other occasions. I have tried only to present a forceful sketch of an overall line of defense for what I consider a plausible but largely ignored theory of punishment. The heart of the theory is, as we have seen, the special justificatory structure described in this section. This structure may be, and I think is, present in moral and quasi-moral phenomena other than punishment. But in no other part of morality is its presence more plausible or, given that it is valid, its recognition of greater practical importance. I say this because I not only believe, as my objections to the standard theories have indicated, that punishment has been misconceived philosophically, but also that it has suffered from these misconceptions in practice. Our major mistake, I have argued, is to have focused too much on the punishing and too little on the creation of the threat of it. My hope is that with the correction of this faulty focus, we may be able to see that punishment requires of us neither an act of faith in the justice of retribution nor any neglect of rights for the sake of effects.

C. S. NINO

A Consensual Theory
of Punishment

I. A DILEMMA

Underlying most discussions of the justification of punishment is a dilemma pitting a certain general conception of the aims of a liberal and rational system of criminal law against intuitions about distinctions and requirements that this system ought to take into account. These intuitions—for example, that an innocent person should never be punished or that certain subjective attitudes are required for criminal responsibility—do not appear to be supported by a view of the criminal law which is mainly concerned with the protection of society in general.

In the face of this dilemma some thinkers rely on their intuitions, refusing to accept a general conception which, although initially attractive, threatens to usher us into a Brave New World. Others remain faithful to the principles they consider essential to a liberal and rational morality, dismissing their intuitive convictions as outmoded superstitions.

This article proposes an escape from the dilemma. What will be expounded here is the part of a general theory of criminal responsibility which deals with the justification of punishment.[1] The theory endeavors to reflect some basic liberal ideals while satisfying many of our deepest moral intuitions about these matters.

II. PUNISHMENT AND SOCIAL PROTECTION

Punishment is one species of the large family of measures involving intentional deprivation of a person's normally recognized rights by official institutions, using coercive means if necessary. This general class also

1. The whole of that general theory is found in my Ph.D. thesis.

includes quarantines, the confinement of dangerous mental defectives, requisitions in time of war, and the like.

The justification of these measures on the grounds of social protection is rarely attacked as a general principle, provided some minimum conditions are met. These conditions take into account the fact that this is a sort of protection that requires causing harm to the very thing which is thereby protected from still greater harms. For example, if we say that society suffers harm when some of its members contract a disease, obviously we should say the same when someone is deprived of his freedom by virtue of a quarantine. The imposition of these measures, therefore, must not occur before the following requirements are met: it must be certain or highly probable that what is taken to be an evil will occur; the protective measures must be both necessary and effective for preventing that evil; and the measures must involve lesser evils than those they are intended to prevent. If there is no dispute about the evaluation of evils involved, it would simply be self-defeating to protect society from a harm by using a measure which either involves a greater harm, is ineffective, or is unnecessary.

In the case of nonpunitive measures involving the coercive deprivation of rights, it is beyond doubt that these measures constitute a lesser evil than those they seek to prevent. When this is so, few people would object to such measures. Although there are some complications that this hasty acceptance overlooks (some of which I shall mention below), it is undeniable that considerations of social protection provide a prima facie justification for the coercive deprivation of some rights.

The obvious question is, To what extent can the legitimacy of punishment be defended on the same grounds as the legitimacy of, say, quarantines? This leads us, of course, to an evaluation of the well-known utilitarian justification of punishment.

I shall not survey here the arguments which object that the prudential requirements governing all protective measures listed above are hardly met in the case of punishment. These objections depend on empirical claims, and will not be discussed in this essay.

Yet other arguments against justifying punishment on grounds of social protection seem to lose much of their weight when they are examined in the context of other compulsory and generally unpleasant deprivations of rights. For instance, the argument that social protection would allow extremely harsh penalties for preventing even the most trifling offenses[2] is clearly absurd: hanging a motorist for the sake of preventing parking offenses would be self-defeating as a measure of social protection on the assumption that one accepts the scale of values which is crucial to the argument (the death of a person is worse than a congested traffic flow).[3]

A much more serious argument is the commonly invoked one[4] pointing out that the utilitarian justification of punishment allows for cases in which innocent people could be punished in order to prevent greater harms to society. But it is striking that problems raised by such cases (which are fairly unlikely if the prudential conditions are observed) have been a source of such deep doubts about social protection as a justification of punishment, when we consider that in actual fact the victims of non-punitive compulsory measures are always innocent. The burden of showing the relevant difference between punishment and other coercive measures rests on those who allege this argument.

Nevertheless, the justification of punishment based solely on social protection faces a further objection, which I consider decisive, and which applies to the punishment not only of innocent people but to that of the guilty as well. Although it is seldom invoked in present discussions of punishment, it is the same objection being made increasingly against utilitarianism in general.[5]

In the same way that a measure increasing the national product at the cost of a highly inequitable distribution of wealth could be questioned as unfair, a measure diminishing the overall harm that the community would suffer at the cost of selectively harming some of its members could likewise be attacked as unfair. Such measures are condemned by the Kantian

2. See this argument, for instance, in K. G. Armstrong, "The Retributionist Hits Back," in *The Philosophy of Punishment*, ed. H. B. Acton (London: Macmillan & Co., 1973).

3. Except that we considered, as Rousseau and others did, that the individual who commits an offense is automatically excluded from society and, therefore, is not counted any longer in the calculation of benefits and harms affecting that society. See a critical appraisal of this view in C. S. Nino, "La justificación de la legítima defensa," *Doctrina Penal* 2, no. 6 (1979).

4. This argument is advanced, among others, by J. D. Mabbott, "Punishment," in *The Philosophy of Punishment*, ed. H. B. Acton, and K. G. Armstrong, "The Retributionist Hits Back," p. 155.

5. See, especially, John Rawls, *A Theory of Justice* (Oxford: Oxford University Press, 1971), pp. 26, 27; and Robert Nozick, *Anarchy, State and Utopia* (New York: Basic Books, 1974), pp. 28, 29, 32, 33.

injunction against using men only as means and not as ends in themselves.

Without pursuing the arguments and rejoinders that this appeal to distributive justice provokes, I am convinced this appeal is valid. Unless we adhere to the mythical view that society is a sort of living organism,[6] there is no reason for seeing it as the basic moral unit, whose comparative well-being—independent of the well-being of each of its members—is the ground on which political action can be justified. If individuals are taken to be those basic moral units and not simply as the basic psychological ones (in the sense of being the sole source of pleasure and displeasure), it is their comparative well-being that should ground political action.

Accordingly, to justify quarantines or penalties it is not enough to point out that society, as a whole, will be better off. A leper could rightly appeal to the unfairness of having his condition aggravated by depriving him of his freedom while others enjoy health and freedom because of his deprivation.

However, in the case of the nonpunitive deprivation of rights this objection can be overcome by observing certain conditions in the imposition of these measures. In some cases a procedural mechanism could be designed that achieved a fair allocation of burdens (we might, for instance, resort to a lottery to decide whose goods are to be requisitioned). In other cases the unpleasantness of the measure could be reduced to a minimum. But the most general way of qualifying measures of social protection so as to overcome the problem of distributive unfairness is to offer compensation to the individuals who suffer the deprivation.[7]

The problem, however, is that no similar devices can be envisaged for supplementing punishment in order to make it compatible with the requirement of a fair distribution of benefits and burdens among the members of society. If punishment is justified by its capacity to diminish future crimes against society, and if this objective is pursued by means of general and special deterrence, the unpleasantness of punishment is not a mere side-effect (as in the case of other measures) but is essential to the purposes being pursued.[8] To offer compensation to the people who are

6. D. Gauthier, *Practical Reasoning* (Oxford: Oxford University Press, 1963), p. 126.

7. See this point in Nozick, *Anarchy*, pp. 142–46.

8. I think that this is also a conceptual requirement, distinguishing punishment from other coercive legal measures.

subjected to punishment would, obviously, be incompatible with the reason for imposing it.

Thus, it seems that unless we surrender to the retributivist claim that considerations of desert (according to the evaluation of the moral character of people as reflected in their acts) should be taken into account, punishment necessarily implies an unfair distribution of burdens and benefits among members of society.

However, I think that there is a line of argument which shows that the practice of punishment can be patterned after a commonly accepted principle of distribution that does not rely on the moral blameworthiness of people and does not require us to relinquish the conception of punishment as a measure of social protection. Section III will be dedicated to the analysis of that general principle, and in Section IV its application to punishment will be discussed.

III. Distribution According to Consent

Appeals to an equitable distribution of benefits and burdens are out of place when the individuals concerned have consciously acquiesced in a balance which is not egalitarian. For we recognize fairness according to consent[9] as a separate justification of political action, and it may be combined with other criteria of fairness. No doubt, this is an area of morality that needs much more exploration than it has so far received. I can only present here some general remarks about the matter.

One obvious category of cases (though not the only one) in which we accept what could, but for its origin, be considered an unfair distribution of goods, is that of contracts. The scope of social relationships recognized as permissible objects of contract could vary greatly, but the validity of such contracts, apart from this, is not dependent in any legal system on whether or not they represent a perfectly equitable distribution of burdens and benefits among the parties; the validity basically depends instead on whether those parties have freely consented to the distribution involved.

There is indeed a strong and praiseworthy trend in modern legal systems which could be described as aiming to prevent gross inequality of bargaining power. But, this trend responds to an increasing concern over

---

9. A. M. Honoré, "Social Justice," *McGill Law Journal* 8, no. 2 (1962), distinguishes from among different principles of justice what he calls "justice according to choice," connecting this principle to the justification of punishment.

the extent to which it can be maintained that the will of the parties is free and conscious even in the absence of such traditional defenses as duress or necessity.

Quite obviously the emphasis on the parties' actual freedom to contract is due to the fact that only the presence of such freedom can justify a departure from the requirement that social distributions of benefits and burdens should be equitable, taking into account such circumstances as needs, desert, and so forth. When an equitable distribution is being pursued, as in systems of social security, the will of the persons involved may be overridden. Certainly the limits to which voluntary and possibly inequitable distributions are to be permitted, and equitable but possibly compulsory ones are to be enforced, arouse well-known ideological controversies. Nevertheless, few would deny that if inequitable distributions are to be upheld, one of the firmest grounds for upholding them would be their consensual character, and that if compulsory distributions are enforced, the equity of their content would be a good argument in their favor.

The nature of the consent required for the validity of contracts is a matter of permanent controversy among jurists. Rather than comment on the details of those discussions, I shall simply reiterate some basic guidelines for what constitutes consent (even when, in practice, some departures from those guidelines are tolerated for a variety of pragmatic considerations).

It is often supposed that for an individual to consent to the assumption of some duty or responsibility he must necessarily make a statement such as, "I consent to this." Such a supposition is a mistake. Aside from what may be legally required for the validity of a special class of contracts, the consent of the individual to some duty or responsibility is shown by the performance of *any* voluntary act with the knowledge that the act has as a necessary consequence the assumption of the duty or responsibility in question. For instance, the act can be to sign a document, to take a taxi, to lift a hand in an auction, all of which may have as consequence having incurred the obligation to pay for something.

What is required in the first place is, therefore, that the act implying consent be voluntary. (Of course, this requirement is excluded in some cases of defense, such as automatism, coercion, and insanity.) Obviously, the voluntariness of the act is not enough to constitute consent: the agent must be aware of the relevant circumstances in relation to which the action is described. An individual entering into a contract must not only sign a certain document without being forced, but he must also know what he is doing. This knowledge must include, in particular, awareness of the obligations or liabilities he is assuming with his act.

A person consents to all the consequences that he knows are necessary effects of his voluntary act. As Hobbes put it: "Whoever voluntarily doth any action, accepteth all the known consequences of it."[10] Therefore, the person who voluntarily performs an act knowing that it has the undertaking of certain obligations as a necessary consequence consents to undertake those obligations.

Obviously, the consent to undertake a contractual obligation is independent of the attitudes of the person toward the acts that are the object of the obligation. An individual may consent to undertake the obligation of performing an act despite the fact that he greatly dislikes performing it or that he does not intend to perform it when the occasion arrives; consenting to undertake a contractual obligation can even be accompanied by the belief that the obligation will never be enforced.

It is generally accepted that the fact that a contractual obligation has been consented to provides at least a prima facie moral justification for enforcing it. We can test our convictions about the matter with the following example of a covenant that may have quite dramatic effects: the voluntary enlistment of an individual in the army of a country at war. If the volunteer dies defending the country, one might indeed say that he shouldered a very unequal share of the burdens of protecting his society compared with the benefits he obtained. But few would consider this, in contrast to the case of conscription, morally problematic because the person has consented to undertake the obligation of fighting. This is obviously so even when the individual has miscalculated the risks involved or had intended to desert; we would agree that to enforce the obligation by compelling him to stay in the battlefield, for instance, is prima facie right.

A quite similar idea, though it does not involve an obligation, is the basis for the principle of the law of torts, recognized to some extent by most legal systems, that the consent to assume a certain risk on the part of the injured party may exclude the responsibility of the tort-feasor for the harm caused through the realization of the risk. One application of

---

10. *Leviathan*, ed. Michael Oakeshott (London: Collier Macmillan, 1977), p. 218.

the principle is represented by the well-known maxim *volenti non fit injuria*. Here, as in the case of contracts, it is important to note that the decisive factor is not the expectation of some *factual* consequences (which can only serve as evidence of the consent of the individual[11]) but rather that the person has consented to assume some *normative* consequences. The voluntary act of the individual must involve consent to exonerate the other party from his legal duties and liabilities.

The situation given in all these cases can be described in the following way: We have a voluntary act which may or may not be intended to change legal relationships. That act may have some factual consequences, such as the risk of suffering harm which the volunteer who enlists in the army or the gambler who places a bet or the person who accepts a lift from a drunken driver brings upon himself. As we shall see later, the knowledge that a factual consequence may *possibly* follow from an act is not a morally relevant reason that justifies placing the legal burdens attached to that consequence on an individual. Specifically, consent to run the risk of some harm does not necessarily imply consent to suffer that harm. But the act can also have legal normative consequences. It is a matter of law that in certain circumstances saying voluntarily, "I bind myself to pay to you one hundred dollars for your work," involves the obligation to pay one hundred dollars, that taking something voluntarily from the stall of the supermarket involves the obligation to pay the price of the item, that knowingly accepting a lift from a drunken driver involves (in one view) renouncing the right to obtain compensation if an accident occurs. When that particular legal consequence of the voluntary act is known by the agent, we may say that he has consented to it. And it is that consent which is taken to be morally relevant and to justify enforcing the normative consequence in question against the person who has consented to it. Another way of describing the situation is to say that the consent to certain *legal* normative consequences involves *moral* normative consequences.[12] The individual who, for instance, consents to undertake some legal obligation is, in principle, morally obliged to do the act which is the object of that obligation.

11. See A. M. Honoré, "Causation and Remoteness of Damage," *International Encyclopedia of Comparative Law* (New York: Oceana Publications, n. d.), vol. 11, chap. 7, p. 114.

12. Dr. Joseph Raz suggested the distinctions between the factual, the legal normative, and the moral normative consequences of an act.

IV. THE CONSENT TO ASSUME A LIABILITY TO PUNISHMENT

If we look at the case of punishment, it is easy to find analogies with the cases mentioned above. Punishment is not something that befalls its 'victim' through some fortuitous happening or the actions of third parties without the possibility of control on his part. Among other things, it is the product of the will of the person who suffers it, at least when certain requirements related to the agent's state of mind are met.

Some authors suggest that there is a sense in which it is possible to say that the criminal wants to be punished. That sense was explained in such an obscure way that little was done to dissipate the instinctive reaction against the suggestion. It is as preposterous to think that criminals generally want to be punished as to think that volunteers want to die in battle.

A case of punishment, however, can be described in terms preserving the analogy with either the case of contracts or the case in which the injured party has consented to assume the risk of some harm. Here too we must examine not the factual consequences of an offense but the normative ones. We might say that a criminal brings the risk of being punished upon himself. This however, provides as little moral justification for actually punishing him as the fact that the volunteer brings upon himself the risk of dying in battle provides a moral justification for killing him in battle.

A necessary legal consequence of committing an offense is the loss of immunity from punishment that the person previously enjoyed. This loss of immunity is obviously correlative—in Hohfeldian terms—to the legal power on the part of certain public officials to punish the offender. The individual who commits a crime assumes a legal liability to suffer punishment and relinquishes the right that he would otherwise enjoy of seeking compensation or criminally prosecuting the official for the deprivation of rights involved in punishment.

This is merely a description in the simplest terms of the normative legal situation in which the individual finds himself after committing an offense. This description does not itself provide a moral justification for attaching these legal consequences to those acts. The fact that the offender loses his legal immunity from punishment does not imply that he also loses the moral immunity deriving from the principle that it is prima facie wrong to sacrifice an individual for the benefit of others. The assertion that an offense involves losing this moral immunity must be grounded on something more than the mere fact that the law gives officials the power to punish offenders.

The individual who performs a voluntary act—an offense—knowing that the loss of his legal immunity from punishment is a necessary consequence of that act consents to that normative consequence in the same way that a contracting party consents to the normative consequences following from the contract. This consent to assume a legal liability to suffer punishment is, as in the case of contracts and in the voluntary assumption of a risk, an irrevocable one, and it is independent of the attitude of the agent toward the event which is the object of the normative characterization. The individual may believe that his actual punishment is extremely improbable, or he may intend to evade it. This is irrelevant to his consent to lose his immunity from punishment, as is the attitude of the gambler, who is sure that he will win or who intends to cheat, in relation to his consent to undertake the obligation to pay the bet if he loses.

Therefore, the relevant consent here is the consent to the normative consequences of the act, that is to say, in the case of an offense, the consent to assume a liability to punishment. This consent is given when the act is voluntary and the agent knows that the normative consequence in question ensues *necessarily* from the performance of the act. The mere belief that the liability to punishment (or, in general, any consequence of the act) is a *possible* or *probable* outcome of the action is not sufficient in itself for concluding that the agent has consented to assume that liability. This feature of the notion of consent is relevant in determining whether or not any consequence of a voluntary act is consented to by the agent. The belief that the consequence may possibly follow from the act may justify the assertion that the agent has consented to run the *risk* of generating that consequence, but it is not enough to support the conclusion that the agent has consented to bring it about. This latter consent cannot be inferred from the former consent alone (though I think—but cannot argue here—that it can be inferred when, in addition, the agent is disposed to act the same in the counterfactual case of foreseeing the consequence as certain). This implies that a person who, for instance, unknowingly commits an offense of strict liability, being aware that the law creates this sort of offense and that, consequently, a liability to punishment may be a possible consequence of his acts, does not necessarily consent to assume that liability. This view requires making some plausible maneuvers, which I shall not undertake here,[13] for dealing with crimes of negligence.

My contention is that insofar as the agent's consent to forgo his immunity against punishment is required before that punishment is imposed, the gap in the moral justification of the practice, left by pure considerations of social protection, can be bridged. When the protection of the community requires necessary and effective punitive measures involving lesser harms than the harm feared, the consent of the recipient of those measures makes an appeal to an equitable distribution of those burdens out of place. If the punishment is attached to a justifiable obligation, if the authorities involved are legitimate, if the punishment deprives the individual of goods he can alienate, and if it is a necessary and effective means of protecting the community against greater harms, then the fact that the individual has freely consented to make himself liable to that punishment (by performing a voluntary act with the knowledge that the relinquishment of his immunity is a necessary consequence of it) provides a prima facie moral justification for exercising the correlative legal power of punishing him.

The principle of distribution, which that moral justification presupposes, is the same as that which justifies the distribution of advantages and burdens ensuing from contracts and the distribution achieved in the law of torts when the burdens that follow from a tort are placed on the consenting injured party. This justification of course presupposes that several conditions have been satisfied. First, the person punished must have been capable of preventing the act to which the liability is attached (this excludes the rare case of punishing an innocent person that pure social protection might allow). Second, the individual must have performed the act with knowledge of its relevant factual properties. Third, he must have known that the undertaking of a liability to suffer punishment was a necessary consequence of such an act. This obviously implies that one must have knowledge of the law, and it also proscribes the imposition of retroactive criminal laws.

Because this is not the first time that the justification of punishment

13. The core of the account of the punishability of negligence, which I developed elsewhere in my doctoral dissertation, does not differ much from that of J. L. Mackie in "The Grounds of Responsibility," *Law, Morality and Society: Essays in Honour of H.L.A. Hart*, ed. P.M.S. Hacker and J. Raz (Oxford: Oxford University Press, 1977), p. 184.

has been connected with the requirement of subjective attitudes, I would like to distinguish the thesis advanced here from some others. I require more than a certain subjective attitude toward the offense committed; I demand a subjective attitude toward punishment itself. (Indeed, it is precisely the need for this latter attitude which justifies requiring particular attitudes toward the offense.) Furthermore, my requiring subjective attitudes is not based on a utilitarian calculus, nor on the value of such things as freedom of choice or predictability of the future.[14] Finally, I cannot agree with current retributivist views which demand subjective attitudes on the grounds that punishment should be a reaction against an immoral act and, consequently, requires a wicked state of mind (under the justification of punishment suggested here, the blameworthiness of the agent is as little relevant as it is in the case of contracts).[15]

V. Some Possible Objections

The variety of situations in which this principle applies precludes raising certain objections against its application to punishment. It might be alleged that in contracts the parties consent to undertake obligations and to grant correlative rights, whereas all that the offender consents to is to relinquish an immunity. But, apart from the fact that it is not easy to see why this difference in the characterization of the normative consequences should have moral significance, one must recall that there are several contracts—like the contract of agency—some of whose consequences can be described in terms of relinquishing certain immunities. It could further be said that the consent involved in the commission of an offense is merely a unilateral manifestation of will rather than a bilateral agreement, as in the case of contracts. However, most legal systems attach normative consequences to unilateral acts involving consent (notable examples of these in English law are conveyances of land and declarations of trust), and the doctrine of assumption of risk by the injured party in the law of torts is sometimes applicable to unilateral acts.[16] Finally, it could be al-

14. In this respect, among others, this view differs from that of H.L.A. Hart: see his *Punishment and Responsibility* (Oxford: Oxford University Press, 1968).

15. In my doctoral dissertation I defended the opinion that the liberal view, which excludes the moral self-degradation of people as a basis for the State's interfering with their conduct, implies that the blameworthiness of the agent should be disregarded, not only as a sufficient condition of punishment, but also as a necessary one.

16. See A. M. Honoré, "Causation and Remoteness of Damage," p. 117.

leged that the consent to forgo one's immunity from punishment is always implicit (the law does not attach that normative consequence to an explicit declaration to that effect), which marks a clear difference from the case of contracts, most of which require an explicit consent to the normative effects. Again the answer must be that there are many contracts (in fact most of the contracts that we undertake every day, such as traveling on a bus) where implicit consent is enough, and that the doctrine of assumption of risk expressly contemplates cases of implicit consent.[17] Furthermore, one may well argue that the difference between explicit and implicit consent has no moral significance even in the case of contracts (quite apart, of course, from its relevance for dealing with evidential problems). The basic difference is that in the case of explicit consent the voluntary action to which normative consequences are attached is a specific speech act performed with the intention of generating normative consequences as a means to some further end, whereas in the case of implicit consent that action is an act of some other sort performed with the knowledge that certain normative consequences will necessarily follow. Insofar as the action is voluntary and the normative effects are known, the distinctive features mentioned do not seem to have any moral relevance to the justification for enforcing contracts.

However, I am not denying that punishment presents peculiarities that are not shared by other institutions covered by this principle of distribution. Punishment is *threatened* and not *offered* to individuals who contemplate committing a crime. Furthermore, in contrast to the case of contracts, an alternative course of action open to the individual seeking to avoid punishment involves compliance with a legal restriction which may be perceived by that person as a burden. Do these facts imply that the choice of the agent who decides to commit a crime assuming a liability to suffer punishment is not entirely free, and, therefore, that consent to this consequence cannot be given?

The current discussion about the distinction between threats and offers, inaugurated in a lucid article by Nozick,[18] illuminates our present problem little since it is oriented toward the elucidation of the case in which the threatened person decides not to defy the threat but to do what

17. Honoré, "Causation," p. 115.

18. Robert Nozick, "Coercion," in *Philosophy, Politics and Society*, ed. P. Laslett, W. G. Runnciman, and Q. Skinner (Oxford: Oxford University Press, 1972), p. 101.

he is told. It does not follow from the fact that the individual is coerced in the latter case that he is also coerced when he defies the threat. On the contrary, one would say that when he defies the threat, the individual is resisting coercion, and that this resistance, far from being unfree, is the result of a great strength of will.

There is, however, a perturbing aspect of the distinction between threats and offers. Nozick calls our attention to the relevance of looking not only at the choice the person who received a threat or an offer has, but also at the choice he would have made about moving from a situation in which the threat or the offer had not been made to a situation to which it has been.[19] According to Nozick, the fact that the threatened person would not normally have chosen to go from the prethreat to the threat situation whereas the person who receives an offer would normally have chosen to move from the preoffer to the offer situation is decisive in discriminating between the two cases in relation to the voluntariness of that person's action. This criterion seems to call into question the voluntariness of the assumption of a liability to punishment on the part of an offender, since he or she would not normally choose to move from a situation in which the action is not punishable to a situation in which it is. However, the same can be said in the case of contracts, since a contracting party would normally prefer to achieve the object of his or her contract without entering into it and without the correlative obligations that, in absence of the relevant legal rules (like property laws), he would not have to assume. If an offender might claim that the law coerces him into assuming a liability to punishment should he want a certain prohibited advantage, a contracting party might also claim that the law coerces him into accepting the terms of an offer should he want something over which the offerer has legal power. In the case of contracts we do not allow such a claim when the relevant laws are considered just; the justification of particular distributions based on the free choices of the parties presupposes the fairness of the legal framework within which those choices are made.[20] The same can be said in the case of the criminal law: a particular distribution of punishment can only be justified on the basis of the consent of the recipients when the legal prohibition of the act to which punishment is attached is just (it should not be, for instance, discriminatory

19. See ibid., pp. 127ff.
20. This presupposition might create some difficulties for those who seek to justify the fairness of the legal framework itself on the basis of consent.

and should not proscribe actions that people have the moral right to do).

It is also important to consider the circumstance in which the action required if one is to avoid the punishable action itself carries a certain burden or restriction. The analysis of a rather peculiar case of punishment will illustrate the relevance of the consequences of the alternate choice of the individual in determining whether his assumption of punishment is free. Suppose that the law makes punishable both an act and its omission. So far, there is nothing in the characterization of consent that precludes saying that, in a case like this, whatever course of action the individual adopts, he consents to make himself liable to punishment. Yet, the case is not substantially different from that in which the individual is punished for something over which he has no control, such as the color of his skin. One may propose some further qualification of the range of actions which can be consented to by people. If voluntariness is excluded when the action is empirically necessary, it should be excluded with even greater reason when the action is logically necessary. The prescription of a penalty for an action and its omission is equivalent to the prescription of that penalty for the complex action resulting from the disjunction of the action and the omission in question; and this complex action is logically necessary.

Quite apart from the above qualification, there is a substantive principle underlying our intuitive rejection of a case like the foregoing, which applies as well to different situations. According to this principle, a liability, burden, or obligation can only be justified on the basis of the consent of the agent when the alternative course of action open to him either does not involve any liability, burden, or obligation, or, if it does, those consequences can be justified, without recourse to the fact that the individual has chosen this alternative. The idea behind this principle is, obviously, that the choice of a certain action is not free when the alternative one implies relinquishing rights that the agent would otherwise enjoy; this is not the case when the burdens attached to the alternative action are burdens that the individual ought to assume, whether he consents to them or not. This principle proscribes putting individuals in a situation such that, whatever they decide to do, their choice would be taken as the basis for depriving them of certain rights.

This principle has a general consequence with regard to the justification of the legal obligations which are complied with by the individual who decides to avoid the liability to suffer punishment (and the further burdens and obligations which may follow from that compliance). They cannot be justified by taking into account the decision not to forgo the immunity from punishment. If they are justified at all, it should be on the basis of reasons that are independent of this choice.

This consequence is obvious in the case of obligations such as those related to killing, stealing, or raping. But it may be less obvious in the case of other legal obligations and restrictions. Take the case of conscription mentioned above, for instance. An individual who decides not to assume the liability to punishment attached to the evasion of conscription chooses to comply with the requirement of military service, and this, in its turn, implies assuming a complex of specific duties and burdens (such as wearing a military uniform). One may be tempted to justify compliance with conscription and the assumption of the subsequent specific duties and burdens on the basis of the choice of the individual; in the end, he is not physically compelled to that compliance. But the principle we are discussing precludes that justification, since the opposite choice would imply certain penalties (both in the case of evading conscription altogether and of violating the subsequent duties), and those penalties need to be justified on the basis of the consent of the agent. If conscription and the specific duties and burdens that it involves (as opposed to the penalties attached to the violation of these duties) are at all justifiable, they must be justified on grounds other than the consent of the individual. This justification is, in its turn, necessary for justifying the penalties attached to the evasion of conscription and the violation of the military duties, in addition to the requirement that the agent had consented to make himself liable to those penalties.

This principle does not preclude the possibility that in some cases the obligation the individual complies with when he decides to avoid the liability to suffer punishment can be grounded on a *previous and different* choice of the individual. This is so, for instance, in the case of the army volunteer also mentioned earlier. If the volunteer decides to face the impending battle, the subsequent restrictions on his freedom of action can be justified on the basis of his *previous* choice to enlist in the army; the alternative to such a choice did not involve assuming any obligations or burdens. But the choice to enlist was a different choice from that, for instance, of facing a battle; this latter choice cannot by itself serve to justify the restrictions on his freedom, since the opposite choice (namely deserting) would be taken as grounds for justifying the corresponding punishment.

The case of the volunteer serves to clarify an important aspect of the general thesis here advanced. The thesis does not involve the hypothesis of a social contract in any of the varieties defended by political philosophers. It does not rely on an explicit or implicit acceptance by the citizens of the criminal laws imposing obligations or stipulating penalties for noncompliance. It does not assert that every case of punishment is like the case of the punishment of the volunteer who deserts, consequently violating obligations he has previously voluntarily assumed. The grounds on which the obligations that the offender violates can be justified are irrelevant to this thesis: they may be either consensual or independent of the consent of the people subject to them; in most cases, as in the case of conscription or the obligation not to kill other people, those grounds are independent of a choice of the agent; in some exceptional cases, such as the case of the volunteer, those obligations are grounded on a previous and different choice from that of deciding to commit an offense. The focus of this thesis is on this latter choice. The justification of punishment defended in this article relies on the consent to assume the liability to suffer punishment involved in the voluntary commission of an offense with the knowledge that that liability is a necessary consequence of it.

Obviously, following out these suggestions would lead to a discussion of the extent to which the consent of the person affected can justify measures and political arrangements which may imply inequitable burdens upon him.[21] I shall not develop this theme here; but I venture to say that the discussion of the justification of punishment could be considerably expanded and illuminated if it embraced this topic.

If we think of the matter in this way, we will eventually understand the truth behind the superficial absurdity that criminals want to be punished. This claim is intended to support the idea that we punish criminals as people, respecting their moral autonomy, and not as mere things to be manipulated.[22] I would like to put the matter the other way round:

21. See some interesting remarks about the extent to which *hypothetical* consent may or may not justify certain arrangements or measures in Ronald Dworkin, "The Original Positions," in *Reading Rawls*, ed. Norman Daniels (Oxford: Oxford University Press, 1975).
22. See Jonathan Glover's discussion on manipulation in *Responsibility* (London: Routledge & Kegan Paul, 1955), pp. 155ff.

*A Consensual Theory
of Punishment*

unless we rely on the moral autonomy of the individual, making his liability to punishment depend on his free and conscious undertaking of it, all the burdens imposed on offenders, even in the name of treatment, would be unfair even if they are not accompanied by tangible countervailing benefits. Otherwise such burdens would be exacted gratuitously for the exclusive profit of others and would fall under Kant's condemnation of practices which treat men only as means and not as ends in themselves.[23]

I think that it is in keeping with Kant's spirit though not with his letter, to interpret that condemnation as applicable not to every use of punishment as a measure of social protection but only to those uses that fail to take into account the individual's consent. Only when that consent is respected do we treat individuals as ends, since only then do we recognize their own ends.

23. *Philosophy of Law*, trans. W. Hastie (Edinburgh, 1887), pp. 195–98.

This article is a modified version of one chapter of my thesis submitted to Oxford University for the Doctor of Philosophy degree. I express my gratitude to Professor A. M. Honoré, Dr. J. M. Finnis, Professor H. L. A. Hart, and Dr. P. F. Skegg, for their illuminating comments and criticisms. My thanks are also due to the Editors of *Philosophy & Public Affairs* for their very helpful advice.

JEAN HAMPTON

The Moral Education Theory of Punishment

> We ought not to repay injustice with injustice or
> to do harm to any man, no matter what we may
> have suffered from him.
>
> Plato, *Crito*, X, 49

There are few social practices more time-honored or more widely accepted throughout the world than the practice of punishing wrongdoers. Yet if one were to listen to philosophers discussing this practice, one would think punishment impossible to justify and difficult even to understand. However, I do not believe that one should conclude that punishment as a practice is morally unjustifiable or fundamentally irrational. Instead I want to explore the promise of another theory of punishment which incorporates certain elements of the deterrence, retributivist, and rehabilitation views, but whose justification for punishment and whose formula for determining what punishment a wrongdoer deserves are distinctive and importantly different from the reasons and formulas characterizing the traditional rival theories.

This view, which I call the moral education theory of punishment, is not new. There is good reason to believe Plato and Hegel accepted something like it,[1] and more recently, Herbert Morris and Robert Nozick have maintained that the moral education which punishment effects is at least part of punishment's justification.[2] I want to go further, however, and

---

1. See Hegel, *Philosophy of Right*, trans. T. Knox (Oxford: Clarendon Press, 1952), sections 90–104 (pp. 66–74); and see Plato, in particular the dialogues: *The Laws* (bks. 5 and 9), *Gorgias* (esp. pp. 474ff.), *Protagoras* (esp. pp. 323ff.) and Socrates's discussion of his own punishment in the *Apology*, and the *Crito*. I am not convinced that this characterization of either Hegel's or Plato's views is correct, but I do not have time to pursue those issues here. J. E. McTaggart has analyzed Hegel's position in a way that suggests it is a moral education view. See his "Hegel's Theory of Punishment," *International Journal of Ethics* 6 (1896), pp. 482–99; portions reprinted in *Philosophical Perspectives On Punishment*, ed. Gertrude Ezorsky (Albany, NY: State University of New York Press, 1972). In her *Plato on Punishment*, M. M. Mackenzie's presentation of Plato's position suggests it is not a strict moral education view.

2. Recently Morris has been explicitly advocating this view in "A Paternalistic Theory of Punishment," *American Philosophical Quarterly* 18, no. 4 (October 1981), but only as *one*

suggest that by reflecting on the educative character of punishment we can provide a full and complete justification for it. Hence my discussion of the moral education theory in this paper is meant to develop it as a complete justification of punishment and to distinguish it from its traditional rivals. Most of my discussion will focus on the theory's application to the state's punishment of criminal offenders, but I will also be looking at the theory's implications for punishment within other societal institutions, most notably the family.

I will not, however, be able to give an adequate development of the theory in this paper. It is too complex, and too closely connected to many difficult issues, including the nature of law, the foundation of ethical reasoning, and the way human beings develop ethical concepts. Hence what I shall do is simply to *introduce* the theory, sketching its outlines in the first half, and suggesting what seem to be certain advantages and drawbacks of the view in the second half. Much more work needs to be done before anyone is in a position to embrace the view wholeheartedly, hence I won't even attempt to argue in any detailed way here that it is superior to the three traditional views. But I hope my discussion will show that this theory is promising, and merits considerably more discussion and study by the larger intellectual community.

I. THE JUSTIFICATION

Philosophers who write about punishment spend most of their time worrying about whether the *state*'s punishment of criminals is justifiable, so let us begin with that particular issue.

When does punishment by the state take place? The answer to this question seems simple: the state carries out punishment upon a person when he or she has broken a *law*. Yet the fact that the state's punishment always follows the transgression of a law is surely neither coincidental nor irrelevant to the understanding and justification of this practice. What

---

aspect of the justification of punishment. Morris argues that punishment is sufficiently complicated to require a justification incorporating all of the justificatory reasons offered by the traditional theories of punishment as well as by the moral education view. I do not think this sort of patchwork approach to punishment will work and, in this article, I explore the idea that the moral education view can, by itself, give an adequate justification of punishment.

See also Nozick's recent book *Philosophical Explanations* (Cambridge: Harvard University Press, 1981), pp. 363–97.

is the nature of law? This is a thorny problem which has vexed philosophers for hundreds of years. For the purposes of this article, however, let us agree with Hart that there are (at least) two kinds of law, those which are power-conferring rules, for example, rules which specify how to make a contract or a will, and those which are "rules of obligation."[3] We are concerned with the latter kind of rule, and philosophers and legal theorists have generally analyzed the structure of this sort of law as "orders backed by threats" made by the state.

What is the subject matter of these orders? I will contend (consistent with a positivist account of law) that the subject matter *ought* to be (although it might not always be) drawn either from ethical imperatives, of the form "don't steal," or "don't murder," or else from imperatives made necessary for moral reasons, for example, "drive on the right"—so that the safety of others on the road is insured, or "advertise your university job in the professional journals"—so that blacks and women will not be denied an opportunity to secure the job.[4] The state makes these two kinds of commands not only to define a minimal set of duties which a human being in that community must follow in his or her dealings with others, but also to designate actions which, when followed by all members of the society, will solve various problems of conflict and coordination.[5]

And the threat? What role does it play? In the end, this is the central question for which we must have an adequate answer if we are to construct a viable theory of punishment.

The threat, which specifies the infliction of pain if the imperative is not obeyed, gives people a nonmoral incentive, that is, the avoidance of pain, to refrain from the prohibited action. The state hopes this incentive will block a person's performance of the immoral action whenever the ethical incentive fails to do so. But insofar as the threat given in the law is designed to play this kind of "deterring" role, carrying out the threat, that is, punishing someone when he or she has broken the law, is, at least in part, a way of "making good" on the threat. The threat will only deter the disobedience of the state's orders if people believe there is a good chance the pain will be inflicted upon them after they commit the

3. See Hart, *The Concept of Law* (Oxford: Clarendon Press, 1961), chaps. 5 and 6.

4. As stated, this is a positivist definition of law. However, with John Chipman Gray I am maintaining that morality, although not the same as law, should be the source of law. (See Gray's *The Nature and Source of Law* [New York: Macmillan, 1921], p. 84.)

5. See Edna Ullman-Margalit, *The Emergence of Norms* (Oxford: Clarendon Press, 1977) for a discussion of how law can solve coordination and conflict problems.

crime. But if the state punishes in order to make good on its threats, then the deterrence of future crime cannot be wholly irrelevant to the justification of punishment. And anyone, including Kant, who analyzes laws as orders backed by threats must recognize that fact.[6]

Moreover, I believe we must accept the deterrence theorist's contention that the justification of punishment is connected with the fact that it is a necessary tool for preventing future crime and promoting the public's well-being. Consider standard justifications of the state: philosophers from Plato to Kant to Hart have argued that because a community of people cannot tolerate violent and destructive behavior in its midst, it is justified in establishing a state which will coercively interfere in people's lives for publicly announced and agreed-upon reasons so that an unacceptable level of violence and harm can be prevented. Whereas we normally think the state has to respect its citizens' choices about how to live, certain choices, for example, choices to rape, to murder, or to steal, cannot be respected by a community which is committed to preserving and pursuing the well-being of its members. So when the state annexes punishment to these damaging activities, it says that such activities are not a viable option for anyone in that community.

But to say that the state's punishment is needed to prevent crime is not to commit oneself to the deterrence justification of punishment—it all depends on what one takes prevention to entail. And, as Hegel says, if we aimed to prevent wrongdoing only by deterring its commission, we would be treating human beings in the same way that we treat dogs.[7] Consider the kind of lesson an animal learns when, in an effort to leave a pasture, it runs up against an electrified fence. It experiences pain and is conditioned, after a series of encounters with the fence, to stay away from it and thus remain in the pasture. A human being in the same

6. Although Kant's position on punishment is officially retributive (see his *Metaphysical Elements of Justice*, trans. J. Ladd [Indianapolis: Bobbs-Merrill, 1965], p. 100, Academy edition, p. 331), his definition of law conflicts with his retributivist position. Note, for example, the deterrent flavor of his justification of law:

> if a certain use of freedom is itself a hindrance to freedom according to universal laws (that is, unjust), then the use of coercion to counteract it, inasmuch as it is the prevention of a hindrance to freedom according to universal laws, is consistent with freedom according to universal laws; in other words, this use of coercion is just (p. 36, Academy edition, p. 231; see also *Metaphysical Elements of Justice*, pp. 18–9, 33–45; Academy edition, pp. 218–21, 229–39).

7. Hegel, *Philosophy of Right*, addition to par. 99, p. 246.

pasture will get the same message and learn the same lesson—"if you want to avoid pain, don't try to transgress the boundary marked by this fence." But, unlike the animal in the pasture, a human being will also be able to reflect on the reasons for that fence's being there, to theorize about *why* there is this barrier to his freedom.

Punishments are like electrified fences. At the very least they teach a person, via pain, that there is a "barrier" to the action she wants to do, and so, at the very least, they aim to deter. But because punishment "fences" are marking *moral* boundaries, the pain which these "fences" administer (or threaten to administer) conveys a larger message to beings who are able to reflect on the reasons for these barriers' existence: they convey that there is a barrier to these actions *because* they are morally wrong. Thus, according to the moral education theory, punishment is not intended as a way of conditioning a human being to do what society wants her to do (in the way that an animal is conditioned by an electrified fence to stay within a pasture); rather, the theory maintains that punishment is intended as a way of teaching the wrongdoer that the action she did (or wants to do) is forbidden because it is morally wrong and should not be done for that reason. The theory also regards that lesson as public, and thus as directed to the rest of society. When the state makes its criminal law and its enforcement practices known, it conveys an educative message not only to the convicted criminal but also to anyone else in the society who might be tempted to do what she did.

Comparing punishments to electrical fences helps to make clear how a certain kind of deterrent message is built into the larger moral point which punishment aims to convey. If one wants someone to understand that an offense is immoral, at the very least one has to convey to him or her that it is prohibited—that it ought not to occur. Pain is the way to convey that message. The pain says "Don't!" and gives the wrongdoer a reason for not performing the action again; an animal shocked by a fence gets the same kind of message and the same kind of incentive. But the state also wants to use the pain of punishment to get the human wrongdoer to reflect on the moral reasons for that barrier's existence, so that he will make the decision to reject the prohibited action for *moral* reasons, rather than for the self-interested reason of avoiding pain.

If those who are punished (or who watch the punishment take place) reject the moral message implicit in the punishment, at least they will learn from it that there is a barrier to the actions they committed (or are tempted to commit). Insofar as they choose to respond to their punishment (or the punishment of others) merely as a threat, it can keep them within moral boundaries in the same way that fences keep animals in a pasture. This deterrent effect of punishment is certainly welcome by the state whose role is to protect its citizens, and which has erected a "punishment barrier" to certain kinds of actions precisely because those actions will seriously harm its citizens. But on the moral eduation view, it is incorrect to regard simple deterrence as the aim of punishment; rather, to state it succinctly, the view maintains that punishment is justified as a way to prevent wrongdoing insofar as it can teach both wrongdoers and the public at large the moral reasons for *choosing* not to perform an offense.

I said at the outset that one of the reasons any punishment theory is complicated is that it involves one in taking stands on many difficult ethical and legal issues. And it should be quite clear already that particular positions on the nature of morality and human freedom are presupposed by the moral education view which distinguish the theory from its traditional rivals. Given that the goal of punishment, whether carried out by the state on criminals or by parents on children, is the offender's (as well as other potential offenders') realization of an action's wrongness, the moral education view naturally assumes that there is a fact of the matter about what is right and what is wrong. That is, it naturally rests on ethical objectivism. Perhaps certain sophisticated subjectivists could adapt the theory to accommodate their ontological commitments (punishment, they might say, teaches what society defines as right and wrong). But such an accommodation, in my view, does real damage to the theory, which purports to explain punishment as a way of conveying when an action *is* wrong. Given that the theory holds that punishment is a way of teaching ethical *knowledge*, if there is no such thing, the practice seems highly suspect.

The theory also takes a strong stand on human freedom. It rests on the idea that we can act freely in a way that animals cannot. If we were only like animals, attempts at punishment would affect us in the way that electrical fences affect animals—they would deter us, nothing more. But this theory assumes that we are autonomous, that we can choose and be held accountable for our actions. Thus it holds that punishments must attempt to do more than simply deter us from performing certain offenses; they must also, on this view, attempt to provide us with moral reasons for our *choosing* not to perform these actions. Only creatures who are free to determine their lives according to their moral values can choose not to do an action because it is wrong. Insofar as the moral education view justifies punishment as a way of promoting that moral choice, it assumes that punishment is (and ought only to be) inflicted on beings who are free in this sense.[8] It might be that human beings who have lost their autonomy and who have broken a law can be justifiably treated in a painful way so as to deter them (even as we would deter dangerous animals) from behaving similarly in the future, but this theory would not call such treatment punishment.

Thus one distinction between the moral education view and the deterrence justification of punishment is that on the moral education view, the state is not concerned to use pain coercively so as to progressively eliminate certain types of behavior; rather, it is concerned to educate its citizens morally so that they choose not to engage in this behavior. Moreover, there is another important difference between the two views. On the deterrence view, the infliction of pain on certain individuals is justified as a way of promoting a larger social end. But critics of the deterrence view have pointed out that this is just to say that it is all right to *use* certain individuals to achieve a desirable social goal. The moral education theory, however, does not sanction the use of a criminal for social purposes; on the contrary, it attempts to justify punishment as a way to benefit the person who will experience it, a way of helping him to gain moral knowledge if he chooses to listen. Of course other desirable social goals will be achieved through his punishment, goals which include the education of the larger community about the immorality of the offense, but none of these ends is to be achieved at the expense of the criminal. Instead the moral good which punishment attempts to accomplish within the wrongdoer makes it something which is done *for* him, not *to* him.

There are also sharp differences between the moral education view and various rehabilitative theories of criminal "treatment." An advocate of the moral education view does not perceive punishment as a way of treating a "sick" person for a mental disease, but rather as a way of sending a moral message to a person who has acted immorally and who is to be

8. Kantians who see a close connection between autonomy and moral knowledge will note that this connection is suggested in these remarks.

held responsible for her actions.[9] And whereas both theorists are concerned with the good which punishment can do for the wrongdoer, they disagree about what that good is, one defining it as moral growth, the other as the wrongdoer's acceptance of society's mores and her successful operation in the community. In addition, as we shall discuss in Section II, they disagree about what methods to use to achieve these different ends.

Some readers might wonder how close the moral education view is to the old retribution theory. Indeed references in the literature to a view of this type frequently characterize it as a variant of retribution.[10] Nonetheless, there are sharp and important differences between the two views, which we will explore in more detail in Section II. Suffice to say now that whereas retributivism understands punishment as performing the rather metaphysical task of "negating the wrong" and "reasserting the right," the moral education theorist argues that there is a concrete moral *goal* which punishment should be designed to accomplish, and that goal includes the benefiting of the criminal himself. The state, as it punishes the lawbreaker, is trying to promote his moral personality; it realizes that "[h]is soul is in jeopardy as his victim's is not."[11] Thus, it punishes him as a way of communicating a moral message to him, which he can accept or not, as he chooses.

Certain retributivists have also been very attracted to the idea that punishment is a kind of speech act. For example, Robert Nozick in his book *Philosophical Explanations* has provided a nice nine-point analysis of punishment which presents it as a kind of communication and which fits the account of meaning put forward by H. P. Grice.[12] Yet if punishment is a way of (morally) speaking with a wrongdoer, then why doesn't this show that it is fundamentally justified *as a communication*, in virtue

9. Rehabilitationists disagree about exactly what disease criminals suffer from. See for example the various psychiatric diagnoses of Benjamin Karpman in "Criminal Psychodynamics: A Platform," reprinted in *Punishment and Rehabilitation*, ed. J. Murphy (Belmont, CA: Wadsworth, 1973) as opposed to the behaviorist analysis of criminal behavior offered by B. F. Skinner in *Science and Human Behavior* (New York: Macmillan, 1953), pp. 182–93 and 446–49.

10. See for example Nozick's characterization of the view as "teleological retributivism," pp. 370–74 and Gertrude Ezorsky's use of that term in *Philosophical Perspectives on Punishment*.

11. Morris, "The Paternalistic Theory of Punishment," p. 268.

12. Nozick, pp. 369–80.

of what it is trying to communicate, rather than, in Nozick's view, as some kind of symbolic "linkage" of the criminal with "correct values"?[13]

Indeed, I would maintain that regarding punishment as a kind of moral communication is intuitively very natural and attractive. Consider, for example, what we say when we punish others: a father who punishes his child explains that he does so in order that the child "learn his lesson"; someone who has been physically harmed by another demands punishment "so that she will understand what she did to me"; a judge recently told a well-known user of cocaine that he was receiving a stiff sentence because his "matter-of-fact dabbling in cocaine . . . tells the whole world it is all right to use it."[14] These kinds of remarks accompanying our punishment efforts suggest that our principal concern as we punish is to get the wrongdoer to stop doing the immoral action by communicating to her that her offense was immoral. And the last remark by the judge to the cocaine user shows that when the state punishes it is important that these communications be public, so that other members of society will hear the same moral message. Even people who seem to be seeking revenge on wrongdoers behave in ways which show that they too want to make a moral point not only to the wrongdoer, but to anyone else who will listen. The hero seeking revenge in a Western movie, for example, never simply shoots the bad guy in the back when he finds him—he always confronts the bad guy first (usually in the presence of other people) and tells him *why* he is about to die. Indeed, the movie would be unsatisfying if he didn't make that communication. And surely, the hero's desire to explain his actions is linked with his desire to convey to the bad guy and to others in society that the bad guy had "done him wrong."[15]

Moreover, if one understands punishment as a moral message aimed at educating both the wrongdoer and the rest of society about the immorality of the offense, one has a powerful explanation (at least as powerful as the one offered by retributivism) of why victims so badly want

13. Ibid., pp. 374ff. The point is that if one is going to accept the idea that punishment is a communication, one is connecting it with human purposive activity, and hence the *purpose* of speaking to the criminal (as well as to the rest of society) becomes central to the justification of the communication itself. To deny this is simply to regard punishment as something fundamentally different from a species of communication (for example, to regard it as some kind of "value-linkage device") which Nozick seems reluctant to do.

14. *Los Angeles Times*, 30 July 1981, part 4, p. 1.

15. Nozick has also found the "communication" element in comic book stories about revenge; see *Philosophical Explanations*, pp. 368–69.

their assailants punished. If the point of punishment is to convey to the criminal (and others) that the criminal *wronged* the victim, then punishment is implicitly recognizing the victim's plight, and honoring the moral claims of that individual. Punishment affirms as a *fact* that the victim has been wronged, and as a *fact* that he is owed a certain kind of treatment from others. Hence, on this view, it is natural for the victim to demand punishment because it is a way for the community to restore his moral status after it has been damaged by his assailant.

Thus far, I have concentrated on how the state's punishment of criminals can be justified as an attempt at moral education. But I want to contend that punishment efforts by *any* institution or individual should be perceived as efforts at moral education, although the nature and extensiveness of the legitimate educative roles of these institutions and individuals might differ sharply. For example, I believe it is quite clear that parents want to make such a moral communication through their punishments.[16] Suppose for example, that a mother sees her daughter hitting another child. After stepping in to stop this violent behavior, the mother will reflect on what she can do to prevent its reoccurrence. If the mother chooses to try to do this by punishing her daughter, one of the things she "says" through the punishment is, "if you do this again, you will experience the same unpleasantness," and this message is directed at any other children in the family, as well as at this daughter. Hence, one of the things the mother is doing is introducing the incentive of avoiding pain into the children's "calculations" about how to act if and when they are tempted in the future to hurt each other. If a genuine concern for each other's well-being is absent from the children's minds, at least this incentive (as well as fear of losing her approval) might be strong enough to prevent them from hurting each other in the future.[17] But clearly the mother is also trying to get her children to appreciate that

16. Parental punishment can take many forms; although spanking and various kinds of corporal punishment are usually what spring to mind when one thinks of parental punishment, many parents punish through the expression of anger or disapproval, which can be interpreted by the child as a withdrawal of love or as the (at least temporary) loss of the parent's friendship. Such deprivations are in many ways far more serious than the momentary experience of bodily pain or the temporary loss of certain privileges, and hence, although they seem to be mild forms of punishment, they can in actuality be very severe. I am indebted to Herbert Morris for suggesting this point.

17. Because children are not completely responsible, rational beings, punishing them can also be justified as a way of encouraging in them certain kinds of morally desirable habits, insofar as it has "conditioning like" effects. Aristotle seems to regard punishment

there is a *moral* reason for prohibiting this action. The punishment is supposed to convey the message, "don't do this action again because it is *wrong*; love and not hatred or unwarranted violence is what one should display towards one another." The ultimate goal of the punishment is not merely to deter the child from performing the bad action in the future, but to deter her *by convincing her* (as well as the other children) to renounce the action because it is wrong. And the older and more ethically mature the child becomes, the less the parent will need to resort to punishment to make her moral point, and the more other techniques, like moral suasion, discussion, or debate, will be appropriate.

However, although both state and parental punishment should, according to this theory, be understood as efforts at moral communication and education, the theory does not regard the two kinds of punishment as exactly the same. While punishment should always be regarded as moral education, the "character" of that education can vary enormously, depending in particular on the nature of the institution or individual charged with inflicting the punishment. For example, a parent who is responsible for the full maturation and moral development of her child is naturally thought to be entitled to punish her children for many more offenses and in very different ways, than the children's schoolteacher, or the neighbor down the street. We also think of a university as having punishment rights over its students, but we certainly reject the idea that this sort of institution acts *in loco parentis* towards its students generally. Hence, the theory would not have us understand the punishment role of all institutions, and particularly governments, as the *same* as punishment by parents.[18] None of us, I believe, thinks that the state's role is to teach its citizens the entire content of morality—a role we might characterize as "moral paternalism." A variety of considerations are important in limiting the mode and extent of the state's punishment.

Nonetheless, some readers still might think the moral education theory implies a paternalistic theory of the state—after all, doesn't it maintain that the state can interfere in people's lives for their own good? But when such philosophers as John Stuart Mill have rejected paternalism, what

---

of children as, at least in part, playing this role. See for example *Nicomachean Ethics*, bk. I, chap. 4. I would not want to deny that aspect of parental punishment.

18. It is because I believe there are sharp and important differences between parental and state punishment that I eschew Herbert Morris's title for this type of punishment theory (that is, his title "the paternalistic theory of punishment").

they have rejected is a certain position on what should be law; specifically, they have rejected the state's passing any law which would restrict what an individual can do to *himself* (as opposed to what he can do to another). They have not objected to the idea that when the state justifiably interferes in someone's life *after* he has broken a law (which prohibited harm to another), it should intend good rather than evil towards the criminal. Now it is possible they might call this theory paternalistic anyway, not because it takes any stand on what should be law, but because it views the state's punishment as interference in his life plans without his consent for his own good. But why should paternalism in this sense be offensive? It would be strange indeed if philosophers insisted that the state should only try to prevent further harm to the community by actively intending to harm, or use, or at least be indifferent to, the people it punishes!

But, Mill might complain, if you are willing to allow the state to morally educate those who harm others, why not allow it to morally educate those who harm themselves? This is a good question, but one the moral education theory cannot answer. Indeed, answering it is the same as answering the question: What ought to be made law? Or, alternatively, what is the appropriate area for legislation? Though central to political theory, these questions are ones to which the moral education theory can give no answer, for while the theory maintains that punishment of a certain sort should follow the transgression of a law, it is no part of the theory to say *what* ethical reasons warrant the imposition of a law. Indeed, one of the advantages of the theory is that one can adopt it no matter what position one occupies on the political spectrum.

But, critics might insist, isn't this theory arguing that the state should be in the business of deciding and enforcing morality, overriding the autonomous moral decisions of its citizens? Yes, that is exactly the theory's point, the state *is* in that business in a very limited way. Imagine a murderer saying: "You, the state, have no right to tell me that my murder of this man is wrong," or a rapist protesting: "Who is the state to tell me that my rape of this woman is immoral?" These statements sound absurd, because we believe not merely that such actions are wrong, but that they are also heinous and morally appalling. The state is justified in punishing rapists and murderers because their choices about what to do betray a serious inability to make decisions about immoral and moral actions, which has resulted in substantial harm to some members of that community. And while some readers might find it offensive to contemplate the state presuming to morally educate anyone but serious felons, is this not exactly the kind of sentiment behind the libertarians' call for extensive constraints on the state's role and power?

Moreover, I wonder whether, by calling this theory paternalistic, one might not be irritated more by the thought of being governed than by the thought of what this particular theory says being governed involves. Yet, unless one is prepared to be an anarchist, one must admit that being governed is necessary as long as we, as human beings, are prone to immoral acts. We do not outgrow cruelty, or meanness, or the egoistic disregard for others when we reach the age of majority. On this view, the state exists because even adults need to be governed, although not in the way that children require governing by their parents. (Indeed, these ideas suggested by the theory form a germ of an argument against anarchism, which I can only pursue in another place.)

But, critics might insist, it is this theory's view of what governing involves that is objectionable. Who and what is the state, that it can presume to teach us a moral lesson? Yet I regard this question not as posing a challenge to the moral education view itself, but rather as posing a challenge *by* that theory to any existing state. Not only does the theory offer a partial explanation of the state's role, but it also proposes a view of what the state *ought* to be like if its punishment activities have any legitimacy. For example, insofar as the state should be morally educating when it punishes, this theory implies that the state's laws should be arrived at by reflection on what is right or wrong, and not on what is in the best interest of a particular class, or race, or sex. That this is not always true of the laws of our society is an indictment of our state, and punishments inflicted as a way of enforcing these biased laws cannot be justified. Moreover, if we accept the idea that the state is supposed to morally educate its citizens, it is natural to argue that all of its citizens should participate either directly or through representatives in the legislative branch of that institution in order to control and supervise its moral enforcement so that the resulting laws reflect the moral consensus of the community rather than the views of one class. Hence the moral education view can underlie an argument for the democratic structure of a state.

Finally, I would contend that the moral education theory illuminates better than any of its theoretical rivals the strategy of those who are civilly disobedient. Martin Luther King, Jr. wrote that it is critical for anyone who wants to be civilly disobedient to accept the penalty for his or her lawbreaking, not only to express "the very highest respect for law" but also "to arouse the conscience of the community over its injustice."[19] The moral education theory explains how both these objectives are achieved. The civilly disobedient person, when she accepts the penalty for law-breaking, is respecting the state's right to punish transgressors of its laws, but she is also forcing the state to commit itself, in full view of the rest of society, to the idea that her actions show she needs moral education. And when that person is protesting, as Gandhi or King did, offensive and unjust laws, she knows the state's punishment will appear morally outrageous and will arouse the conscience of anyone sensitive to the claims of justice. Therefore, the civilly disobedient person is, on this view, using the idea of what the state and its laws ought to be like if its punishment activities have legitimacy in order to effect moral improvement in the legal system.

II. Questions and Criticisms

Although I will not fully develop and defend the moral education view in this article, I now want to put some flesh on the skeletal presentation of the view just given by considering some questions which spring naturally to mind as one reflects on the theory.

   1. What is this theory's punishment formula? Punishment formulas always follow directly from punishment justifications. If punishment is justified as a deterrent, then it follows from that justification that particular punishments should be structured so as to deter. But if punishment is justified as a way of morally educating the wrongdoer and the rest of society about the immorality of the act, then it follows that one should punish in ways that promote this two-part goal. But how do we go about structuring punishments that morally educate? And would this way of determining punishments yield intuitively more just punishments than those yielded by the formulas of the traditional theories?

One reason these formulas of all the traditional theories have been attacked as unjust is that all of them fail to incorporate an acceptable upper bound on what punishments can be legitimately inflicted on an

19. Martin Luther King, Jr., "Letter from a Birmingham Jail," from *Civil Disobedience*, ed. H. A. Bedau (New York: Pegasus, 1969), pp. 78–9.

offender. Consider that, once the deterrence theorist has defined his deterrence goal, any punishment that will achieve this goal is justified, including the most brutalizing. Similarly, the retributivist's *lex talionis* punishment formula (dictating that punishments are to be somehow equal to the crime) would seem to recommend, for example, torturing the torturer, murdering *all* murderers, and such recommendations cast serious doubt on the formula's moral adequacy.[20] Even the rehabilitation theory does not place strict limits on the kinds of "treatments" which can legitimately be given to offenders. If the psychiatric "experts" decide that powerful drugs, shock treatments, lobotomies or other similar medical procedures are legitimate and necessary treatments of certain criminals, why shouldn't they be used? The only upper bound on the treatments inherent in this theory derives from the consciences of psychiatrists and their consensus about what constitutes "reasonable" treatment, and many contend that history has shown such an upper bound to be far too high.[21]

The moral education theory, however, does seem to have the resources to generate a reasonable upper limit on how much punishment the state can legitimately administer. Because part of the goal of punishment is to educate the criminal, this theory insists that as he is educated, his autonomy must be respected. The moral education theorist does not want "education" confused with "conditioning." Shock treatments or lobotomies that would damage or destroy the criminal's freedom to choose are not appropriate educative techniques. On this view the goal of punishment is not to destroy the criminal's freedom of choice, but to persuade him to use his freedom in a way consistent with the freedom of others. Thus, any punishment that would damage the autonomy of the criminal is ruled out by this theory.

20. Some retributivists have tried to argue that the *lex talionis* needn't be regarded as a formula whose upper bound *must* be respected; see, for example, K. C. Armstrong, "The Retributivist Hits Back," *Philosophy of Punishment*, ed. H. B. Acton (London: Macmillan, 1969). However, critics can object that Armstrong's weaker retributivist position still does not *rule out* barbaric punishments (like torture) as permissible, nor does it explain why and when punishments which are less in severity than the criminal act can be legitimately inflicted.

21. Consider the START program used in a Connecticut prison to "rehabilitate" child molesters: electrodes were connected to the prisoner's skin, and then pictures of naked boys and girls were flashed on a screen while electric shocks were applied. The Federal Bureau of Prisons canceled this program just before they were about to lose a court challenge to the program's constitutionality (see David J. Rothman's discussion of this in "Behavior Modification in Total Institutions," *Hastings Center Report* 5, no. 1 [1975]: 22).

In addition, it is important to remember that, on this view, punishments should be designed to convey to the criminal and to the rest of society the idea that the criminal's act was wrong. And it seems difficult if not impossible for the state to convey this message if it is carrying out cruel and disfiguring punishments such as torture or maiming. When the state climbs into the moral gutter with the criminal in this way it cannot credibly convey either to the criminal or to the public its moral message that human life must always be respected and preserved, and such actions can even undercut its justification for existing. Note that both of these considerations indicate this theory rules out execution as punishment.[22] (Of course, the moral education theory says nothing about whether the execution of criminals might be justified not as punishment but as a method of "legitimate elimination" of criminals who are judged to have lost all of their essential humanity, making them wild beasts of prey on a community that must, to survive, destroy them. Whether such a justification of criminal execution can be morally tolerable is something I do not want to explore here.)

But, the reader might wonder, how can inflicting *any* pain upon a criminal be morally educational? And why isn't the infliction of mild sorts of pains and deprivations also climbing into the moral gutter with the criminal? The moral education theorist must provide an explanation of why certain sorts of painful experiences (whose infliction on others we would normally condemn) may legitimately be inflicted in order to facilitate moral growth. But is such an explanation possible? And even if it is, would the infliction of pain always be the right way to send a moral message? If a criminal's psychological make-up is such that pain would not reform him, whereas "inflicting" a pleasurable experience would produce this reform, are we therefore justified only in giving him that pleasurable experience? Retributivists like Robert Nozick think the answer to this last question is yes, and thus reject the view as an adequate justification of punishment by itself.[23]

---

22. Apart from the fact that killing someone is hardly an appropriate technique for educating him, it is likely that this action sends a poor message to the rest of society about the value of human life. Indeed, in one of their national meetings, the Catholic bishops of the United States argued that repeal of capital punishment would send "a message that we can break the cycle of violence, that we need not take life for life, that we can envisage more human and more hopeful and effective responses to the growth of violent crime." ("Statement on Capital Punishment," *Origins* 10, no. 24 [27 November 1980]: 374.)

23. Nozick, pp. 373–74.

All three of these worries would be allayed if the moral education theorist could show that only the infliction of pain of a certain sort following a wrongdoing is *necessarily* connected with the promotion of the goal of moral education. In order to establish this necessary connection between certain sorts of painful experiences and moral growth, the moral education theorist needs an account of what moral concepts are, and an account of how human beings come to acquire them (that is, what moral education is). I cannot even attempt to propose, much less develop, answers to these central ethical issues here. But I will try to offer reasons for thinking that painful experiences of a particular sort would seem to be necessary for the communication of a certain kind of moral message.

It is useful to start our discussion by getting a good understanding of what actions count as punishment. First, if we see punishment from the offender's standpoint, we appreciate that it involves the loss of her freedom. This is obviously true when one is locked up in a penitentiary, but it is also true when, for example, parents stop their child's allowance (money that had previously been defined as hers is withheld—whether she likes it or not) or when they force her to experience a spanking or a lecture. I would argue that this loss of freedom is why (autonomous) human beings so dislike punishment. Second, whereas it is very natural to characterize punishment as involving pain or other unpleasant consequences, the infliction of what we intuitively want to call punishment might involve the wrongdoer in performing actions which one would not normally describe as painful or unpleasant. For example, a doctor who cheated the Medicare system and who is sentenced to compulsory weekend service in a state-supported clinic would not be undergoing what one would normally describe as a painful or unpleasant experience (he isn't being incarcerated, whipped, fined). Nonetheless, insofar as some of his free time is being taken away from him, the state is depriving him of his freedom to carry out his own plans and to pursue the satisfaction of his own interests. In this case, the state is clearly punishing an offender, but it sounds distorted to say that it is inflicting pain on him. Thus we need a phrase to describe punishment which will capture better than "infliction of pain" all of the treatments which we intuitively want to call punishment. For this purpose I propose the phrase "disruption of the freedom to pursue the satisfaction of one's desires," a phrase which is suitably general and which fits a wide variety of experiences that we want to call

experiences of *punishment*. (It may well be *too* general, but I do not want
to pursue that issue here.)[24]

Thus I understand punishment as an experience which a wrongdoer
is forced by an authority to undergo in virtue of the fact that he has
transgressed (what ought to be) a morally derived rule laid down by that
authority, and which disrupts (in either a major or a minor way) the
wrongdoer's freedom to pursue the satisfaction of his desires. Given that
punishment is understood in this way, how do coercion and the disruption
of one's self-interested pursuits convey a *moral* message?

Before answering this question, it is important to make clear that punishment is only *one* method of moral education. Upon reflection, it is
clear, I think, that we choose to employ this method only when we're
trying to teach someone that an action is *wrong*, rather than when we
are trying to teach someone what (imperfect) moral duties he or she
ought to recognize. (We punish a child when he kicks his brother; we
don't punish him in order to get him to give Dad a present on Father's
Day.)

What is one trying to get across when one wants to communicate an
action's wrongness? The first thing one wants to convey is that the action
is forbidden, prohibited, "fenced off." Consider a mother who sees her
child cheating at solitaire. She might say to the child, "You mustn't do
that." Or if she saw her child putting his left shoe on his right foot, she
would likely say, "No, you mustn't dress that way." In both cases it would
be highly inappropriate for her to follow these words with punishment.
She is communicating to her child that what he is doing in these circumstances is inadvisable, imprudent, not playing by the rules, but she
is not communicating (and not trying to communicate) the idea that such
actions violate one's moral duty to others (or, for that matter, one's moral
duty to oneself). Now consider this mother seeing her son kick the neighbor's young daughter. Once again she might say, "You mustn't do that,"

24. George Fletcher, in *Rethinking Criminal Law* (Boston: Little, Brown, 1978), p. 410,
worries about defining punishment so that it doesn't include too much (for example, it
should not include the impeachment of President Nixon, despite the fact that it would be
a case of unpleasant consequences inflicted on Nixon by an authority in virtue of a wrongdoing). I do not have time here to consider how to hone my definition such that it will not
encompass impeachments, deportation, tort damages, and so forth. Indeed, perhaps the
only way one can do this is to bring into the definition of punishment its justification as
moral education.

to the child, but the "mustn't" in the mother's words here is unique. It is more than "you shouldn't" or "it isn't advisable" or "it's against the rules of the game." Rather, it attempts to convey the idea that the action is forbidden, prohibited, intolerable.

But merely telling the child that he "mustn't do that" will not effectively convey to the child that there is this profound moral boundary. Without punishment why shouldn't the child regard the "mustn't" in the parent's statement just as he did the "mustn't" in "You mustn't cheat at solitaire"? The mother needs to get across to the child the very special nature of the prohibition against this immoral act. How can she do this? Consider the fact that someone who (for no moral reason) violates a positive duty to others is not acting out of any interest in the other's well-being. A teenager who steals from a passer-by because she needs the money, a man who rapes a woman so that he can experience a sense of power and mastery—such people are performing immoral acts in order to satisfy their own needs and interests, insensitive to the needs and interests of the people they hurt. The way to communicate to such people that there is a barrier of a very special sort against these kinds of actions would seem to be to link performance of the actions with what such people care about most—the pursuit of their own pleasure. Only when disruption of that pursuit takes place will a wrongdoer appreciate the special force of the "mustn't" in the punisher's communication. So the only effective way to "talk to" such people is through the disruption of their own interests, that is, through punishment (which has been defined as just such a disruption).

What conclusions will a person draw from this disruption of his pleasure? At the very least he will conclude that his society (in the guise of the family, the state, the university, etc.) has erected a barrier to that kind of action, and that if he wants to pursue the satisfaction of his own desires, he won't perform that action again. So at the very least, he will understand his punishment as society's attempt to deter him from committing the action in the future. Such a conclusion does not have moral content. The person views his punishment only as a sign of society's condemnation of the act, not as a sign of the act's *wrongness*. But it is a start, and a *necessary first start*. If a wrongdoer has little or no conception of an action's wrongness, then the first thing one must do is to communicate to him that the action is prohibited. We must put up the electrical fence in an attempt to keep him out of a forbidden realm.

But given that we want the offender to understand the moral reasons for the action's condemnation, how can punishment communicate those reasons? The punisher wants the wrongdoer to move from the first stage of the educative process initiated by punishment—the realization that society prohibits the action—to a second stage, where the moral reasons for the condemnation of the action are understood and accepted. Can punishment, involving the disruption of a person's self-interested pursuits, help an offender to arrive at this final moral conclusion, to understand, in other words, why this fence has been erected?

What is it that one wants the wrongdoer to see? As we noted before, someone who (for no moral reason) violates her (perfect) moral duty to others is not thinking about the others' needs and interests, and most likely has little conception of, or is indifferent to, the pain her actions caused another to suffer. Hence, what the punisher needs to do is to communicate to the wrongdoer *that* her victims suffered and how much they suffered, so that the wrongdoer can appreciate the harmfulness of her action. How does one get this message across to a person insensitive to others? Should not such a person be made to endure an unpleasant experience designed, in some sense, to "represent" the pain suffered by her victim(s)? This is surely the intuition behind the *lex talionis* but it best supports the concept of punishment as moral education. As Nozick admits,[25] it is very natural to regard the pain or unpleasantness inflicted by the wrongdoer as the punisher's way of saying: "This is what you did to another. You hate it; so consider how your victim felt." By giving a wrongdoer something like what she gave to others, you are trying to drive home to her just how painful and damaging her action was for her victims, and this experience will, one hopes, help the wrongdoer to understand the immorality of her action.

Of course, the moral education formula does not recommend that punishments be specifically *equal* to the crime—in many instances this doesn't even make sense. But what does the "representation" of the wrongful act involve, if not actual equality? This is a terribly difficult question, and I find I can only offer tentative, hesitant answers. One way the moral education theorist can set punishments for crimes is to think about "fit." Irrespective of how severe a particular crime is, there will sometimes be a punishment that seems naturally suited to it; for example, giving a

25. Compare Nozick's discussion of the content of the Gricean message of punishment, pp. 370–74.

certain youth charged with burglarizing and stealing money from a neighbor's house the punishment of supervised compulsory service to this neighbor for a period of time, or giving a doctor charged with cheating a government medical insurance program the punishment of compulsory unremunerated service in a state medical institution. And probably such punishments seem to fit these crimes because they force the offender to compensate the victim, and thus help to heal more effectively the "moral wound" which the offense has caused. Another way the moral education theorist can make specific punishment recommendations is to construct an ordinal scale of crimes, going from most offensive to least offensive, and then to link determinate sentences to each crime, respecting this ordinal comparison, and insuring proportionality between crime and punishment. But it is not easy to use either method to fashion a tidy punishment table because it is not easy to determine which painful experiences will be educative but not cruel, both proportional to the offense committed and somehow relevant to that offense. Indeed, our society has been notoriously unsuccessful in coming up with punishments that are in any way morally educative. And I would argue that it speaks in favor of this theory that it rejects many forms of incarceration used today as legitimate punishments, insofar as they tend to make criminals morally worse rather than better.

But even if this theory can tell us how to represent wrongdoing in a punishment, it must still handle other questions which I do not have time to pursue properly in this article. For example, how does that representation help the wrongdoer to understand and *accept* the fact that she did wrong and should do otherwise in the future? And if we want to send the most effective message possible in order to bring about this acceptance, should we try to tailor punishments to the particular psychological and moral deficiencies of the wrongdoer, or must considerations of equal treatment and fairness override this? Finally, does the view justify the state's punishing people who are innocent of any illegal act but who seem to need moral education?

The theory has a very interesting and complicated response to this last question. We have said that punishment is not the appropriate method to teach every sort of moral lesson, but only the lesson that a certain action is wrong. But on whom is the state justified in imposing such a lesson?—clearly, a person who has shown she needs the lesson by committing a wrong which the state had declared illegal, and clearly *not* a person who has shown she already understands this lesson (at least in some sense) by conscientiously obeying that law. We also believe that the state is justified in imposing this lesson on a person who has not broken that law but who has *tried* to do so. She might, for example, be punished for "attempted murder" or "attempted kidnapping." (And do we make the punishments for such attempts at wrongdoing less than for successful wrongdoings because we're not sure the attempts provide conclusive evidence that such people would have carried through?) But what about a person who has not broken a law or even attempted to do so but who has, say, talked about doing so publicly? Is that enough evidence that she needs moral education? Probably—by *some* person or institution, but not by the state. The point is that we believe the state should refrain from punishing immoral people who have nonetheless committed no illegal act, not because they don't need moral education but because the state is not the appropriate institution to effect that education. Indeed, one of the reasons we insist that the state operate by enacting laws is that doing so defines when it may coercively interfere in the lives of its citizens and when it may not; its legislation, in other words, defines the extent of its educative role (and there might exist constitutional rules guiding this legislation). So if the state were to interfere with its citizens' lives when they had not broken its laws, it would exceed its own legitimate role. In the end, the state may not punish immoral people who are innocent of any crime not because they don't need moral education, but because the state is not justified in giving it to them.

However, there is another question relevant to the issue of punishing the innocent. Given that I have represented the moral education theory as having a two-part goal—the moral education of the criminal and the moral education of the rest of society—it might be that a punishment which would achieve one part of this goal would not be an effective way of realizing the other part. Must we choose between these two objectives, or is it possible to show that they are inextricably linked? And if they are not, could it be that in order to pursue the goal of morally educating *society*, it would be necessary to punish an innocent person? More generally, could it be justifiable on this view to punish a wrongdoer much more (or much less) severely than her offense (if any) would seem to warrant if doing so would further society's moral education? If this were true, the theory would not preserve proportionality between crime and punishments. However, there are reasons for thinking that educating the criminal and educating the community are inextricably linked. For example, if the state aims to convey a moral lesson to the community about how other human beings should be treated, it will completely fail to do so if it inflicts pain on someone innocent of any wrongdoing—indeed, it would send a message exactly contrary to the one it had intended. But even if we suppose, for the sake of argument, that these educational objectives could become disengaged, we can preserve proportionality between a person's crime and her punishment by making the moral education of the criminal lexically prior to the moral education of the community (after all, we *know* she needs the lesson, we're less sure about the community).[26]

However, giving adequate arguments for solutions to any of the problems I have posed in this section requires a much more fully developed account of what moral education is and of how punishment would help to effect it. Some readers might think that developing such an account is simply an empirical rather than a philosophical task. But before we can know how to morally educate, we need a better theoretical understanding of what moral knowledge is, and why human beings do wrong. (Is it because, as Kant insists, we choose to defy the power of the moral law or because, as Socrates argues, we are morally ignorant?) Moreover, we need a better appreciation of the source and extent of the state's authority if we are to understand its legitimate role as moral educator. Further work on this theory has to come to grips with these issues in moral and political philosophy before we can know whether to embrace it. But I have tried to suggest in my remarks in this section that certain kinds of approaches to these issues are at least promising.

2. *Is the moral education of most criminals just a pipe dream?* How can we really expect hard-core criminals convicted of serious offenses to be able to change and morally improve? In answer to this last question, the moral education theorist will admit that the state can predict that many of the criminals it punishes will refuse to accept the moral message it delivers. As I have stressed, the moral education theory rests on the assumption of individual autonomy, and thus an advocate of this theory must not only admit but insist that the choice of whether to listen to the moral message contained in the punishment belongs to the criminal.

26. I have profited from discussions with Katherine Shamey on this point.

Thus it is very unlikely that society will be 100 percent successful in its moral education efforts, no matter how well it uses the theory to structure punishments.

But at least the punishment the state delivers can have a deterrent effect; even if the criminal refuses to understand the state's communication about why there is a barrier to his action, at least he will understand *that* the barrier exists. Hegel once wrote that if a criminal is coerced by a punishment, it is because he *chooses* to be so coerced; such a person rejects the moral message and accepts instead the avoidance of pain as his sole reason for avoiding the action.[27] In the end, punishments might only have deterrent effects because that is all wrongdoers will let them have.

However, neither the state nor anyone else can determine who the "losers" are. None of us can read another's mind, none of us knows the pressures, beliefs, and concerns motivating another's actions and decisions. The state cannot, even with the help of a thousand psychiatrists, *know for sure* who is a hopeless case and who isn't. Nor is this just a simple epistemological problem. Insofar as the state, on this view, should regard each person it punishes as autonomous, it is committed to the view that the choice of whether to reform or not is a free one, and hence one the state cannot hope to predict. Finally, the state's assumption that the people it is entitled to punish are free means it must never regard any one it punishes as hopeless, insofar as it is assuming that each of these persons still has the ability to choose to be moral. Thus, as Hegel puts it,[28] punishment is the criminal's "right" as a free person—to refuse to punish him on the grounds that he has been diagnosed as hopeless is to regard him as something other than a rational human being.

But even if it seems likely that punishing some criminals will not effect their moral growth, and may not even deter them, the moral education of the community about the nature of their crimes can still be promoted by their punishment. Indeed any victim of crime is going to be very sensitive to this fact, insofar as he has been the one against whom the wrong has been committed, and is the one who is most interested in having the community acknowledge that what happened to him *shouldn't* have happened. And as long as the person whom we punish is admitted to be an autonomous human being, we cannot be convicted of using her

27. See Hegel, *Philosophy of Right*, sec. 91.
28. Ibid., sec. 100, p. 70.

as we educate the community about the wrongness of her offense, because we are doing something to her which is *for* her, which can achieve a great deal of good for her, if she will but let it.

3. *Shouldn't the moral education theory imply an indeterminate sentencing policy?* Throughout your discussion, rehabilitationists might complain, you have been assuming that punishment by the state should proceed from determinate sentences for specific crimes. But isn't indeterminate sentencing fairer? Why keep a criminal who has learned his moral lesson in jail just because his sentence has not run out, and why release a criminal who is unrepentant and who will probably harm the public again, just because his sentence has run out?

However, the moral education theorist has very good reasons, provided by the foundations of the theory itself, for rejecting the concepts of indeterminate sentencing and parole boards. First, this theorist would strongly disagree with the idea that a criminal should continue to receive "treatment" until his reform has been effected. Recall that it is an important tenet of the view that the criminals we punish are free beings, responsible for their actions. And you can't *make* a free human being believe something. In particular, you can't coerce people to be just for justice's sake. Punishment is the state's attempt to teach a moral lesson, but whether or not the criminal will listen and accept it is up to the criminal himself.

The moral education theorist takes this stand not simply because she believes one ought to respect the criminal's autonomy, but also because she believes one has no choice but to respect it. The fact that parole boards in this country have tried to coerce repentance is, from the standpoint of this theorist, a grave and lamentable mistake. (Consider James McConnell's claim, in an article in *Psychology Today*, that "Somehow we've got to *force* people to love one another, to force them to want to behave properly.")[29] Indeed, critics of present parole systems in the United States maintain that these systems only open the way for manipulation.[30] The parole board uses the threat of the refusal of parole to get the kind of behavior it wants from the criminal, and the criminal manipulates

29. From "Criminals Can be Brainwashed—Now," *Psychology Today*, April 1970, p. 14; also quoted in Rick Carlson's *The Dilemma of Corrections* (Lexington, MA: Lexington Books, 1976), p. 35.

30. See "The Crime of Treatment," American Friends Service Committee from *The Struggle for Justice*, chap. 6 (New York: Hill and Wang, 1971) reprinted in *Punishment: Selected Readings*, eds., Feinberg and Gross.

back—playing the game, acting reformed, just to get out. In the process, no moral message is conveyed to the criminal, and probably no real reformation takes place. The high recidivism rate in the United States tells the tale of how successful parole boards have been in evaluating the rehabilitation of prisoners. As one prisoner put it: "If they ask if this yellow wall is blue, I'll say, of course it's blue. I'll say anything they want me to say if they're getting ready to let me go."[31]

The moral education theorist doesn't want the state to play this game. A sentence for a crime is set, and when the criminal breaks a law, the sentence is inflicted on him as a way of teaching him that what he did was wrong. When the sentence is up, the criminal is released. The state hopes its message was effective, but whether it was or not is largely up to the criminal himself.

There is another important reason why the moral education theorist does not want to insist on repentance before release. Even a good state can make mistakes when it enacts law. It is not just possible but probable that the state at one time or another will declare a certain action immoral which some of its citizens will regard as highly moral. These citizens will often decide to disobey this "immoral" law, and while being punished, will steadfastly refuse to repent for an action they believe was right. Martin Luther King, Jr., never repented for breaking various segregation laws in the South while he was in jail; few draft resisters repented for refusing to go to Vietnam when they were in prison. By not insisting on the repentance of its criminals, the state is, once again, respecting the freedom of its citizens—particularly each citizen's freedom of conscience, and their right, as free beings, to disagree with its rulings. Hence, the moral education theorist doesn't want the state to insist on repentance because it doesn't want Solzhenitsyns rotting in jail until they have "reformed."[32]

How can the moral education theorist justify the punishment of a criminal who is already repentant prior to his sentencing, or who repents

31. Quoted by Carlson, p. 161; from David Fogel, *We Are the Living Proof* (Cincinnati: W. H. Anderson, n.d.).

32. Jeffrie Murphy has argued that instituting a rehabilitationist penal system would deny prisoners many of their present due process rights. See "Criminal Punishment and Psychiatric Fallacies," especially pp. 207–209, in *Punishment and Rehabilitation*, ed. J. Murphy. The American Friends Service Committee has also charged that the California penal system, which was heavily influenced by the rehabilitation theory, has in fact done this. See "The Crime of Treatment," pp. 91–93, in Feinberg et al.

before his sentence is completely served? The theorist's response to this question is complicated. Because it is difficult to be sure that a seemingly repentant criminal is *truly* repentant, and thus because a policy of suspending or shortening sentences for those who seem repentant to the authorities could easily lead the criminal to fake repentance before a court or a parole board, the moral education theorist would be very reluctant to endorse such a policy.

Moreover, it might well be the case that, prior to or during sentencing, a criminal's experience of repentance is produced in large part by the expectation of receiving the full punishment, so that the state's subsequent failure to inflict it could lead to a weakening of the criminal's renunciation of the action. Like a bad but repentant child who will conclude, if he is not punished by his parents, that his action must not have been so bad, the repentant criminal might well need to experience his complete sentence in order to "learn his lesson" effectively.

Finally, the lesson learning effected by punishment can also involve a purification process for a wrongdoer, a process of healing. As Herbert Morris has written, experiencing the pain of punishment can be a kind of catharsis for the criminal, a way of "burning out" the evil in his soul.[33] Novelists like Dostoevsky have explored the criminal's need, born of guilt and shame, to experience pain at the hands of the society he has wronged in order to be reconciled with them. Thus the rehabilitationist who would deny the criminal the experience of pain at the hands of the state would deny him what he may want and need to be forgiven—both by society and by himself. And punishment understood as moral education would explain how it could be perceived as a purification process. For how is it that one overcomes shame? Is it not by becoming a person *different* from the one who did the immoral action? The subsiding of shame in us seems to go along with the idea, "Given who I was, I did the action then, but I'm different now—I'm *better* now—and I wouldn't do the same act again." But how do we become different, how do we change, improve? Insofar as punishment is seen as a way of educating oneself about the offense, undergoing that experience is a way of changing for the better. It might well be the yearning for that change which drives a person like Raskolnikov towards his punishment.

Nonetheless, if there were clear evidence that a criminal was very

33. See Morris's discussion of certain wrongdoers' need to experience punishment in "The Paternalistic Theory of Punishment," p. 267.

remorseful for his action and had already experienced great pain because of his crime (had "suffered enough"), this theory would endorse a suspension of his sentence or else a pardon (*not* just a parole). His moral education would have already been accomplished, and the example of his repentance would be lesson enough for the general public. (Indeed, punishment under these circumstances would make the state appear vindictive.) In addition, because the state conceives itself to be punishing a wrong, it is appropriate for it to allow certain sorts of excuses and mitigating circumstances to lessen the penalty normally inflicted for the crime in question.

4. *Does the moral education theory actually presuppose the truth of retribution?* Retributivists have a very interesting criticism of the moral education theory available to them. Granted, they might maintain, that punishment is connected with moral education, still this only provides an additional reason for punishing someone—it does not provide the fundamental justification of punishment. That fundamental justification, they would argue, is retributive: wrongdoers simply *deserve* to experience pain for the sake of the wrong they have committed. As Kant has argued, however much good one intends one's punishment to effect,

> yet it must first be justified in itself as punishment, i.e. as mere harm, so that if it stopped there, and the person punished could get no glimpse of kindness hidden behind this harshness, he must yet admit that justice was done him, and that his reward was perfectly suitable to his conduct.[34]

Moreover, such modern retributivists as Walter Moberly have argued that it is only when the wrongdoer can assent to his punishment as already justified in virtue of his offense that the punishment can do him any good.[35]

In a certain sense, Moberly's point is simply that a criminal will perceive his punishment as vindictive and vengeful unless he understands or accepts the fact that it is justified. But should the justification of punishment be cashed out in terms of the retributive concept of desert, given that it has been difficult for retributivists to say what they mean by the

34. Kant, *Critique of Practical Reason*, "The Analytic of Pure Practical Reason," Remark II. (Abbott trans. in *Kant's Theory of Ethics* [London: Longman, 1959], p. 127; Academy edition, p. 38.)

35. Walter Moberly, *The Ethics of Punishment*, (London: Faber & Faber, 1968), p. 141.

criminal's "deserving" punishment simply in virtue of his offense? Robert Nozick tries to cash out the retributive link between crime and "deserved" punishment by saying that the punishment represents a kind of "linkage" between the criminal and "right values."[36] But why is inflicting pain on someone a way of effecting this linkage? Why isn't the infliction of a pleasurable experience for the sake of the crime just as good a way of linking the wrongdoer with these right values? And if Nozick explains the linkage of pain with crime by saying that the pain is necessary in order to communicate to the criminal that his action was wrong, he has answered the question but lost his retributive theory. Other philosophers, like Hegel,[37] speak of punishment as a way of "annulling" or "canceling" the crime and hence "deserved" for that reason. But although Hegel's words have a nice metaphorical ring to them, it is hard to see how they can be given a literal force that will explain the retributivist concept of desert. As J. L. Mackie has written, insofar as punishment occurs after the crime, it certainly cannot cancel it—past events are not eliminated by later ones.[38]

It is partly because retributivists have been at a loss to explain the notion of desert implicit in their theory of punishment that I have sought to propose and explore a completely nonretributivist justification of punishment. But my reasons for rejecting retributivism are deeper. The retributive position is that it is somehow morally appropriate to inflict pain for pain, to take an eye for an eye, a tooth for a tooth. But how is it ever morally appropriate to inflict one evil for the sake of another? How is the society that inflicts the second evil any different from the wrongdoer who has inflicted the first? He strikes first, they strike back; why is the second strike acceptable but the first not? Plato, in a passage quoted at the start of this article, insists that both harms are wrong; and Jesus attacks retributivism[39] for similar reasons:

36. Nozick, pp. 374ff.

37. For example, see Hegel, *The Philosophy of Right*, sec. 101–103.

38. J. L. Mackie, "Morality and the Retributive Emotions," in *Criminal Justice Ethics* 1, no. 1 (Winter/Spring 1982): 3–10. In the face of the retributivists' failure to explain why punishment is deserved, Mackie wants to argue that our retributive intuitions spring from fundamental retributive emotions, which are part of a human being's fundamental moral make-up (and he gives a sketch of how our evolution as a species could have generated such emotions). But many retributivists, particularly the Kantian sort, would eschew such an explanation which, in any case, is hardly a *justification* of the retributive impulse itself.

39. Jesus rejected not only "negative retributivism," that is, the idea that we deserve bad

You have learned that they were told, 'Eye for eye, tooth for tooth'. But
what I tell you is this: Do not set yourself against the man who wrongs
you. . . . You have heard that they were told 'Love your neighbor, hate
your enemy'. But what I tell you is this: Love your enemy and pray for
your persecutors; only so can you be children of your heavenly father,
who makes the sun rise on good and bad alike, and sends the rain on
the honest and dishonest. [Matt. 5:38–9, 43–6]

In other words, both reject retributivism because they insist that the only
thing human beings "deserve" in this life is *good*, that no matter what
evil a person has committed, no one is justified in doing further evil to
her.

But if one accepts the idea that no one can ever deserve ill, can we
hope to justify punishment? Yes, if punishment can be shown to be a
good for the wrongdoer. The moral education theory makes just such an
attempt to explain punishment as a good for those who experience it, as
something done *for* them, not to them, something designed to achieve a
goal that includes their own moral well-being. This is the justification of
punishment the criminal needs to hear so that he can accept it as legitimate rather than dismiss it as vindictive. Therefore, my interest in the
moral education theory is connected with my desire to justify punishment
as a good for those who experience it, and to avoid any theoretical justification of punishment that would regard it as a deserved evil.[40] Reflection on the punishment activities of those who truly love the people
they punish, for example, the infliction of pain by a parent on a beloved
but naughty child, suggests to me that punishment should not be justified
as a deserved evil, but rather as an attempt, by someone who cares, to
improve a wayward person.

Still, the moral education theory can incorporate a particular notion of
desert which might be attractive to retributivists. Anyone who is punished
according to this theory would know that his punishment is "deserved,"
that is, morally required, insofar as the community cannot morally tolerate
the immoral lesson that his act conveys to others (for example, the mes-

---

for doing bad, but also "positive retributivism," that is, the idea that we deserve good for
doing good, but I cannot go into that here.

40. Indeed, I believe that it is because retribution would justify punishment as a deserved
evil that it strikes many as much too close to revenge.

sage that raping a woman is all right if it gives one a feeling of self-mastery) and cannot morally allow that he receive no education about the evil of his act.

So the theory's point is this: Wrong occasions punishment not because pain deserves pain, but because evil deserves correction.

I have many people to thank for their help in developing the ideas in this paper; among them: Warren Quinn, Thomas Hill, Judith De Cew, Marilyn Adams, Robert Adams, Richard Healey, Christopher Morris, Norman Dahl, Julie Heath, George Fletcher, Robert Gerstein, David Dolinko, and especially Herbert Morris. I also want to thank the Editors of *Philosophy & Public Affairs* for their incisive comments, and members of my seminar on punishment at UCLA in the Spring of 1983 for their lively and helpful discussions of the theory. Portions of the article were also read, among other places, at the 1982 Pacific Division APA Meeting, at C.S.U. Northridge, and at the University of Rajasthan, Jaipur, India.

PART II

Problems of Punishment

MARTHA C. NUSSBAUM   Equity and Mercy

> We stomp on the rape magazines or we invade
> where they prostitute us, where we are herded
> and sold, we ruin their theatres where they have
> sex on us, we face them, we scream in their fuck-
> ing faces, we are the women they have made
> scream when they choose. . . . We're all the same,
> cunt is cunt is cunt, we're facsimiles of the ones
> they done it to, or we are the ones they done it to,
> and I can't tell him from him from him . . . so at
> night, ghosts, we convene; to spread justice,
> which stands in for law, which has always been
> merciless, which is, by its nature, cruel.
>   Andrea Dworkin, *Mercy*

> This second doctrine [of mercy]—counterdoctrine
> would be a better word—has completely exploded
> whatever coherence the notion of 'guided discre-
> tion' once had. . . . The requirement [of mitiga-
> tion] destroys whatever rationality and predict-
> ability the . . . requirement [of aggravation] was
> designed to achieve.
>   Justice Scalia, in *Walton v. Arizona*

> "O child . . . do not cure evil with evil. Many peo-
> ple have preferred the more equitable to the more
> just."
>   Herodotus, *History*

I

I begin with the plot of a novel whose title is *Mercy*.[1] By the author's deliberate design, it is not really a novel, and there is no mercy in it. These facts are connected. My plan is to pursue this connection. The

This paper was delivered as a Dewey Lecture at the University of Chicago Law School, as a Boutwood Lecture at Cambridge University, as a Whitehall-Linn Lecture at Bryn Mawr College, and at a Legal Humanities conference at Stanford University. I am grateful to these audiences for their questions and comments, and especially to Ronald Allen, Albert Alshuler, Allen Boegehold, Daniel Brudney, Myles Burnyeat, Scott Crider, John Lawless, Richard Posner, John Roemer, Cass Sunstein, and the Editors of *Philosophy & Public Affairs* for comments that have been very helpful to me in revising an earlier draft, and to Susan Wolf and Joyce Carol Oates for valuable discussions.

1. Andrea Dworkin, *Mercy* (New York: Four Walls, Eight Windows, 1991); see my review in *The Boston Review* (May–June 1992). In the September–October issue I reply to letters defending Dworkin's position.

author of this "novel" is the feminist writer and antipornography activist Andrea Dworkin. Its narrator is also named Andrea—a name that, as she tells us, means "courage" or "manhood." At the age of nine, Andrea is molested by an anonymous man in a movie theater. At fourteen, she is cut with a knife by a sadistic teenage lover. At eighteen she sleeps with many men for money; she finds a tender black lover, but is brutally raped by his roommate. Jailed for antiwar activity, she is assaulted and tortured by prison doctors. She goes to Crete and has a passionate loving relationship with a Greek bartender, but when he discovers that she has been making love casually with many men he rapes her and gives her up. Returning to New York, she lives a marginal life of sex, drink, and drugs. Threatened by a gang one night, she tries to make peace with its leader. He holds her hostage at knifepoint in her own bed. Apparently rescued by a man who turns up at her door, she finds herself raped by her rescuer.

At twenty-two she marries a tender young revolutionary. As soon as they are husband and wife, he finds himself unable to make love without tying her up and hitting her. She leaves him for street life. Some years later, after many other abuses, she takes karate lessons and becomes adept at kicking drunken homeless men to death. We encounter at this point the passage that I have quoted as an epigraph to this article; it expresses Andrea's angry refusal of mercy, her determination to exact retribution without concern for the identity of the particulars. ("I can't tell him from him from him.") Although one might wonder whether the point is that terrible experiences have corrupted Andrea's perception, it appears that her refusal of mercy is endorsed by the novel as a whole.

This novel does not read like a traditional novel, because its form expresses the retributive idea that its message preaches. That is, it refuses to perceive any of the male offenders—or any other male—as a particular individual, and it refuses to invite the reader into the story of their lives. Like Andrea, it can't tell him from him from him. The reader hears only the solitary voice of the narrator; others exist for her only as sources of her pain. Like the women in the male pornography that Dworkin decries, her males have no history, no psychology, no concrete reasons for action. They are just knives that cut, arms that beat, penises that maim by the very act of penetration. Dworkin's refusal of the traditional novelist's attention to the stories of particular lives seems closely connected with her heroine's refusal to be merciful to any of those lives, with her doctrine that justice is cruel and hard.[2] But the nature of the connection between mercy and a vision of the particular is not yet evident; my hope is to make it evident—and, in the process, to make a case for the moral and legal importance of the novelist's art.

In order to do this, however, I must begin with a historical inquiry into the origins, in the Western tradition, of the close connection between equitable judgment—judgment that attends to the particulars—and mercy, defined by Seneca as "the inclination of the mind toward leniency in exacting punishment." I begin with a puzzle in ancient Greek thought about law and justice. Solving this puzzle requires understanding some features of the archaic idea of justice that turn out to be highly pertinent to Andrea Dworkin's project. This sort of justice is soon criticized, with appeal to both equity and mercy. After following the arguments of Aristotle and Seneca on this question, I shall return to contemporary issues, using these ideas to make a case for the moral and legal importance of narrative art in several areas of contemporary legal and political relevance, defending the equity/mercy tradition as an alternative both to retributive views of punishment and to some modern deterrence-based views.

II

There is a puzzle in the evidence for ancient Greek thought about legal and moral reasoning. Two concepts that do not appear to be at all the same are treated as so closely linked as to be aspects of the same concept, and introduced together by one and the same moral term. The moral term is *epieikeia*.[3] The concepts are the two that I have already identified as my theme: the ability to judge in such a way as to respond with sensitivity to all the particulars of a person and situation, and the "inclina-

2. I note that we do not find this refusal in some of Dworkin's best essays on sexuality, in particular the essays on Tennessee Williams and James Baldwin in *Intercourse*.

3. For an excellent discussion of the term and its philosophical and legal history in Greece and Rome, see Francesco D'Agostino, *Epieikeia: Il Tema Dell'Equità nell'Antichità Greca* (Milan: A. Giuffre, 1973). An excellent study that focuses on fourth-century B.C. oratory and its relationship to Aristotle is John Lawless, *Law, Argument and Equity in the Speeches of Isaeus*, Ph.D. diss., Brown University, 1991. Both D'Agostino and Lawless have extensive bibliographies. *Epieikeia* is usually translated into Latin by *clementia* (see below). Modern scholars generally render it into German with "Billigkeit," Italian by "equità," French by "équité" or (translating the Latin) "clémence."

tion of the mind" toward leniency in punishing—equity and mercy.[4] From the beginning, the idea of flexible particularized judgment is linked with leniency. *Epieikeia*, which originally designated the former, is therefore said to be accompanied by the latter; it is something mild and gentle, something contrasted to the rigid or harsh. The Herodotean father, in my epigraph, contrasts the notion of strict retributive justice with *epieikeia*, at a time when that word was already clearly associated with situational appropriateness.[5] The orator Gorgias, praising the civic character of soldiers fallen in battle, says of them that "on many occasions they preferred the gentle equitable (*to praon epieikes*) to the harshly stubborn just (*tou authadous dikaiou*), and appropriateness of reasoning to the precision of the law, thinking that this is the most divine and most common law, namely to say and not say, to do and to leave undone, the thing required by the situation at the time required by the situation."[6] He too, then, links the ability to do and say the right thing in the situation with a certain mildness or softness; opposed to both is the stubborn and inflexible harshness of law. By this time, the original and real etymology of the word *epieikeia*—from *eikos*, the "plausible" or "appropriate,"[7]—is being supplemented by a popular derivation of the term from *eikô*, "yield," "give way." Thus even in writing the history of the term, Greek thinkers discover a connection between appropriate judgment and leniency.[8]

4. Both equity and mercy can be spoken of as attributes of persons, as features of judgments rendered by a person, or as moral abstractions in their own right. Thus a person may be praised as *epieikês*; his or her judgments or decisions display *to epieikes*, or show a respect for *to epieikes*.

5. Hdt. III.53; for discussion, see D'Agostino, *Epieikeia*, p. 7. See also Soph. fr. 770 (Pearson), which contrasts "simple justice" (*tên haplôs dikên*) with both equity and grace (*charis*). All translations from the Greek are my own.

6. Gorgias, *Epitaphios*, fragment Diels-Kranz 82B6. The passage has occasioned much comment and controversy: see D'Agostino, *Epieikeia*, p. 28ff. for some examples. It seems crucial to understand the passage as pertaining to the civic virtue of the fallen, not their military attributes.

7. See P. Chantraine, *Dictionnaire etymologique de la langue grecque: Histoire des mots*, vol. 2 (Paris: Klinksieck, 1970), p. 355. For other references, see D'Agostino, *Epieikeia*, pp. 1–2, n. 3. *Eikos* is the participle of *eoika*, "seems." (The English word "seemly" is an instructive parallel.) In early poetry, the opposite of *epieikes* is *aeikes*, "outrageous," "totally inappropriate," "horrible."

8. In addition to the passages discussed below, see Pseudo-Plato, *Definitiones* 412A, the first known definition of *epieikeia*, which defines it as "good order of the reasoning soul with respect to the fine and shameful," as "the ability to hit on what is appropriate in contracts," and also as "mitigation of that which is just and advantageous."

The puzzle lies, as I have said, in the unexplained connection between appropriate situational judgment and mercy. One might well suppose that a judgment that gets all the situational particulars correct will set the level of fault sometimes high up, sometimes low down, as the situation demands. If the judgment is a penalty-setting judgment, it will sometimes set a heavy penalty and sometimes a light one, again as the situation demands. If the equitable judgment or penalty are being contrasted with a general principle designed beforehand to fit a large number of situations—as is usually the case—then we might expect that the equitable will sometimes be more lenient than the generality of the law, but sometimes harsher. For, as that not-very-merciful philosopher Plato puts it in the *Laws*, sometimes the offender turns out to be unusually good for an offender of that sort, but sometimes, too, unusually bad.[9] Plato has a modern ally in Justice Scalia, who feels that it is absurd that aggravation and mitigation should be treated asymmetrically in the law. The very same requirements should hold for both; presumably, once we begin looking at the specific circumstances, we will be about as likely to find grounds for the one as for the other.[10]

But this is not what many Greek and Roman thinkers seem to think. They think that the decision to concern oneself with the particulars is connected with taking up a gentle and lenient cast of mind toward human wrongdoing. They endorse the asymmetry that Justice Scalia finds absurd and incoherent. We must now ask on what grounds, and with what rationality and coherence of their own, they do so.

III

We can make some progress by looking at what *epieikeia* opposes or corrects. We see in our passages a contrast between *epieikeia* as flexible situational judgment and the exceptionless and inflexible mandates of law or rule. We also find these laws or rules described as "harsh," "harshly stubborn," a "cure of evil with evil." This goes to the heart of

9. Plato, *Laws* 867d, on regulations concerning the recall of an exiled homicide.

10. Justice Scalia, in *Walton v. Arizona*: "Our cases proudly announce that the Constitution effectively prohibits the States from excluding from the sentencing decision *any* aspect of a defendant's character or record or *any* circumstance surrounding the crime: [for example] that the defendant had a poor and deprived childhood, or that he had a rich and spoiled childhood" (at 3062).

our puzzle, clearly, for what we need to know is how that sort of justice comes to be seen as *harsh* in its lack of fit to the particulars, rather than as simply imprecise.

Let us think, then, of the archaic conception of justice. And let us examine the first surviving philosophical text to use the notion of justice, for in its metaphorical application of *dikê* to cosmic process it illustrates very vividly what *dikê*, in human legal and moral matters, was taken to involve. Writing about the cyclical changes of the basic elements into one another—as the hot, the cold, the wet, and the dry succeed one another in the varying combinations that make up the seasons of the year—the sixth-century B.C. philosopher Anaximander writes, "They pay penalty and retribution (*dikên kai tisin*) to one another in accordance with the assessment of time."[11]

Anaximander describes a process in which "encroachments" by one element are made up in exact proportion, over time, by compensatory "encroachments" of the corresponding opposite element. We are, it seems, to imagine as neutral a state of balance in which each element has, so to speak, its own—its due sphere, its due representation in the sphere of things. Next the balance is thrown off, in that one or more of the elements goes too far, trespasses on the preserve of the other—as, for example, winter is an invasion by the cold and the wet into the due preserve of the warm and the dry. (Thus the root notion of injustice, already in the sixth century, is the notion of *pleonexia*, grasping more than one's due share, the very notion that Plato exploits in the *Republic*, trying to capture its opposite with the notion of "having and doing one's own.")[12] Winter is an imbalance, and in order for justice or *dikê* to be restored, retribution (*tisis*) must take place; the elements that encroached must "pay justice and retribution" to the ones they squeezed out. What this seems to mean is that a corresponding encroachment in the other direc-

11. Anaximander DK fragment BI, the first surviving verbatim fragment of ancient Greek philosophy. (We know it to be verbatim because Simplicius, who reports it, also comments with some embarrassment about its language, saying "as he said using rather poetic terms.") For an excellent account of Anaximander's idea and its connection with ideas of justice and equality in law and morals see Gregory Vlastos, "Equality and Justice in Early Greek Cosmologies," in *Studies in Presocratic Philosophy*, ed. David Furley and Reginald Allen, vol. 1 (London: Routledge, 1970), 56–91.

12. See G. Vlastos, "Plato's Theory of Social Justice," in *Interpretations of Plato: A Swarthmore Symposium*, ed. H. North (Leiden: Brill, 1977).

tion must take place, in order that "the doer should suffer."[13] Summer is
the due retribution for the imbalance of winter; mere springtime would
not right the balance, because cold and wet would not be duly squeezed
out in their turn.

In short, this cosmology works with an intuitive idea that derives from
the legal and moral sphere. It is the idea that for encroachment and pain
inflicted a compensating pain and encroachment must be performed.
The primitive sense of the just—remarkably constant from several ancient cultures to modern intuitions such as those illustrated in our Andrea Dworkin passage—starts from the notion that a human life (or,
here, the life of the cosmos) is a vulnerable thing, a thing that can be
invaded, wounded, or violated by another's act in many ways. For this
penetration, the only remedy that seems appropriate is a counterinva-
sion, equally deliberate, equally grave. And to right the balance truly, the
retribution must be exactly, strictly proportional to the original encroachment. It differs from the original act only in the sequence of time and in
the fact that it is a response rather than an original act—a fact frequently
obscured if there is a long sequence of acts and counteracts.

This retributive idea is committed to a certain neglect of the particulars. For Anaximander, it hardly matters whether the snow and rain that
get evaporated are in any sense "the same" snow and rain that did the
original aggressing. The very question is odd, and Anaximander seems
altogether uninterested in the issues of individuation and identity that
would enable us to go further with it. Nor are things terribly different in
the human legal and moral applications of retributive *dikê*. Very often
the original offender is no longer on the scene, or is inaccessible to the
victim, and yet the balance still remains to be righted. What then happens is that a substitute target must be found, usually some member of
the offender's family. The crimes of Atreus are avenged against Agamemnon, Agamemnon's offense burdens Orestes. The law that "the doer
must suffer" becomes, in this conception of justice as balanced retribution, the law that for every bad action some surrogate for the doer must
suffer; and, like Andrea Dworkin's narrator, the ancient concept of *dikê*
can't "tell him from him from him." A male has raped Andrea; then another male will get a karate kick. The substitution is usually justified

13. *Ton drasanta pathein*, Aeschylus, *Choephoroi*, l. 313. A similar idea is expressed in
many other places; see, for example, Aes., *Agamemnon* 249, 1564.

through an intuitive notion that the real offender is "the line of X" or "the house of X," or, in Dworkin, "the gender of X." But this alleged justification entails neglect of the particularity of the so-called offender; it neglects, too, questions of motive and intention that one might think crucial in just sentencing.

A closely related sort of neglect can arise even if the original offender is around to receive the punishment. For suppose that the offender committed an act that is in some sense heinous, but did so with extenuating circumstances. (Oedipus committed both parricide and incest, but with an excusable ignorance of crucial information.) *Dikê* says that parricide and incest have occurred here, and the balance must be righted. The eyes that saw their mother's naked body must be blinded. Now in this case the doer and the sufferer are the same individual, but notice that Oedipus's particularity is still in a significant sense neglected. For he is being treated the same way, by *dikê*, as a true or voluntary parricide would be treated, and crucial facts about *him*, about his good character, innocent motives, and fine intentions, are neglected. But to neglect all this is to neglect *him*: substitution again, though of a more subtle sort, neglecting crucial elements of the person's individual identity.[14]

If we start thinking this way, the asymmetry we asked about begins to arise naturally. For looked at in this way, *dikê* is always harsh and unyielding. Sometimes the harshness is merited, sometimes excessive. But it is rarely too soft, for it begins from the assumption that the doer *should* suffer, that any wrong should be "made up" by a penalty that befits a deliberate wrong. The particulars of the case, more closely inspected, lead toward extenuation or mitigation far more frequently than in the opposite direction. If *dikê* has got the right person, well and good; nothing more need be added. If, however, *dikê* has got hold of the wrong person, a more flexible and particularized judgment will let that person off. So too in the Oedipus case: for *dikê* assumes that Oedipus *is* a parricide; there is nothing more we can find out about him that will aggravate his offense. We can and do, on the other hand, find out that in a most relevant sense he is *not* a parricide, because the act that he intended and chose was not the act that we have judged him to have performed. Once again, the more flexible judgment of *epieikeia* steps in to

14. One might wonder whether parricide and incest have actually been committed, for one might argue that intention is relevant to the categorization of the act.

say, be gentle with this man, for we cannot assume without looking further that he really did the awful thing for which strict justice holds him responsible. Getting the right life and getting the life right are not two separate issues, but two aspects of a single process of appropriate scrutiny.

In effect, the asymmetry arises from the fact that the circumstances of human life throw up many and various obstacles to meeting the tough standards of justice; if we set a high standard of good action, the very course of life will often make it difficult for mere human beings to measure up. To put it another way, the asymmetry arises from a certain view about the common or likely causes of wrongdoing: the asymmetrist claims that a certain number of wrongful acts are fully deliberate wrongs and that a certain number are produced by obstacles such as failure of knowledge, mistaken identification, bad education, or the presence of a competing moral claim. There may be some cases of parricide and incest that are produced by an especially or unusually blameworthy degree of hatred or wickedness, going beyond the responsible deliberateness assumed by the law, but the claim is that this is likely to be a smaller class than the Oedipus-type class, given the character of human life and the nature of human motivation.

The world of strict *dikê* is a harsh and symmetrical world, in which order and design are preserved with exceptionless clarity. After summer comes fall, after fall comes winter, after day comes the night; the fact that Agamemnon was not the killer of Thyestes' children is as irrelevant to *dikê* as the fact that the night did not deliberately aggress against the day; the fact that Oedipus acted in ignorance is as irrelevant to *dikê* as the fact that the winter came in ignorance of its crimes against the summer. It is a world in which gods are at home, and in which mortals often fare badly. As a fragment of Sophocles puts it, "The god before whom you come . . . knows neither equity nor grace (*oute toupieikes oute tên charin*), but only cares for strict and simple justice (*tên haplôs dikên*)."[15] The world of *epieikeia* or equity, by contrast, is a world of imperfect human efforts and of complex obstacles to doing well, a world in which humans sometimes deliberately do wrong, but sometimes also get tripped up by ignorance, passion, poverty, bad education, or circumstan-

15. Sophocles fr. 770 (Pearson). See D'Agostino, *Epieikeia*, p. 8ff. for other related passages.

tial constraints of various sort. It is a world in which bad things are sometimes simply bad, sometimes extremely bad, but sometimes—and more
often, when one goes into them—somewhat less bad, given the obstacles
the person faced on the way to acting properly. *Epieikeia* is a gentle art
of particular perception, a temper of mind that refuses to demand retribution without understanding the whole story; it responds to Oedipus's
demand to be seen for the person he is.

IV

So far we have been dealing only with a contrast between the equitable
and the just. Justice itself is still understood as strict retribution, and
therefore the equitable, insofar as it recognizes features of the particular
case that the strict law does not cover, stands in opposition to the just.
But justice or *dikê* is by the fifth century a venerated moral norm, associated in general with the idea of giving to each his or her due. We would
expect, then, as the conflict between equity and strict retributive justice
assumed prominence, an attempt to forge a new conception of justice,
one that incorporates the insights of equity. This project was pursued to
some extent by Plato, in his late works the *Statesman* and the *Laws*.[16]
Even more significant for our purposes, it was pursued, albeit unsystem-
atically, by the Attic orators in their arguments over particular cases in
front of citizen juries.[17] But it was Aristotle who made the major contribution.

Aristotle's discussion of the equitable in the *Nicomachean Ethics* occurs within his account of justice. It begins with an apparent dilemma.
The *epieikes*, he says, is neither strictly the same as the just nor altogether different in kind (*EN* 1137a33–4). On the one hand, it looks as if
it would be strange to separate *epieikeia* from justice, for we praise both

16. See *Statesman* 294A–95A, *Laws* 757E, 867D, 876A–E, 925D–26D. Like Aristotle,
Plato recognizes the importance of *epieikeia* both in the judgment of whether a certain
offense was committed and in the assessment of penalties. He suggests that laws are written deliberately in such a way as to leave gaps to be filled in by the judgment of judges or
juries. He compares the prescriptions of law to the general instructions that an athletic
trainer has to give when he cannot deal with each pupil one by one and also to a trainer or
a medical doctor who has to go out of town and therefore leaves instructions that cannot
anticipate all the circumstances that may arise. This being so, it is in the spirit of law that
when one *does* look into the particular case, one will modify the prescription to suit the
differing conditions.

17. See Lawless, *Law, Argument and Equity*, with comprehensive bibliography; for
some particulars, see below.

people and their judgments for the quality of *epieikeia*, recognizing it as a normatively good thing. But in that case it will be odd if *epieikeia* turns out to be altogether opposed to the just. Then we would either have to say that justice is not a normatively good quality, or withdraw our normative claims for *epieikeia* (1137a34–b8).[18] Aristotle's solution to the dilemma is to define equity as a kind of justice, but a kind that is superior to and frequently opposed to another sort, namely strict legal justice (1137b8ff.). Equity may be regarded as a "correcting" and "completing" of legal justice.[19]

The reason for this opposition, he continues, is that the law must speak in general terms, and therefore must err in two ways, both leaving gaps that must be filled up by particular judgments, and sometimes even getting things wrong. Aristotle says that this is not the fault of the lawgiver, but is in the very nature of human ethical life; the "matter of the practical" can be grasped only crudely by rules given in advance, and adequately only by a flexible judgment suited to the complexities of the case. He uses the famous image of the good architect who does not measure a complicated structure (for example a fluted column) with a straightedge. If he did, he would get a woefully inadequate measurement. Instead he uses a flexible strip of metal that "bends to the shape of the stone and is not fixed" (1137b30–32). Exactly in this way, particular judgments, superior in flexibility to the general dictates of law, should bend round to suit the case.[20]

Aristotle ends the discussion with some remarks that seem ill-suited to their context, but by now we should be prepared to understand how they fit in:

> It is also clear from this [account of the equitable] what sort of person the equitable person is. For a person who chooses and does such things, and who is not zealous for strict judgment in the direction of

18. Strictly speaking, there is another possibility: that they are both valuable norms that pervasively conflict in their requirements. Aristotle does recognize contingent conflicts of obligation, but not this more deep-seated value conflict.

19. *Epanorthôma* suggests both things: the image is of straightening up something that has fallen over or gone crooked a bit. Equity is putting law into the condition to which it aspires in the first place.

20. On the role of this passage in Aristotle's ethical theory generally, see my essay "The Discernment of Perception: An Aristotelian Model for Public and Private Rationality," in *Love's Knowledge: Essays on Philosophy and Literature* (New York: Oxford University Press, 1990). There I discuss in greater detail Aristotle's reasons for thinking that general rules cannot be sufficient for the complexities of particular cases.

the worse, but is inclined to mitigation, even though he can invoke the law on his side—such a person is equitable, and this trait of character is equity, being a kind of justice and not a distinct trait of character. (1137b34–1138a3)

Here Aristotle alludes to and endorses the tradition that links perception of the particular with mitigation, and by now we can see on what grounds he does so. But Aristotle makes a new contribution, for he insists that this is the way a truly *just* person is. In keeping with his insistence throughout his ethical and political writings that justice, as a virtue of character, is a peculiarly human virtue, one that gods neither possess nor comprehend, and indeed would think "ridiculous" (*EN* 1178b11), he now gives the just a definition suited to an imperfect human life.[21]

In the *Rhetoric* discussion of *epieikeia*, having given a very similar account of the equitable as that which corrects or supplements—and thereby fulfills—the written law, Aristotle adds a somewhat more detailed account of equitable assessment, telling us that the equitable person is characterized by a sympathetic understanding of "human things." He uses the word *suggnômê*, "judging with." He links this ability with particular perception, and both of these with the ability to classify actions in accordance with the agent's motives and intentions (1374b2–10).[22]

The logic of these connections seems to be as follows. To perceive the particular accurately, one must "judge *with*" the agent who has done the alleged wrong. One must, that is, see things from that person's point of view, for only then will one begin to comprehend what obstacles that person faced as he or she acted. In this sense, it takes *suggnômê* to deliver a "correct discrimination" of the equitable. When one looks at the person's case with *suggnômê*, certain distinctions that do not play a part in the archaic conception of *dikê* assume a remarkable salience. Equity, like the sympathetic spectatorship of the tragic audience, accepts Oedipus's plea that the ignorant and nonvoluntary nature of his act be acknowledged; it acknowledges, too, the terrible dilemmas faced by characters such as Agamemnon, Antigone, and Creon, and the terrible moral defectiveness of all their options. Recognizing the burden of these "hu-

---

21. See *EN* VII.1 on ethical excellence in general; *Pol.* I.1 on the social excellences, and *EN* X.8, 1178a9–b18 on virtue and justice as purely human and not divine.

22. Cf. also *EN* 1143a19–20, connecting *suggnômê* and equity, and both with perception of the particular; cf. also *EN* 1110a24–25, 1111a1–2, on *suggnômê* in tragic situations.

man things," the equitable judge is inclined not to be "zealous for strict judgment in the direction of the worse," but to prefer merciful mitigation.

I have already illustrated Aristotle's argument by alluding to tragedy and tragic spectatorship. And since I shall go on to develop my own account of the equitable with reference to literature, it seems well worth pointing out that Aristotle's account of *suggnômê* and *epieikeia* in these passages has close links with his theory of tragedy. For in his theory the spectator forms bonds of both sympathy and identification with the tragic hero.[23] This means that "judging with" is built into the drama itself, into the way in which the form solicits attention. If I see Oedipus as one whom I might be, I will be concerned to understand how and why his predicament came about; I will focus on all those features of motive and agency, those aspects of the unfortunate operations of chance, that I would judge important were I in a similar plight myself. I would ask *how* and *why* all this came about, and ask not from a vantage point of lofty superiority, but by seeing his tragedy as something "such as might happen" in my own life.[24] Tragedy is thus a school of equity, and therefore of mercy. If I prove unable to occupy the equitable attitude, I will not even enjoy tragedy, for its proper pleasure requires emotions of pity and fear that only *suggnômê* makes possible.

Aristotle's attitude to law and equity was not simply a theoretical fiction. There is evidence that it both shaped legal practice and, even more clearly, built upon an already developed and developing tradition of Athenian legal thought.[25] We have, of course, almost no records of the actual outcomes of jury trials, and no record at all of the deliberations of jurors. The process did not encourage lengthy or communal deliberation, as

23. See Stephen Halliwell, *Aristotle's Poetics* (London: Duckworth, 1986), and "Pleasure, Understanding, and Emotion in Aristotle's *Poetics*," in *Essays on Aristotle's Poetics*, ed. A. Rorty (Princeton: Princeton University Press, 1992), 241–60.

24. See *Poetics*, ch. 9, and the excellent discussion in Halliwell, "Pleasure." Aristotle remarks that neither pity nor fear will be experienced by a person who believes that he or she is above the uncertainties of life and can suffer no serious reversal. See *Rhet.* 1382b30ff., 1385b21–22, 31: he calls this state of mind a *hubristikê diathesis*, an "overweening disposition."

25. Among the legal and rhetorical figures mentioned, Lysias predates Aristotle and is active in the late fifth century, while both Isaeus and Isocrates are contemporaries of Aristotle; their period of activity overlaps with the likely period of composition of Aristotle's *Rhetoric*, which is prior to Aristotle's first departure from Athens in 347. Isaeus's earliest and latest works, for example, can be dated approximately to 389 and 344/3 B.C.

each juror cast a separate vote after hearing the various arguments, apparently without much mutual consultation.[26] We do, however, have many examples of persuasive speeches delivered to such juries. Since the orator's reputation rested on his ability to persuade a jury of average citizens chosen by lot, we can rely on these speeches for evidence of widespread popular beliefs about legal and ethical concepts. These speeches show the orators relying on a concept of law and even of justice that is very much like the one that Aristotle renders explicit and systematic. Thus litigants frequently call for a justice tailored to the circumstances of their own case, and frequently use the expression *ta dikaia* ("those things that are just") in that sense.[27] They often proceed as if the written law is understood to be a set of guidelines with gaps to be filled in or corrected by arguments appealing to the notion of equity.[28] In this process, frequent appeal is made to the jurors' sense of fairness, as if, once the particular circumstances of the case are understood, they can be expected to see that justice consists in an equitable determination.

This is a deep insight, one that I support. For it seems wrong to make a simple contrast between justice and equity, suggesting that we have to choose between the one and the other.[29] Nor, in a deep sense, do we have to choose between equity and the rule of law as understandings of what justice demands. The point of the rule of law is to bring us as close as possible to what equity would discern in a variety of cases, given the dangers of carelessness, bias, and arbitrariness endemic to any totally discretionary procedure. But no such rules can be precise or sensitive enough, and when they have manifestly erred, it is justice itself, not a departure from justice, to use equity's flexible standard.

26. On all this, see Lawless, *Law, Argument and Equity*, with copious references to sources ancient and modern.

27. See Michael Hillgruber, *Die zehnte Rede des Lysias: Einleitung, Text und Kommentar mit einem Anhang über die Gesetzesinterpretation bei den attischen Rednern* (Berlin and New York: Walter de Gruyter, 1988), 116–17. Hillgruber cites passages in the orators where an appeal to *ta dikaia* is used to persuade the jurors that obedience to the letter of the law is not required by their oath. These passages are: Andocides 1.31, Lysias 15.8, Demosthenes 21.4, 21.212, 23.194, 24.175, [Dem.] 58.61. Lawless, *Law, Argument and Equity*, p. 78, discusses this material and adds Isaeus 1.40 to the list.

28. See K. Seeliger, "Zur Charackteristik des Isaios," *Jahrb. für Philologie* 113 (1876): 673–79, translated in Lawless, *Law, Argument and Equity*: "The principle of equity is almost always maintained, while the letter of the law is not infrequently circumvented, however much the orator is accustomed to holding his opponents to it."

29. For examples of such contrasts, see Richard Posner, *Law and Literature* (Cambridge, Mass.: Harvard University Press, 1988), 108ff., on which see further below.

V

We are still not all the way to a doctrine of mercy. For what Aristotle recommends is precise attention to the circumstances of offense and offender, both in ascertaining whether or not there is any guilt and in assessing the penalty if there is. He is prepared to let people off the hook if it can be shown that their wrongdoing is unintentional, or to judge them more lightly if it is the result of something less than fully deliberate badness. But the point of this is to separate out the fully and truly guilty from those who superficially resemble them. In effect, we are given a more precise classification of offenses, a classification that takes intention and motive into account. But once a particular offense is correctly classified, the offender is punished exactly in proportion to the actual offense.

By contrast to the archaic conception of justice, this is indeed merciful, but it does not suffice, I think, for all that we mean by mercy, which seems to involve a gentleness going *beyond* due proportion, even to the deliberate offender. With his emphasis on sympathetic understanding, Aristotle is on his way to this idea. And he insists that the virtuous disposition in the area of retributive anger is best named "gentleness" (using the same word that Gorgias had used in connection with *epieikeia*). He stresses that "the gentle person is not given to retribution [*timôrêtikos*], but is rather inclined to sympathetic understanding [*suggnômonikos*]" (*EN* 1126a2–3). But retribution will still play an important role, where the circumstances demand it. For "people who do not get retributively angry[30] at those at whom they should look like fools. . . . For they seem to have no perception and no feeling of pain . . . and to allow oneself and one's loved ones to be kicked around, and overlook it, is slavish" (1126a4–8). The demand to avoid the slavish is certain to play a role in the public world of the law, as well as in the private world of the family. This demand makes Aristotelian *suggnômê* stop short of mercy. For the full development of that idea, we must wait for Roman Stoicism and for Seneca.[31]

Stoic moral theory accepts and builds on the Aristotelian insight that

30. I am translating *orgizesthai* this way because Aristotle defines *orgê* as a desire for retribution, on account of the pain of a believed slight.

31. I have discussed Seneca's views on mercy in "Seneca on Anger in Public Life," chapter 11 of *The Therapy of Desire: Theory and Practice in Hellenistic Ethics* (Princeton: Princeton University Press, forthcoming 1994).

rules and precepts are useful only as guidelines in both private and public thought. Any fully adequate moral or legal judgment must be built
upon a full grasp of all the particular circumstances of the situation, including the motives and intentions of the agent. Like Aristotle, Stoics are
fond of using an analogy between medicine and ethics to illustrate this
point: general ethical or legal rules are about as useful as medical rules
and precepts—which is to say, useful as outlines, but no substitute for a
resourceful confrontation with all the circumstances of the case. Both
the Greek and the later Roman Stoics stress that an act is fully correct
and moral, what they call a *katorthôma*, only if it is done with the appropriate motives and the appropriate knowledge; a *kathêkon* or (in Latin)
officium is an act of (merely) the right general type, without consideration of the agent's thoughts and motivations. Rules can tell you what
the *kathêkonta* are, but to get all the way to a full *katorthôma* you need
to become a certain sort of person. The same goes in reverse for bad
actions. This means that the Aristotelian idea of justice as equity is already built into the moral schema from the beginning, and it will automatically influence the classification of offenses in public reasoning and
in the law.[32]

The Greek Stoics stop there, and in their moral rigor they explicitly
reject any application of *epieikeia* that goes beyond the careful classification of offenses. The soul of the good Stoic judge is a hard soul that
protects itself from all impulses that might sway it from the strict path of
virtue and duty. "All wise men," they announce, "are harshly rigorous
[*austêroi*]."[33] They "never permit their soul to give way or to be caught
by any pleasure or pain."[34] This hardness cordons them off from any
yielding response to the defects of another person. The wise man, they
announce, does not forgive those who err, and he never waives the punishment required in the law. An unyielding judge, the Stoic will do exactly what strict justice requires. In this connection, *epieikeia* is explic-

32. One possible difference: Aristotle's ethical schema makes a big distinction between
adikêmata, for which it is necessary to have a bad *character*, and lesser wrongdoings that
will be classified as among the blameworthy *hamartêmata*. The latter class will include
bad acts done from weakness of will with respect to some passion. Stoic moral theory is
harsher toward the passions, treating them as types of false judgment that are always in
an agent's power to refuse. Thus the distinction between *akrasia* and wrongdoing from
bad character is significantly weakened, if not altogether eroded.
33. Diogenes Laertius VII.117 = *Stoicorum Veterum Fragmenta* (SVF) III.637.
34. Clement, *Strom.* VII.7 = SVF III.639.

itly rejected: the Stoic will never waive the punishment that is mandated
for that particular type of offense.[35]

Many Greek Stoic texts show us this attitude of detachment and hardness to offenders, an attitude far removed from the Aristotelian norm of
suggnômê. One can see this emerge with particular clarity in the treatment of tragedy, which Stoics are permitted to watch, so long as they
watch it from a vantage point of secure critical detachment (like Odys-
seus, they say, lashed to the mast so that he can hear, but not be swayed
by, the sirens' song).[36] From this secure vantage point they view the dis-
asters and vulnerabilities of ordinary mortals with amusement and even
scorn, defining tragedy as what happens "when chance events befall
fools."[37] To Oedipus, the wise man says, "Slave, where are your crowns,
where your diadem?" To Medea, the wise man says, "Stop wanting your
husband, and there is not one of the things you want that will fail to
happen."[38] There is no inevitability in tragedy, for if one has the proper
moral views there is no contingency in the world that can bring one
low.[39]

Here Seneca steps in, perceiving a serious tension in the Greek Stoic
position. On the one hand, Stoicism is deeply committed to the Aristotelian position that good moral assessment, like good medical assessment,
is searchingly particular, devoted to a deep and internal understanding
of each concrete case. On the other hand, the Stoic norm of critical detachment withholds psychological understanding, treating deep and
complex predicaments as easily avoidable mistakes, simply refusing to
see the obstacles to good action from the erring agent's own viewpoint.

Seneca opts for the medical side of this dilemma, offering a complex
account of the origins of human wrongdoing that leads to a new view of
the proper response to it. Seneca begins his argument in *De ira* as an
Aristotelian would, asking the judge to look at all the circumstances of
the offense (1.19.5–8). At this point he still seems to be a symmetrist,

35. *SVF* III.640.
36. Plutarch, *On How the Young Person Should Listen to Poetry* 15CD. I argue that this
work represents some of the contents of Chrysippus's lost work of the same title, in my
"Poetry and the Passions: Two Stoic Views," in *Passions & Perceptions*, ed., J. Brunschwig
and M. Nussbaum (Cambridge: Cambridge University Press, 1993), 97–149.
37. Epictetus, *Diss.* 2.26.31. Though a Roman Stoic, Epictetus is loyal to the original
views of the Greek Stoics.
38. Epictetus 1.24.16–18, 2.17.19–22.
39. The proper view is that virtue by itself is sufficient for *eudaimonia*.

urging that sometimes a closer look makes the person look better, sometimes worse. But he then continues his reflections, in the second book,
in a manner that makes our asymmetry open up. People who do bad
things—even when they act from bad motives—are not, he insists, simply making a foolish and easily corrigible error. They are yielding to pressures—many of them social—that lie deep in the fabric of human life.
Before a child is capable of the critical exercise of reason, he or she has
internalized a socially taught scheme of values that is in many ways diseased, giving rise to similarly diseased passions: the excessive love of
money and honor, angers connected with slights to one's honor, excessive attachment to sex (especially to romanticized conceptions of the
sexual act and the sexual partner), anger and violence connected with
sexual jealousy; the list goes on and on.[40]

These cultural forces are in error, and in that sense someone who is in
their grip is indeed a "fool," as Epictetus holds. But there is not much
point in giving a little sermon to Medea as to a docile child; such errors,
taught from an early age, take over the soul and can be eradicated, if at
all, only by a lifetime of zealous and obsessive self-examination. And,
furthermore, Seneca suggests that anger and the desire to inflict pain—
the worst, in his opinion, of the errors of the soul—are not in any simple
way just the result of a corrigible error, even at the social level. He re-
peatedly commits himself to the view that they do not result from innate
instinct. On the other hand, they "omit no time of life, exempt no race of
human beings" (*De ira* III.22).

In a crucial passage, Seneca says that the wise person is not surprised
at the omnipresence of aggression and injustice, "since he has examined
thoroughly the circumstances of human life" (*condicio humanae vitae*,
II.10). Circumstances, then, and not innate propensities, are at the origins of vice. And when the wise person looks at these circumstances
clearly, he finds that they make it extremely difficult not to err. The
world into which human beings are born is a rough place, one that confronts them with threats to their safety on every side. If they remain attached to their safety and to the resources that are necessary to protect
it—as is natural and rational—that very attachment to the world will almost certainly, in time, lead to competitive or retaliatory aggression. For

40. Most of my argument in this passage is based on the *De ira* (*On Anger*), though
there are many similar passages in other works.

when goods are in short supply and people are attached to them, they compete for them. Thus aggression and violence grow not so much inside us as from an interaction between our nature and external conditions that is prior to and more deeply rooted than any specific form of society.

Seneca now uses this view as the basis for his argument against retributive anger and in favor of mercy. Given the omnipresence of aggression and wrongdoing, he now argues, if we look at the lives of others with the attitudes typical of the retributive tradition of justice—even in its modified particularist form—if, that is, we are determined to fix a penalty precisely proportionate to the nature of the particular wrongdoing, then we will never cease to be retributive and to inflict punishment, for everything we see will upset us. But this retributive attitude, even when in some sense justified, is not without its consequences for the human spirit. A person who notes and reacts to every injustice, and who becomes preoccupied with assigning just punishments, becomes, in the end, oddly similar to the raging ungentle people against whom he reacts. Retributive anger hardens the spirit, turning it against the humanity it sees. And in turning against humanity, in evincing the rage and hardness of the angry, one then becomes perilously close to the callous wrongdoers who arouse rage in the first place. Thus in Seneca's examples we find acts of horrifying vindictiveness and cruelty committed by people whose anger is initially justified, according to a precise assessment of the nature of the crime. Sulla's acts of retribution were first directed against legitimate enemies; they ended in the murder of innocent children (II.34). Caligula was justified in his anger over the imprisonment of his mother, and yet this led him to cruelty and destruction. Cambyses had just cause of battle against the Ethiopians, but in his obsession with revenge he led his men on a fatal campaign that ended in cannibalism (III.20). Andrea Dworkin's heroine would be right at home here, for she reacts in some sense appropriately to real wrongs, but becomes in the process an engine of revenge, indifferent to the face of humanity.[41]

Seneca's famous counterproposal, announced at the very end of *De*

41. Insofar as she punishes people who are totally innocent of crime, she is not even a good Greek Stoic judge, for whom the particulars of the crime and offender must be correct. But the Greek Stoic would say that once some basic criteria of responsibility are met, a tough punishment is in order without a search for mitigating factors, and here her judicial procedure is like theirs.

ira, is that we should "cultivate humanity" (*colamus humanitatem*, III.43). He elsewhere describes this as the proposal to "give a pardon to the human species" (II.10). It is this attitude that he now calls by the name of mercy, translating Greek *epieikeia* with the Latin word *clementia*. Rejecting the austerity and rigor of the Greek Stoic, he makes a sympathetic participatory attitude central to the norm of good judging. Senecan *clementia* does not fail to pass judgment on wrongdoing; this is continually stressed. Seneca does not hold that the circumstances of human life remove moral and legal responsibility for bad acts. We may still convict defendants who fulfill some basic conditions of rationality in action. But, looking at the circumstances of human life, one comes to understand how such things have happened, and this "medical" understanding leads to mercy.

Clementia, mercy, is even defined in a manner that makes its difference from Greek Stoic harshness evident: it is an "inclination of the soul to mildness in exacting penalties," and also, "that which turns its course away this side of that which could be justly determined" (*De clem.* II.3). The Greek Stoic soul, by contrast, never bends aside, never inclines away from hardness. The somewhat more gentle Aristotelian soul does bend, but inconstantly, conscious always that it is slavish to allow oneself and one's loved ones to be kicked around. Given that Seneca defines mercy as the opposite of cruelty, and given that cruelty is held to be a frequent outgrowth of retributive anger, we can say, putting all this together, that mercy, *clementia*, is opposed at one and the same time both to strictness in exacting penalties and also to retributive anger, as if that strictness does indeed lie very close to anger in the heart. As Seneca says, "It is a fault to punish a fault in full" (*culpa est totam persequi culpam, De clem.* II.7, fr.).[42]

One might, of course, adopt this attitude as a practical strategy to keep the self pure from anger without endorsing it as just or correct toward the offender. Seneca sometimes appears to oscillate between these two positions, since he can commend the practical strategy even to those who do not accept his position about correctness. But in the end his position is clearly that it is right and correct to assign punishments in ac-

---

42. Unlike Aristotle, Seneca does not endorse pity or compassion as a correct response to the misfortunes of human life. In his view, to do so would be to give too little credit to the person's own will and dignity and, frequently, too much importance to external events.

cordance with mercy, both because of what it means for oneself and because of what it says about and to the offender.

The merciful attitude, as Seneca develops it, entails regarding each
particular case as a complex narrative of human effort in a world full of
obstacles. The merciful judge will not fail to judge the guilt of the offender, but she will also see the many obstacles this offender faced as a
member of a culture, a gender, a city or country, and, above all, as a
member of the human species, facing the obstacles characteristic of
human life in a world of scarcity and accident. The starting point is a
general view of human life and its difficulties, but the search for mitigating factors must at every point be searchingly particular. The narrative-
medical attitude asks the judge to imagine what it was like to have been
that particular offender, facing those particular obstacles with the resources of that history. Seneca's bet is that after this imaginative exercise
one will cease to have the strict retributive attitude to the punishment of
the offender. One will be inclined, in fact, to gentleness and the waiving
of the strict punishment mandated in the law. The punishments that one
does assign will be chosen, on the whole, not for their retributive function, but for their power to improve the life of the defendant.[43]

This merciful attitude requires, and rests upon, a new attitude toward
the self. The retributive attitude has a we/them mentality, in which
judges set themselves above offenders, looking at their actions as if from
a lofty height and preparing to find satisfaction in their pain. The good
Senecan judge, by contrast, has both identification and sympathetic understanding. Accordingly, a central element in Seneca's prescription for
the judge is that he should remind himself at every turn that he himself
is capable of the failings he reproves in others. "If we want to be fair
judges of all things, let us persuade ourselves of this first: that none of
us is without fault. For it is from this point above all that retributive anger arises: 'I did nothing wrong,' and 'I did nothing.' No, rather, you don't
admit to anything" (II.28).

This part of Seneca's argument reaches its conclusion in a remarkable
passage in which Seneca confronts himself with the attitude of merciful
judgment that he also recommends, describing his own daily practice of

43. Some ameliorative punishments, according to Seneca, can be extremely harsh. Indeed, in a peculiar move, he defends capital punishment itself as in the interest of the
punished, given that a shorter bad life is better than a longer one; he compares it to merciful euthanasia.

self-examination in forensic language that links it to his public recommendations:

> A person will cease from retributive anger and be more moderate if he
> knows that every day he has to come before himself as judge. What
> therefore is more wonderful than this habit of unfolding the entire
> day? How fine is the sleep that follows this acknowledgment of one-
> self, how serene, how deep and free, when the mind has been either
> praised or admonished, and as its own hidden investigator and asses-
> sor has gained knowledge of its own character? I avail myself of this
> power, and plead my cause daily before myself. When the light has
> been removed from sight, and my wife, long since aware of this habit
> of mine, has fallen silent, I examine my entire day and measure my
> deeds and words. I hide nothing from myself, I pass over nothing. For
> why should I fear anything from my own errors, when I can say, "See
> that you don't do that again, this time I pardon you." (III.36)

Seeing the complexity and fallibility of his own acts, seeing those acts as
the product of a complex web of highly particular connections among
original impulses, the circumstances of life, and the complicated psychological reactions life elicits from the mind, he learns to view others, too,
as people whose errors emerge from a complex narrative history. Seneca's claim is that he will then moderate his retributive zeal toward the
punishment of their injustices and intensify his commitment to mutual
aid.

This part of Seneca's work seems very private. But there is no doubt
that the primary aim of this work, and of the later *De clementia* as well,
is the amelioration of public life and public judgment. The *De ira* was
written at the start of the reign of the emperor Claudius. It responds to a
well-known speech by Claudius on the subject of anger and irascibility,
and obviously contains advice for the new regime.[44] Moreover, its explicit
addressee and interlocutor is Novatus, Seneca's own brother, an aspiring
orator and public man. Thus its entire argumentative structure is built
around the idea of showing a public judge that the retributive attitude is
unsuitable for good judging. As for the *De clementia*, its explicit addressee is none other than the new emperor Nero Caesar himself, and

44. See J. Fillion-Lahille, *Le De ira de Sénèque* (Paris: 1984), and the summary of the
evidence in Nussbaum, *Therapy*, ch. 11.

its explicit task is to persuade this young man to use his immense power in merciful, rather than retributive, ways. The private material provides the basis for a new sort of public and judicial life.

VI

But instead of pursuing this history further, I want now to suggest some implications of these ideas for contemporary political and legal issues. First I shall develop a general thesis concerning the connection between the merciful attitude and the literary imagination; then I shall apply it to some particular questions. The Greco-Roman tradition already made a close connection between equity and narrative. The person who "reads" a complex case in the manner of the reader of a narrative or the spectator at a drama is put in contact—by the structure of the forms themselves as they solicit the reader's or spectator's attention—with two features of the equitable: its attentiveness to particularity and its capacity for sympathetic understanding. This means that the spectator or reader, if he or she reads well, is already prepared for equity and, in turn, for mercy.

I could illustrate these points about the relationship between form and content in many ways. Instead I want to choose just two examples, which show with particular clarity the connection between mercy and the art of the novelist, for the novel has been in recent times an especially vigorous popular literary form. The novel goes beyond tragic drama in its formal commitment to following complex life histories, looking at the minute details of motive and intention and their social formation—all that Seneca would have the good judge examine. This means that the novel, even more than tragic drama, is an artificial construction of mercy.

My first example is from Charles Dickens's *David Copperfield*.[45] James Steerforth, we know, is a bad person, one who deserves blame for some very serious bad actions. He humiliates the kind teacher, Mr. Mell; he uses his charm to get power over those younger and weaker than himself; he uses his wealth to escape discipline and criticism. And, above all, he destroys the life of Em'ly, by convincing her to run away with him with a false promise of marriage—betraying, in the process, both David's

45. These issues are discussed in more detail in my essay "Steerforth's Arm," in *Love's Knowledge*.

trusting friendship and the simple kindness of the Peggotty family. These bad actions are seen and judged by Agnes Wickfield in the straightforward way characteristic of the strict moral code that is her guide in life. A reader of religious books rather than of novels and stories, Agnes has no interest in the psychology of Steerforth's acts, or in seeing them from his point of view. She simply judges him, and judges him harshly, calling him David's "bad angel," and urging David (even before the serious crime) to have no further association with him. (It is a subtle point in the novel that moralism here allies itself with and provides a screen for the operations of jealousy; Agnes resents the romantic hold that Steerforth has over David and uses her moral condemnation to get revenge.) David's view is more complex.

The novel—represented as written by David some years after the event, during a tranquil marriage to Agnes—does present its reader with Agnes's moral judgment of Steerforth and the reasons for that judgment. The reader is led, at times—even as David shows himself being led—into the strict moral point of view, and is inclined at such times to judge Steerforth harshly. But these times are moments within the novel; they do not define the overall attitude with which the novel leaves us. David tells and shows the reader that the novelist's imagination is of a certain sort—very different, in fact, from the moral imagination of Agnes. And this imagination leads to a different way of judging.

The central characteristic of the narrative imagination, as David depicts it, is that it preserves as a legacy from childhood an ability to attend closely to the particulars and to respond to them in a close and accurate manner. Like our ancient tradition, David immediately goes on to link this "power of observation" with gentleness: adults who retain it retain also "a certain freshness, and gentleness, and capacity of being pleased, which are also an inheritance they have preserved from their childhood" (p. 61).[46] The nature of the connection is apparent in the manner in which the younger David sees Steerforth, and in which the mature novelist David depicts him for the reader's imagination.[47] We do become aware of Steerforth's crimes, but we see them as episodes in the life of an extremely complicated character who has enormous ability, awesome

46. All citations from the novel are taken from the Penguin edition, ed. Trevor Blount (Harmondsworth: Penguin, 1966).

47. These are not precisely the same, since the mature novelist has achieved an integration of the erotic and the moral that eludes the character earlier on.

powers of attraction, great kindness and beneficence to his friends, and an extremely unfortunate family history. We do judge Steerforth's arrogance, duplicity, and self-destructiveness. But we know also, as readers of the novel, that he grew up with no father to guide him, and with the misguided and uncritical affection of a willful and doting mother who indulged his every whim. We know, too, that his position and wealth compounded this ill fortune, exempting him for too long from the necessity to discipline his character and to cooperate with others. We are led to see his crimes as deliberate in the immediate sense required by strict legal and even moral judgment, but we also know that behind these crimes is a tangled history that might have been otherwise, a history that was not fully chosen by Steerforth himself. We imagine that with a different childhood Steerforth might have made an altogether different use of his abilities—that he might have had, in short, a different character. Like Seneca's reader, we are led to see character itself as something formed in society and in the family, something for which strict morality rightly holds individuals responsible, but something over which, in the end, individuals do not have full control.[48]

The result of all this is mercy. Just before Steerforth leaves to run off with Em'ly, in the last conversation he has with David, we have the following exchange:

> "Daisy, if anything should ever separate us, you must think of me at my best, old boy. Come! Let us make that bargain. Think of me at my best, if circumstances should ever part us!"
>
> "You have no best to me, Steerforth," said I, "and no worst. You are always equally loved, and cherished in my heart." (p. 497)

David keeps the bargain, loving Steerforth with the unconditional attention and concern of his narratorial heart. When, years later, the tempest washes Steerforth's body ashore, and he recognizes it, David exclaims:

48. Compare the ideas on moral responsibility developed in Susan Wolf, *Freedom Within Reason* (New York: Oxford University Press, 1990). Wolf holds—like the ancient tradition described here—that there is an asymmetry between praise and blame, that it is legitimate to commend people for achievements that are in large part the outgrowth of early education and social factors, but not legitimate to blame them when such forces have made them into bad characters who are unable to respond to reason. In Wolf's view, as in mine, this asymmetry will sometimes mean not holding individuals responsible for their bad acts. Unlike her, however, I make a distinction between culpability and punishment, holding that a defendant's life story may give reasons for mitigating punishment even when requirements for culpability are met.

No need, O Steerforth, to have said, when we last spoke together, in that hour which I so little deemed to be our parting-hour—no need to have said, "Think of me at my best!" I had done that ever; and could I change now, looking on this sight! (p. 866)

Just as the character David suspends punitive judgment on Steerforth's acts, so the imagination of the narrator—and of the reader—is led to turn aside, substituting for punishment an understanding of Steerforth's life story. David makes it very clear that the activity of novel writing causes him to relive this moment of mercy, and that its "freshness and gentleness" can be expected to be its reader's experience as well.[49] In this sense the novel is about itself, and the characteristic moral stance of its own production and reception. That stance is the stance of equity, and of mercy.

My second example is contemporary. Last year the novelist Joyce Carol Oates visited my seminar at Brown to speak about the moral and political dimensions of her fiction. As we discussed her recent novel *Because It Is Bitter and Because It Is My Heart*, a student, silent until then, burst in with a heated denunciation of Oates's character Leslie, a well-meaning but ineffectual liberal photographer. Isn't his life a complete failure really? Isn't he contemptible for his inability to *do* anything significant out of his antiracist intentions? Isn't he to be blamed for not more successfully combating racism in his family and in his society? Oates was silent for a time, her eyes peering up from behind her round glasses. Then she answered slowly, in her high, clear, girlish voice, "That's not the way I see it, really." She then went on to narrate the story of Leslie's life, the efforts he had made, the formidable social and psychological obstacles in the way of his achieving more, politically, than he had—speaking of him as of a friend whose life inhabited her own imagination and whom, on that account, she could not altogether dismiss or condemn. Here, I believe, was mercy and, lying very close to it, the root of the novelist's art. The novel's structure is a structure of *suggnômê*, of the penetration of the life of another into one's own imagination and heart. It is a form of imaginative and emotional receptivity, in which the reader, following the author's lead, comes to be inhabited by the tangled

---

49. See especially p. 855, shortly preceding the discovery of Steerforth's death: "As plainly as I behold what happened, I will try to write it down. I do not recall it, but see it done; for it happens again before me."

complexities and struggles of other concrete lives.[50] Novels do not withhold all moral judgment, and they contain villains as well as heroes. But
for any character with whom the form invites our participatory identification, the motives for mercy are engendered in the structure of literary
perception itself.

VII

Now to contemporary implications. Up until now, I have been talking
about a moral ideal, which has evident implications for publicly promulgated norms of human behavior and for public conduct in areas in which
there is latitude for judicial discretion. I have suggested that in many
ways this norm fulfills and completes a conception of justice that lies
itself at the basis of the rule of law; it was to prevent incomplete, defective, and biased discretionary reasoning that the rule of law was introduced and defended. But at this point and for this reason caution is in
order, for the moral ideal should not be too simply converted into a norm
for a legal system. First of all, a legal system has to look out for the likelihood that the moral ideal will not always be perfectly realized, and it
should protect against abuses that moral arbitrariness and bias can en-
gender. This suggests a large role for codified requirements in areas in
which one cannot guarantee that the equity ideal will be well implemented. The equity tradition supports this. Second, a system of law must
look to social consequences as well as to the just judgment on particular
offenders. Thus it may need to balance an interest in the deterrent role
of punishments against the equity tradition's interest in punishments
that suit the agent. Both the balance between codification and discretion
and the balance between equity and deterrence are enormously complex
matters, with which my analysis here cannot fully grapple. What I do
wish to offer here are some representative suggestions of what the equity
tradition has to offer us as we think about these issues.

50. Of course the novelist's stance is traditionally linked with compassion, as well as
with mercy. Sometimes, that is, the response will be to sympathize with the plight of a
character without blaming, whereas in other cases there may be both blame and a merciful
punishment. The line is, and should be, difficult to draw, for the factors that make mercy
appropriate also begin to cast doubt on full moral responsibility. (In other cases, of course,
there is not even a prima facie offense, and therefore we will have pity without mercy.)

1. A Model of Judicial Reasoning

In other recent work,[51] I have been developing the idea that legal, and especially judicial, reasoning can be modeled on the reasoning of the concerned reader of a novel.[52] Following in some respects the lead of Adam Smith in *The Theory of Moral Sentiments*,[53] I argue that the experience of the concerned reader is an artificial construction of ideal moral and judicial spectatorship, with respect both to particularity of attention and to the sort and range of emotions that will and will not be felt. Identifying with a wide range of characters from different social circumstances and concerning oneself in each case with the entire complex history of their efforts, the reader comes to have emotions both sympathetic and participatory toward the things that they do and suffer. These emotions will be based on a highly particularized perception of the character's situation. On the other hand, since the reader is not a character in the story, except in the Henry Jamesian sense of being a "participator by a fond attention,"[54] she will lack emotions relating to her own concrete placement in the situation that she is asked to judge; her judgments will thus, I argue, be both emotionally sympathetic and, in the most appropriate sense, neutral.

My current inquiry into mercy takes Smith's model one step further, where judgment on the wrongdoing of others is concerned, going beyond his rather austere construction of emotional spectatorship. For it construes the participatory emotion of the literary imagination as emotion that will frequently lead to mercy, even where a judgment of culpability has been made. And this merciful attitude derives directly, we can now see, from the literary mind's keen interest in all the particulars, a fact not much stressed by Smith in his account of the literary (perhaps because he focuses on classical drama, in which the concrete circumstances of daily life are not always so clearly in view). My literary judge sees defendants as inhabitants of a complex web of circumstances, cir-

51. The development of this idea begins in "The Discernment of Perception," in *Love's Knowledge*; it continues in "The Literary Imagination in Public Life," the Alexander Rosenthal Lectures, Northwestern University Law School, 1991 and forthcoming. Lecture 1 has appeared under the series title, in *New Literary History* 23 (1991).

52. Or the spectator at a play. I discuss some reasons for focusing above all on the novel in "The Literary Imagination in Public Life."

53. Discussed in "Steerforth's Arm," in *Love's Knowledge*.

54. The citation is from the preface to *The Princess Casamassima*; see James, *The Art of the Novel* (New York: Charles Scribner's Sons, 1909), p. 62.

cumstances which often, in their totality, justify mitigation of blame or punishment.[55]

This attitude of my ideal judge is unashamedly mentalistic. It does not hesitate to use centrally the notions of intention, choice, reflection, deliberation, and character that are part of a nonreductive intentionalist psychology. Like the novel, it treats the inner world of the defendant as a deep and complex place, and it instructs the judge to investigate that depth. This approach is opposed, in spirit if not always in outcome, to an approach to the offender articulated in some well-known writings of Justice Holmes, and further developed recently by Richard Posner.[56] According to this approach, the offender should be treated as a thing with no insides to be scrutinized from the internal viewpoint, but simply as a machine whose likely behavior, as a result of a given judgment or punishment, we attempt, as judges, to predict.[57] The sole proper concern of punishment becomes deterrence. As law becomes more sophisticated, and our predictive ability improves, states of mind play a smaller and smaller role in judgment.

55. John Roemer has made the following important point to me in conversation: insofar as my literary judge treats many of a person's abilities, talents, and achievements as products of circumstances beyond his or her control, this reinforces and deepens the novel's commitment to egalitarianism. (In "The Literary Imagination" I had argued that the novel is already egalitarian in asking us to identify successively with members of different social classes and to see their needs without being aware of where, in the social scheme we are to choose, we ourselves will be.) For we will then see the talents and dispositions in virtue of which people earn their greater or lesser social rewards as not fully theirs by desert, given the large role played by social advantages and other external circumstances in getting to these dispositions; we will be more inclined to treat them as social resources that are as subject to allocation as other resources. (Not, obviously, in the sense that we will take A's talents from A and give them to B, but we will regard A's talents as like a certain level of wealth, on account of which we may require A to give back more to society in other ways.) On all this, see Roemer, "Equality of Talent," *Economics and Philosophy* 1 (1985): 151–86; "Equality of Resources Implies Equality of Welfare," *Quarterly Journal of Economics* (November 1986): 751–83; "A Pragmatic Theory of Responsibility for the Egalitarian Planner," *Philosophy & Public Affairs*, pp. 146–66, this issue.

56. The most important sources for Holmes's view are "The Path of the Law" and "The Common Law," now printed (the latter in extracts) in *The Essential Holmes*, ed. Richard A. Posner (Chicago: University of Chicago Press, 1992), 160–77, 237–64. For Posner's views, see *The Problems of Jurisprudence* (Cambridge, Mass.: Harvard University Press, 1990), pp. 161–96.

57. Posner approvingly comments on Holmes's view: "We would deal with criminals as we deal with unreasonably dangerous machines. . . . [I]nstead of treating dangerous objects as people, he was proposing to treat dangerous people as objects" (*Essential Holmes*, p. 168).

Holmes's defense of this idea takes an interesting form, from our point of view. For it begins from an extremely perceptive description and criticism of the retributive idea of judgment and punishment.[58] His own deterrence-based view is advanced as an alternative—he seems to think it the only plausible one—to retributivism, and much of the argument's force comes from the connection of the positive recommendation with the effective negative critique. The trouble begins when he conflates the retributive idea with the idea of looking to the wrongdoer's state of mind, implying that an interest in the "insides" invariably brings retributivism with it.[59] As we have seen, matters are far more complicated, both historically and philosophically. It is, I think, in order to extricate judging from the retributive view—felt by Holmes, rightly, to be based on metaphysical and religious notions of balance and proportion, and to be an outgrowth of passions that we should not encourage in society—that he feels himself bound to oppose all mentalist and intention-based notions of punishment.[60] In "The Common Law" he argues that far from considering "the condition of a man's heart or conscience" in making a judgment, we should focus on external standards that are altogether independent of motive and intention. Here he insists on the very sort of strict assessment without mitigation that the entire mercy tradition opposes:

> [The external standards] do not merely require that every man should get as near as he can to the best conduct possible for him. They require him at his own peril to come up to a certain height. They take no account of incapacities, unless the weakness is so marked as to fall into well-known exceptions, such as infancy or madness. They assume that every man is as able as every other to behave as they command. If they fall on any one class harder than on another, it is on the weakest.[61]

58. See especially "The Common Law," in *Essential Holmes*, p. 247ff. Holmes does not mention the ancient Greek debate; he focuses on Hegel's account of retributivism.

59. See ibid., p. 247: "The desire for vengeance imports an opinion that its object is actually and personally to blame. It takes an internal standard, not an objective or external one, and condemns its victim by that."

60. Holmes notes that the retributive view of the criminal law has been held by such eminent figures as Bishop Butler and Jeremy Bentham. He then quotes, without comment, Sir James Stephen's view that "The criminal law stands to the passion of revenge in much the same relation as marriage to the sexual appetite" (p. 248). Presumably this means that it allows for the satisfaction of this passion in an institutionalized and civilized form, not that it causes the passion's decline.

61. Ibid., p. 253.

From our viewpoint this dichotomy between intentionalism and retributivism leaves out the real opponent of retributivism, both historical and philosophical, simply putting in its place a strict external assessment that looks suspiciously like the old Anaximandrean *dikê* in modern secular dress, despite its evident differences.

Posner follows Holmes's view in most essential respects, developing it in much more detail, referring to modern behaviorist theories of mind. Like Holmes, Posner is motivated above all by the desire to describe an alternative to retributivism, which he criticizes eloquently, with appeal to both history and literature.[62] His argument is highly complex and cannot even be accurately summarized, much less appropriately criticized, in the space available here. What is most important for our purposes is that Posner makes explicit that his behaviorist view of the criminal law requires rejecting—for legal purposes—the Kantian idea that people are to be treated as ends rather than means. It requires, in fact, treating them as objects that through their behavior generate either good or bad social consequences. This, we can easily see, is profoundly opposed to the stance of the literary judge, who may differ from some Kantians in her focus on particular circumstances, but who certainly makes the Kantian insight about human beings central to her entire project. Posner also makes it clear that the case for his account of external standards stands or falls with the case for behaviorism (perhaps eliminative materialism as well?) as an adequate and reasonably complete theory of human behavior. Since I think it is fair to say that the best current work in the philosophy of the mind and in cognitive psychology—like the best work on mind in classical antiquity—finds serious flaws in the behaviorist and reductionist views, this explicitness in Posner makes the vulnerable point in the Holmes/Posner argument especially plain. On the other hand, unlike Holmes, Posner does not seem to claim that the behaviorist view is the only available alternative to retributivist views of punishment. He shows an awareness, in fact, of the mercy tradition—strikingly enough, not in the chapter dealing with the criminal law, but in his chapter dealing with "Literary and Feminist Perspectives."[63] Posner demonstrates some sympathy with this tradition, arguing that what the law should really seek is an appropriate balance between strict legal jus-

---

62. See especially Posner, *Law and Literature: A Misunderstood Relation* (Cambridge, Mass.: Harvard University Press, 1988), 25–70.

63. Posner, *Problems of Jurisprudence*, 393–419; see also *Law and Literature*, 105–15.

tice and a flexible and merciful discretion.[64] He is, however, pessimistic about the role that latitude for mercy is likely to play in actual cases, holding that a discretionary approach on the part of judges will frequently be harsher to defendants—especially minority defendants—than will an approach based on strict rules.[65] This is a valuable insight, and I shall return to it shortly. But first I must conclude the story, where Holmes is concerned.

Holmes's "The Common Law" was written in 1881, "The Path of the Law" (where Holmes argues for a related view) in 1897.[66] It is worthy of note that toward the end of his life, in a remarkable letter, Holmes appears to endorse the mercy tradition, as a result of his reading of Roman philosophy. Writing on March 28, 1924, to his friend Harold Laski, Holmes begins by speaking of the large impression made on him by Seneca's "cosmopolitan humanity."[67] He suggests (correctly) that this notion came to Christianity from Roman philosophy, rather than vice versa. He confirms the impression by reading Plutarch in order to get the Greek perspective. After making an obligatory shocking remark—that "the literature of the past is a bore"—he vigorously praises Tacitus. Then, appended to the account of his Roman reading, comes the arresting insight: "Before I leave you for the day and drop the subject let me repeat if I have said it before that I think the biggest thing in antiquity is 'Father forgive them—they know not what they do.' There is the modern transcending of a moral judgment in the most dramatic of settings."

It is not terribly clear to what extent Holmes means to connect this remark about Jesus with his observations concerning the debt owed by Christianity to Roman thought. My argument has shown that he certainly could do so with justice. Nor is it clear how or whether he would

---

64. Posner, *Law and Literature*, 108ff.

65. There is another reason for Posner's skepticism about mercy: he feels that it implies a kind of interfering scrutiny of the "insides" that sits uneasily with the libertarian hands-off attitude to government intervention he has long defended. I think this is wrong: wanting to know the relevant facts in no way entails additional curtailment of individual liberty of choice.

66. In "The Path of Law" Holmes advances his famous "bad man" theory of the law: in order to figure out the deterrent aspect of punishment correctly, the judge should think, in each case, of what a bad person, completely insensitive to legal or moral requirement except in calculating personal costs and benefits, would do in response to a particular set of legal practices. Thus he endorses the basic strictness in assessing penalties that gave rise to our asymmetry in the ancient tradition.

67. *Essential Holmes*, pp. 59–60.

apply his insight to concrete issues in the law. What is clear is that by this time in his life Holmes recognized that the transcendence of strict moralism that he recommended throughout his career need not be captured through a reliance on external behavioral standards. It seems to him to be most appropriately captured in the "dramatic setting" in which Jesus takes up, toward his enemies, the attitude of Senecan mercy.[68] I think that he is right.[69]

In short, in order to depart from a retributivism that is brutal in its neglect of human complexity, we do not need to embrace a deterrence-only view that treats people as means to society's ends, aggregating their good and ill without regard to what is appropriate for each. The deterrence view is all too close to the retributive view it opposes, in its resolute refusal to examine the particularities of motive, intention, and story, in its treatment of people as place-holders in a larger social or cosmic calculus.[70] A merciful judge need not neglect issues of deterrence, but she is above all committed to an empathetic scrutiny of the "insides" of the individual life.

2. Mercy and the Criminal Law

I have already begun to speak about the criminal law, since the focus in mercy is on wrongdoing and the wrongdoer. The implications of the mercy tradition for issues in the criminal law are many and complex, and I can only begin here to suggest what some of them might be. I shall do this by focusing on a pair of examples: two recent Supreme Court cases involving the death penalty which raise issues of mitigation and aggravation in connection with discretionary sentencing. One is *Walton v. Arizona*;[71] the other is *California v. Brown*.[72] At stake are the roles to be

68. Senecan influence on Christianity begins with the work of writers such as Clement of Alexandria and Augustine. I mean to point to a resemblance, which is later developed in explicitly Stoic terms.

69. For the distinction between forgiveness and mercy, see my discussion of Seneca above; a good modern discussion is in Jean Hampton and Jeffrie Murphy, *Forgiveness and Mercy* (Cambridge: Cambridge University Press, 1988). The attitude of Jesus toward sinners appears to be more one of mercy than of forgiveness: for sinners will certainly be condemned and punished, not let off the hook.

70. In many cases this view is harsher than the retributivist view, since a deterrence-based view will often punish attempts at crime that do not succeed, or punish harshly a relatively minor crime if there is reason to think him or her a dangerous repeat offender.

71. 110 S. Ct. 3047 (1990).

72. 479 U.S. 538 (1987). For discussion of both of these cases I am indebted to Ronald

played by discretion in deciding capital cases and the criteria to be used in analyzing the aggravating and mitigating features of the case. Walton was convicted by a jury of first-degree murder and sentenced to death, in accordance with an Arizona statute that requires the judge first to ascertain whether at least one aggravating circumstance is present—in this case two were found[73]—and then to consider all the alleged mitigating circumstances advanced by the defendant, imposing a death sentence if he finds "no mitigating circumstances sufficiently substantial to call for mercy." The defendant is required to establish a mitigating circumstance by the preponderance of the evidence, and it was this that was the central issue in Walton's appeal. Since previous Supreme Court decisions had rejected a requirement of unanimity for mitigation, Walton contended that the preponderance of the evidence test was also unconstitutional.[74] His claim was rejected by a plurality of the court. My concern is not so much with the result as with some interesting issues that emerge from the opinions.

First, it is plain that the Arizona system, which the decision in effect upholds, establishes a lexical ordering, in which a finding of aggravation—which must be based upon criteria explicitly enumerated in the law—is used to classify an offense as a potential death-penalty offense; mitigation is then considered afterwards, in a discretionary manner. In other words, the whole range of potentially mitigating circumstances will be brought forward only when it has already been established that an offense falls into a certain class of extremely serious offenses. Discretionary concern for the entirety of the defendant's history will enter the picture only in the mitigation phase. Justice Stevens comments on this feature in his dissenting opinion, arguing that once the scope of capital punishment is so reduced, the risk of arbitrariness in sentencing is sufficiently reduced as well to permit very broad discretion and individuated

---

J. Allen, "Evidence, Inference, Rules, and Judgment in Constitutional Adjudication: The Intriguing Case of *Walton v. Arizona*," *Journal of Criminal Law and Criminology* 81 (1991): 727–59. For later thoughts about the role of logic in judicial inference, see Allen, "The Double Jeopardy Clause, Constitutional Interpretation and the Limits of Formal Logic," *Valparaiso University Law Review* 26 (1991): 281–310.

73. The murder was committed in an "especially heinous, cruel or depraved manner," and it was committed for pecuniary gain. Note that even here, in the nondiscretionary and codified portion of the judgment, intentional notions are prominently used.

74. *Mills v. Maryland*, 486 U.S. 367 (1988), and *McKoy v. North Carolina*, 110 S. Ct. 1229 (1990).

decision making with the remaining class. This seems to be a correct and valuable observation. Indeed, the mercy tradition stresses that merciful judgment can be given only when there is time to learn the whole complex history of the life in question and also inclination to do so in a sympathetic manner, without biases of class or race. The tradition wholeheartedly endorses decision making by codified requirement where these requirements cannot be met. (Here Posner's warnings about arbitrariness in equity seem perfectly appropriate, and they are reflected in the move away from unguided discretion represented by the federal sentencing guidelines.)[75] We should not, however, say, as Stevens seems to, that the main function of such criteria is to reduce the number of cases that are eligible for the death penalty. What they do is, of course, more substantial: they eliminate from the death-eligible group many cases for which death would clearly not be an *appropriate* penalty, leaving the judge free to turn his or her attention to those that are more problematic, requiring a more fine-tuned deliberation.[76]

A second significant feature, and a more problematic one, is the plurality's unquestioning acceptance of the preponderance of the evidence test, which, as Allen has shown here and elsewhere, has grave defects when we are dealing with a case having multiple relevant features.[77] Suppose a defendant advances three grounds for mitigation, each of which is established to a .25 probability, and therefore to be thrown out under Arizona's rule. The probability that at least one of the factors is

75. I have not committed myself here on the ideal scope for discretion in other areas of the law. This is an issue I feel I need to study further before making concrete claims. I focus on the capital cases because they have been the focus of an especially interesting debate about mercy, in which the penalty-setting phase has a special weight. I do think that a similar approach could be tried in another group of cases to which a finding of aggravation is pertinent, namely hate crimes. Here I think one would want to describe the grounds for aggravation very explicitly and systematically, either by setting up a special class of crimes or in the guidelines for sentencing. Once one had determined that particular offense was of this particularly severe kind, one could then consider whether the defendant's youth, family background, and so forth gave any grounds for mitigation.

76. See Allen, *"Walton,"* p. 741. I agree with this point against Stevens, but disagree with an earlier one. On p. 736, Allen argues that "the primary thrust of [Stevens's] argument . . . is for categorical rather than discretionary sentencing." This seems to me inaccurate: it is, instead, a statement about the conditions under which discretionary sentencing can be well done.

77. See also Allen, "A Reconceptualization of Civil Trials," *B.U. Law Review* 66 (1986): 401ff.

true, assuming they are independent, is, as Allen shows, .58.[78] If each of three factors is proved to a probability of .4, the probability that at least one is true is .78. On the other hand, if the defendant proves just one of the mitigating factors with a probability of .51 and the others with probability o, he is successful, even though the probability that the decision is correct is in fact lower here than in the previous cases.[79] The law asks the judge to treat each feature one by one, in total isolation from any other. But human lives, as the literary judge would see, consist of complex webs of circumstances, which must be considered as wholes.

This same problem is present in Justice Scalia's scathing attack on the whole notion of mitigation. For Scalia thinks it absurd that we should have codified criteria for aggravation, apply these, and *then* look with unguided discretion to see whether a mitigating factor is present. If the criteria for aggravation are enumerated in the law, so too should be the criteria for mitigation. Only this explicitness and this symmetry can prevent total irrationality. Scalia here ignores the possibility—which Stevens recognizes—that the functions of aggravation-criteria and of mitigation are not parallel: aggravation serves to place the offense in the class to which mitigation is relevant.[80] Furthermore, in ridiculing the entire notion of discretionary mercy, Scalia adamantly refuses the forms of perception that we have associated with the literary attitude. That is, he treats mitigating factors as isolated units, unconnected either to one another or to the whole of a life. It is in this way that he can arrive at the conclusion that unbridled discretion will (absurdly) be permitted to treat traits that are polar opposites as, both of them, mitigating: for example, "that the defendant had a poor and deprived childhood, or that he had a rich and spoiled childhood."[81] Scalia's assumption is that both of these

78. See Allen, *"Walton,"* pp. 734–35. This is the assumption that the current test in effect makes. If they are not independent, this probabilistic analysis does not follow, but there is also, then, no justification at all for treating them in isolation from one another. In either case, then, the conclusion for which I am arguing follows: the life must be considered as a whole.

79. One might also point out that different jurors might be convinced by different factors, so long as they are treated as isolated units. One could have a situation in which all jurors agree that there is at least one mitigating factor present but, if they disagree enough about which one it is, the defendant's attempt fails. I owe this point to Cy Wasserstrom.

80. Here the similarity to the ancient tradition is striking, especially to Seneca's insistence on separating the determination of guilt and its level from the assignment of (merciful) punishment.

81. 110 S. Ct. at 3062.

cannot be mitigating, and that it is a sign of the absurdity of the current state of things that they might both be so treated. But the alleged absurdity arises only because he has severed these traits from the web of circumstances in which they actually figure. In connection with other circumstances either a trait or its opposite might, in fact, be mitigating.[82] This, in Allen's argument and in mine, is the reason why categories for mitigation should not be codified in advance: it will be impossible for such a code to anticipate adequately the countless ways in which factors interweave and bear upon one another in human reality.[83] Telling the whole story, with all the particulars, is the only way to get at that.[84]

In reality, of course, the mercy tradition has serious reservations about the whole idea of capital punishment. Although some of its major exponents, including Seneca, endorsed it, they did so on the basis of very peculiar arguments comparing it to euthanasia (n. 43 above). If we reject these arguments we are left, I think, with no support for capital punishment from within that tradition, and strong reasons to reject retributivist justifications. Indeed, the tradition strongly suggests that such punishments are always cruel and excessive. The question would then have to be whether the deterrence value of such punishments by itself justifies their perpetuation, despite their moral inappropriateness. Furthermore, the deterrence-based argument has never yet been made out in a fully compelling way.

82. See Allen, "*Walton*," p. 739; also p. 742: "Any particular fact is of very little consequence standing alone. The web of facts is what matters." In *David Copperfield* we see a very clear example of a rich and spoiled childhood as a mitigating factor: Steerforth has no opportunity to learn moral self-restraint, and is encouraged to use his talent and charm in a reckless manner.

83. I am not claiming that knowledge of the whole story should never give rise to aggravation of punishment. By focusing on capital cases I have left undiscussed a number of lesser cases in which such thinking might figure. One is a very interesting case recently heard by the Seventh Circuit, in which Posner defends an upward departure from the sentencing guidelines in a case of blackmail, on the ground that the blackmailer's victim, a married homosexual, fit the category of "unusually vulnerable victim" that justifies such aggravation. Detailed consideration of the whole story, and of American homophobia, was required in order to establish that this victim was really more vulnerable than other types of people with sexual secrets to conceal (*U.S. v. Sienky Lallemand*, Seventh Circuit, March 29, 1993).

84. Another point against Scalia is the structure of the pardon power: a governor can pardon a criminal, but not increase a criminal's sentence or condemn someone who was acquitted. Indeed, asymmetry is built into the entirety of the criminal justice system, in the requirement to prove guilt beyond a reasonable doubt, in the safeguards surrounding the admissibility of confessions, and so forth.

California v. Brown raises a different issue: that of jury instruction, where emotion is concerned. The Court reviewed a state jury instruction stipulating that the jury in a capital case (in the sentencing phase) "must not be swayed by mere sentiment, conjecture, sympathy, passion, prejudice, public opinion or public feeling."[85] From the point of view of our account of literary judging, this instruction is a peculiar and inappropriate mixture. For the juror as "judicious spectator" and merciful reader would indeed disregard conjecture, prejudice, public opinion, and public feeling. On the other hand, sentiment, passion, and sympathy would be a prominent part of the appropriate (and rational) deliberative process, where those sentiments are based in the juror's "reading" of the defendant's history, as presented in the evidence. It would of course be right to leave aside any sentiment having to do with one's own involvement in the outcome, but we assume that nobody with a personal interest in the outcome would end up on the jury in any case. It would also be correct to leave aside any mere gut reaction to the defendant's appearance, demeanor, or clothing, anything that could not be made a reasoned part of the "story" of the case. But the vast majority of the passional reactions of a juror hearing a case of this kind will be based on the story that is told; in this sense, the law gives extremely bad advice.[86] The Court, however, approved the instruction, concluding that "[A] reasonable juror would . . . understand the instruction . . . as a directive to ignore only the sort of sympathy that would be totally divorced from the evidence adduced during the penalty phase."[87] On the one hand, this seems to me a perfectly reasonable way of articulating the boundaries of appropriate and inappropriate sympathy. On the other hand, the likelihood is so high that the sentiments of the juror would be of the appropriate, rather than the inappropriate, sort—for what else but the story told them do they have to consider?—that approving the regulation creates a misleading impres-

85. Note that for a juror the case at issue is likely to be a rare event, and thus there is reason to think that jury deliberations will be free from at least some of the problems of callousness and shortness of time that may limit the advisability of discretion in cases involving judges. On the other hand, the limits of juror sympathy with people who are unlike themselves remains a clear difficulty. This is why I sympathize, to the extent that I do, with parts of the warning in the California juror instruction.

86. Compare the advice given to the prospective juror in the state of Massachusetts, in the "Juror's Creed" printed in the Trial Juror's Handbook: "I am a JUROR. I am a seeker of truth . . . I must lay aside all bias and prejudice. I must be led by my intelligence and not by my emotions."

87. 479 U.S. 542–43 (1987).

sion that some large and rather dangerous class of passions are being excluded.[88] The other opinions in the case confirm the general impression of confusion about and suspicion of the passions. Thus Justice O'Connor argues that "the sentence imposed at the penalty stage should reflect a reasoned *moral* response to the defendant's background, character, and crime rather than mere sympathy or emotion." She goes on to state that "the individualized assessment of the appropriateness of the death penalty is a moral inquiry into the culpability of the defendant, and not an emotional response to the mitigating evidence."[89] This contrast between morality and sympathy is a nest of confusions, as my argument by now should have shown. Justice Brennan, too, holds that "mere sympathy" must be left to one side—though he does hold (dissenting) that the instruction prohibits the juror from considering exactly what he or she should consider.[90] Justice Blackmun does somewhat better, defending the juror's ability to respond with mercy as "a particularly valuable aspect of the capital sentencing procedure." But he, too, contrasts rationality with mercy, even in the process of defending the latter: "While the sentencer's decision to accord life to a defendant at times might be a rational or moral one, it also may arise from the defendant's appeal to the sentencer's sympathy or mercy, human qualities that are undeniably emotional in nature."[91] The confusion persists: in a more recent case, the Court now speaks even more suspiciously and pejoratively of the juror's emotions, contrasting them with the "actual evidence regarding the crime and the defendant"[92]—as if these were not the source of and basis for these emotions.[93]

88. Thus I agree in part with Allen, "*Walton*," p. 747, although I do think it reasonable to stipulate this restriction on sentiment and believe that it is possible to think of cases where sentiments would be of the inappropriate sort.

89. 479 U.S. at 545.

90. Ibid. at 548–50.

91. Ibid. at 561–63. Thus I do not agree with Allen that Blackmun "gets it right" ("*Walton*," p. 750). Allen, like Blackmun, is willing to give the normative term "rational" to the opposition, granting that merciful sentiment is not rational. But why not? Such merciful sentiments are based on judgments that are (if the deliberative process is well executed) both true and justified by the evidence.

92. *Saffle v. Parks*, 110 S. Ct. 1257 (1990) at 1261.

93. One might think that my view entails admitting victim impact statements, for they are certainly part of the whole story, even though the victim is often no longer around to tell it. I am dubious. A criminal trial is about the defendant and what will become of him or her. The question before the court is what the defendant did, and the function of narrative is to illuminate the character and origins of that deed. What has to be decided is not what to do about the victim, but what to do about the defendant. Now of course the victim's

In short, the insights of the mercy tradition can take us a long way in understanding what is well and not well done in recent Supreme Court writings about sentencing. It can help us to defend the asymmetry between mitigation and aggravation that prevailed in *Walton*, as well as *Walton*'s moderate defense of discretion. But it leads to severe criticism of the categories of analysis deployed in the juror-instruction cases, which employ defective conceptions of the rational.

3. Feminist Political Thought

It is now time to return to Andrea Dworkin and to feminism. Dworkin's novel has been in the background throughout this paper, providing us with a striking modern example of the strict retributivist position and showing us how the retributive imagination is opposed to the literary imagination. But Dworkin's book is, after all, called a novel. One might well wonder how I can so easily say that the novel form is a construction of mercy.

The problem is only apparent. For Andrea Dworkin's "novel" is not a novel but an antinovel. By deliberate design, it does not invite its reader to occupy the positions of its characters, seeing their motivations with sympathy and with concern for the entire web of circumstances out of which their actions grow. It does not invite its reader to be emotionally receptive, except to a limited degree in the case of its central figure. But this figure is such a solipsistic, self-absorbed persona that to identify with her is to enter a sealed world of a peculiar sort, a world in and from which the actions of others appear only as external movement, without discernible motive. As for the men who people the novel, the reader is enjoined to view them as the narrator views them: as machines that produce pain. We are forbidden to have an interest in their character, origins, motives, or points of view. We are forbidden all sympathy and even all curiosity. We are refused perception of the particular, for, as in the male pornography that Dworkin's activism opposes, her male characters are not particulars, but generic objects.[94] In effect, we are refused novelistic readership.

---

experience may be relevant to ascertaining the nature of the offense, and to that extent it is admissible anyway. But the additional information imported by victim impact statements seems primarily to lie in giving vent to the passion for revenge, and the emotions they seek to arouse are those associated with that passion.

94. In "Defining Pornography," *University of Pennsylvania Law Review* forthcoming, James Lindgren shows that none of the standard definitions of pornography works terribly well in separating feminist fiction from pornography, if (as MacKinnon has urged) the

Indeed, the very form of Dworkin's work causes us, as readers, to in-habit the retributive frame of mind and to refuse mercy. The inclination to mercy is present in the text only as a fool's inclination toward collab-oration and slavery. When the narrator, entering her new profession as a karate-killer of homeless men, enunciates "the political principle which went as follows: It is very important for women to kill men," a voice within the text suggests the explanations that might lead to mercy.[95] As the return of the narrator quickly makes clear, this is meant to be a par-ody voice, a fool's voice, the voice of a collaborator with the enemy:

> He didn't mean it; or he didn't do it, not really, or not fully, or not knowing, or not intending; he didn't understand; or he couldn't help it; or he won't again; certainly he will try not to; unless; well; he just can't help it; be patient; he needs help; sympathy; over time. Yes, her ass is grass but you can't expect miracles, it takes time, she wasn't perfect either you know; he needs time, education, help, support; yeah, she's dead meat; but you can't expect someone to change right away, overnight, besides she wasn't perfect, was she, he needs time, help, support, education; well, yeah, he was out of control; listen, she's lucky it wasn't worse, I'm not covering it up or saying what he did was right, but she's not perfect, believe me, and he had a terrible mother; yeah, I know, you had to scrape her off the ground; but you know, she wasn't perfect either, he's got a problem; he's human, he's got a prob-lem.[96]

The only alternative to the retributive attitude, Dworkin implies, is an attitude of foolish and hideous capitulation. The novelist's characteristic style of perception is in league with evil.

This is an unsuccessful and badly written book. It is far less success-ful, both as writing and as thought, than the best of Dworkin's essays.[97] And yet it is in another way an important book, for it brings to the surface

---

test is applied to passages taken out of the context of the whole work. MacKinnon's and Dworkin's definition works better than others to separate Dworkin's own fiction from por-nography, but only because Lindgren has selected a rare Dworkin passage in which the woman is in control of what takes place and is not subordinated.

95. Dworkin, *Mercy*, p. 328.

96. Ibid., p. 329.

97. In my *Boston Review* piece on Dworkin, I discuss some of the essays in *Intercourse*, which express a view of sexuality far more subtle and particularized than the views ex-pressed here, especially where women are not in the picture and Dworkin is discussing male homosexuality.

for scrutiny the strict retributive attitude that animates some portions of
feminist moral and legal thought, and allows us to see this attitude as a
reasonable response to terrible wrongs. Dworkin is correct in stressing
the pervasiveness of male violence against women, and correct, too, in
insisting that to deny and conceal these wrongs is to condemn women of
the present and future to continued bodily and psychological suffering.
She is correct in protesting loudly against these wrongs and in refusing
to say that they are not wrongs. The only remedy, Dworkin suggests, is
to refuse all sympathy and all particular perception, moving over to a
conception of justice so resolute in its denial of particularity that it resembles Anaximandrean *dikê* more than it resembles most modern retributive schemes. The narrator announces, "None of them's innocent
and who cares? I fucking don't care." And it is Dworkin's position, re-
peatedly announced in the novel as in her essays, that all heterosexual
males are rapists and all heterosexual intercourse is rape. In this sense,
there really is no difference between him and him, and to refuse to see
this is to collaborate with evil.

But Dworkin is wrong. Retributivism is not the only alternative to cow-
ardly denial and capitulation.[98] Seneca's *De ira* is hardly a work that denies evil where it exists; indeed, it is a work almost as relentlessly ob-
sessed with narrating tales of evil as is Dworkin's work. Like Dworkin's
work, it insists on the pervasiveness of evil, the enormous difficulty of
eradicating it, and the necessity of bringing it to judgment. Mercy is not
acquittal. In what, then, does its great difference from Dworkin's work
consist? First of all, it does not exempt itself. It takes the Dworkin parody
line "She wasn't perfect either" very seriously, urging that all human
beings are the products of social and natural conditions that are, in certain ways, subversive of justice and love, that need slow, patient resistance. This interest in self-scrutiny already gives it a certain gentleness,
forces it out of the we/them mentality characteristic of retributivism.
Second, it is really interested in the obstacles to goodness that Dworkin's
narrator mocks and dismisses: the social obstacles, deeply internalized,
that cannot be changed in an instant; the other more circumstantial and
particular obstacles that stand between individuals and justice to those

98. One might argue that Dworkin's style of retributivism, even if not morally precise,
has strategic value, in publicizing the pervasiveness of harms done to women. I doubt this.
For if, with Dworkin, we refuse to make distinctions we commonly make between consensual heterosexual intercourse and coercion, we are likely to get fewer convictions for rape,
not more.

they love. It judges these social forces and commits itself to changing them but, where judgment on the individual is concerned, it yields in mercy before the difficulty of life. This means that it can be in its form a powerful work of narrative art. If you really open your imagination and heart to admit the life story of someone else, it becomes far more difficult to finish that person off with a karate kick. In short, the text constructs a reader who, while judging justly, remains capable of love.

What I am really saying is that good feminist thought, in the law and in life generally, is like good judging: it does not ignore the evidence, it does not fail to say that injustice is injustice, evil evil[99]—but it is capable of *suggnômê*, and therefore of *clementia*. And if it is shrewd it will draw on the resources of the novelist's art.

I shall end by returning to Seneca's *De clementia*. Toward the end of the address to Nero Caesar, Seneca asks him a pointed question: "What . . . would living be if lions and bears held the power, if serpents and all the most destructive animals were given power over us?" (I.26.3) These serpents, lions, and bears, as Seneca well knows, inhabit our souls in the forms of our jealous angers, our competitiveness, our retributive harshness.[100] These animals are as they are because they are incapable of receiving another creature's life story into their imagination and responding to that history with gentleness. But those serpents, lions, and bears in the mind still play a part today, almost two thousand years after Seneca's treatise was written, in determining the shape of our legal institutions, as the merciful attitude to punishment still comes in for ridicule, as the notion of deliberation based on sentiment still gets repudiated and misunderstood, as a simple form of retributivism has an increasing influence on our legal and political life. As judges, as jurors, as feminists, we should, I argue with Seneca, oppose the ascendancy of these more obtuse animals and, while judging the wrong to be wrong, still cultivate the perceptions, and the gentleness, of mercy.[101]

99. Contrast Dworkin, *Mercy*, p. 334, where, in an epilogue entitled "Not Andrea," a liberal feminist attacks Andrea Dworkin as "a prime example, of course, of the simple-minded demagogue who promotes the proposition that *bad things are bad*."

100. For Seneca's use of this animal imagery elsewhere, see my "Serpents in the Soul: A Reading of Seneca's *Medea*," in Nussbaum, *Therapy*, ch. 12; and also in *Pursuits of Reason: Essays in Honor of Stanley Cavell*, ed. T. Cohen, et al. (Lubbock: Texas Tech Press, 1993). On related imagery in Lucretius, see Nussbaum, *Therapy*, ch. 7.

101. Cf. also *De clementia* I.17.1: "No animal has a more troublesome temperament, none needs to be handled with greater skill, than the human being; and to none should mercy more be shown."

MICHAEL DAVIS   Harm and Retribution

Recently, a respected legal theorist, Hugo Bedau, was asked to evaluate a proposed revision of Pennsylvania's penal code. He began by noting: "The classification [of crimes and punishments] . . . has been assumed to be fundamentally retributive, and so its penalty schedule must be based on two basic retributive principles: (1) the severity of the punishment must be proportional to the gravity of the offense, and (2) the gravity of the offense must be a function of fault in the offender and harm caused the victim."[1] These two "basic principles" (or part of them) are often referred to as "*lex talionis.*"

What interests me here are two of Bedau's three uses of "must." Because the classification of crimes and punishments is retributive, it *must*, Bedau says, be based on *lex talionis.* And, for the same reason, the penalties provided *must* be a function of fault in the offender and harm done the victim (and, except in special cases, nothing else). My thesis is that there is no "must" about either.

Some retributivists, most notably F. H. Bradley, may seem to have argued something similar.[2] But the upshot of their arguments was that retribution needs a utilitarian principle to proportion punishment to

I should like to express my appreciation to the National Endowment for the Humanities for the year of support without which this article could not have been written; and to the University of Chicago for according me the privileges of a visiting scholar which made writing the paper much easier than it might otherwise have been.

1. H. A. Bedau, "Classification-Based Sentencing: Some Conceptual and Ethical Problems," *NOMOS XXVII: Criminal Justice* (1985): 102.

2. F. H. Bradley, *Ethical Studies*, 2d ed. (London: Oxford University Press, 1962), pp. 26–27. (Whether Bradley meant to make such a compromise is another question. My impression is that he has been misread.) Cf. B. Bosanquet, *The Philosophical Theory of the State*, 4th ed. (London: Macmillan, 1965), p. 212; and Bedau, p. 103.

crime. Those retributivists defended a compromised retributivism. I shall not. I shall not because there is, I believe, a better *retributive* principle for proportioning punishment to crime. That principle proportions punishment to the unfair advantage the criminal takes just by committing his crime. Let us call it "the unfair-advantage principle."

The unfair-advantage principle superficially resembles *lex talionis* enough that, as far as I can tell, no one has clearly distinguished them. Yet the differences are important. Or, at least, that is what I shall try to show. I proceed in this way. First, I distinguish *lex talionis* from the unfair-advantage principle. Second, I show that the unfair-advantage principle can explain a variety of criminal laws better than *lex talionis* can. Third, I show that *lex talionis* is virtually unusable in large areas of criminal law while the unfair-advantage principle should be equally usable everywhere. Last, I consider saving *lex talionis* by leaving the measurement of harm to intuition or empirical survey. I argue that it cannot be saved in that way.

I shall not explain (or defend) the unfair advantage principle more than necessary to make clear how it differs from *lex talionis*. Space forbids me to do here what has already been done elsewhere.[3]

My thesis, if proved, should be important to retributivists in at least three ways. First, it should help to establish that the unfair-advantage approach to punishment is significantly different from other forms of (uncompromised) retributivism (since it gives up *lex talionis* while other forms do not). Second, given the problems of *lex talionis*, the argument here should help to establish the superiority of the unfair-advantage approach over other forms of retributivism. And third, because critics of (uncompromised) retributivism tend to treat *lex talionis* as retributivism's chief weakness,[4] my argument should also help to dissuade such critics from treating it as a weakness of retributivism as such. They would have to treat *lex talionis* merely as a weakness of some forms of retributivism. If they still chose to reject retributivism categorically, it would have to be for reasons independent of *lex talionis*.

3. See, for example, Herbert Morris, "Persons and Punishment," *Monist* 52 (1968): 475–501 (to whom the recent popularity of the principle seems to be due). For a defense of the principle against the utilitarian charge that it is incapable of giving content to the concept of proportion, see Michael Davis, "How to Make the Punishment Fit the Crime," *Ethics* 93 (1983): 726–52.

4. See, for example, Michael H. Mitias, "Is Retribution Inconsistent Without *Lex Talionis*?" *Rivista internazionale di filosofia del diritto* 56 (1983): 211–30.

While this article is supposed to be a contribution to retributive theory, much of what is said should also be relevant to "utilitarian" (or "consequentialist") theories of punishment in which desert limits what may be done to the criminal. Such "mixed" theories need not interpret "desert" as requiring proportion between punishment and the harm the criminal did.

But (I should add) this article is not supposed to be relevant only to theory. Retributivism is not merely a subject for theorists. As Bedau's commentary on the proposed revision of Pennsylvania's penal code should suggest, retributivism is again a principle helping to shape and justify the way punishment is in fact administered. So, what I say here should be useful to legislators, criminologists, and others who are concerned to make punishment as just as possible.

I. What is *Lex Talionis*?

Lex talionis (or *jus talionis*) may once have referred unequivocally to a certain principle defining or limiting the right of retaliation, but it has long since become equivocal. *Lex talionis* may now refer either to a general principle of corrective justice or to a particular principle of criminal law. As a general principle of corrective justice, *lex* requires the wrongdoer to suffer as much as (but no more than) he has wrongfully made others suffer. This principle is more at home in the mountains of Corsica or in a schoolyard fight than in the criminal law. ("He hit you once, so you should hit him just once in return.")[5] This is not the *lex talionis* that concerns me. My concern is a principle of criminal law, one that is supposed to explain what statutory penalties and judicial sentences must be to be justified as acts of a relatively just legal system. Whatever light that principle sheds on natural justice, poetic justice, divine justice, or the like is, while welcome, gratuitous.

Lex talionis, understood as a principle of criminal law, is still equivocal. It may be understood either "formally" or "materially." Understood formally, it is the first of Bedau's "two basic principles," that is, the principle that punishment should be proportioned to the gravity of the offense or otherwise made to "fit the crime." This *lex talionis* is simply a reminder

5. For a recent, extensive, and highly sophisticated discussion of this principle of morality, see Robert Nozick, *Philosophical Explanations* (Cambridge, MA: Harvard University Press, Belknap Press, 1981), pp. 363–93.

that criminal justice consists primarily in punishing violations of the criminal law, not in punishing faults of character, deterring antisocial behavior, or doing other sorts of good. Other good may be done as well, of course, but doing it is secondary, not to be achieved by punishment greater than the crime deserves (however desert happens to be measured). Bedau was certainly right to include that principle among the "basic principles" of retributivism. So understood, *lex talionis* is essential to any retributive theory.[6] Differences among retributivist theories are largely in how to measure desert, not in whether desert is what punishment should be measured against. For example, some retributivists have held that deserved punishment is determined by the moral wrong the criminal did when he broke the law; others, that it is the special moral wrong involved in breaking a particular criminal law as such.

Lex talionis may also be understood "materially," that is, as a principle requiring punishment to be proportioned (in part at least) to harm done (or, perhaps, to be limited by the harm done). This is Bedau's second "basic principle." Different retributive theories differ concerning what shall count as harm (and how important harm is for determining punishment). But, any theory for which *lex talionis* is not purely formal will have to understand "harm" as existing *independent of a particular criminal statute*. Harm will have to be something a statute can protect against by forbidding (or requiring) certain acts. The loss of an eye is an example of such a harm. For most retributivists, the invasion of a right would be another. What else may be is controversial.

Lex talionis is so often invoked as the principle that requires an eye for an eye, a tooth for a tooth, that it may be worth a moment to point out that even those among its defenders who talk that way, do not mean what they seem to say. For example, Kant states the "law of retribution" as "any undeserved evil that you inflict on someone else among the people is one that you do to yourself."[7] Yet, his examples of retribution include apology followed by solitary confinement as punishment for attacking a social inferior without just cause, penal servitude as punishment for theft, and death as punishment for treason. Accompanying each example is an

6. And not only to retributive theories. John Rawls makes the point that utilitarian theories such as Bentham's also include (something like) the formal version of *lex talionis*. "Two Concepts of Rules," in (among other places) *The Philosophy of Punishment*, ed. H. B. Acton (London: Macmillan, 1969), p. 114n.

7. Immanuel Kant, *The Metaphysical Elements of Justice*, trans. John Ladd (Indianapolis: Liberal Arts Library, 1965), pp. 101–102 (VI, 332–33) and pp. 132–33 (VI, 363–67).

explanation of how the suggested punishment would satisfy the "spirit," if not the letter, of *lex talionis*.[8] Plainly, even Kant understood *lex talionis* to require an *equivalent* "evil," not the *same* "evil."

Of course, retributivists *are* divided on whether *lex talionis* requires the punishment to *be* equivalent or merely specifies eqivalence as the *most* justice will allow. Kant left little room for clemency. For him, justice generally required a certain punishment and the sovereign had no right to do more or less. Most modern retributivists would reject Kant's rigorism. But that need not concern us. Now we may complete our explanation of *lex talionis* by contrasting it with the unfair-advantage principle.

The unfair-advantage principle assumes that each criminal law (or perhaps the criminal law as a whole) creates a system of cooperation. Some people forbear doing what they would otherwise do because the law has given them reasonable assurance that others will do the same (and everyone will be better off if everyone abstains). Such a system imposes burdens insofar as people do forbear doing what they would otherwise do. Anyone who breaks a law does not bear the same burden the rest do. Unless he is punished, he will, in effect, have gotten away with doing less than others. He will have an advantage they do not.

According to the unfair-advantage principle, it is this advantage the criminal law is supposed to take back by punishing the criminal for his crime. The advantage bears no necessary relation to the harm the criminal actually did. For example, he may have done great damage and only committed theft; or no damage at all even though he tried to commit murder. According to the unfair-advantage principle, the damage a criminal actually does is between him and his victim, a private matter to be settled by civil suit (or the moral equivalent). His *crime* consists only in the unfair advantage he necessarily took over the law-abiding by breaking the law in question. The measure of punishment due is the relative value of *that* unfair advantage. The greater the advantage, the greater the punishment should be. The focus of the unfair-advantage principle is on what the *criminal* gained; the focus of *lex talionis*, on what *others* lost.[9]

In one respect, however, the two principles are alike. Neither the unfair-advantage principle nor *lex talionis* distinguishes sharply between laying down rules for punishment and applying those rules to particular cases.

8. Ibid.
9. Cf. Davis, "How to Make the Punishment Fit the Crime," pp. 736–46.

Under either principle, a legislature has little or no discretion concerning *how much* the crime should be punished (though it may have wide discretion concerning the form of that punishment). That a legislature requires a certain penalty for a certain crime does not mean that the criminal deserves it for the crime in question or that it would be just for a judge to impose it even under an otherwise just procedure. The principle of punishment, whether *lex talionis* or unfair-advantage principle, determines that. From the perspective of either principle, there is only one continuous process of proportioning punishment to crime once a legislature has made an act criminal. The judge completes whatever the legislature has left undone.

The rule-act distinction seems to belong to utilitarian, rather than to retributive, theories of punishment. I shall say nothing more of it here. For retributivists, the important distinction seems to be between (a) the legislative decision to make a class of acts criminal, (b) the legislative or judicial decision that a certain crime deserves (no more than) a certain punishment, and (c) the judicial decision that the actual sentence should be such and such (the judge taking into account the criminal as well as his crime to determine whether the sentence should be less than what the crime itself deserves).[10]

II. Harm, "Harm," and No "Harm"

Harm is the engine of *lex talionis*. To determine how much (or how little) *lex talionis* can help us understand the criminal law, we must consider the place of harm in the criminal law. Is it the right place for *lex talionis* to provide an adequate theory of how much to punish?

I suggest that, while trying to answer that question, we confine ourselves to the criminal law as we know it. This limitation is not meant to foreclose the possibility that a retributive theory might provide a criticism of practice.[11] Rather, it serves to remind us of the practice we are trying to understand. We may wish to criticize some of it, perhaps all of it. But criticism not founded on understanding will hardly convince. So, whether

10. Cf. ibid., pp. 750–52; and Michael Davis, "Sentencing: Must Justice Be Even-Handed? *Law and Philosophy* 1 (1982): 77–117.

11. Indeed, I have elsewhere provided examples of the critical power of retributivism. See, for example, "Setting Penalties: What Does Rape Deserve?" *Law and Philosophy* 3 (1984): 62–111; and "Guilty But Insane?" *Social Theory and Practice* 10 (1984): 1–23.

our ultimate aim is understanding or reform, we should begin with the criminal law as it is.

Harm certainly has a significant place in the criminal law even if "harm" is understood strictly as physical injury to some person or physical damage to some thing. Many common crimes do harm in this sense. Murder and mayhem require that some individual suffer physical injury: arson and wanton destruction of property, that some property be damaged.

But many common crimes do no harm—if "harm" is understood that strictly. Kidnapping, robbery, theft, burglary, and perhaps even battery may leave no mark on any person or reduce the value of anything. Such crimes do harm, if they do harm, only in a looser sense of "harm." They invade the *right* of some individual. A kidnapper must deprive his victim of liberty, for example, by carrying the victim off against his will. A robber must deprive her victim of property by force. And so on. The rights in question (liberty, property, or the like) are rights existing independent of the particular criminal statute. They would be enforceable by civil suit whether or not protected by criminal statute. So, extending "harm" to include what such crimes do is certainly consistent with *lex talionis*.[12]

But, extended only in this way, "harm" is still not broad enough for anything like a full theory of deserved punishment. Some serious crimes do not seem to be an invasion of anyone's right but merely a beneficial restraint on commerce. For example, a blackmailer may have a right (that is, a "liberty-right") to publish the information he uses to blackmail and a similar right to accept payment for silence. What right (what "claim-right") could one have (all else equal) to the helpful silence of another if one is not willing to pay for it? What right not to be given an opportunity to pay for it?

The law—civil or criminal—is ordinarily not concerned to prevent publication of the sort of (truthful) information a blackmailer uses, nor is it generally concerned with people receiving money to keep silent. The blackmail statute simply forbids a blackmailer's volunteering to sell his silence. Here, it seems, if we are still to talk of "harm," we must understand "harm" as violating a (preexisting) *interest*, that is, an interest in not having someone force you to choose between paying for his silence

12. See W. D. Ross, *The Right and The Good* (London: Oxford University Press, 1930), pp. 62–63, for an example of someone who expressly limits justified punishment to the vindication of rights.

and having your reputation blasted, not as violating a (preexisting) right. The point of prohibiting blackmail seems to be to remove a certain temptation to destroy the reputation of others. The law against blackmail may be said to protect an individual from the "harm of lost reputation," but that "harm" is to an interest, not (like the harms discussed earlier) harm that constitutes "breach of the peace" or invades a right.

But extending "harm" to include protecting (some) interests of individuals still does not extend the concept enough to explain punishing all serious crimes. Some serious crimes do not seem to invade the interest of any individual (at least, not in anything like the full-blooded sense of "interest" we have been considering so far). For example, treason seems to be a crime against government, a corporate person, not an individual. The same seems to be true of tax evasion, smuggling, and the like "social crimes." Here it is natural to talk of "harming the interests of society" ("society" referring to the corporate entity, not to any particular individuals). The interests of society may, it seems, be distinct from those of any individual (though still connected with them in certain complex ways). I may, for example, commit treason by giving some rebels a bed for the night and a few crumbs in the morning (if I do it in part to help their cause). I may in this small way help impede the government's efforts to starve the rebellion into submission. Yet, it is hard to see how the interests of any individual would be harmed by my kindness (at least, in the way their interests would be harmed by my blackmailing them). Who in particular would be worse off? One can, of course, imagine situations in which my kindness adversely affected someone (for example, by giving the rebels enough encouragement to persevere until they engaged in some deadly attack on government facilities they would not otherwise have attacked). But those would not be the only cases, or even the most common.

It might, however, be argued that any act of treason, even my seemingly harmless kindness, necessarily harms the interests of some individuals, for example, the interests of those individuals who cooperate to produce the shared good of political stability. What are we to make of this argument? We must, I think, distinguish two forms of it. One form is in fact an appeal to the unfair-advantage principle, not *lex talionis*, and so cannot threaten any claim we may make concerning the infirmity of *lex talionis*; the other, while an appeal to *lex talionis*, is so only supposing a sense of "harm" we have yet to consider.

Let us begin with the first form of the argument. The claim it makes is that I harm those who cooperate to produce political stability by taking *unfair* advantage of that stability while refusing to do my share. The advantage must be "unfair" because we ordinarily do not consider taking fair advantage to deserve punishment. If we now ask how one is to know that the advantage is "unfair," the answer seems to be that the system of cooperation producing that stability is (in part at least) defined by the criminal statute prohibiting treason. My act of kindness to the rebels would not take unfair advantage of anyone if the criminal law allowed such kindness. My kindness is not cooperation because, and it seems simply because, it is prohibited. The harm it is said my kindness does cannot, then, on this analysis, be defined apart from the criminal statute in question. Since *lex talionis* (as we have understood it) is supposed to provide a measure of harm (and so, of deserved punishment) *independent* of the existence of the particular criminal statute in question, this form of the argument cannot be an appeal to *lex talionis*. And indeed, as the explicit reference to "unfair advantage" suggests, it is nothing more than a special form of appeal to the unfair-advantage principle itself.

That brings us to the other form of the argument. The claim is that, treason statute or not, my kindness to the rebels harms the interests of those cooperating to maintain political stability. My kindness does that by at least *risking* that political stability (whether fairly or unfairly). We have already had to adopt a relatively abstract notion of harm, that is, harm as damage to some interest of an individual or society (an individual's rights being among those interests). But this second form of the argument asks us to go further. Or, rather, it asks us to go further in one way (by having "harm" include "risk of harm") so as not to go further in another (by having "harm" include "harm to society"). Since I do not think we can avoid that second extension anyway, I think we may allow those who hope to keep *lex talionis* from becoming unusable to deny that "harm" includes "harm to society" (strictly speaking). There are, after all, many other crimes in which the only plausible harm is a "*risk* of harm to person or property."

Consider, for example, the crime of reckless driving. If I drive recklessly on an empty highway, I do not in fact invade anyone's interest in safety (since I endanger no one). I also do not invade any interest of government in the way my earlier act of kindness did (since what I do does not endanger the government even to the degree helping rebels does). What

I do is *risk endangering* anyone who *might* be on the highway (even though it happens that no one is there). If we are to describe what I am doing in terms of preexisting interest, we shall have to say that I am violating the interest of all those who might have used the highway in not having me risk endangering them, or perhaps society's interest in not having people risk endangering each other. If the interests we have discussed so far may be described as "primary," this is a "secondary interest," that is, an interest in not having a primary interest put at risk (where "risk" refers to the harm reasonably foreseeable given what the actor knows or, perhaps, should know, and "danger" refers to the harm reasonably foreseeable given—something like—full information).

Perhaps we can explain punishing attempts in the same way. By definition, an attempt does not do the harm the complete crime would have done. Some attempts violate no primary interest at all. For example, an attempted murder might consist of no more than putting sugar, believed to be poison, in the coffee of one's senile aunt or trying to shoot one's enemy from ambush with an empty gun believed to be loaded. While such crimes do not in fact endanger, they could, like reckless driving, endanger someone under other circumstances and, for all the actor knew, the other circumstances prevailed. So, it seems reasonable to say that attempts violate a secondary interest in not having our safety or control of property risked (whether it is in fact endangered or not).

There are, however, other crimes, some serious, that seem not to harm even a secondary interest. Consider, for example, the crime of conspiracy. A conspiracy may be no more than an agreement to attempt an ordinary crime, for example, robbery or murder. Two would-be criminals can be guilty of such a conspiracy if, having agreed to commit the crime, they buy rope or do some other (ordinarily) lawful act in preparation for carrying out the planned crime. They need not do anything amounting to an attempt. Since two would-be criminals cannot lawfully do some acts one would-be criminal can lawfully do, the "harm" of conspiracy seems to be harm in a sense different from that in which attempt does harm. It is, it seems, an invasion of the interest in not having people join together to undertake a criminal attempt. Perhaps we can call this a "tertiary interest."

If so, we shall have to talk of "fourth-degree interests" too. Consider the crime of solicitation. You commit this crime by (in effect) attempting to commit conspiracy, that is, by going about trying to get others to agree to attempt a crime for you. ("Try," because if you succeed, there is a conspiracy.) The "harm" done by solicitation seems very far from harm strictly so called. Of course, if solicitation of a certain sort were allowed, there might be more successful attempts of the corresponding primary crime. That possibility is something that rightly concerns a legislature. But, more than in conspiracy or attempt, it seems odd to talk about that sensible concern in terms of someone's (fourth-degree) interest a particular criminal harms by a particular solicitation.

We have, it seems, already stretched the concept of harm pretty far. But we have not yet stretched it far enough to cover the whole criminal law. There are some crimes that do not seem to involve harm even in this most extended sense. Consider, for example, recidivism. A recidivist statute may punish as a separate crime being guilty of an ordinary crime when one has previously been convicted of others. The recidivist commits the same "underlying" crime a first offender would if he did the same act. But the recidivist commits two crimes, the "underlying" crime and recidivism, where the first offender would commit only one.

Because *lex talionis* includes both harm and fault in its calculation of deserved punishment, it might seem that punishment for recidivism can be justified under *lex talionis* by supposing that repeat offenders deserve greater punishment because repetition demonstrates greater fault. In fact, such a justification will work for only one class of recidivist statute, that is, those that treat repetition as an aggravating factor. Most recidivist statutes do not treat repetition that way. Instead they treat repetition as a separate crime. The punishment allowable under the recidivist statute is *in addition to* the maximum punishment for the underlying crime and can be many times that *maximum* (indeed, it can be considerably more than the maximum for all the preceding offenses together). For example, conviction for three thefts might require a mandatory life sentence even though the maximum punishment for each theft would have been ten years imprisonment (and even though the criminal in fact served the maximum each time). Explaining such hugely enhanced punishments as a function merely of increased fault certainly looks *ad hoc* (especially in the absence of any independent measure of fault).

It seems, then, that if we are to explain recidivist statutes under *lex talionis*, we must explain them (at least in large part) as punishing invasion of an interest not invaded by a first offender committing the same "underlying" crime. Such an explanation will require some ingenuity. What interest could potential victims have in suffering a crime at the hands of a first offender *rather than* at the hands of a recidivist? What interest could society have in having a particular crime committed by a first offender rather than by a recidivist?

So, if the recidivist deserves more punishment than a first offender, he must, it seems, deserve it for reasons independent of the harm *he* does. At least two contemporary retributivists have drawn that conclusion. Both George Fletcher and Hyman Gross have argued that the "recidivist premium" cannot be explained by the principles of punishment (Gross adding that recidivist statutes are best thought of as "crude counterparts of civil commitment").[13]

To say that it is hard to find the interest an individual recidivist invades by being a recidivist (in addition to the interest he invades by the "underlying" crime) is, of course, not to say that there may not be good reason to punish recidivism in the way we do. It is not hard to think of such reasons. For example, recidivist statutes may give us a means of incapacitating those criminals most likely to contribute most to the rate of crime. The problem is to turn such a general reason, suitable for justifying criminalization, into a harm (that is, an injury to a preexisting interest) suitable for proportioning punishment to the crime. That is the problem because *lex talionis* proportions punishment (in part at least) to the harm a particular criminal did. Where we cannot find an interest the criminal invaded, we cannot invoke *lex talionis*—except to justify no punishment whatever.

Perhaps, if we thought long and hard, we could discover an interest recidivists invade. "Interest" is an extraordinarily flexible category. But, it seems unlikely that our discovery would have enough intuitive appeal to justify the very substantial penalties with which recidivism is in fact punished. Our concern is not a question far from experience. *Lex talionis* is itself supposed to be common sense. If the interest *lex talionis* requires can be discovered only by much hard thought, it is unlikely to be what a legislator (or judge) would take into account. And if it is not that, it is unlikely to explain the criminal law as it is. So, even this brief and impressionistic survey of the criminal law seems to have stretched the concept of harm to the breaking point (or beyond).

13. George Fletcher, "The Recidivist Premium," *Criminal Justice Ethics* 1 (1982): 54–59; and Hyman Gross, *A Theory of Criminal Justice* (New York: Oxford University Press, 1979), p. 40.

Recidivist statutes provide a clear example of the superiority of the unfair-advantage principle over *lex talionis*. According to the unfair-advantage principle, the recidivist deserves punishment, if he deserves punishment, because committing another crime after he has been convicted of others takes an advantage a first offender would not take just by committing the same "underlying" crime. It is perhaps analogous to going back for seconds when not everyone has had a first helping. There is nothing unfair about it unless it is against "the rules." But if it is against the rules (that is, there is a recidivist statute), it is unfair to take that advantage and so there is something to deserve punishment.[14] Whether the state should prohibit criminals from "going back for seconds" is (according to the unfair-advantage principle) an independent question. Moreover, it is a question for the theory of legislation (that is, for the theory demarking what should be prohibited from what should not be), not for the theory of punishment.

Here, it seems, *lex talionis* reveals disturbing prelegal roots the unfair-advantage principle does not have. According to *les talionis*, a law, even if itself not unjust, can*not* make an act punishable unless the act is "punishable" law or not, that is, unless it invades a (legitimate) interest existing independent of the criminal law in question. The criminal law cannot make a "harmless" act punishable because without harm there is, according to *lex talionis*, nothing to measure deserved punishment against. Since it would be unjust to punish to any degree what cannot deserve punishment to any degree, for *lex talionis* prelegal conditions limit what the law can punish. The law cannot add to what deserves punishment, only select a subset of punishable acts to make punishable at law. *Lex talionis* is, in effect, a theory of legislation as well as a theory of how much to punish.

The unfair-advantage principle is not (or, at least, not to the same degree). The principle is consistent with any theory of what the criminal law should forbid or allow (provided the criminal law is conceived as part of a relatively just legal system). That is so because (ordinarily) any law within a relatively just legal system creates a cooperative scheme most departures from which would take unfair advantage. Of course, a particular departure for special reason may not amount to taking such advan-

14. For a full defense of this claim, see Michael Davis, "Just Deserts for Recidivists," *Criminal Justice Ethics* 4 (Summer/Fall 1985): 29–50.

tage (for example, because the departure constitutes a "mere technical violation" or because enforcing the law in that case would be discriminatory or otherwise unfair). In such cases, the unfair-advantage principle would provide the basis for excuse or justification. Such special cases, while an important problem for any adequate theory of criminal law, present a problem different from the one we are now considering. The category of excuse or justification presupposes that punishment for the crime in question is generally deserved. The problem we have been considering until now is whether *lex talionis* or the unfair-advantage principle better explains how punishment for various *sorts* of crime can be deserved.

Because the unfair-advantage principle is concerned with unfair advantage taken by disobeying the law rather than with harm done against the law, the unfair-advantage principle automatically separates (most) questions of demarcation from those of proportion. Because separating such questions seems more judicious than implicitly supposing that what justifies making an act criminal will also provide the measure of punishment for doing the act once doing it is a crime, I take this difference between the unfair-advantage principle and *lex talionis* to be an advantage of the unfair-advantage principle.[15]

III. Doing Harm or Failing to Help Prevent Harm?

Lex talionis limits the criminal law to protecting (preexisting) interests. A law which does not protect some such interest cannot be understood as part of the criminal law; what it "punishes" cannot be understood as a crime; and so, what is done to the "criminal" cannot be justified *as punishment* even though what is done is obviously part of the ordinary processes of the criminal law. Given the criminal law as we know it, that is a significant limitation. The point of legislation does not always translate easily into an interest a particular criminal invades by a particular crime. Recidivist statutes provide one example of that, an example of the difficulty of finding an *interest* the criminal invades. I should now like to consider a class of crimes in which the difficulty is not finding an interest

15. For those who see no advantage in separating those questions, I would suggest considering the advantages of separation as illustrated in my "Why Attempts Deserve Less Punishment than Complete Crimes," *Law and Philosophy*, forthcoming, and "Strict Liability: Deserved Punishment for Faultless Conduct," also forthcoming.

but finding an *invasion*. Some crimes consist of no more than an intentional *non*doing, for example, refusing to aid a police officer when asked, "misprison of treason," or failure to report a bribe. Let us consider the last of these examples briefly to see how *lex talionis* may not explain why such a crime deserves punishment.

In Illinois, anyone ". . . connected with any professional or amateur contest, sporting event or exhibition, who fails to report [to an appropriate official] . . . any offer or promise made to him [with the intent, understanding, or agreement that he will not use his best efforts in connection with such contest]" commits the class-A misdemeanor of failing to report a bribe.[16] The point of this statute is plain enough. If more people reported bribe attempts, fewer bribes would be offered and more would-be bribers would be caught. Preventing bribes would, in turn, help to preserve the integrity of contests, sporting events, and the like. It is also plain that the statute helps to protect certain interests. The statute helps to protect our interest in not being misled concerning the nature of the contest or sporting event we might attend, participate in, or bet on (and, if we have such an interest, our interest in not being forced to decide whether or not to take a bribe). But the statute provides that protection by requiring ordinary citizens to report any attempt at a certain sort of solicitation.

How might *lex talionis* apply here? If bribe attempts were never reported but bribes were never accepted, the contests or events the statute is supposed to protect would still be as fair as they could be. So, someone failing to report a bribe does not, as would someone who took a bribe, *increase* the danger that a contest or event will be less fair than it would be if he had not been offered the bribe. He merely does not increase the probability that the contest will be fair. He does not aid in apprehending those who make such contests unfair. That is harm only if failure to do good (or prevent harm) can constitute doing harm (or *invading* an interest).

There are cases in which failure to act does harm—or, more accurately, is part of doing harm. For example, if relying on your promise to report any attempt to bribe and hearing nothing of the bribe you were offered, I state publicly that there has been no attempt to bribe, I would suffer loss of credibility when the attempt later became known. And you would be one cause of that loss. I would be harmed, law or no law. And you would have caused that harm.

16. *Ill. Rev. Stat.* Ch. 38, sec. 29–3.

The ordinary case of failing to report a bribe is, however, not like that. Ordinarily, the expectation that anyone offered a bribe will report it does not exist or, if it exists, exists only because the statute makes failing to report the bribe a crime. Without the statute, there does not seem to be a larger act that could constitute doing harm (unless we are willing to give up the distinction between doing harm and letting it happen). Someone who fails to report the bribe attempt could have helped prevent invasion of certain interests and did not. But he does not seem to have *invaded* any interest at all. He has not done harm, only let it happen.

Because *lex talionis* proportions punishment to the harm the criminal *does*, it seems to forbid punishing someone who has done no harm. That is certainly inconsistent with a significant part of the criminal law as we know it. Statutes imposing duties to act are not, like retroactive criminal statutes or secret laws, mere oddities, more often discussed by legal theorists than invoked in a courtroom. Any theory of just punishment that cannot explain such common statutes as part of the criminal law is already substantially less desirable, all else equal, than one that can.

So, it is worth noting that, unlike *lex talionis*, the unfair-advantage principle is immune to such problems. The principle does not require a statute to protect against invasion of an interest for the statute to be part of the criminal law. All the principle requires is that the statute be part of a system of cooperation (and that the statute include criminal penalties). Even a statute the legislature has adopted without good reason may create a system of cooperation. If it does (and if the statute allows criminal penalties), the unfair-advantage principle applies.

Of course, a particularly silly statute may not create a system of cooperation. People may just scoff at the statute (while letting it remain "on the books" out of misplaced piety, disinterest, or who knows what). If the statute is a "dead letter," the unfair-advantage principle would not recognize it as part of the criminal law (except in some sense too extended to justify punishment). One can take no advantage by violating a "dead law" and so, according to the unfair-advantage principle, one cannot deserve punishment even if one does violate it. And that is so even, contrary to what we are now assuming, the statute would prevent invasion of some significant interest if it were obeyed.[17]

17. This result seems to accord with practice. Courts do not respond to silly statutes by reducing the maximum penalty for violation. Instead, either they reinterpret the statute so that it is no longer silly, as in *City of St. Louis v. Fritz*, 53 Mo. 582 (1873) or *People v.*

It might also happen that a silly statute, though it does not deserve to be enforced, is being enforced and, because it is being enforced, is generally being obeyed. If so, the statute is part of a system of cooperation and, for the unfair-advantage principle, that is all that is necessary for the penalties to apply (supposing the legal system as a whole to be relatively just). People will be shouldering burdens they would not otherwise shoulder. Unless the criminal is a special case, his failure to shoulder the same burden will give him an unfair advantage over others. That advantage is all the unfair-advantage principle requires that punishment be proportioned to.

So, according to that principle, the important distinction is not between doing harm and letting it happen (or between invading an interest and failing to help prevent such an invasion), but between cooperating and not cooperating with the criminal law (by obeying or disobeying it). The criminal law punishes failure to report a bribe for exactly the same reason it punishes reckless driving or recidivism. All are failures to cooperate, failures to abide by the rules of the cooperative scheme constituting the criminal law within a relatively just legal system. The reckless driver fails to drive as the law requires. The recidivist fails to abstain from "taking seconds" the law has forbidden. And the person who does not bother to report a bribe attempt fails to do what the law says he should. Each benefits from the cooperation of others but does not respond as they have. Each makes himself an exception and, according to the unfair-advantage principle, punishment is supposed to undo that exceptional status.

IV. HARM AS THE MEASURE OF DESERT

The last two sections compared *lex talionis* and the unfair-advantage principle as explanations of *what* the criminal law punishes. We learned that *lex talionis* cannot make sense of certain kinds of criminal law the unfair-advantage principle can. We may now inquire which principle is better at helping us understand *how much* punishment a crime deserves. To be fair to *lex talionis*, we must, given the results of the last two sections,

---

Johnson, 6 N.Y. 2d 549, 161 N.E. 2d 9 (1959), or they invalidate the statute, as in *Park v. State*, 42 Nev. 386, 178 P. 389 (1919) or *Meyer v. Nebraska*, 262 U.S. 390 (1923). Courts seem to be concerned about the penalty only when the statute is neither silly nor "fallen into desuetude." See, for example, *Weems v. United States*, 217 U.S. 349 (1910) or *Solem v. Helm*, 463 U.S. 277, 103 S.Ct. 3001, 77 L. Ed. 2d 637 (1983).

limit our inquiry to those crimes for which there is an identifiable harm (or invasion of interest). That, as we saw, is a significant limitation, but one about which we have said enough already.

Does the concept of harm give us insight into how much punishment a criminal deserves for what he did? The answer seems to be that it certainly does—sometimes. For example, it seems only simple good sense to explain why murder deserves more punishment than battery by pointing out that the harm done by killing someone is greater than the harm done by hitting him. The simpler the legal system, the more likely it is that the relation among crimes will be like that, one crime differing from another only in the seriousness of harm done. Perhaps this explanation's good sense has something to do with the enduring appeal of *lex talionis*.

Unfortunately, modern systems of criminal law are not simple. They include many laws differing from one another in more than harm. Consider, for example, whether killing someone through reckless operation of an automobile deserves more or less punishment than grabbing someone with the intention of throwing acid in his face. The automobile driver has, it seems, done more harm strictly speaking. He has caused a death while the would-be acid thrower may not actually have thrown the acid because, say, someone knocked the bottle from his hand just in time. The driver has recklessly violated the primary interest in life; the would-be acid thrower, only a secondary interest in not having acid thrown in one's face and a primary interest in not being grabbed and put in fear of serious injury. So, who deserves the greater penalty, the reckless driver or the would-be acid thrower?

Most defenders of *lex talionis* would, I think, answer that the would-be acid thrower deserves the greater penalty. If that is their answer, they have the support of many systems of criminal law. For example, in Illinois, the reckless driver who kills is guilty of a class-4 felony (one to three years imprisonment) while the would-be acid thrower is guilty of a class-1 felony (four to fifteen years imprisonment).[18] But, of course, giving the "right answer" is not enough. The defenders of *lex talionis* must also be able to get that answer in a way that helps us to understand why the criminal law does what it does (or, occasionally, why it should not do what it does). How would they get their answer?

The defenders of *lex talionis* would, I think, point out that there is more to proportioning punishment to crime than proportioning it to harm.

18. *Ill. Rev. Stat.* Ch. 38, secs. 9–3 and 12–4.1 (and sec. 1005–8–1).

All else equal, they might say, the ranking of harms corresponds to the ranking of deserved punishments. But in the case I have put, all else is not equal. I have, first, mixed different kinds of "*mens rea*" (and so, different kinds of "wickedness," "culpability," or "fault"). The driver was only reckless while the would-be acid thrower committed his crime intentionally. According to (what we may call) "the principle of culpability," a crime done intentionally deserves more punishment, all else equal than one done recklessly. Second, I have also mixed kinds of harm, a secondary interest in bodily integrity with a primary interest in life. That too affects deserved punishment. All else equal, an injury to a secondary interest deserves less punishment than an injury to the corresponding primary interest but not necessarily less than injury to *any* primary interest.

We must, I think, agree with the defenders of *lex talionis* that this is so. Having agreed, however, we must add that taking such considerations into account makes using *lex talionis* more difficult than seems desirable. For example, to determine whether the reckless driver or the would-be acid thrower deserves more punishment, we need to take into account not only the harm each did or threatened, but the *mens rea* of each. How are we to do that?

Defenders of *lex talionis* have had surprisingly little to say on this question. Kant simply urges that the criminal be made to suffer "according to the spirit—even if not the letter [of *lex talionis*] . . ." and then gives the examples of that spirit mentioned earlier.[19] The long history of retributism does not, I believe, provide any better explanation of how to apply *lex talionis* to "hard cases" of setting penalties (though much of criminal law consists of such hard cases).[20] If it were impossible to provide a better explanation as part of a theory otherwise at least as satisfactory as *lex talionis*, that failing would be no more unfortunate than our mortality, a misfortune to be lived with if we are to live at all. But, if there is an alternative theory that is otherwise at least as satisfactory and has more to say about scaling penalties than does *lex talionis*, the same failing

19. Kant, p. 133.
20. See, for example, Gross. On p. 438, he proposes to proportion punishment to "culpability" (which, for him, includes harm done or risked as well as *mens rea*), while on the next, he proposes to proportion punishment so that the criminal does not get away with his crime. But he can say nothing about how to do either except to argue that it is a "rational" decision. Perhaps he could have said more if he had seen that he had failed to distinguish *lex talionis* ("culpability") from the unfair-advantage principle (taking back the unfair advantage so the criminal does not get away with his crime).

is a serious weakness. I believe the unfair-advantage principle provides the basis for such an alternative theory.

Why have the defenders of *lex talionis* had so little to say about setting particular penalties? The answer is obvious. It is hard to say anything more helpful so long as one depends on *lex talionis*. What we need is some way to weigh a variety of considerations (at least four kinds of interest and several kinds of *mens rea* including purposefulness, intention, recklessness, and negligence). The problem bears an unpleasant likeness to that which a utilitarian theory of punishment faces. We could, for example, think of the weight of a certain secondary interest as equal to the product of the primary interest threatened and the probability of that threat being realized. So, if I attempt a crime with a fifty-fifty chance of success, my attempt would (all else equal) be half as bad as the complete crime. But, thinking in such terms requires cardinal numbers (or something very like them). *Lex talionis* would have to be arithmetic and so, to apply it, we would have to find some way to assign cardinal numbers to the various primary harms. We would, for example, have to be able to say how much worse is being killed than being disfigured by acid. Fifty percent worse? Two hundred percent worse? Or what? And we would have to be able to do the same for kinds of *mens rea* as well. Is intentionally committing a certain crime twice as bad as committing it recklessly?

The absurdity of such questions suggests either a deeper absurdity in any version of retributivism assuming *lex talionis* or a mistake in our understanding of *lex talionis*. My view is that it reveals a deeper absurdity. But, to be fair, let us assume that defenders of *lex talionis* can work out the mathematics necessary to handle comparison of different kinds of interest and different mental states, and then examine *lex talionis* under the most favorable conditions, that is, holding *mens rea* and kind of interest constant. Intentional crime will be compared with intentional crime, complete crime with complete crime, and so on.

Consider two crimes in which *mens rea* and kind of interest seem identical. For example, Illinois distinguishes between (ordinary) involuntary manslaughter and what is often called "vehicular homicide" (though Illinois calls it "reckless homicide"). While vehicular homicide is a class-4 felony (one to three years imprisonment), involuntary manslaughter is a class-3 felony (two to five years imprisonment).[21] Does *lex*

---

21. *Ill. Rev. Statutes*, Ch. 38, sec. 9–3 (and sec. 1005–8–1).

talionis help us to understand why these two kinds of manslaughter are punished as they are? It *seems* not. Manslaughter, whether "involuntary" or "vehicular," requires exactly the same *mens rea*, "recklessness," and the same harm, death. So, how can the defenders of *lex talionis* defend against what seems to be a clear counterexample to their version of retributivism?

They have at least three strategies open to them. One is to dismiss the distinction between "involuntary manslaughter" and "vehicular homicide" as an "anomaly," that is, as an indefensible distinction. The second strategy is to show that the two crimes, contrary to all appearances, violate different interests. The third strategy is to show that our example is not as "clean" as it should be, that is, that there is in it another factor *lex talionis* recognizes as relevant.

The first strategy would be tempting if Illinois were alone (or almost alone) in distinguishing between involuntary manslaughter and vehicular homicide. Unfortunately, the distinction has long been part of the criminal law of many jurisdictions, both American and foreign. So, dismissing the distinction as an anomaly would appear *ad hoc* without a powerful argument. That argument cannot (on pain of begging the question) rest on the principle that, all else equal, punishment should be proportioned to harm done. And it is hard to see on what other ground it could rest. So, the strategy of dismissal looks uninviting.

If the first strategy looks uninviting, so does the second. It is hard to guess what interest (ordinary) involuntary manslaughter violates that vehicular homicide would not violate as well. Death by automobile is seldom pretty and is often as painful as death by any means by which involuntary manslaughter is commonly committed. Still, with enough ingenuity, perhaps we could find some way to distinguish the interest harmed by involuntary manslaughter from the interest harmed by vehicular homicide. But the ingenuity required signals another problem with the second strategy. The greater the ingenuity required, the less intuitive what we find is likely to be.

That leaves the third strategy, showing the example not to be as "clean" as it seems. The strategy has some promise. It seems that, as soon as cars became common, juries began to refuse to convict of involuntary manslaughter drivers who recklessly caused death. Legislatures responded by creating a less serious crime of which juries were willing to convict drivers. Whether juries were reluctant to convict drivers of involuntary manslaughter because they thought, "There but for the grace of God go I," or because they considered driving to constitute a partial excuse for manslaughter, a cousin of duress or extreme temptation, or because of some other reason, is open to debate. It is, however, easy to see why juries might have thought driving a partial excuse. Living would be far less convenient if we did not drive, yet driving puts us in circumstances where it is easier to be reckless with life than it is in (ordinary) involuntary manslaughter. Since this is a general feature of conduct, it should be recognized by law as other such excuses are, not left to the discretion of the judge when sentencing.

This third strategy is not as *ad hoc* as it may seem. Legal theorists have long explained the distinction between ("second degree") murder and *voluntary* manslaughter in just this way. Voluntary manslaughter differs from murder neither in the harm caused, death, nor in the intention to kill. An intentional killing is voluntary manslaughter rather than murder if there are certain extenuating circumstnaces. In Illinois, for example, a killer commits voluntary manslaughter if he kills "under a sudden and intense provocation" or because he "wrongly believes himself to be acting in self-defense."[22]

Though obviously promising, the third strategy is not without problems. One problem is that thinking of voluntary manslaughter as partially excused murder seems more informative than thinking of vehicular homicide as partially excused involuntary manslaughter. "Provocation" or "mistake of fact" sounds more like an excuse than does "driving a vehicle" (or even "the convenience and difficulty of driving"). A more substantial problem is simply an extension of one discussed earlier. It now seems that *lex talionis* cannot be applied without a theory of excuses. Since that is so, we have a new layer of complexity in the setting of statutory penalties. We must weigh not only various kinds of interests and various kinds of *mens rea* but also partial excuses if likely to be widely shared by those doing the harm in question (all this without any guidance on how to weigh such things). The problem would be even more complex for a judge imposing sentence if the legislature left him with full discretion.

Any theory upon which intelligent people have long labored is likely to have the resources to answer almost any objection. The objections

22. *Ill. Rev. Statutes*, Ch. 38, sec. 9–2 (and sec. 1005–8–1).

made here are probably no exception. But, if each answer is bought at the cost of new complexity, the theory may become too expensive to hold, at least if there is a simpler alternative available. So, it would be useful to contrast the complexity to which *lex talionis* has already driven us here with the *relative* simplicity with which the unfair-advantage principle handles the same examples.

The unfair-advantage principle does not require us to distinguish harm, *mens rea*, and excuse in a statute like that prohibiting vehicular homicide. To find *what*, according to the unfair-advantage principle, we are to proportion punishment to, we need only determine the unfair advantage the criminal would take by violating the statute in question. One way to do that is to formulate a license that would pardon in advance one instance of that crime. Ordinarily, the formula of the license will be a simple paraphrase of the statute itself. Having formulated the license, we can determine *how much* unfair advantage the crime takes by comparing the value of licenses pardoning similar crimes (for example, with the value of a license pardoning involuntary manslaughter). That would place the crime in question (in our case, vehicular homicide) in a ranking of crimes.

But how (it may be asked) are we to compare the advantages such licenses represent without the same arithmetic *lex talionis* requires? The answer is simple. *Lex talionis* requires cardinal numbers because it requires us to agree (at least approximately) on both the degree we would assign each harm, *mens rea*, and excuse and the weight we would assign these factors relative to one another. The *lex talionis* presupposes a single point of view from which all this can be done. The unfair-advantage principle presupposes no such thing. Instead, it provides guidance on how to *construct* such a point of view (or, rather, its equivalent). Unfair advantage is, of course, a function of physical act, degree of *mens rea*, and so on just as harm (and fault) are in *lex talionis*. But, under the unfair-advantage principle, these factors can be weighed differently by different people (just as people may have widely different views about the relative value of houses and apartments) and yet provide the basis for agreement on what punishment is deserved (just as people can agree on what "the going rate" for this house or that apartment would be). How much unfair advantage an act takes is primarily a function of the social circumstances in which the act is committed (just as market price is). One way to represent that function, one I have found useful elsewhere, is as the result of auctioning pardons in advance for the relevant crimes under circumstances otherwise as close as possible to those of the society in question, consistent with getting a reasonable result. The procedure permits comparison (to the degree necessary) of relative seriousness of crimes without use of any numbers beyond what is necessary to indicate ordinal rank.[23]

Consider again the problem of explaining why vehicular homicide is punished less than involuntary manslaughter. According to the unfair-advantage principle, we can solve that problem by explaining why a license to commit the crime would be worth less than a license to commit similar crimes ranked above it. So, to explain why vehicular homicide should be punished less than involuntary manslaughter, we need only explain why a license to commit vehicular manslaughter would not be worth as much as a license to commit involuntary manslaughter. The explanation is obvious if we think of vehicular homicide as a special case of involuntary manslaughter (that is, as involuntary manslaughter with the "partial excuse" of "done with a vehicle"). A license to commit involuntary manslaughter would be more valuable than a license to commit vehicular homicide because (and just insofar as) a license to commit involuntary manslaughter in any way whatever is more useful than a license to commit it in only one way, by use of a vehicle. The unfair-advantage principle does not need a theory of excuses to reach this result (that is, a theory of what should count as an excuse). Whatever lowers the value of a license is relevant, whether it fits the general category of excuse or not. For example, the requirement that the involuntary manslaughter be done with a vehicle would reduce the value of a license to do involuntary manslaughter because committing involuntary manslaughter with a vehicle is inherently more risky than committing it in the other ways in which it is commonly committed (for example, by failure to provide one's patient with adequate medical attention or by careless use of a rifle). A rational person choosing between various acts of recklessness would, all else equal, prefer to be reckless in some way other than driving. If that is so, licenses for reckless driving would, all else equal, be worth less than licenses to kill by other means (even if a substantial portion of drivers did not share that preference). That being so, vehicular manslaughter would, according to the unfair advantage prin-

---

23. For examples of this, see papers cited above on rape, recidivism, attempts, and strict liability.

ciple, deserve less punishment than (ordinary) involuntary manslaughter (all else equal).

I have, it should be noticed, framed the problem as one of comparing a general license to commit manslaughter with a special license to commit a certain kind of manslaughter. This frame fits one statutory scheme, that is, the one in which a reckless driver who has killed someone could be charged under either the involuntary manslaughter statute or the vehicular homicide statute. This is not the only statutory scheme. Another scheme expressly excludes vehicular homicide from coverage under the involuntary manslaughter statute. I have not framed the problem to fit that scheme because doing so would have meant an argument more complicated than necessary for my limited purpose here. The argument I have given, whatever its faults, is enough to show how much easier to use than *lex talionis* the unfair-advantage principle can be. The argument also shows that the two principles are quite different in the way they work. We would not, for example, expect *lex talionis* to be as sensitive to the details of a statutory scheme as the unfair-advantage principle here seems to be.

V. Testing *Lex Talionis* Against Intuition

We have compared the ability of harm and unfair advantage to provide a measure of deserved punishment. While doing that, we implicitly considered whether the measure each provided fit our intuitive notions of justice. Discussion was limited to two crimes, recidivism and failing to report a bribe, but the results are worth recalling. It seemed the legislature could have good reason to make recidivism or failure to report a bribe criminal, good reason even though neither crime seems to constitute invasion of an interest. We did not consider whether punishment for such crimes would be just, and we must admit that there could well be controversy about how much punishment such crimes deserve. But neither example would have raised doubts about the adequacy of *lex talionis* as an explanation of the criminal law if punishing such crimes was clearly unjust. All retributive theories are theories of *just* punishment. They undertake to *explain* the criminal law only as an element of a relatively just legal system. If the crimes in question should not be crimes, we are not likely to be much concerned whether our theory of punishment can find a punishment for them or not. Our concern is more likely to be pointing out the anomaly and calling for repeal of the offending statute.

So, insofar as our earlier discussion succeeded in raising doubts about *lex talionis* as a measure of deserved punishment, it presupposes that punishing recidivism or failure to report a bribe could be just. We could, of course, now reject that presupposition. But, we could not reject it because of a *clear* intuition that punishing such crimes is unjust. If we had a clear intuition of that, we would have rejected those examples as they were presented. Since we did not, whatever reason we may have for rejecting them now, if we want to reject them now, the reason cannot be intuition. So, we must conclude from that earlier discussion that *lex talionis* seems to forbid punishment of some offenses as unjust the punishment of which does not seem unjust to us. *Lex talionis* is, in that respect at least, inconsistent with our intuitive notions of justice.

Of course, recidivism and failing to report a bribe, while not mere oddities, are not paradigms of crime. They cast doubt on the ability of *lex talionis* to help us understand the criminal law as we know it. But they still leave *lex talionis* wide scope. They make it harder to accept *lex talionis* without making it unreasonable. If we are to find anything more decisive, we shall have to find it among crimes constituting the central cases of criminal law. Yet, as we saw, finding appropriate examples there will be troublesome. Because application of *lex talionis* to such crimes is at least complicated, we are not likely to know what punishment *lex talionis* would recommend for such crimes. If we cannot know that, we cannot tell whether our intuitions diverge from what *lex talionis* would recommend. And if we cannot tell that, we cannot test *lex talionis* any more than we have already.

It may seem that this disposes of further testing too quickly. We can (it might be said) work case by case, making comparisons just as we would for the unfair-advantage principle. There would be no decision procedure, but we could know when we had an answer. If our arguments for a particular crime being "worse" than another succeeded in convincing all rational persons concerned, we would know what *lex talionis* required. We could then test that answer against the criminal law as it is, the unfair-advantage principle, or our own sense of justice, as we chose. There might (it would be admitted) be some cases where rational persons disagreed, but surely (it would be added) there are many about which all can agree.

Unfortunately, this approach to using *lex talionis* must be rejected here, though it might serve in another context.[24] Our concern now is to test *lex talionis* (and the unfair-advantage principle) against *our* intuitions. What the suggested approach amounts to is also determining what *lex talionis* says by our intuition. That would be permissible if the relevant intuition of justice were *not* closely related to our judgments of how bad crimes are. But, since these are virtually the same intuitions, the suggested approach would simply beg the question we wish to answer. For all we would know, the intuitive judgments upon which we had to rely could import the whole unfair-advantage principle into *lex talionis*. We could not know what we were testing.

Though this approach seems to beg the question, something much like it might not. I think we could avoid begging the question by using intuitions of gravity of offense other than our own and adopting some mechanical procedure to apply *lex talionis* to these. For example, we might conduct a survey of the general population to determine the ranking of common crimes according to harm (in the extended sense). If we selected common crimes so that all had the same *mens rea* (and none included any recognizable excuse), we could translate that ranking of crimes by harm into a ranking of crimes by criminal desert as *lex talionis* understands it. The ranking would, of course, be incomplete. We would not know how crimes of different *mens rea* or with an excuse would be ranked relative to the crimes already ranked. We would also not know what punishment the crimes actually ranked would deserve. We would only know that what was ranked lower deserved no more than what was ranked above. But, even that would be enough to test *lex talionis*. If the ranking (more or less) fit our intuitions about what crimes deserved more punishment, *lex talionis* would at least be shown to fit our intuitions about what some common crimes deserve in punishment relative to one another. If, however, the ranking did not fit those intuitions, that would leave *lex talionis* with very little support where most of its support should be.

Sociologists can rarely provide the information legal theorists wish for. The technical problems tend to be insurmountable. Rarer is the wish granted before a theorist makes it. Yet, our wish for a survey of the general population concerning the ranking of crimes seems to have been granted several times over. For at least two decades now, sociologists have been

---

24. For example, this seems to be what Gross has in mind, pp. 439–440.

conducting such surveys. The results are intriguing. There seems to be a surprising degree of agreement among those surveyed concerning the ranking of crimes according to "seriousness." And this agreement itself seems to be principled rather than a mere reflection of what those surveyed happen to hear about existing statutes.[25]

Wishes granted are often like good fish filleted. There is always at least one bone to catch in your throat. The research in question is not all we could wish. Most researchers only asked those surveyed to rank crimes according to "seriousness." None provided a definition of "seriousness." Only one seems to have asked informants to go on to rank penalties according to "severity" or to assign penalties to crimes (and this survey was not intended to produce a ranking of crimes extensive enough for our purposes). No researcher asked informants to rank crimes according to harm done (or according to importance of interest invaded).

So, to use any of these surveys in the way we wish, we must make an assumption. We must assume that those surveyed meant by "seriousness" what we mean by "harm" or "importance of invaded interests" (that is, that they were answering a question about deserved punishment as *lex talionis* understands it). The assumption is not unreasonable. Researchers may be forgiven for not asking informants to rank crimes according to harm done. Asking that might well have led informants to consider only the primary interests invaded or even only the physical harm done. In contrast, "seriousness" seems a fair translation of "importance of invaded interests." Or, at least, it should seem so to one who believes (as defenders of *lex talionis* seem to) that *lex talionis* is common sense and if the crimes to be ranked all have the same *mens rea* (as indeed most do) and include no excusing conditions (as most do not). We have as good a test of *lex talionis* as we are likely to get. What follows?

The survey results do correspond in a rough way with normal statutory schemes and with our intuitions of what crimes deserve most punishment. But there are also striking disparities. And, the more detailed the crime descriptions used in the survey, the greater the disparities. One survey will be enough for our purposes. Consider the highly respected and often cited 1974 study by Rossi, Waite, Bose, and Berk: "Planned killing of a policeman" and "selling heroin" are among the top three

25. V. Lee Hamilton and Steve Rytina, "Social Consensus on Norms of Justice: Should the Punishment Fit the Crime?" *American Journal of Sociology* 85 (1980): 1117–44.

crimes. "Assault with a gun on a policeman" and "kidnapping for ransom" are ranked eleventh and twelfth, respectively. Ranked fifteenth is "*assassination* of a public official," just *below* "killing someone after an argument over a business transaction" and just above "making sexual advances to young children." "Beating up a child" is ranked thirtieth, between "armed holdup of a taxi driver" and "armed robbery of a neighborhood druggist." "Spying for a foreign government" is ranked forty-fifth, just between "armed robbery of an armored truck" and "killing a pedestrian while exceeding the speed limit." "Forcible rape of a former spouse" is sixty-second, just below "neglecting to care for own children" (and substantially below "selling pep pills"). At 103 is "bribing a public official to obtain favors," between "using false identification to obtain goods from a store" and "passing worthless checks involving less than $100."[26]

There are other oddities in this ranking of 140 crimes. But I think these are enough to show that, if this ranking is indeed a ranking by importance of invaded interest, *lex talionis* is not a principle of the criminal law as we know it (or, at least, not an important one). What legal system we know of would, for example, treat assassinating a public official as substantially *less* serious than assaulting a police officer with a gun? Such examples also make clear that there is a significant difference between *lex talionis* and our judgment of which crimes deserve most punishment. Even someone who favors capital punishment for assassins is unlikely to favor it for merely assaulting a police officer (and perhaps not even for selling heroin).

But there is something else about this list that deserves notice, something that may help to explain the enduring appeal of *lex talionis*. We can, I think, often understand why those surveyed might have responded as they did, even though we would not want (legal) punishment to be apportioned according to those responses. Indeed, often we might have responded similarly. But if we did, it would, it seems, be because we were answering a question about something other than deserved punishment,

26. Peter H. Rossi et al., "The Seriousness of Crimes: Normative Structure and Individual Differences," *American Sociological Review* 39 (1974): 224–37, esp. pp. 228–29. These results are so bizarre that many philosophers are tempted to dismiss them out of hand (when it is necessary to understand both their appeal and ultimate irrelevance). So, perhaps it is worth pointing out that it is not only foggy-minded sociologists who have taken this study seriously. Among those citing it respectfully is the U.S. Supreme Court in *Solem v. Helm*, p. 292.

for example, about what we consider morally more blameworthy or personally more threatening. While it seems reasonable that such considerations should have some place in determining deserved punishment if a legal system is to maintain the allegiance of its subjects, it also seems that, as a matter of fact, they need not have all that large a place. That is why our intuitions of what the law should be do not seem to fit *lex talionis*, at least as represented in this survey's results.

We must conclude then that *lex talionis* cannot be the principle by which we proportion punishment to crime or the principle according to which we make intuitive judgments of proportion between punishment and crime. Must we draw the same conclusion concerning the unfair-advantage principle? Are the survey results we have been examining as damaging to that principle?

The answer is, I think, no. There are at least two reasons: First, such survey results cannot damage the unfair-advantage principle the way they damage *lex talionis* because the surveys asked the wrong question for determining relative unfair advantage. To get results directly relevant to the unfair-advantage principle, a survey would, for example, have to ask people to rank licenses to commit various crimes according to how much they would be willing to pay for them (as in so-called "market research surveys"). Second, the resulting ranking would itself only be raw material. The ranking would have to be fed into some economic model to determine what the fair market price of each license would be. Such a model would have to take into account both demand for the crime (that is, how many potential criminals are willing to commit the crime at a certain price) and supply (that is, how many such crimes society is willing to license). It seems then that the ranking such a model would generate is not likely to have more than the roughest resemblance to a ranking derived directly from the survey.

While the economic model is only one way to represent the constraints the unfair-advantage principle puts on what can be deserved punishment, it does provide an especially graphic way to understand both the critical power of that principle and the relation of unfair advantage to *lex talionis*. The harm the criminal might do is, of course, relevant to how much of a certain sort of crime society will want to tolerate (and so to how many licenses it might put up for sale). Societies fear harm and will want to keep it to that minimum consistent with its other objectives, for example, a reasonable liberty or reasonable police budget. That is why *lex talionis* can make some sense of the criminal law as it is. The reason it cannot make more sense of it is that considerations of fairness do not allow society to apportion punishment simply to prevent harm. There is more to criminal desert than that. *Mens rea* is also relevant, as most forms of *lex talionis* recognize. But so is the "price" a criminal pays to undertake a certain crime (apart from the possibility of punishment). If committing a crime itself involves considerable risk to the criminal, then (all else equal) he deserves less punishment than would someone else committing an equally harmful crime with the same *mens rea* but with less risk to himself. *Lex talionis* cannot recognize such considerations except in the catchall category of "excuse." That is why it has such difficulty explaining the penalty for crimes like vehicular homicide. *Lex talionis* makes harm more central to punishment than it should be.

My frequent appeal to economics may suggest another objection to the unfair-advantage principle. That principle cannot (it might be said) be the principle implicit in the criminal law as we know it because the economic models appealed to seem to require more information than legislators usually have and more mathematical sophistication than they have had at their command until quite recently. The objection is correct insofar as it rejects the possibility that legislators (and judges) could explicitly engage in the sort of reasoning our auction involves. But I do not claim otherwise. All I claim is that such models provide a way of picturing their (and our) conception of criminal desert in much the way that economic models help us to understand why prices are what they are. I have elsewhere set out the procedures I think legislators (and judges) actually follow.[27] These correspond to the very rough-and-ready way most of us decide what price to pay for this or that. They do not require the sort of information my auction requires. But they also do not contribute to our understanding of what we do in the way that a model can, even if the model requires assuming that in practice we have information (or other resources) we can at best only approximate. Interestingly, *lex talionis* seems never to have suggested any model, only regulative metaphors like "an eye for an eye."

I conclude that retributivists should give up *lex talionis* for the unfair-advantage principle.

27. "How to Make the Punishment Fit the Crime," esp. pp. 736–42.

A. JOHN SIMMONS

Locke and the
Right to Punish

I

Most philosophical discussions of punishment focus in one way or another on the question, "When is punishment just?" Even a brief glance
at these discussions, however, reveals the many different ways in which
that question may be understood. We might, for instance, take it to be a
question about the *kind or amount* of punishment that is just in response to various offenses, or a question about *who* can be justly punished, or a question about *when* (if) punishment is the proper response
to crime or wrongdoing at all. The array of possible answers to these
three versions of the question, and observations about the ways in which
these answers must be related to one another, are well displayed in contemporary philosophical literature on punishment. There is, however, a
fourth way of understanding the question, which is not so often touched
on in the literature on punishment because it places the question more
squarely within the province of political philosophy. This interpretation
makes the question one about authority and the "right to punish." What
makes it just for a particular person or group to punish us, instead of
some other person or group?

What is distinctive about this fourth interpretation of the question
"When is punishment just?" is that the kinds of answers often given to
the other three interpretations seem quite feeble when offered as answers to this one. While one may be convinced that the practice of pun-

This article is a shortened version of a chapter in my forthcoming book, *The Lockean
Theory of Rights*, to be published by Princeton University Press. I am grateful to Nancy
Schauber, George Klosko, Julian Franklin, and the Editors of *Philosophy & Public Affairs*
for their very helpful comments on recent drafts of the article, and to audiences at many
schools for their questions about much older drafts.

ishment is justified by its social utility (its deterrent value), it is much harder to believe that just *anyone* may rightfully punish (and so deter) others, or that the person or group that may rightfully punish another individual is that person or group whose doing the punishing would maximize total happiness (or most effectively deter crime). This latter position might entail that citizens of country A could be justly punished for their ordinary crimes by the government of country B, provided only that this arrangement would be maximally useful. And again, while one might be convinced that only those who deserve punishment may be justly punished, and only then to the extent deserved, it is much harder to believe that just anyone may rightfully punish those citizens who deserve it, or that those who most deserve to do the punishing are the ones entitled to do so. Neither one's general level of virtue nor one's particular talents in the area of punishing (e.g., special aptitude for being a judge, jailer, or executioner) are normally taken to establish any special claim to be the one who should punish others.

When we ask what makes it just for a particular person or group, rather than another, to punish some person, the answer that seems most natural concerns neither utility nor desert. It is not that our governments deserve to punish us, or that their doing so maximizes happiness; it is rather that they have authority or the right to do so. Locke put the point thus: "To justify bringing such evil [i.e., punishment] on any man two things are requisite. First, that he who does it has commission and power to do so. Secondly, that it be directly useful for the procuring of some greater good. . . . Usefulness, when present, being but one of those conditions, cannot give the other, which is a commission to punish."[1] The natural answer to our question makes central reference to authorization and rights, and it has been the natural rights tradition in political philosophy that has emphasized this point most forcefully. According to that tradition, one person (A) may justly punish another (B) only if either (1) A has a natural right to punish the crimes (wrongs) of B, or (2) B has alienated to A or created for A by forfeiture a right to punish B for B's

---

1. *A Second Letter Concerning Toleration,* in *The Works of John Locke* (London: Thomas Davison, 1823), 6:112. Locke seems to have the same point in mind when he distinguishes between the justifications of punishment on the separable grounds that "it is effectual" and "it is just" (Lord Peter King, *The Life of John Locke* [London: Colburn and Bentley, 1830], 2:113).

crimes (wrongs). This position cannot, I think, adequately be characterized as either purely utilitarian or purely retributivist.[2]

It will not be my purpose here to evaluate the entire natural rights
position on punishment, or to explore its relations to other views (e.g.,
whether it is consistent with or even reducible to retributivist or deterrence views).[3] I wish to concentrate on only one aspect of natural rights
theory's claims about punishment, a position shared by classical natural
rights theorists (such as Grotius and Locke) and contemporary ones
(such as Nozick and Rothbard). All persons in a state of nature, these
authors claim, have a moral right to punish moral wrongdoers. This "natural executive right," of course, plays a central role in Locke's account of
how a government can come to have the right to punish its citizens (as
it must in any Lockean account of these matters), and Locke's defense
of the executive right is the best known of the classical defenses. I will,
accordingly, focus much of my attention on Locke's arguments and possible extensions or developments of them. But any theory of punishment
must either accommodate or reject this right, so my discussion of
Locke's views should prove of more than purely historical interest.

The motivation for defending the natural executive right seems reasonably clear. Locke and other philosophers in the natural rights tradition have normally wanted to claim that all political authority (or
"power") is artificial, and so must be explained in terms of more basic,
natural forms of authority. Governments have rights to limit our liberty,
for instance, only insofar as they have been granted those rights by us;
we, however, possess these rights naturally (or, rather, are "born to" a
basic set of moral rights). Governmental rights, then, are simply composed of the natural rights of those who become citizens, transferred to
government by some voluntary undertaking (e.g., contract, consent, or

2. By which I do *not* mean to claim that, e.g., utilitarians do not have alternative accounts of authority and the right to punish.

3. Ted Honderich, *Punishment: The Supposed Justifications* (Harmondsworth, Eng.:
Penguin, 1971), pp. 158–62. I do not believe that rights theories of punishment collapse
(as Honderich argues) into retributivism. I trust that my argument below (Section IV) will
show why this need not happen, since fairness, not desert, is the central notion at work.
Honderich now classes rights theories as "rights retributivism," one form of the "new retributivism," with another being "restorative retributivism" ("Punishment, the New Retributivism, and Political Philosophy," in *Philosophy and Practice*, ed. A. P. Griffiths [Cam-
bridge: Cambridge University Press, 1985], pp. 117–47). The theory I outline below utilizes
both "rights" and "restorative" elements. Contemporary defenders of rights theories of punishment include Alan Goldman, Thomas Hurka, Vinit Haksar, and Warren Quinn.

the granting of a trust). This transfer of rights may go unobserved by some (as when consent is "tacit" only), but it must take place if government is to have any *de jure* power. However beneficial and fair the practices and policies a government enforces, it has no right or authority to enforce them against an uncommitted "independent."[4]

The same story can be told about a government's right to punish criminals. This right, like all governmental rights, must be composed of the redistributed natural rights of citizens, rights that the citizens must therefore have been capable of possessing in a nonpolitical state of nature. It is hard to deny that governments do, at least sometimes, have (or are capable of having) the *de jure* authority or right to punish criminals. But if they do, the argument continues, persons in a state of nature must also, at least sometimes, have the right to punish wrongdoers. From what other source could a government have obtained its right?

Locke was surely correct when he guessed that this would seem "a very strange doctrine to some men."[5] Critics in Locke's own day were uncomfortable with the idea of a natural right to punish, and contemporary philosophers have been quite solidly against it. We naturally tend to think of the right to punish as something denied private persons and possessed only by special authorities within a carefully defined institutional framework. The "private application of force," at least in matters of punishment, seems both institutionally and morally indefensible.[6] But these views are mistaken, according to the natural rights theorist; they are true only of private punishment in *civil* society, where government must have a "monopoly on force."[7] Perhaps the view that *all* private pun-

---

4. John Hodson, *The Ethics of Legal Coercion* (Dordrecht: Reidel, 1963), p. 117.

5. *Second Treatise*, para. 9. Subsequent references to the *Two Treatises* will be by I or II, followed by paragraph number.

6. Hugo Grotius, *De Jure Praedae Commentarius*, trans. G. Williams and W. Zeydel (Oxford: Oxford University Press, 1950), bk. VIII (question VII, article I), p. 89. Grotius's purpose here is to explore the general justifications for the private use of force (i.e., in his terms, what "causes justly give rise to private wars"). In discussing "the fourth cause" of just private war, namely, wrongdoing, Grotius is led to a defense of the natural executive right. Parallel, but less complete, discussions of these matters occur in *De Jure Belli ac Pacis Libri Tres*, trans. W. Kelsey (Oxford: Oxford University Press, 1925), bk. II, chap. xx. Grotius's views were, of course, extremely influential within the natural rights tradition. See Richard Tuck, *Natural Rights Theories* (Cambridge: Cambridge University Press, 1979), pp. 62–63.

7. Note Locke's claim: "For all force (as has often been said) belongs only to the magistrate, nor ought any private persons at any time to use force unless it be in self-defense against unjust violence" (*A Letter Concerning Toleration*, in *"The Second Treatise of Civil*

ishment is indefensible arises solely from the fact of our constant exposure to institutionalized forms of punishment. Be that as it may, the institutional authority can be explained only by conceding the existence of
a natural executive right. And further, when we really set our minds to
the task, the idea of a nonpolitical or prepolitical right to punish seems
less and less counterintuitive. For the early natural rights theorist, it was
not at all implausible to point to the prepolitical authority to punish
wrongdoers possessed by God and by fathers. And there are ample scrip-
tural grounds for concluding that God intended all persons to have such
authority, as the earthly executors of his law.[8] But even if we insist on a
secular foundation for natural rights theory, "Is the general right to punish so counterintuitive? If some great wrong were committed in another
country which refuses to punish it (perhaps the government is in league
with, or is itself, the wrongdoer), wouldn't it be all right for you to punish
the wrongdoer, to inflict some harm on him for his act?"[9]

Is Locke's "very strange doctrine" defensible after all? It is important
to see from the start that, properly understood, the idea of a natural right
to punish can have a strong intuitive appeal; it can seem hard to deny
that free and equal persons would have a right (or be morally at liberty)
to punish in at least certain kinds of states of nature (remembering now
that persons can be in the state of nature not only *before* the institution
of government, but also after its collapse or during the rule of a despotical government).[10] Imagine that, for whatever reason, your society "dis-
solved" into disorder and chaos. Once again in your natural state, unpro-

---

Government" and "A Letter Concerning Toleration," ed. J. Gough [Oxford: Blackwell,
1947], p. 132).

8. Grotius, for instance, cites Judges 15 (Samson's punishment of the Philistines) and
Genesis 9 ("Whoso sheddeth man's blood, by man shall his blood he shed") as supporting
a natural executive right (*De Jure Praedae Commentarius*, bk. VIII, p. 90). Locke follows
Grotius in citing Genesis 9:6 (along with Genesis 4:14) for support (II, 11). Neither author
cites those passages that seem to support the view that only God has the right to punish:
e.g., Romans 12:19 ("Vengeance is mine, I will repay, says the Lord") or Genesis 4:15 ("If
anyone slays Cain, vengeance shall be taken on him sevenfold"). See Thomas Pangle, *The
Spirit of Modern Republicanism* (Chicago: University of Chicago Press, 1988), p. 303.

9. Robert Nozick, *Anarchy, State, and Utopia* (New York: Basic Books, 1974), p. 137.
The "wouldn't it be all right" formulation here suggests a liberty to punish, rather than a
full claim right to do so. As we will see, however, Locke *disagrees* with Nozick about the
rights of *citizens* in legitimate polities to punish alien citizens. Locke's claims (and mine)
in fact concern only the rights of some individuals in the state of nature.

10. Some take such a denial to be "implausible on its face" (Charles Sayward, "Anarchism and Rights Violations," *Crítica*, April 1982, p. 110).

tected by the rule of law, you witness a man brutally robbing and murdering a defenseless victim. If it were within your power to do so, would you not feel justified in seeing to it that the murderer suffered for his crime? Would there be anything morally objectionable in your inflicting on him some harm, either to save others from his atrocities or (supposing you somehow know that he will commit no more) simply as a response to *what he did*? Would not anyone in that state of nature have a right to *punish* him for his moral crime? If you are in any way tempted to answer yes, there are obvious reasons to think more about the executive right. But even if your inclination is to say no, theoretical considerations may persuade you to excise this belief from your set of "considered judgments" about morality. And if you eventually accept the idea that there is such a right, as we will see, you will be hard-pressed to reject the natural rights tradition's account of the origin of the *state's* right to punish.

Now I would not want to appear to be placing too much weight on (as yet) undefended intuitions. They are, at best, only a provisional starting point. If there are sound theoretical grounds for rejecting the idea of a natural right to punish, then we must, of course, discount intuitions to the contrary. And contemporary philosophers have certainly argued that there are such theoretical grounds. Their criticisms of the natural right to punish can, I think, fairly be reduced to three main claims: (1) The very idea of a natural right to punish involves a fundamental confusion, or even incoherence; (2) One cannot, in any event, give a satisfactory account of the origin and nature of the natural right to punish; and (3) If we begin with a private right of punishment, we can give no persuasive account of how a just government can come to have an *exclusive* moral right to punish wrongdoers. I deal with the first of these criticisms elsewhere.[11] Here I will try to respond to (2) and (3), arguing that a Lockean theory of rights has available to it the resources to deal with these attacks.

In addition to these quite basic complaints, of course, it may seem that even those who *share* my intuitions in the case just described will probably also have intuitions about punishment that Locke and the natural rights tradition would seem to want to reject—for instance, that private citizens even in a just state would be justified in punishing a criminal

11. In chap. 3, sec. 3, of my forthcoming book, *The Lockean Theory of Rights*.

whose cleverness made legal punishment impossible, or that private citizens in one country might justifiably punish a criminal in another, if
both governments refuse to punish him. I believe that none of the objections mentioned above is convincing and that there is good reason to take
seriously the idea of a natural right to punish. I begin this task by examining the case for a natural executive right as it was presented by its
most famous advocate.[12]

II

In chapter II of the *Second Treatise*, Locke argues that in the state of
nature all persons enjoy an equal right to punish violators of the law of
nature, that is, those who "invade" the rights of others:[13] "The execution
of the law of nature is in that state [i.e., the state of nature], put into
every man's hands, whereby everyone has a right to punish the transgressors of that law to such a degree, as may hinder its violation" (II, 7).

While the exercise of this right in a state of nature is necessary to give
force to natural law, it is also a great inconvenience. Because people will
tend to be partial toward themselves and their friends, they will not always properly use this right to punish. They may punish excessively, or
where there is no guilt at all, which will prompt a similar response from
the ones punished, and "confusion and disorder" (or a state of war) will
follow (II, 13). What is needed, of course, is a common judge standing
over them all, and authorized to decide the proper remedy for conflicts
between them.[14] If each surrenders his right to punish to such a judge,
each will profit from the greater security and consistency of decision that
will result. This, of course, is one of Locke's main arguments for the
desirability of civil society, his main response to the anarchist. Life under
government is preferable to life in a state of nature at least largely because of the improved procedures for the rightful punishment of criminals. Indeed, the transfer of the executive right from citizen to common

---

12. For a concise recent summary of Locke's views on punishment, see James Tully,
"Political Freedom," *Journal of Philosophy* 87 (1990): 517–18.

13. Locke calls this right the "executive power of the law of nature" (II, 89).

14. This view—i.e., that the partiality of each in judging for himself is what makes government necessary—was already present in Locke's early *Two Tracts on Government*
(Cambridge: Cambridge University Press, 1967). See *First Tract*, pp. 137–38.

judge (i.e., the state) is so important to Locke's justification of civil society that he at times seems to *define* political society in terms of this transfer having occurred. The citizens' executive rights, once entrusted to government, become the executive power of the state.

Locke's defense of a natural executive right, then, lies at the very heart of his political philosophy.[15] For this reason, if no other, we should be careful to understand his claims. First, Locke is not claiming that each person in a state of nature has an unlimited right to treat a criminal however he pleases. While "every man in the state of nature has a power to kill a murderer" (II, 11), "lesser breaches" of the law of nature must be punished less severely (II, 12). The executive right is a right "only to retribute to him, so far as calm reason and conscience dictates, what is proportionate to his transgression, which is so much as may serve for reparation and restraint" (II, 8). Locke seems unconcerned about having here identified the limits to rightful punishment at once in both retributivist terms ("retribute" what is "proportionate" to the crime) and consequentialist terms (what is sufficient for "restraint"). During the remainder of the chapter, Locke talks almost exclusively like a consequentialist; but later in the text, retributivist language seems to dominate.[16] Similarly, while we have seen Locke's claim (in the *Second Letter Concerning Toleration*) that punishment, to be justified, must "be directly useful for the procuring of some greater good," in other portions of the same work he talks like a pure retributivist.[17] It may be, of course, that Locke is simply—and not very carefully—following the lead of Grotius, who maintained that while punishment should "fit the crime" as far as possible, punishment that accomplishes no substantial good end, in

15. Richard Ashcraft characterizes Locke's defense of the executive right (and of the possibility of others assisting in enforcing natural law) as "the whole point of the *Second Treatise*," since it is this position that legitimizes popular resistance against the king (*Revolutionary Politics and Locke's "Two Treatises of Government"* [Princeton: Princeton University Press, 1986], p. 332). I would put the point slightly differently. Locke cannot give up his defense of the natural executive right without surrendering as well the right of the people to punish a deposed king.

16. As in his talk of crimes "which deserve death" (e.g., II, 23). See also II, 11 and II, 87: "Man . . . hath by nature a power . . . to judge of, and punish the breaches of [the law of nature] . . . as he is persuaded the offense deserves. . . ." These passages are hard to square with Daniel Farrell's claim that Locke "neither suggests nor needs" the idea that punishment should be proportionate to desert ("Punishment Without the State," *Nous* 22 [1988]: 452). Farrell's Locke seems to be a pure consequentialist.

17. E.g., *A Second Letter Concerning Toleration*, pp. 71, 105.

terms of future consequences, should be avoided as unjust.[18] But we should notice that when Locke *employs* the right to punish in the arguments of the *Treatises*, he employs it as if it were a right to punish *all* wrongdoing, *not* as if it were a right to punish only when punishment can be shown to be directly useful.

Second, we should be sure that we remember what Locke means when he says that each person possesses the executive right in a *state of nature*. The state of nature is, of course, that state in which prepolitical man existed, but it is also the state into which each of us is born today, and in which we remain until we consent to join some commonwealth. It is the state to which we return when our political society dissolves (as in times of civil war), and perhaps also when our political leaders overstep the bounds of their rightful authority (i.e., cases of tyranny). It is the state in which all political rulers stand with respect to one another, and in which all citizens of one state stand with respect to citizens of another state.[19]

Third, Locke's position is not really that *all* persons in the state of nature with respect to others have the natural right to punish those others for their crimes. Children (those below the "age of reason") do not possess this executive right in spite of being in the state of nature with respect to all persons. Presumably the same is true of idiots, madmen, warmakers, and any other "persons" who do not qualify for Locke as full right-holders. Perhaps more important, Locke believes that when we join together to form a political society we must be understood not only to be agreeing to allow a common judge to exercise our executive rights in conflicts between us. We must also be understood to be entrusting to government the right to punish transgressors of natural law who are *not* members of our commonwealth. That right, thus entrusted, becomes the state's *federative* power (II, 145–48). As members of a legitimate civil society, then, we have no right to punish anyone. Our natural right to punish certain persons (those who become our fellow citizens) is entrusted to government as its executive power, while the natural right to

18. *De Jure Praedae Commentarius*, bk. VIII, pp. 93–104; *De Jure Belli ac Pacis*, bk. II, chap. xx. I take Locke to be committed to a moral theory that is neither purely consequentialist nor purely deontological. I discuss this in *The Lockean Theory of Rights*, chaps. 1 and 2.

19. Defense and explanation of these claims is provided in my "Locke's State of Nature " *Political Theory* 17 (1989): 449–70.

punish all other persons is similarly entrusted as the government's federative power.[20] In short, we have a natural right to punish those who
breach natural law only after we reach the age of reason (and while we
remain committed to the law of reason), and during those times when
we are not members of some legitimate political society.

We have seen one reason why Locke was so eager to defend the natural right to punish: it is difficult to understand how an artificial body
like a state could possess the moral authority to punish unless it received
this authority from persons who possessed it naturally.[21] But surely, it
seems reasonable to respond, a government might receive the right to
punish from citizens without it following that each person, prior to becoming a citizen, had a right to punish every wrongdoer. Locke's first
reply to such concerns—that the state of nature is a state of equal rights,
so that if anyone has a right to punish another, everyone must have that
same right (II, 7)—will not suffice. For might it not be the case that we
all equally possess a more *limited* right to punish—say, the right to punish criminals who victimize *us* (i.e., a right to punish held only by the
victim of a crime, not all mankind)? There would then be equal natural
rights, but no general right to punish just any violator of natural law;
and by entrusting these more limited rights to government, we would
still grant to our governors the right to punish any who violated the
rights of a citizen of the commonwealth.

Locke's response to this proposal has two parts. To the suggestion that
the victim has special rights against the criminal, Locke agrees, as we
will see. But the victim cannot hold the sole right to punish a wrongdoer,
for the victim is not the only one who suffers from a crime. In a sense,
Locke claims, mankind as a whole is the victim of every crime; every
offense is "a trespass against the whole species" (II, 8). Those who violate the rights of others cast aside reason as a guide to their actions, mak-

20. Locke earlier calls these two powers "the power of making laws" and "the power of
war and peace" (II, 88), though the first of these must also incorporate some of the *legislative* power.

21. There is, of course, a clear sense in which *the state* for Locke is perfectly "natural"—
i.e., there is every reason to suppose that persons (acting "naturally") will in fact create
states where they do not exist (indeed, they will be "driven" into them). See M. Seliger,
The Liberal Politics of John Locke (London: Allen and Unwin, 1968), pp. 221–23. But the
moral authority of states is for Locke created or artificial, not natural. Against Robert Fil-
mer, Locke argues that "governments must be left again to the old way of being made by
contrivance and the consent of men" (I, 6).

ing themselves a danger to all persons. Every person has a stake in protecting himself and others from future attacks, so every person shares in the right to punish the criminal.

These claims may seem extravagant. In what way can a harmless petty thief (or even a local bully) be seen as a threat to all mankind? The idea that someone who commits any kind of wrong against another is therefore liable to do all manner of immoral things to people far and wide seems a bit farfetched. On the other hand, if your neighbor (the victim of a violent assault, say) had sole authority to punish his sadistic attacker, and chose to be lenient, you might well feel that the "public element" of the crime gave you a right to try to more effectively deter that criminal from future attacks. Much more needs to be said about Locke's claim that every crime is against all mankind, and I will return to it later.

No one but the most eager disciple of Locke would be persuaded by the arguments thus far advanced that there is a natural executive right, or that we can explain a government's right to punish only in terms of a transfer of the executive right. Locke's insistence that God must have intended each person to be executor of His law obviously requires further support. And there are, of course, other arguments in the *Second Treatise* designed to provide this support. While only one of these is prominent in the text, it might be reasonable to ascribe to him two others as well.

1. Locke's language (in II, 7) might suggest to one the following view (though Locke nowhere in the *Treatises* explicitly states it): the ideas of duty and right (and, more generally, of morality) imply the existence of law. But there can be a real law only where there are sanctions attached to disobedience, where violations of the law are rightfully punished: "Where the laws cannot be executed, it is all one as if there were no laws" (II, 219). If, then, the law of nature is to be a genuine law, and the duties and rights it defines genuine, the law must rightly be backed up by physical force. Since it *is* a genuine law, binding even in a man's natural state, Locke supposes, someone in the state of nature must have the right to enforce natural law (and if someone has that right, everyone must have it, as we have seen). The internal sanction of the pangs of conscience that sometimes accompanies wrongdoing is insufficient to constitute real enforcement of the law. While little of this is stated in the *Treatises*, Locke does say such things in the *Essay*: "What duty is, cannot be understood without a law; nor a law be known or supposed with-

out a lawmaker, or without reward and punishment. . . . Since it would
be utterly in vain to suppose a rule set to the free actions of men, without
annexing to it some enforcement of good and evil to determine his will,
we must, wherever we suppose a law, suppose also some reward or punishment annexed to that law" (*An Essay Concerning Human Understanding*, 1.2.12, 2.28.6). The very idea of morality (and of law), Locke
seems to be claiming, implies a natural executive right.[22]

2. It is clear from the text that Locke believes there to be a strong
connection between the executive right and the right we have to preserve ourselves and others. The idea that a right to punish is somehow
implied by our right to defend ourselves or others was neither new with
Locke nor confined to philosophers in earlier centuries. Grotius, in the
earliest systematic defense of a natural right to punish, argued in this
way,[23] as do many of the most recent such defenses.[24] The idea they
share, presumably, is that insofar as punishment can serve as a means
for deterring future crime (both crime committed by the criminal punished and by others, suitably impressed by the example of his punishment), it is a way of defending ourselves against aggression by others. If
we have a right to defend ourselves, then, certainly we have a right to
employ one *means* of self-defense, namely, punishment of criminals.

It might be natural to respond to the line of argument suggested above
as we earlier responded to the claim that every crime threatens all mankind. Surely it is *not* true that our right of self-defense could justify punishing just any violator of natural law, as the executive right allows; for
some criminals seem to pose no real threat to our safety at all. Simple
considerations of self-defense are insufficient to derive a general right to
punish.

22. Leo Strauss has written as if this were Locke's *only* (or at least central) defense of
the executive right (*Natural Right and History* [Chicago: University of Chicago Press,
1953], p. 222). The text, of course, does not support such an extravagant claim (if, indeed,
Strauss intended to make it). But there are also reasons, as we will see, to doubt that Locke
had any such argument in mind.

23. *De Jure Praedae Commentarius*, bk. VIII, p. 91: "The causes for the infliction of
punishment are natural, and derived from that precept which we have called the First
Law." (The First Law is: "It shall be permissible to defend [one's own] life and to shun that
which threatens to prove injurious" [p. 369].)

24. See, e.g., Murray Rothbard, *The Ethics of Liberty* (Atlantic Highlands, N.J.: Humanities Press, 1982), p. 89 ("All rights of punishment derive from the victim's right of
self-defense"), and Farrell, "Punishment Without the State," pp. 443–44. Farrell's case is
actually (like Locke's) the more complicated view that self-defense is justified by the same
principle that justifies defense of other innocents, and hence punishment.

Locke seems sensitive to this worry, for his position is more complicated than the one just summarized. He in fact distinguishes between
two separate aspects of our executive right. Two legitimate aims of punishment, remember, are "reparation and restraint"; these two aims define distinct rights. All men have the natural right to punish transgressors of natural law for the purpose of restraining (deterring) criminals;
this right, however, derives *not* from our right of self-defense but from
our right of "preserving all mankind." From the narrower right of self-
defense (or self-preservation) that each of us possesses, Locke thinks,
we derive only a right to take reparation from a criminal when we have
been his victim: "The damnified person has this power of appropriating
to himself the goods or services of the offender, by right of self-preservation, as every man has a power to punish the crime, to prevent its being committed again, by the right he has of preserving all mankind" (II,
11).²⁵ Locke is not, then, committed to holding that considerations of
self-defense justify my punishing just any criminal in a state of nature;
such considerations do not, strictly speaking for Locke, justify *punishment* at all, but only the exacting of compensation. Whether this claim
is defensible or not, the important point for our purposes is that the executive right *is* implied, according to Locke (and more plausibly, I
think), by the more general right to preserve mankind.

3. We arrive finally at Locke's most prominently presented argument
for the executive right. Unless there is a natural right to punish, Locke
maintains, the ruler (government) of a state could never rightfully punish an alien who commits a crime in that state. Since rulers clearly *can*
rightfully punish alien criminals when they break the laws of the countries they are visiting, there must be a natural executive right (II, 9).
Locke's thinking here runs as follows: An alien is not bound by the laws
of the states he visits; he has not consented to the authority of those
states' governments. The alien remains in the state of nature with respect to those governments. If that is true, however, the government can
rightfully punish the alien only if it could rightfully punish him in the
state of nature (i.e., if the citizens who gave the government its rights

25. Note Locke's apparent claim that this second right cannot be transferred to civil
authorities, so that they might remit the requirement of compensation (II, 11). Locke is, I
think, better read here as saying that the transfer of this right is not to be *presumed* to be
part of *any* contract of government than as saying that the right literally cannot be transferred.

could have punished him in the state of nature). Since we all believe that the government *can* legitimately punish in such cases, we must accept the natural executive right as the only possible explanation of this fact. In punishing the alien, the state is merely doing what its citizens would have been entitled to do had they not left the state of nature by entrusting their executive rights to their government.[26]

III

We have now seen Locke's arguments for a natural right to punish. Let me examine them in turn.

1. Take first Locke's apparent argument that we cannot understand the idea of duty, or moral ideas generally, without supposing a natural right to enforce the duty (by punishing offenders). The argument really proceeds in three stages:

(a) Moral duty implies the existence of law.
(b) True law requires the likely application of rightful sanctions for breach of the law.
(c) The only possible sanction for natural (moral) law that is likely to be applied at all times is punishment by other men. For this punishment to be rightful, men must have a right to punish wrongdoers.

Even granting Locke the truth of (a) and (b) (and, of course, many of Locke's contemporaries would have done so), the truth of (c), the crucial

26. This argument will not, of course, convince anarchists or any who doubt that the state *can* legitimately punish aliens. Let me conclude this explanation of Locke's case for the executive right with a purely historical observation. In his notes to the argument just considered, Peter Laslett comments that Locke's language announced "that his doctrine of punishment was, or was intended by him to be, a novelty" (*Two Treatises of Government* [Cambridge: Cambridge University Press, 1963], p. 313n). On this point, see Wolfgang Von Leyden, "Locke's Strange Doctrine of Punishment," in *John Locke: Symposium Wolfenbuttel 1979*, ed. R. Brandt (Berlin: de Gruyter, 1981). Philosophers and political scientists have, by and large, accepted at least Locke's *arguments* for his "strange doctrine" as a novelty (see, e.g., Geraint Parry, *John Locke* [London: Allen and Unwin, 1978], p. 58). But it is worth noting that even Locke's last, central argument (concerning the punishment of aliens) was used previously by Grotius (*De Jure Praedae Commentarius*, bk. VIII, p. 92); and, as the earlier portions of my discussion have suggested, much of the rest of Locke's position seems also to have been borrowed from Grotius. Locke's original contribution on this subject lay not so much in the formulation or defense of the executive right as in his systematic presentation of its importance for political philosophy.

claim in the argument, still seems doubtful. Why is an appropriate sanction for natural law not the rightful sanction of divine punishment (or reward)? That God backs up natural law with sanctions "of infinite weight and duration" (*An Essay Concerning Human Understanding*, 2.28.8) is surely sufficient for it to count as "true law"; indeed, this seems to be *precisely* what Locke had in mind in the passages from the *Essay* quoted earlier. There is no need for the sanctions of a general executive right in order to explain the possibility of moral duty (and natural law), and Locke seems, rightly, not to insist that there is such a need in the *Treatises*.

What Locke *does* say in the *Second Treatise* is that "the law of nature would, as all other laws that concern men in this world, be in vain, if there were nobody that in the state of nature had a power to execute that law" (II, 7). While Locke is not holding that the sanction of the law is what *makes* it obligatory, he does hold that the law has no *point* without sanctions.[27] And God surely wants his law to have a point. But God's sanctions are not sufficient to compel widespread obedience, so the law of nature will not be effectively enforced in the state of nature. What we need is sanctions immediately applied in this life, not the next. Now Locke undoubtedly means all of this, but he *cannot* mean to conclude that there can be no "real" law of nature or true morality *unless* men enforce that law in the state of nature. For in the *Essay*, immediately after insisting that law requires sanctions, and that in the case of moral (divine) law the relevant sanctions are those applied by God, Locke comments that "the penalties that attend the breach of God's laws some, nay perhaps most men, seldom seriously reflect on: and amongst those that do, many, whilst they break the law, entertain thoughts of future reconciliation" (2.28.12). This observation that God's sanctions are insufficient to compel obedience does *not* lead Locke to doubt that the law of nature is a true law; quite the contrary.

The ineffectiveness of God's sanctions does not seem to force us to choose between accepting the executive right and rejecting natural law, on Locke's view. What Locke is thinking, I believe, is that where a good law is not being obeyed by those bound to do so, those to whom the law applies have a duty and right to assist in its enforcement. The only ap-

---

27. E.g., in *An Essay Concerning Human Understanding*, 2.28.6, and *Essays on the Law of Nature* (Oxford: Oxford University Press, 1965), p. 173.

parent basis for such a claim in the case of natural law, however, would be that since natural law promotes the well-being of those to whom it applies, our general duty and right to help preserve mankind requires and permits that we enforce that law. This, of course, brings us to the second of Locke's arguments for the executive right, and forces the conclusion that the first argument we considered neither has any independent force (as a defense of the executive right) nor was intended by Locke to have any.

2. I turn now to Locke's second argument for the executive right: that it is implied by our right and duty to preserve all mankind. This right is for Locke a particularly "fundamental" one, a trivial consequence of the fundamental law of nature (II, 6, 11). So let us accept it for the moment. Does a right to preserve mankind imply a natural executive right?

First, how are we to understand the idea of a right to preserve mankind? Presumably, like the right of self-defense, this right could be taken at least two ways. Construed narrowly, the right to preserve others might be viewed as a right only to help defend them when they are actually being attacked by others. More broadly, the right to preserve others could be taken to include not only the right to defend them, but also the right to protect them in other ways—such as by creating a "deterrent climate" or by preemptive attacks against those whose presence endangers them.

It is difficult to see how the former of these versions of the right to preserve mankind could naturally yield a right to punish, for punishment of a criminal involves far more than defending someone against his attacks; punishment begins where defense leaves off. Much more than the narrow right to preserve will be required to derive a right to punish. What about the broader version of the right? It would clearly justify more than simply punishment, since preemptive attacks on the dangerous might well include harming those who have not yet broken the natural (moral) law (in order to prevent their doing so in the future). But Locke's remarks elsewhere suggest that he might well be comfortable with this sort of consequence: people "have not only a right to get out of [tyranny], but to *prevent* it" (II, 220; emphasis mine). And while the broad version of our natural right to preserve mankind justifies *more* than punishment, it appears *also* to justify punishment. It will (sometimes) explain our right to harm in response to wrongdoing, since doing this will (sometimes) help to preserve mankind (by virtue of having, in many instances, beneficial deterrent effects).

Here, then, we have a first, Lockean argument for the natural executive right. This argument, of course, will not satisfy *secular* concerns
about the right to punish without independent derivation of the right to
preserve mankind (a derivation that may well be possible). But whether
presented in its religious or secular form, this argument simply cannot
account directly for *all* of what Locke wants in a natural executive right.
Locke seems most often to want to defend a right to punish *any* wrongdoer, not a right to punish that is conditional on the direct usefulness of
particular acts of punishing. But it is manifestly false that punishment
of wrongdoers will *always* be causally related to effective deterrence.
Some punishment neither advances nor can be reasonably believed to
advance the preservation of mankind. Only by further employment of
rule-consequentialist reasoning (i.e., by arguing that punishment *tends*
to deter crime) will a Lockean be able to draw from the right to preserve
mankind a right to punish every breach of natural law. And the appeal
of this style of reasoning is clearly limited.

3. Now for Locke's third and most prominent argument: that we cannot explain the rightful punishment of aliens unless there is a natural
executive right. What is striking about Locke's prominent presentation
of this argument is his total failure to see how badly it fits the overall
position he defends in the *Second Treatise* (indeed, it looks as if Locke
may have simply taken the argument from Grotius without seriously
considering its implications). For there seems to be an incredibly simple
refutation of the argument available, one that can be found in Locke's
own text. Locke is well known for his theory of tacit consent, according
to which any person who has "any possession or enjoyment of any part
of the dominions of any government" can be taken to have consented to
the authority of that government over him, "whether this his possession
be of land, to him and his heirs forever, or a lodging only for a week; or
whether it be barely travelling freely on the highway; and in effect, it
reaches as far as the very being of anyone within the territories of that
government" (II, 119).

The implication of these passages is clear: any alien, merely by freely
entering the territories of the state, can be taken to consent to its authority over him. The alien, we might say, has authorized the state to punish
him should he violate its laws. We can, then, explain the government's
right to punish aliens entirely in terms of Locke's own account of the

tacit agreement between government and alien.[28] No reference to a natural executive right seems necessary. The state's laws do "reach" (i.e., bind) the alien, for he is not in a state of nature with respect to the state once he enters its territories. He is a sort of "temporary member" of the commonwealth, like any resident or visitor who has not *expressly* consented to be a full member (II, 121–22).

Even more embarrassing for Locke is the following question: if we can explain the state's right to punish aliens without reference to a natural executive right, can we not similarly explain its right to punish *citizens*? Instead of starting with the assumption that each citizen has a right to punish everyone else, which he entrusts to government, why not assume that each citizen begins with only a right to control his own life (as it were, he has a right only to "punish" himself). Each citizen then entrusts a portion of this natural right of self-government to the state, authorizing government to punish him (i.e., control his life) for violations of its laws. The net result of all citizens so authorizing government, of course, would be that the government had the right to punish all citizens. This is the conclusion that Locke wants to reach; but, contrary to Locke's suggestions, it seems possible to reach it without appealing to a natural executive right. We can explain the right of governments to punish both citizens and aliens without having to suppose that any "natural man" ever had the right to punish another. And we can explain it in a way that is consistent with Locke's desire to show that all governmental rights are derived (by transfer in trust) from the citizens of the state.

This alteration in Locke's program seems even more desirable when we remember that if the government's right to punish is merely its citizens' executive rights, suitably transferred, the government's power to punish must be limited to cases where the law of nature has been transgressed. This, after all, was all that the natural executive right allowed. And while much of the behavior that a state will want to make criminal surely violates natural law, some clearly does not—for instance, violation of at least some tax laws, drug and "morals" laws, traffic and parking laws, and many other regulatory statutes hardly seems naturally immoral. How can we explain the government's right to punish in such areas? It is easy to reply that in addition to giving the state the right to

28. This seems to be what Jeffrie Murphy has in mind in "A Paradox in Locke's Theory of Natural Rights," *Dialogue* 8 (1967): 267. Farrell also notes the availability of this argument to Locke ("Punishment Without the State," p. 451).

punish violations of natural law, each citizen also gives up some further
portion of his right to control his life (justifying punishment in these
additional areas). This seems to be what Locke has in mind (e.g., II,
128–30).[29] But surely, if we must appeal to transfers of our natural right
of self-government to explain *parts* of the state's right to punish, it would
be theoretically more elegant to explain *all* of its right to punish in these
terms. We would also thus spare ourselves the effort of defending
Locke's "strange doctrine" of the executive right, telling Locke's story
entirely in terms of citizens entrusting to government portions of their
rights to govern themselves.[30]

What is wrong with this simpler, more elegant, revised Lockean account I have just outlined? Why did Locke not choose this course, with
all of its apparent advantages? We might speculate about his reasons.
First, Locke seems to have confusedly supposed that if all governmental
rights come from the citizens, and the government has the right to punish everyone, then some citizen must have had the right to punish everyone. And if any citizen had it, everyone must have had it. He seems not
to have considered that the government's right to punish might be composed, piecemeal, from the many and much more limited rights of citizens to "punish" themselves only. Second, there seems to be a serious
problem, on our revised account, about capital punishment. No person,
according to Locke, has the moral right to kill himself (nor is this morally
permissible) (II, 6). How, then, could government come to have the right
to punish us with death, if this right must have come from each citizen?[31] The natural executive right, of course, included the right to punish *others* with death (where appropriate), not ourselves. It might thus
be supposed to be transferred to government, justifying capital punishment, without Locke having to defend a right to commit suicide. I will

29. Contrary to C. B. Macpherson's apparent claim that Lockean government can do no
more than enforce natural law (*The Political Theory of Possessive Individualism* [Oxford:
Oxford University Press, 1962], p. 218).

30. This seems to be roughly the solution proposed by J.E.J. Altham (as a remedy to
problems in Nozick, not in Locke). Nobody has a right to punish others in a state of nature;
the government's right arises from individual contracts ("Reflections on the State of Nature," in *Rational Action*, ed. R. Harrison [Cambridge: Cambridge University Press, 1979],
pp. 140–41).

31. See Cesare Beccaria's related difficulties in deriving the state's right to punish
crimes with death from the individual transfer of rights in a contract of government (*On
Crimes and Punishments* [Indianapolis: Bobbs-Merrill, 1963], pp. 45–52).

say about this problem only that there are quite general difficulties in
Locke about capital punishment, of which this is only one.[32] Perhaps the
proper resolution of them, within a broadly Lockean framework, will require the abandonment of Locke's prohibition on suicide (which seems
to me, on independent grounds, a good idea). Third, Locke may have
been concerned about the revised account's apparent inability to ground
a *federative* right of government. Insofar as the federative right includes
a right to punish noncitizens, it is unclear how this could in any way be
derived from citizens' rights over themselves only.

There is, I think, a final and much more interesting problem with the
revised account proposed above, one of which Locke may well have been
aware (as I argue in Section VI). The revised account can succeed only
if there is no natural right to punish. My remarks thus far have suggested only that the revised account obviates the need to defend a natural executive right, but the point must be put more strongly. It is not just
that a defense of our revised account saves us the trouble of proving
Locke's "strange doctrine"; the revised account cannot *be* defended, if
there *is* a right of all to punish. I will elaborate on this point more fully
and explain the shortcomings of the apparently superior revised account
in Section VI.

IV

Locke does not always talk of our natural right to punish as something
derivable from our right to preserve mankind, itself a consequence of
God's positive authorization. There is in Locke another line about the
right to punish, one that he does not really distinguish from those we
have considered thus far. Sometimes, particularly where he is concerned
with war, Locke talks not as if the right to punish were a *general* right
all persons have as agents of God, but rather as if it were a *special* right
created by the criminal himself, in committing his crime. By breaching
the law of nature, a criminal *forfeits* certain of his natural rights, lowering moral barriers that previously existed against the infliction of harm.
This leaves others with a greater right to interfere in the criminal's life
and makes legitimate the punishment they may impose upon him. This

32. On these problems, see John Dunn, *The Political Thought of John Locke* (Cambridge: Cambridge University Press, 1969), pp. 126–27.

seems, at first blush, a plausible story about how punishment might become morally lawful in a state of nature. What is, perhaps, especially
attractive about this account is that it seems not to require any reference
to God's authority, making it an explanation of a natural right to punish
that would be consistent with even a purely secular theory of natural
rights, and with the secular strain of Locke's own thought, as we will
see.

Remarks about the forfeiture of rights are scattered through both of
Locke's *Treatises*, but no careful formulation of the doctrine is ever
given. In the *Second Treatise*, comments on forfeiture are most prominent in discussion of those cases where an individual forfeits *all* of his
rights by some act that deserves death. Murderers, and those who unjustly put themselves into a state of war against others (by declaring a
wrongful intention to take their lives), lose all of their rights (II, 85, 172–
73). All moral barriers to harming them are lowered, making punishment even by death rightful. It is only thus that arbitrary, despotical
power of one man over another is possible. (Locke also, however, keeps
the fundamental law of nature always in mind, for he observes that "even
the guilty are to be spared, where it can prove no prejudice to the innocent" [II, 159].) In the *First Treatise*, Locke speaks of less complete and
dramatic cases of the forfeiture of rights, as when a father forfeits his
rights over his children (I, 100). Presumably, the idea is that by performing acts contrary to natural law one forfeits that portion of one's own
rights against others that will make an interference in one's own life,
proportionate to one's interference in others' lives, morally permissible.[33]
The most serious offenses leave a criminal altogether rightless, like some
lesser animal, which may be used or killed at will.

This kind of account of the forfeiture of natural rights seems very
much like what some contemporary libertarians have had in mind. Murray Rothbard, for instance, writes that "the criminal, or invader, loses his
own right to the extent that he deprived another man of his."[34] And Robert Nozick puts it only slightly differently: "One might take a contract-

---

33. Locke does not have in mind (as we saw in Section II) that just *any* crime, no matter
how small, results in a forfeiture of *all* rights. See, e.g., T. H. Green, *Lectures on the Principles of Political Obligation* (Ann Arbor: University of Michigan Press, 1967), sec. 177,
and Alan H. Goldman, "The Paradox of Punishment," *Philosophy & Public Affairs* 9, no. 1
(Fall 1979): 44–45.
34. *The Ethics of Liberty*, p. 80.

like view of moral prohibitions and hold that those who themselves violate another's boundaries forfeit the right to have certain of their own
boundaries respected. On this view, one is not morally prohibited from
doing certain sorts of things to others who have already violated certain
moral prohibitions (and gone unpunished for this). Certain wrongdoing
gives others a *liberty* to cross certain boundaries (an absence of a duty
not to do it); the details might be those of some retributive view."[35] There
is one prominent difference between the views of Rothbard and Nozick
on forfeiture, however. Rothbard believes that the victim of a crime has
a special right, not shared by others, to punish the criminal; Nozick regards the right to punish as shared by "all mankind." This disagreement
in fact reflects a fundamental inconsistency in Locke's theory. Locke
seems to have not one doctrine of forfeiture, but two.

Sometimes Locke presents the simple picture of forfeiture described
above: criminals lose their rights, making punishment by any other person lawful. The criminal's right(s) simply disappears—for a time, that is;
it presumably returns to him when he has received his just punishment,
or perhaps when he is forgiven. This seems to be Nozick's version of
Locke, and a version consistent with Locke's insistence that *all* persons
in a state of nature have the right to punish criminals. At other times,
however (and, indeed, in the most prominent passages on forfeiture—
e.g., II, 23, 172), Locke talks as if the criminal's right were not simply
lost, but rather forfeited *to* or *with respect to* a particular party—namely,
the victim of the crime. The victim is the only person with the right to
punish, though he may, of course, enlist the aid of willing assistants.
This seems to be something like Rothbard's view. It implies, among other
things, that if Morton wrongs Swanson, and I attempt to punish Morton
for this, I wrong Morton by doing so, even if the punishment I apply to
Morton is the one he deserves (or the one that would otherwise be lawful
in kind and amount). Morton's moral barriers have been lowered only
with respect to Swanson, not the rest of mankind. Locke also talks as if
the victim of the crime has the right *not* to punish the criminal if he so
decides, which seems to make room for the virtue of *forgiveness*.[36]

35. *Anarchy, State, and Utopia*, pp. 137–38. Notice that W. D. Ross, like Nozick, characterizes the right to punish as a *liberty* (*The Right and the Good* [Oxford: Oxford University Press, 1930], p. 61).

36. "If [the criminal deserving death] be once allowed to be master of his own life, the
despotical, arbitrary power of his master ceases" (II, 172; see also II, 24). Locke also talks

However we may feel about forgiveness, it has to be admitted that this second line on forfeiture conflicts with many of Locke's most important claims about punishment. It is inconsistent with his view that the natural right to punish a wrongdoer is held by all persons, and it implies that one man may forgive (or be lenient in response to) what is a "trespass against the whole species." And it conflicts with Locke's claim that the victim's special right, entailed by his right to preserve himself, is a right to *reparation*. Nor is it a plausible position considered on its own merits. It has serious difficulty in cases where the victim is killed by the wrongdoer (who then has a right to punish?).[37] And, as Nozick has observed, punishment is "owed" to the criminal, not to the victim;[38] the criminal does not deserve to be punished *by the victim*. Locke, by noting the victim's special right to reparation, has already taken account of what is unique about the victim's position. We must, then, reject this second line of argument about forfeiture in Locke as perhaps implausible in its own right and as certainly inconsistent with more important features of Locke's theory.[39]

I have spoken approvingly of the first Lockean line about forfeiture, where rights are simply lost for a time. But much about this line of argument remains unexplained—and goes largely unexplained by Locke and most of the libertarian authors who have followed his lead. For instance, it should be made clear how heavily this account relies not only on a theory of natural *rights*, but on whatever theory is used to determine

---

as if magistrates (II, 11) or rulers (II, 159) may decide *not* to punish the guilty (and they are, after all, also only exercising the natural executive right). The possibility of forgiveness might seem to modify an essentially Old Testament conception of punishment with some New Testament sentiments.

37. Perhaps the solution might be that whoever inherits the other rights (i.e., property) of the deceased also inherits the right to punish his killer. But this solution seems to conflict with the general limits on inheritance Locke elsewhere discusses (see, e.g., I, 74, 98). Warren Quinn has suggested to me that we might understand the victim to have tacitly transferred the right to punish his murder in advance, as an obvious act of prudential rationality.

38. *Anarchy, State, and Utopia*, p. 138; Altham, "Reflections on the State of Nature," p. 142.

39. This is not to say that the second line is without advantages of its own. In addition to those mentioned below concerning exclusivity, for instance, the second line obviates some (but not all) concerns, also discussed below, about the *reasons* for which we may harm others. If the unjust aggressor simply forfeits rights (not *to* anyone), his *fellow* aggressors, who share his evil aims, may justly harm or kill him, for whatever bad reasons they may have. I try to show below that the first line can handle such worries.

what punishments fit the crime (a subject on which I will not even begin to comment here). As I have outlined it, the Lockean line on forfeiture makes central use of certain aspects of a retributivist theory of punishment; moral desert determines the degree of right-forfeiture that results from moral wrongdoing. Of course, this does not mean that the Lockean position just reduces to a pure retributivism, insofar as those who are rightly punishable are not simply those who *deserve* punishment, but only those who have also first violated the rights of another. (Thus, one who might seem to *deserve* punishment more than some minor violator of rights—such as one who constantly and deliberately humiliated others—might not be punishable on the Lockean account.) Desert determines only the extent of the forfeiture, by determining what constitutes an appropriate response to wrongdoing.[40] But only another's forfeiture of rights can give one (in Locke's language) a "commission" to punish him. Forfeiture makes it legitimate to give wrongdoers what they deserve.[41]

This may still leave us wondering, however, about *why* the violation of another's rights causes us to lose our own (to the extent deserved). The answer is surely not obvious, as defenders of the doctrine of forfeiture seem to assume. It is the "mystery" or apparent emptiness of the idea of forfeiture that has led critics in this century to reject it (e.g., critics of W. D. Ross and other intuitionists). When asked why punishment is justified, defenders of forfeiture say: because the criminal has forfeited his rights. But no account is forthcoming of *why* the criminal loses his rights on this occasion. As a result, it appears that saying the criminal forfeits his rights is saying nothing *more* than that punishing him is justified.[42] But we naturally want to be shown *why* this is justified, not simply have it asserted in a mysterious way.

Locke would appear to have several accounts available of why a criminal loses rights. One is that God has granted us our rights and chooses

40. This may, of course, be a more strongly retributivist view than Locke would have been happy with, given the consequentialist character of some aspects of his moral theory. It is possible to replace this retributivist account of the proper kind and amount of punishment with a consequentialist one, without altering the basic character of the Lockean program. But the result would, in my view, be a less plausible position.

41. Of course, to the extent that retributivism is taken to *include* the view that neither punishability nor the authority to punish is to be determined *simply* by considerations of moral desert, this is a "retributivist" stance.

42. Warren Quinn, "The Right to Threaten and the Right to Punish," *Philosophy & Public Affairs* 14, no. 4 (Fall 1985): 332–33.

to withdraw them when we violate his law.[43] Another is that rationality is a condition for being subject to natural law and a possessor of the rights that law defines. Since acting wrongly demonstrates some measure of irrationality (on Locke's view), it involves a loss of some part of the rights enjoyed by the fully rational. Neither line of argument is entirely persuasive. The first line, while it is clearly consistent with Locke's premises, will not help us in any attempt at a *secular* theory of forfeiture (and it retains a rather mysterious quality itself). The second line is unconvincing because wrongdoing is neither a necessary nor a sufficient condition for lack of full rationality.

But it is possible to give other accounts of forfeiture within a secular natural rights theory. Perhaps the most "natural" way to view forfeiture involves maintaining that any reasonable or fair system of protective, right-defining rules (laws, conventions) must specify that one's status under the rules depends on respecting them. Protection under the rules is contingent on our obeying them; any rights the rules may define are guaranteed only to those who refrain from violating them (independent, of course, of unanimous agreement to alternative arrangements). Surely no one could reasonably complain of being deprived of privileges under rules he refuses to live by. Indeed, to extend such privileges to those who break the rules would seem to involve serious and straightforward *unfairness* to those who limit their own liberty by obeying the rules. Of course, considerations of fairness also seem to dictate that a minor violation of the rules result in only a minor loss of status under the rules, and so on, so that the protection we enjoy under the rules will be proportionate to our own conformity to them. Insofar as there are objective *moral* rules (defining rights) under which all persons originally stand, and protection under the rules depends on others' obedience to them, then, a proportional forfeiture of moral rights may be a *necessary* consequence of infringing the moral rights of others.[44] Valid moral rules do not

---

43. If, as I believe, Locke thinks that rights are entrusted to us by God only for certain uses, it is perfectly natural that when abused, our rights return to God.

44. Thus no *consent* to loss of rights (as in Hegel) is necessary to explain the idea of rights-forfeiture. The moral work in the account is done instead by the idea of fairness. The Lockean can as a result avoid Hegel's problem of having to claim that any inalienable right must also be nonforfeitable. See Allen Wood, *Hegel's Ethical Thought* (Cambridge: Cambridge University Press, 1990), p. 121, on Hegel's problem. For a related forfeiture account of punishment, see Goldman, "The Paradox of Punishment," pp. 43–45. Goldman seems to be discussing legal rights in his account of forfeiture; it is not clear whether he would wish

extend protection to persons unfairly taking advantage of others' willing-
ness to abide by them. Locke occasionally uses language that suggests
an account of forfeiture based in natural fairness, as when he speaks of
punishment as "the abridgement of anyone's *share* of the good things of
the world."[45]

There is, of course, a "Kantian" rendering of this argument that would,
I think, be quite unobjectionable to Locke. One formulation of Kant's
categorical imperative of morality proscribes our using persons merely as
means to our own ends, just as Locke argues that we are not "made for
one another's uses" (II, 6). When we violate protective rules under
which all stand in ways that deprive others of their rights (or violate their
rights), we seem to be using others in a straightforward way. We use
their compliance and forbearance (which is motivated by their recognition of our equal standing under the law) as a means of securing greater
advantage for ourselves.[46] Rights forfeiture can thus be seen as what se-
cures the possibility of natural fairness and what renders impossible ongoing but morally protected patterns of (ab)use of others.[47]

V

Even if these sketchy suggestions about the ground of forfeiture are
found convincing or suggestive, of course, it may seem that serious prob-

---

to extend his analysis to natural rights (along the lines I have suggested). Herbert Morris
discusses punishment in terms of fairness in his well-known paper "Persons and Punishment." But he is not trying either to analyze *forfeiture* or to discuss *natural* punishment.
See also Ross, *The Right and the Good*, pp. 60–64.

45. King, *The Life of John Locke* 2:110 (emphasis mine).

46. See Murphy's discussion of Kant's own views on the unfairness of not punishing the
guilty (which is, of course, slightly different from the unfairness I describe here of persons
enjoying full moral protection while breaching the rights of others), in "Three Mistakes
about Retributivism," *Analysis* 31 (1971): 167–68. *Punishing* the guilty is *not* a case of
using them as mere means to our ends, on this account; for punishment is both required
by a moral principle of fairness (and hence is *not* justified simply by its consequences for
us) and responds to the free choices of persons to violate binding rules with their preestab-
lished sanctions.

47. It is worth noting another reason for suspecting that Locke might have been happy
to subscribe to this account of rights-forfeiture—i.e., to an account that centrally utilizes
the idea of "taking advantage" of others. Locke never suggests that those violations of natural law that involve only harm to *oneself* result in forfeiture of rights; only harm to *others*
is said to have this consequence. But self-harming violations of natural law *are* contrary to
reason and *do* endanger mankind (i.e., oneself as part of mankind), just like other-harming
violations. The only feature of other-harming violations that self-harming violations seem
to *lack* is their taking advantage of the sacrifices of others.

lems for this account will be caused by the fact that the right to punish as I have derived it can only be a "liberty right," not a full "claim right." If my right to punish arises from another's forfeiture of his own right, the right to punish must be only a permission, the absence of an obligation to refrain. It does not imply, as a claim right would, that others must not interfere with my actions. That is, though a wrongdoer's forfeiture of his right leaves me morally free to punish him, it does not obligate others to *allow* me to punish him. They, being also at liberty to punish, may "compete" with me to punish him first.

The situation would be slightly different on the second line about forfeiture, considered and rejected above. For on that account, only the victim has the right to (is at liberty to) punish; the victim's liberty right is thus an *exclusive* liberty, not in competition with the liberties of others. Others could not punish the criminal first (this would violate the *criminal's* rights), nor could they interfere with the victim's lawful punishment of the criminal (for that would infringe the victim's right of self-government—his right not to be hindered by others in his lawful pursuits except by their *competition*). Thus, the exclusive liberty the victim would have on the second (unsatisfactory) account of forfeiture would have moral consequences similar to the victim's having a full claim right to punish. It may seem a shame not to pursue this account further, for is not this kind of exclusivity of the right to punish (i.e., the guarantee of freedom from interference) exactly the property we wish our *government's* right to punish to have? Do we not believe that legitimate governments have a right, in the full sense, to lawfully punish criminals, a right that includes an obligation on citizens not to interfere or try to punish the criminal before the state does (this is the so-called monopoly on force that governments are supposed to claim and that excludes, among other things, vigilantism)? We need to explore the potential of the *first* account of forfeiture (the one I have chosen to defend over the second account) to provide a solution to this problem of explaining the exclusivity of the legitimate government's right to punish.

Suppose, as the first account maintains, that Butch commits crime (moral wrong) C, for which punishment P is appropriate, according to natural law. Butch forfeits certain of his rights, making it morally permissible for me or any other person to impose P upon him (subject to the limit that no more than a total punishment of P be imposed). Just how strong a "right" to punish does this liberty give me? Well, what kinds of justifications might another person, Chico, have for interfering with my imposing P on Butch? First, Chico might think Butch deserved punishment Q, instead of P, and as a result believe himself justified in imposing Q and resisting my imposition of P. Or he might think Butch innocent altogether, and feel justified in defending Butch against me. Or he might oppose punishment generally and argue that he was justified in stopping my punishment of Butch. Finally, Chico might want to punish Butch himself, and compete with me to impose P.

Only the last of these could be a successful defense of Chico's interfering with my punishing Butch with P; and even this would not justify Chico's physically impeding my punishing. Chico's only justification would be for *competitive* interference (where he rushed to Butch's home and punished him with P before I could get there). We must remember that we are not describing a Hobbesian state of nature, in which people have liberty rights *only*. In a Lockean state of nature, each person has a full claim right to freedom from (noncompetitive) interference, provided he acts within the constraints of the moral law. Since my imposing P on Butch would be within those constraints, any interference by Chico other than competitive interference is morally indefensible. My right to punish, then, when combined with my right of self-government, rules out most kinds of interference, and constitutes a reasonably substantial right.

My remarks above have already suggested that I think the proper solution to the problem of competitive liberties is an appeal to the principle "first come, first served." This answer for the system of "open punishment" I have been describing is similar to the Lockean solution for a system of "open property." Where land or natural resources are unowned, those who labor on them first (subject to certain provisos) "make a property" in them. All are initially at liberty to claim parts of the common, and may use only competitive interference (i.e., taking first) in exercising this liberty.[48]

Nozick worries that if we allow the first punisher to preempt the field, sadists will compete to arrive first at the scene of the crime, to get in

48. The well-known Lockean provisos on the creation of property (II, 31–33) are necessary in that case, but *not* in a system of open punishment, because obviously being deprived of access to natural resources endangers one's life, while being deprived of chances to punish criminals, as long as *someone* does it, does not—in fact, it may even enhance one's life prospects.

their licks while the getting's good. This possibility makes one uncomfortable, and not because (as Nozick supposes) the sadists will be hard to control (always imposing excessive punishment in the heat of passion). Sadists who thus lose control will also be punishable. What makes one uncomfortable is the prospect of punishing being done by rational, responsible sadists—who punish only the guilty, and only with the proper kind and amount of punishment, but who delight in doing so. This brings us squarely up against a difficulty I have thus far avoided facing. If the criminal simply forfeits his right not to be harmed in certain ways, then *any* way in which this harm is imposed appears morally acceptable, *any* reason a person has for imposing it is good enough. If Butch and his gang roam the state of nature, cutting throats at random just for the fun of it, and happen to cut the throat of a murderer (who deserves to be punished with a painful death, say), then that particular throat-cutting, but no other, might be morally acceptable. This seems a preposterous implication of the position I have been defending.[49]

We must remember first that punishment is the infliction of harm for (in response to, because of) wrongdoing.[50] At least *part* of what motivates one inflicting harm must be the belief that a wrong has been done and that the response he is making is morally (legally, conventionally) appropriate or deserved, or that infliction of harm cannot possibly count as *punishment*. Butch and his gang *punish* no one; neither do the rational sadists if part of their reason for acting is not the belief that punishment is appropriate. Punishers may have *additional* motives (beyond these beliefs)—anger, a desire to protect society, sadism, and so on. But these cannot be *all* that moves a person to inflict harm on another, if we are to count that infliction of harm as punishment.[51]

Of course, what we *call* the harm Butch and his gang cause is not very important or interesting. What is important is that it is not morally per-

---

49. Quinn, "The Right to Threaten and the Right to Punish," pp. 332–33.

50. On Locke's commitment to this view, see Von Leyden, "Locke's Strange Doctrine of Punishment," p. 121. For a recent general statement of this view of punishment, see Wood, *Hegel's Ethical Thought*, p. 108.

51. Where *institutional* forms of punishment are concerned, matters are not so simple. A criminal can properly be said to be punished, for instance, even if the motives of some judge, jury member, or executioner are purely sadistic. What remains true, however, is that what we might call the overall "institutional" motive must reflect the notion of a justified response to wrongdoing if we are to count the institutional process as one of punishing.

missible. We are permitted to harm wrongdoers only for certain reasons. The situation parallels that of taking reparation for injuries another has caused. If I take property from one who, completely unbeknownst to me, had previously stolen *my* property, my taking is still theft (and morally impermissible)—even though the property I took from him I might have been entitled to take, if I had taken it *as reparation*. Similarly, the throat-cutting Butch imposes is murder, not justifiable punishment, though he might have been entitled to kill if he had done so *as punishment*.

The main difficulty with this suggestion, as far as I can tell, is in motivating the revision it requires of the doctrine of forfeiture. Criminals must be said to forfeit not rights not to be harmed in certain ways (*simpliciter*), but rather rights not to be harmed in certain ways *for certain reasons*. The criminal, after such a forfeiture, has no right to complain about harms done him as punishment; he still has every right to complain (though we will no doubt be less sympathetic than usual) about other kinds of harming. These claims seem to me not unbearably awkward or ad hoc, for we often *voluntarily* transfer to others rights to act only for certain reasons (e.g., you may give your doctor the right to act during your upcoming surgery as he thinks best—but only when he acts for medical reasons, as opposed, say, to his acting for financial reasons or to enhance his professional reputation). If we may voluntarily create a situation where others have rights to act only for certain reasons, it seems plausible to suppose that nonvoluntary forfeiture might result, as I have claimed it must, in rights to harm another only for certain reasons. And the fairness account of forfeiture defended above seems to push us naturally in just this direction. For the unfairness to others that would be involved in allowing the criminal to *retain* his full complement of rights is unfairness only to those who themselves *obey* the relevant rules. Butch, with others who harm for the *wrong* reasons, is *not* obeying the rules in the relevant sense—that is, he is not prepared to deliberately limit his own liberty according to his view of what is required by fair rules. Indeed, he demonstrates his unwillingness to obey the rules in the very act of attempting to inflict the harm, since he *believes* the act *not* to be one of just punishment. There is thus no obvious unfairness to Butch in allowing a criminal to retain his right not to be harmed for Butch's reasons. Fairness (thus forfeiture) is at issue only in relation to those who *do* obey the rules and attempt to harm others only for acceptable reasons.[52]

Again there is, I think, a Kantian (and thus, to the extent noted earlier, a Lockean) motivation for this restriction on rights forfeiture. Harming others (who deserve punishment) for the wrong reasons is morally wrong in the same way that disproportionate punishment of wrongdoers is wrong. Both fail to *respond* to the person and what he did, both fail to respect him and take him seriously. As Jeffrie Murphy puts the claim, "An autonomous person has a right that his punishment be *addressed* to that status—to those unique features of his individual, responsible conduct which occasion the punishment"; otherwise, he is "being *used*" for whatever the purposes are that motivate the excessive punishment (or, in my case, the wrongly motivated harming).[53] Respect or responsiveness is not determined just by the brute, physical description of our acts, but also by our beliefs and intentions. Since the possession of rights is premised on autonomy and moral agency, forfeiture of rights is similarly restricted—we forfeit rights by our misconduct only to the extent that makes possible *respectful* punishment. Only the total forfeiture of personhood affects this restriction for Locke.[54] The same style of argument that Locke could use to justify his insistence on proportionality of punishment (II, 8), then, can be used to justify this limit on the *reasons* for which we may legitimately harm wrongdoers.[55]

52. This argument provides as well, I think, a response to many who have criticized certain aspects of forfeiture theories of the right of self-defense. David Wasserman, for instance, has claimed (following George Fletcher) that there are "serious and well-recognized drawbacks to a forfeiture approach" to self-defense rights ("Justifying Self-Defense," *Philosophy & Public Affairs* 16, no. 4 [Fall 1987]: 361). Among these "drawbacks" is the alleged inability of forfeiture accounts to explain why aggressors' lives may not be taken for just any reason, why they may be taken only by those responding defensively, and then only if such force is necessary to repel the attack (see Judith Thomson's similar criticisms in "Self-Defense and Rights," in *Rights, Restitution, and Risk* [Cambridge, Mass.: Harvard University Press, 1986], pp. 33–37). The style of argument presented above suggests that forfeiture theory has ample resources to deal with such problems as these.

53. "Cruel and Unusual Punishments," in *Retribution, Justice, and Therapy* (Dordrecht: Reidel, 1979), p. 234.

54. Here Locke apparently disagrees with Gregory Vlastos, who claims that "the moral community is not a club from which members may be dropped for delinquency" ("Justice and Equality," in *Social Justice*, ed. R. Brandt [Englewood Cliffs, N.J.: Prentice-Hall, 1962], p. 48).

55. And Locke would here again be following Grotius, who restricts reasons for which one may punish (*De Jure Belli ac Pacis*, bk. II, chap. xx, p. 468).

If my claims to this point have been correct, a system of open punishment is a morally acceptable and morally well-motivated system.[56] But are there difficulties we have not yet considered for a system of open punishment (other than the obvious ones, like defending a theory of natural rights in the first place)? Admittedly, this account of the natural executive right leaves no room for a certain kind of mercy or forgiveness, understood as the right of any individual. While individuals can be forgiving in their hearts and can refrain from punishing, a criminal can be forgiven (in the performative sense, so that punishment is no longer rightful) only if everyone agrees to forgo punishing him. I accept this result without great discomfort. Perhaps someone might wish to argue that this is another reason for favoring civil society (where it will be easier for criminals to be forgiven); I do not.

It may, finally, seem that in spite of the "strength" of this version of a right to punish, in terms of making interference by others impermissible,

56. Nozick, in his discussion of open punishment, very quickly gives up trying to understand how it might work, and retreats instead to a view according to which everyone jointly holds the right to punish (or to empower someone to punish). No one *individually* has such a right (*Anarchy, State, and Utopia*, p. 139). But his apparent retreat turns out to be only a strategic withdrawal. Nozick has good reason to *want* a system of open punishment to be indefensible (which explains his haste in disposing of it). For if everyone jointly holds the right to punish, but people disagree about whom to empower to do their punishing, then the "dominant protective agency" operating in the state of nature has the best claim to do the punishing. For it represents a larger part of the "everyone" who jointly hold the right to punish than any competing agency or individual. And since no *individual* has the right to punish, held separately, no individual's rights are violated when the dominant protective agency does all of the punishing of criminals for us (i.e., for everyone). This is what allows Nozick to claim that the dominant protective agency has "some special legitimacy" and violates no individual's rights (ibid., pp. 139–40).

If, however, the best way to understand the right to punish in a state of nature is in terms of the system of open punishment defended above, Nozick's main argument appears to fail. He can argue neither that the dominant protective agency has a special legitimacy nor that the rights of individuals (who will be prevented by the agency from punishing in their own way) will not be violated by its practices. Even Nozick must have been uncomfortable about suggesting that the right to punish must be held jointly, since he observed that this would make it the *only* right in a state of nature "possessed by people jointly rather than individually" (ibid., p. 139). This has the appearance of a position designed only to produce the desired results. See Gerald Postema's interesting and much more complete discussion of the difficulties with Nozick's main argument in "Nozick on Liberty, Compensation, and the Individual's Right to Punish," *Social Theory and Practice* 6 (1980): 311–37. Some portions of my presentation in this section parallel Postema's work, though we reach quite different conclusions. See also Altham, "Reflections on the State of Nature," pp. 141–44.

it is still too weak a version of the right to punish to satisfy Lockean
ambitions. I will consider two ways in which this might seem to be so.

First, it might be claimed that a mere liberty to punish, even if protected from all but competitive interference, fails to capture the sense
(occasionally suggested by Locke) in which punishment in the state of
nature is not merely morally permissible, but a *duty*.[57] If it is simply *permissible* to punish a thief, say, there seems to be no stronger moral reason to do so than there would be to hit an unruly dog (who also lacks the
right not to be harmed). Punishment seems a matter of moral indifference. What this complaint overlooks is that in the case of the wrongdoer,
but not in the case of the dog, the punishment is not only permissible
but *deserved*. Where it is true both that someone deserves a certain treatment and that it is permissible for us to treat him in that way, we have
good moral reason to act. Thus, punishing the wrongdoer is not a matter
of moral indifference on this account (even if it is not, strictly speaking,
a duty either), for the mere absence (through forfeiture) of rights is not
the whole story.[58] I believe that the natural right to punish, understood
as it has been described in this section, captures all of the force of the
intuition expressed earlier (in Section I) about the justifiability of pun-

57. In the central sections on punishment (II, 7–13), Locke actually almost always talks
of punishment as if it were permissible only, *not* a duty. His use of "may," "right," and
"power" convey this sense. The quotation from Genesis (II, 11) stands out in quite dramatic contrast to this tendency. Punishment seems to be a duty at all only after government
takes over and *agrees* to use the right to punish for the common good (making the duty in
that case *consensual* in nature); and it is not always a duty even then, since the magistrate
may rightfully *decline* to punish wrongdoers in some cases (II, 11) (see below, and note 36
above). Further, the idea that we have no *duty* to punish seems to be central to Locke's
arguments concerning resistance to oppressive government. If there is no duty to punish
in Locke, this is further reason to favor our first (simple) line on forfeiture as the best
reading of Locke, since we can see now that it naturally yields no such duty. On the other
hand, of course, the right to punish is derived by Locke from the right to preserve mankind—a right that is, as we have seen, also a *duty*. This strongly implies that punishment
should also, at least often, be a duty. Perhaps Locke is attracted to a view like that of Grotius, for whom some punishment is required, while other is only permitted, so that forgiving the criminal is only sometimes acceptable (*De Jure Belli ac Pacis*, bk. II, chap. xx, pp.
489–91). But Locke seems never to take any explicit stand on this question.

58. This point provides a partial answer to one of Allen Wood's criticisms of Hegel's
account of punishment—i.e., that Hegel shows how punishing is morally permissible, but
can offer no positive moral reason *for* punishing the guilty. See *Hegel's Ethical Thought*,
pp. 116–17. To the extent that we allow considerations of *deterrence* to function in the
account, of course, there is a *further* reason (the preservation of mankind) for punishing
the thief, but not the dog.

ishment in a nonpolitical state. But can it also be used to explain why a
legitimate government has the *exclusive* right to punish, the other essential part of the Lockean project?

VI

We can, I think, give a Lockean account of these matters (if not precisely
Locke's own) that captures the main ideas Locke was concerned to defend: (a) that a legitimate government's right to punish can be understood only in terms of a redistribution of previously existing natural
rights, and (b) that the natural right to punish *must* be sacrificed (i.e.,
freely alienated) by all members on entrance into civil society.

The Lockean account I have in mind proceeds as follows: As per the
revised Lockean position outlined in Section III, each citizen must en-
trust to government that portion of his right to self-government that is
necessary for effective government, if that government is to be legitimate. The government then holds against each of us a right to interfere
(including, particularly, by punishing) in our lives in the designated areas. But the government *cannot* obtain from us in this way an *exclusive*
right to punish those crimes that are *moral* wrongs. For our rights of self-
government do not include the right of exclusive control over our lives
when we violate the moral law. Our right to be free of interference is only
a right to be free *within* the bounds of natural law. By our wrongdoings
we forfeit the right of control over our lives in some measure, making the
interference of any other lawful. The government can be given by each
of us a right to interfere only where we are *not* violating moral law, for
only in those areas do we begin with a natural right of self-government.
In cases of *moral* wrongdoing, the government has (given what has been
said thus far) only the same liberty to punish that other persons possess.[59] It is thus in competition with private citizens where it seeks to

59. Locke's sensitivity to these issues is best displayed in his early *Second Tract on Government*, where he carefully distinguishes between the magistrate's powers in the areas of
morally obligatory conduct (covering crimes that are also moral wrongs) and "indifferent"
conduct (covering those areas in which our right of self-government originally left us free).
Locke worries that if the magistrate is not free to legislate concerning "things indifferent,"
then he could only re-command and enforce the requirements of natural law, in which
sphere "the power of the magistrate seems to be no greater than that of any private citizen"
(p. 228). This problem is solved by Locke in the *Second Treatise*, where both obligatory
acts and indifferent acts bearing importantly on effective government are taken to be

punish acts that are *mala in se*. The simple transfer of our claim rights
to noninterference cannot give the state an exclusive right to punish.
This requires a remedy, if there is to be one judge over all citizens.

The obvious solution is that (in the Lockean spirit) each citizen must
also surrender on entering civil society his natural liberty to punish
wrongdoers. Each must agree not to *compete* with the state in punishing
moral criminals.[60] In this way, and only in this way, can the government
acquire an *exclusive* liberty to punish moral wrongdoers (the effective
equivalent of a claim right), in addition to the claim right it receives from
each consenting citizen to punish in other necessary areas.[61] The production of the exclusive liberty for government, of course, is in some
ways analogous to Hobbes's account of the origin of the sovereign's right
to punish and to Locke's own account of how a *father* can come to have
title as a prince.[62] But because the Lockean version of man's natural con-

---

proper subjects for legislation. See also King, *The Life of John Locke* 2:109–10, and *A Letter
Concerning Toleration*, p. 126.

60. More precisely, each citizen in his *private* capacity must renounce his natural right
to punish, leaving citizens in their *public* capacities, possibly including himself, free to
exercise a collectively exclusive liberty to punish. The renunciation is thus *conditional* on
not occupying a public executive office.

61. Once the government *has* this right, citizens are no longer free to punish even those
who somehow escape the punishment they deserve. This, however regrettable, must be
understood as part of the price we pay for having one umpire over all citizens. If failure to
punish the deserving is part of a deliberate, unjust program by government, of course,
matters are changed.

62. "And this is the foundation of that right of punishing which is exercised in every
commonwealth. For the subjects did not give the sovereign that right, but only in laying
down theirs strengthened him to use his own as he should think fit for the preservation of
them all; so that it was not given but left to him, and to him only, and (excepting the limits
set him by natural law) as entire as in the condition of mere nature . . ." (*Leviathan*, chap.
28, para. 2). Locke similarly talks as if the father's children could simply "lay down" their
rights to punish, leaving the father free to exercise his own executive right as an exclusive
liberty (II, 74). The strategy I here suggest for Locke (and the Lockean) is similar to the
"Hobbesian account" discussed and rejected by David Schmidtz in *The Limits of Government* (Boulder, Colo.: Westview, 1991), pp. 36–37. Schmidtz appears to reject the account
because it cannot justify state punishment with reference to independents (nonconsenters,
nonclients), since the state's liberty to punish is exclusive only with reference to those who
have surrendered or laid down their similar liberties. But since I take the correct Lockean
position on legitimacy to be precisely that standard state practices such as punishment
typically *cannot* be justified except to those who freely consent to those practices, independents must simply be accepted by the Lockean as remaining in the state of nature and
as being beyond coercive assimilation into the state (see note 63 below). The problem for
the Lockean, then, is not with this account of the legitimate government's right to punish;

dition also includes full claim rights that may be transferred, none of the Hobbesian difficulties about the obligating force of the sovereign's laws arise.

The force of this account might be captured more simply as follows. If it is ever morally permissible to punish wrongdoers—that is, to coercively control them in certain ways—in the state of nature (and, of course, I have argued that, at least often, it is), then our natural rights of self-government must be taken (as Locke took them) to be limited to those areas of our lives where we operate *within* the bounds of natural law. The government cannot, then, obtain in the manner suggested in Section III (by a simple transfer of rights of self-government) an *exclusive* right to punish moral wrongdoers. If it tries to forcibly exclude attempts by private citizens to punish wrongdoers, it invades their natural liberty to use competitive interference in punishing. In the absence of a Lockean "contract" of government, in which this liberty to punish is laid aside by citizens, leaving their governors free to legitimately exercise their liberty to punish (and to force citizens *not* to punish wrongdoers), any government's claim to a "monopoly on force" within its territories must be morally indefensible.[63]

---

it is with the meaning of political consent and with the possible resulting truth of philosophical anarchism.

63. This conclusion does *not* follow, of course, if individuals can justifiably be deprived of or prevented from exercising their rights to punish *without* their consent (i.e., without actual wrongdoing on their part and without their free alienation or renunciation of those rights). Locke, of course, steadfastly opposes such "prescription" of natural rights (see my "Inalienable Rights and Locke's *Treatises*," *Philosophy & Public Affairs* 12, no. 3 [Summer 1983]: 178–79, 185). But Nozick has encouraged us to think instead about this question in terms of the *reliability* of methods of self-help enforcement of natural law, suggesting that the state (or a protective agency, or an individual) may justifiably prohibit and punish enforcement of natural law by others who use methods that are unreliable, thus legitimately eliminating any conflict between its right to punish and that of those independents whose private punishing threatens its clients (*Anarchy, State, and Utopia*, pp. 101–10). But Nozick really provides no justification for prohibiting independents from using *reliable* private punishing methods, or for doing any more than *monitoring* the use of even *unreliable* methods (and intervening only to prevent wrongful punishment). Since Locke's executive right is only a right to punish *correctly* (II, 13), the *proper* use of that right by independents cannot be justifiably infringed without their consent. Their agreement to give up their executive rights is thus still necessary to secure for government a legitimate monopoly on force. I think, then, that Farrell is mistaken in insisting that on Locke's own terms the consent of the governed is *not* really required for legitimate government (see, e.g., his "Punishment Without the State," p. 450, and "Coercion, Consent, and the Justification of Political Power," *Archiv fur Rechts-und Sozialphilosophie* 65 [1979]: 528–29, 532,

However-badly this account may fit with some of the details of Locke's own presentation, it surely captures the central spirit of his views. On the account I have sketched, the government's exclusive right to punish must be understood to be composed of its exclusive liberty to punish moral wrongdoers, plus its claim right(s) to control individual citizens (collectively) in other designated areas of their lives. Similarly, Locke insisted that governments could rightfully punish only if empowered in a fiduciary transaction between citizen and government—and that the rights transferred to government in this transaction must include *both* rights to control our lives and rights connected with the punishment of wrongdoers (II, 128–30). My agreement with Locke is, then, quite substantial. I agree that if there is a natural executive right (and if it is possible to defend the theories of natural rights and desert on which the executive right depends), then this Lockean transaction between government and citizens is necessary for the moral legitimacy of the common practice of punishment within political communities. Since I am further persuaded that there are good reasons to support the natural right to punish, Locke's beliefs about the necessity of this transaction may well be justified.[64]

---

536), both for the reasons suggested above and because the legitimate Lockean state can *at most* prohibit self-help enforcement of natural law, *not* coercively bring independents under the requirements of *civil* law. Similarly, I disagree with Schmidtz's conclusions that the right to punish should really be understood as the right to punish only by the method that is *least risky* to others, and that this may require that independents let the state punish for them (*The Limits of Government*, p. 38). For, in the first place, it is only *acceptably* risky methods of punishment that seem morally permissible, not the *least risky* method in use (which might, of course, be far *too* risky to be allowed). And independent punishment *may* be "acceptably risky." Second, while no individual can be sure that he is a "Charles Bronson type," as Schmidtz rightly claims (ibid., p. 46), state punishment methods can surely not be taken to be exactly risk-free either (given corrupt and overburdened police and courts, crowded and dangerous prisons, etc.). For criticisms of Nozick's approach related to those voiced above, see Sayward, "Anarchism and Rights Violations," pp. 106–9.

64. I have not yet commented on the international implications of the Lockean position—i.e., that, barring international covenants, each legitimate government has the right (i.e., liberty) to punish moral wrongs committed within the territories of other countries by citizens of those countries. This right is not, of course, a right to *interfere* with the legitimate processes of punishment that may be taking place within other countries, but only a right to punish alien wrongdoers who have gone unpunished. If even this limited right seems indefensible, remember the attitude of the Allies at the Nuremberg trials, where German war criminals were prosecuted for *moral* (not legal) crimes against German citizens, committed on German soil. Was it not within the rights of the Allies to punish the monstrous acts of these criminals? The Lockean view implies an affirmative answer. Le-

The results for which I have argued here seem to square well with the central intuition about the justifiability of "natural punishment" expressed in Section I. But what of the apparently conflicting intuitions (e.g., that private citizens *within* civil society might *also* be justified in punishing unpunished wrongdoers)? I suspect that such beliefs arise largely from skepticism about Locke's claims that we have in fact given up our natural right to punish to our government in the kind of transaction he describes. And this skepticism may well be warranted. The Lockean account I have just defended is an account of what must take place if legal punishment is to be *legitimate*. We must not confusedly suppose that it is a *descriptive* account of what in fact occurs in most civil societies (though Locke himself, of course, seems to have supposed just this). It may be true that punishment in many or most civil societies is *not* legitimate, and that private citizens in these societies *are* entitled to punish wrongdoers who go unpunished (either within or without their societies).[65] Lockean consent may be necessary for legitimate legal punishment, but not sufficiently in evidence in real political societies to justify our actual practices.

There are, obviously, many other details of the Lockean program on punishment that need elaboration.[66] But anyone, I think, who finds the

---

gitimate governments have exclusive rights to punish wrongdoers within their territories, but these rights are held only against their own citizens, not against the world at large. Other governments have the right to punish moral wrongs left unpunished by the responsible government, though exercising this right will be sensible and prudent only when (as in the case of Germany) the wrongs in question are serious and numerous.

65. If citizens retain their natural executive rights, of course, they may even have a right to punish wrongdoers *before* the state has a chance to institute legal proceedings. But there will often be good reasons for not doing so—e.g., reasons of prudence, or the fact that it is best (even if not obligatory) to allow more experienced and better-organized punishers to have the first chance to do the job.

66. For instance, it may seem to be an objectionable consequence of our Lockean account that legitimate governments have the right to punish *all* moral wrongs (including, for instance, those that are quite trivial and those that have not been made *legal* wrongs at all). The proper response to such worries is to note that the transaction necessary to create legitimate government involves not only a transfer of rights from citizens to governors. It also includes the specification of *limits* on the government's authority—most importantly, that it not violate the rights of any citizen and that it exercise its authority only for "the common good" (e.g., II, 131). The latter requirement (that it use its power only for the common good) can be understood to constrain the government's exclusive liberty to punish moral wrongdoers. It establishes that governments can rightfully punish only moral wrongs that have been made *legal* wrongs by "promulgated, established laws" (II, 142) ("Or else that law would have been of no use: it being to no purpose to lay restraint or give

Lockean intuitions about natural punishment compelling, who believes in the possibility of a defensible theory of natural rights, or who thinks the arguments of this essay not clearly defective will have reason to consider this program seriously. If it is not, in the end, an acceptable position, there is at least more to be said for it than most contemporary commentators have allowed.

---

privileges to men, in such general terms, as the particular person concerned cannot be known by" [I, 128]), that it should not *make* some moral wrongs (e.g., simple promise-breaking) into legal wrongs, and that it should not punish *trivial* moral wrongs. To do otherwise would be to exercise its authority in ways clearly at odds with the promotion of the common good. As Locke argued much earlier than the *Treatises* (in 1667), the magistrate may tolerate some vices if it is best for society that he do so (*An Essay Concerning Toleration*, in H. R. Fox Bourne, *The Life of John Locke* [London: King, 1876], p. 183). And the government violates no one's rights by *not* punishing certain moral wrongs (at least where it provides *equal* protection from wrongdoing for all of its citizens). Of course, the promotion of the common good requires that punishment be frequent and effective enough to secure a safe and decent life for citizens, but this in no way implies that all moral wrongs must be punished.

PART III

Capital Punishment

DAVID A. CONWAY   Capital Punishment and
                       Deterrence: Some
                       Considerations in
                       Dialogue Form

P: I am happy to learn that our state legislature is trying to restore
   C.P.[1] Many of the legislators think they can pass a bill prescribing
   C.P. that the Supreme Court would not find unconstitutional.

O: Yes, that is true in many legislatures.[2] But it is hardly something
   I am happy about. Not only do I think C.P. is wrong, but I see a
   great danger in the present situation. The prime question in the
   minds of too many legislators seems to be, How do we draft laws
   that the court would not object to? The more basic question, Is
   C.P. ethically justifiable? may be lost sight of altogether.

P: Perhaps, but if necessary, I think C.P. can be justified easily
   enough.

O: Are you some sort of retributivist?

P: Not at all. I hold that deterrence is the aim of punishment and that
   it is the central issue in the minds of legislators. They, as I am, are
   worried about the sheer lack of personal safety in our society.

O: I didn't know that you had any strong feelings on this subject.

P: I didn't until recently. Then I read an interview in a newspaper.
   Ernest van den Haag, in response to questions from Philip Nobile,
   gives some arguments for C.P. that I find very convincing.[3] And I
   would bet that legislators do too.

1. I shall use "C.P." for "capital punishment" throughout this paper.

2. In addition, President Nixon in March of 1973 called for restoration of
C.P., saying that he is convinced that it deters the commission of some types
of crimes.

3. *St. Louis Globe-Democrat*, 6–7 January 1973. The arguments that van den
Haag puts forth in this interview are currently quite popular among "intellec-

I. THE PREFERENCE ARGUMENT

O: How can you think that C.P. is an effective deterrent? What about all of the statistical studies that have failed to show that this is true?[4]

P: I admit that such studies are inconclusive. But I am not relying on them to show the deterrent value of C.P. A simpler fact will do the job. Consider this exchange in the van den Haag interview:

> *Nobile*: Is it true that capital punishment is a better deterrent than irrevocable life imprisonment?
>
> *van den Haag*: Yes, and that I can prove. I noticed a story in the paper the other day about a French heroin smuggler who pleaded guilty in a New York court because, as his lawyer admitted, he preferred irrevocable life imprisonment here to the guillotine in France.
>
> In fact, all prisoners prefer life. For even if the sentence is irrevocable, as long as there's life, psychologically, there's hope.

O: That argument is pretty popular among policemen and some editorial writers. In fact, Hugo Bedau in *The Death Penalty in America* includes a passage from Police Chief Allen which gives this argument. Bedau also mentions it in one of his essays in that volume, but he does not argue against it, although he does argue against some pro-C.P. views of Sidney Hook and Jacques Barzun.[5]

P: What does that mean? That serious philosophers do not bother to argue against policemen and editorial writers? or that this particular argument is too stupid to bother with?

O: I'm not sure what it means. But I do think this argument is worth taking seriously. For it is intuitively plausible, and it rests on an empirical premise which seems to me to be almost indisputably true. That is, almost all of us would, at least consciously, given the pres-

---

tual conservatives" (e.g. writers for the *National Review* and conservative newspapers). The importance of his views is much greater than would be indicated just by the fact that one person happened to express them in a newspaper interview.

4. See, for instance, Hugo Bedau, *The Death Penalty in America* (Garden City: Doubleday, 1967), especially chapters 6 and 7.

5. Ibid., pp. 135–136, 220.

ent choice between being subjected to life imprisonment and to C.P., choose the former. Still, the argument is not convincing.

P: Why not?

O: There are a couple of reasons. First, you are saying that if, given that I must choose between some punishment x and another punishment y, I would strongly prefer y, then it follows that knowing that x will be inflicted on me if I perform some action will more effectively deter me from performing that action than will knowing that y will be inflicted. But consider that, given the choice, I would strongly prefer one thousand years in hell to eternity there. Nonetheless, if one thousand years in hell were the penalty for some action, it would be quite sufficient to deter me from performing that action. The additional years would do nothing to discourage me further.

   Similarly, the prospect of the death penalty, while worse, may not have any greater deterrent effect than does that of life imprisonment. In fact, I would imagine that either prospect would normally deter the rational man, while the man irrational enough not to be deterred by life imprisonment wouldn't be deterred by anything.[6] So, the deterrent value of the two may be indistinguishable in practice even though one penalty may be definitely preferable to the other, if one is forced to choose between them.

P: I see. Still there could be potential killers who are deterred by one and not by the other.

O: Of course there *could be*. But have you forgotten what this discussion is about? You were supposed to have a proof that there are such people.

P: OK. What is your other argument?

O: Well, before, I argued that C.P. may not be an additional deterrent even if we assume that the criminal expects to be caught. But surely most do not expect to be caught or they hold no expectations at all, i.e. they are acting in "blind passion." In these cases, the punishment is irrelevant. If, however, we assume at least minimal rationality on the part of the criminal, he knows that there is some chance that he will be caught. Let us say that he believes that there is a one

6. For a similar supposition, see Bedau, p. 272. There, however, the point is not made specifically in relation to the "Preference Argument."

in ten chance that he will be, and also that the actuality of punishment x is sufficient to deter him from performing some actions from which punishment y would not deter him. It does not follow from this that a one in ten chance of x would deter him from performing any actions that a one in ten chance of y would not. To put it abstractly, we can assign to the death penalty 100 "disutility units" and to life imprisonment 50 "disutility units" to represent a significant difference between their undesirability. If the chance of either punishment actually being inflicted, however, is only one in ten, the difference becomes much less significant (i.e. $1/10 \cdot 100$ vs. $1/10 \cdot 50$, or 10 vs. 5 disutility units). We do not, of course, actually think in such precise terms of probability and utility units, but we do often approximate such reasoning. For instance, if it is important that I get to my destination quickly, I may be willing to (actually) be fined for speeding while I am not willing to (actually) smash up my car and possibly myself. The difference between the two "penalties," if actually inflicted, is very great, great enough that one deters and the other does not. If, however, I know that there is only a slight chance of either occurring, the deterrent effect of the threats may be virtually indistinguishable, and I may speed on my way.

There are, then, at least two reasons for not equating "what we fear the most" with "what will most effectively deter us." Both of these are overlooked by those of you who give the "preference argument."

II. THE RATIONAL PERSON—DETERRENT ARGUMENT

O: What else did you find in the van den Haag interview?

P: Well, there is this.

> *Nobile*: Most capital crimes are crimes of passion in which family members or friends kill each other. You can't stop this sort of thing with the threat of execution.
>
> *van den Haag*: It's perfectly true that the irrational person won't be deterred by any penalty. But to the extent that murder is an act of passion, the death penalty has already deterred all rational persons.

O: And you agree with that?

P: I suppose not. It does seem to be a pretty clear case of *post hoc, ergo propter hoc* reasoning.[7] Still, there is a smaller point to be made here. Van den Haag says that C.P. has deterred rational persons. We do not know that it has. But, we also don't know that it hasn't. You opponents of C.P. are always saying something like, "Virtually all capital crimes are commited by persons in an irrational frame of mind. Therefore, C.P. (or any other punishment) cannot be regarded as a deterrent." So, you say, rational persons just do not (often) murder; I say, maybe they do not because of the threat of C.P. And so you cannot simply cite the fact that they do not as an argument against C.P.

O: I have to grant you that point. What you say has been often enough said before, and, yet, without attempting to answer the point, my fellow opponents of C.P. too often just go on saying "rational people seldom murder." We must seriously try to show that rational people seldom murder even in the absence of C.P., rather than just continuing to recite "rational people seldom murder."

III. THE BEST-BET ARGUMENT

O: Do you have any more arguments to trot out?

P: There is another in the van den Haag interview, and I have been saving the best for last.

O: Let's hear it.

P: All right.

> *Nobile*: You're pretty cavalier about executions, aren't you?
>
> *van den Haag*: If we have capital punishment, our risk is that it is unnecessary and no additional deterrence is achieved. But if we do not have it, our risk is that it might have deterred future murderers and spared future victims. Then it's a matter of which risk you prefer and I prefer to protect the victims.
>
> *Nobile*: But you're gambling with the lives of condemned men who might otherwise live.
>
> *van den Haag*: You're right. But we're both gambling. I'm gambling by executing and you're gambling by not executing.

7. For a more complete critique of the same argument, see Bedau, pp. 268–269.

We can see the force of this more clearly if we specify all of the possible outcomes. ("C.P. works" means "C.P. is a uniquely effective deterrent.")

	C.P. Works	C.P. Does Not Work
We bet C.P. works	(a) We win: Some murderers die, but innocents, who would otherwise die, are spared.	(b) We lose: Some murderers die for no purpose. The lives of others are unaffected.
We bet C.P. does not work	(c) We lose: Murderers live, but some innocents needlessly die.	(d) We win: Murderers live and the lives of others are unaffected.

To make it more clear, suppose that we assign utility values in this way:

Each murderer saved (not executed)	+5
Each murderer executed	−5
Each innocent person saved (not murdered)	+10
Each innocent person murdered	−10

And assume also that, if C.P. works, each execution saves five innocents (a conservative estimate, surely). Potential gains and losses can be represented as:

$$
\begin{array}{ll}
\text{(a)} \quad \begin{array}{r} -5 \\ +50 \\ \hline +45 \end{array} & \text{(b)} \ -5 \\[2em]
\text{(c)} \quad \begin{array}{r} +5 \\ -50 \\ \hline -45 \end{array} & \text{(d)} \ +5
\end{array}
$$

Now we can clearly see that not only do we have less to lose by betting on C.P., but we also have more to gain. It would be quite irrational not to bet on it.

O: Pascal lives.

P: What's that?

O: Nothing. But look, you have to admit that there is an unsavory air about the argument. Nobile is right; the very notion of gambling with human lives seems morally repugnant.

P: Maybe. But the fact is, as van den Haag says, we are also gambling if we do not execute, so you would do so as much as I.

O: If so, then what your argument does is make very apparent the sort of point retributivists have always made. In Kantian terms, this sort of gambling with human lives is a particularly crude form of treating human beings as means rather than ends.

P: You are willing to take a retributivist position in order to avoid the force of the argument?

O: No. I will leave vengeance to the Lord, if he wants it. Anyway, I am not convinced there are not other reasons for rejecting your argument. I cannot get over the feeling that, in some sense, you are gambling with lives in a way that I am not.

P: Maybe that is a feeling that requires therapy to get over. Let me say it once more: If either of us loses our wager, human lives are needlessly lost. Granted, if you win yours, no life is lost at all, while if I win mine, the criminal loses his; but since he loses it and others gain theirs, that cannot be what is disturbing you. There is nothing disturbing about the prospect of saving many innocents.

O: Wait now. I think that I am beginning to see what is going on here. Look at your utility summary again. You rightly say that (a) which represents the situation *if* we bet on C.P. *and win* is the best possible outcome, while (c), the situation which results *if* we bet against it *and lose*, is the worst. Now if this were a case of pure uncertainty, if we had no idea at all whether C.P. deters, these outcomes might be the only thing to consider. But surely this is not such a case: We do have statistical studies; we do have some rudimentary knowledge of criminal psychology; at least, we have some common sense idea of how people behave and why. All of this may be very inconclusive, but still we cannot say we have total uncertainty.

P: No. I never imagined we did have that.

O: So when we are weighing the alternative outcomes, we cannot *just* consider which is most or least desirable; we must consider the probability of that outcome occurring, even though our probability estimates must be very subjective.

P: Of course. I had that in mind all along.

O: It seems to me that that might be at least obscured in van den Haag's statements and in your earlier ones. You sounded as if it were just a matter of both of us gambling and recommending that we decide which to take on the basis of the possible outcomes alone, without taking into account the probabilities of those outcomes occurring. Anyway, can we now, for the sake of argument if nothing else, find a probability we can agree on?

P: I really think that it is at least as likely that it deters as that it does not.

O: I can see no reason at all for such an evaluation.

P: All right. I was going to add that I will not insist on it. Grant me that there is at least a one in five chance that C.P. deters. That is asking little enough. And it is all I need for my argument. In fact, that such a low assessment of the probabilities is all that is needed is, essentially, the point of the argument.

O: Let's see how that works.

P: It's very simple. Even if there is only a .2 probability that C.P. works, the calculations come out this way: if we bet for C.P.,

(a) $.2 \cdot +45 = +9$. That is, there is a one in five chance of gaining 45 utility units. Similarly, there is a .8 chance that I would take a life needlessly.

(b) $.8 \cdot -5 = -4$

And, if we bet against C.P., then

(c) $.2 \cdot -45 = -9$
(d) $.8 \cdot +5 = +4$

So, even if it is improbable that C.P. deters, we should bet that it does.

O: But that calculation is all wrong.

P: Wrong? All I did was multiply possible outcomes by the probability of obtaining those outcomes. What can be wrong with that?

O: In (a), there is not a .2 chance of gaining 45 utility units. There is certainty of there being -5 utility units, a certainty of the criminal losing his life, and a .2 chance of a compensating +50 units, of C.P. being a deterrent. And in (b), there isn't a .8 chance of taking a life needlessly; there is a certainty of taking a life. That it is needless simply means there is no compensating gain. So the outcome for (a) is not +9, it is +5. Let me put the whole thing properly.

(a) $-5 + .2 \cdot +50 = +5$
(b) -5
(c) $+5 + .2 \cdot -50 = -5$
(d) $+5$

This looks very different than it did before.[8] And once the betting situation is put in this way, the correct way, the source of the "worry" that the argument causes becomes clear, and we can seriously evaluate the argument.

P: I see how what you have said changes the advisability of the various wagers, but you seem to mean more than that.

O: I think I do. The argument was put badly from the start. It was put in a way which is reflected in your erroneous utility calculation. Van den Haag says, "It's a matter of which risk you prefer and I prefer to protect the victims." This immediately makes us think of the situation in a misleading way, for it seems to imply that while I would risk the lives of potential victims, he would risk the lives of convicted criminals. Or, minimally, it implies that there are risks of a like kind on both sides. But he isn't *risking* the lives of criminals; he is taking their lives and risking that some further good will come of this.

Put the same thing a slightly different way. It has been said in our discussion that on either bet, the result could be the needless loss of life. This makes the bets look more parallel than they are. If

8. The precise number of utility units assigned to the alternatives is, of course, not significant. What is significant is the difference that results from the two ways of calculating. (I do not think that the rather simple uses I make of utility calculations in this paper assume any particular interpretation of utility theory; whether they are taken as a measure of "satisfaction" on the basis of which we prefer some thing or they simply reflect the fact that we prefer some things, the calculations would be the same and, I take it, at least roughly parallel our rational decision making.)

we bet your way, lives *have been lost*, and the risk is that this is needless. If we bet my way, it is *possible* that *lives may be lost*, needlessly. The difference between *lives lost*, perhaps needlessly, and *perhaps lives lost*, strikes me as a very significant one.

Now it should be clear that there is a sense in which you are gambling and I am not. It is exactly the sense in which I would be gambling if I used my last ten dollars to buy a lottery ticket but would not be if I used the money for groceries. Opting for a certain good, rather than risking it on a chance of a greater future good, is exactly what we mean when we say we refuse to gamble. Not gambling is taking the sure thing.

On the plausible moral principle, gambling with human lives is wrong, I can, then, reject the "Best-bet Argument."

P: But if you understand "gambling" as not taking the sure thing, that moral principal is much too strong. Unless you have infallible knowledge that C.P. deters, on that principle it could never be justified, even under conditions in which you would want to adopt it. For even if it were ninety *percent* certain that it deters, you would still be gambling. And there are other circumstances in which we must gamble with lives in this way. Suppose you were almost, but not quite, certain a madman was about to set off all the bombs in the Western hemisphere. On that principle, you would not be justified in shooting him, even if it were the only possible way to stop him.

O: Yes, I suppose that I must grant you that. But perhaps my suppositions that gambling is taking the risk and that gambling with human lives is wrong, taken together, at least partially account for my intuitive revulsion with van den Haag's argument.

P: That may be. But so far, your intuitions have come to nothing in producing a genuine objection to the argument. I might add that I cannot even agree with your intuition that not gambling is taking the sure thing. Don't we sometimes disapprove of the person who refuses to take out life insurance or automobile liability insurance on the grounds that he is unwisely gambling that he will not die prematurely or be responsible for a highway accident? And he is taking the sure thing, keeping the premium money in his pocket.

So, in common sense terms, failure to take a wise bet is sometimes "gambling."

O: You are right again. And I thank you.

P: For what?

O: For saying just what I needed to hear in order to get straight on this whole business. As I indicated before, once we properly set out the betting situation, it does not appear that you proponents *have* such a good bet. But in addition, I have (along with Nobile) been plagued by the feeling that there is something *in principle* wrong with the argument, that you would gamble with human lives while I would not. Now I understand that these two objections are actually only one objection.

P: How so?

O: Your insurance examples make the point. They show that what we intuitively think of as "gambling" is simply taking the more risky course of action, i.e. making a bad bet. So, my intuitive worry resulted simply from my conviction that your bet on C.P. is "gambling," i.e. that it is the riskier course of action; or, and this comes to the same thing, it is a *bad* bet.

P: So you admit that there is nothing in principle wrong with my argument. That it all depends on whether the bet on C.P. is a good bet.

O: I think I must. But that does not change my views about C.P. Once the bet is clarified, it should be clear that you are asking us to risk too much, to actually take a human life on far too small a chance of saving others. It is just a rotten bet.

P: But it is not. As I have said, the life of each murderer is clearly worth much less than the life of an innocent, and, besides, each criminal life lost may save many innocents.

O: This business about how much lives are "worth" seems pretty suspicious to me. According to some, human life qua human life is sacred and so all lives have the same value. According to others, the continued life of an innocent child is of much less importance than that of a criminal, since it is the criminal, qua criminal, who needs a chance to cleanse his soul. Or we could consider the potential social usefulness of the individual. If we do this, it is by no means obvious that the average murderer has less potential than the average person (consider Chessman or Leopold).

P: How can you talk like that? Have you ever seen the battered, maimed body of an innocent child, raped and brutally murdered? Compare the value of that life against that of the beast who performed the deed, and then can you doubt that the child is worth 10,000 times the criminal?

O: That seems to me to be based on a desire for revenge against "the beast," rather than on any evaluation of the "value of different lives." I admit to sharing such feelings, in some moods, at least, but it is not at all clear how they are relevant. Anyway, let's drop this. I am willing to rely on my feelings and grant, for argument purposes, that the life of a murderer is worth somewhat less than that of an innocent.

The basic problem with your wager is simply that we have no reason to think C.P. does work, and in the absence of such reason, the probability that it does is virtually zero. In general, you proponents seem confused about evidence. First, you say C.P. deters. Then you are confronted with evidence such as: State A and State B have virtually identical capital crime rates but State A hasn't had C.P. for one hundred years. You reply, for instance, that this could be because State A has more Quakers, who are peace-loving folk and so help to keep the crime rate down. And, you say, with C.P. and all those Quakers, State A, perhaps, could have had an even lower crime rate.[9] Since we do not know about all such variables, the evidence is "inconclusive."[10] Here, "inconclusive" can only mean that while the evidence does not indicate that C.P. deters, it also does not demonstrate that it does not.

The next thing we see is you proponents saying that we just do not know whether C.P. deters or not, since the evidence is "inconclusive." But for this to follow, "inconclusive" must mean something like "tends to point both ways." The only studies available, on your own account, fail to supply any evidence at all that it *does* deter. From this, we cannot get "inconclusive" in the latter sense;

9. Neglecting the fact that, with C.P., the crime rate also could have been higher (cf. Sidney Hook, "The Death Sentence," in Bedau, pp. 147–148).

10. For such a use of "inconclusive," see J. Edgar Hoover, in Bedau, p. 134.

we can't say that "we just don't know" whether it deters; we can only conclude, "we have no reason to think it does." Its status as a deterrent is no different from, e.g. prolonged tickling of murderers' feet. It could deter, but why think it does?

P: That's an absurd comparison that only a professional philosopher could think of. Common sense tells us that C.P. is a likely deterrent and foot-tickling is not.

O: I don't see how we can rely very heavily on the common sense of a law-abiding man to tell us how murderers think and why they act. Common sense also tells us that pornography should inflame the passions and therefore increase sex crimes, but Denmark's recent experience indicates quite the opposite.

P: So you demand that we have definite, unequivocal evidence and very high probability that C.P. deters before it could be said to be justifiable.

O: No, I never said that. That is what most of my fellow opponents of C.P. seem to demand. In fact, even though this would probably horrify most opponents, I think the "Best-bet Argument" shows that that demand is too strong. Given the possible gains and losses, if there is even a strong possibility that it works, I do not think it would be irrational to give it another try. But we should do so in full cognizance of the betting situation. We would be taking lives on the chance that there will be more than compensating saving of lives. And, I also think that it is damned difficult to show that there is even a strong possibility that C.P. deters.

P: Not really. Consider the fact that, given a choice between life imprisonment and C.P., prisoners always prefer . . .

O: Good night.

JEFFREY H. REIMAN

Justice, Civilization, and the Death Penalty: Answering van den Haag

On the issue of capital punishment, there is as clear a clash of moral intuitions as we are likely to see. Some (now a majority of Americans) feel deeply that justice requires payment in kind and thus that murderers should die; and others (once, but no longer, nearly a majority of Americans) feel deeply that the state ought not be in the business of putting people to death.[1] Arguments for either side that do not do justice to the intuitions of the other are unlikely to persuade anyone not already convinced. And, since, as I shall suggest, there is truth on both sides, such arguments are easily refutable, leaving us with nothing but conflicting intuitions and no guidance from reason in distinguishing the better from the worse. In this context, I shall try to make an argument for the abolition of the death penalty that does justice to the intuitions on both sides. I shall sketch out a conception of retributive justice that accounts for the justice of executing murderers, and then I shall argue that *though the death penalty is a just punishment for murder*, abolition of the death penalty is part of the civilizing mission of modern states. Before getting to this, let us briefly consider the challenges confronting those who would

This paper is an expanded version of my opening statement in a debate with Ernest van den Haag on the death penalty at an Amnesty International conference on capital punishment, held at John Jay College in New York City, on October 17, 1983. I am grateful to the Editors of *Philosophy & Public Affairs* for very thought-provoking comments, to Hugo Bedau and Robert Johnson for many helpful suggestions, and to Ernest van den Haag for his encouragement.

1. Asked, in a 1981 Gallup Poll, "Are you in favor of the death penalty for persons convicted of murder?" 66.25% were in favor, 25% were opposed, and 8.75% had no opinion. Asked the same question in 1966, 47.5% were opposed, 41.25% were in favor, and 11.25% had no opinion (Timothy J. Flanagan, David J. van Alstyne, and Michael R. Gottfredson, eds., *Sourcebook of Criminal Justice Statistics—1981*, U.S. Department of Justice, Bureau of Justice Statistics [Washington, D.C.: U.S. Government Printing Office, 1982], p. 209).

argue against the death penalty. In my view, these challenges have been
most forcefully put by Ernest van den Haag.

I. THE CHALLENGE TO THE ABOLITIONIST

The recent book, *The Death Penalty: A Debate*, in which van den Haag
argues for the death penalty and John P. Conrad argues against, proves
how difficult it is to mount a telling argument against capital punishment.[2] Conrad contends, for example, that "To kill the offender [who has
committed murder in the first degree] is to respond to his wrong by doing
the same wrong to him" (p. 60). But this popular argument is easily
refuted.[3] Since we regard killing in self-defense or in war as morally
permissible, it cannot be that we regard killing per se as wrong. It follows
that the wrong in murder cannot be that it is killing per se, but that it
is (among other things) the killing of an innocent person. Consequently,
if the state kills a murderer, though it does the same physical act that
he did, it does not do the wrong that he did, since the state is not killing
an innocent person (see p. 62). Moreover, unless this distinction is allowed, all punishments are wrong, since everything that the state does
as punishment is an act which is physically the same as an act normally
thought wrong. For example, if you lock an innocent person in a cage,
that is kidnapping. If the state responds by locking you in prison, it can
hardly be said to be responding to your wrong by doing you a wrong in
return. Indeed, it will be said that it is precisely because what you did
was wrong that locking you up, which would otherwise be wrong, is
right.[4]

2. Ernest van den Haag and John P. Conrad, *The Death Penalty: A Debate* (New York:
Plenum Press, 1983). Unless otherwise indicated, page references in the text and notes
are to this book.

3. Some days after the first attempt to execute J. D. Autry by lethal injection was aborted,
an editorial in *The Washington Post* (14 October 1983) asked: "If the taking of a human
life is the most unacceptable of crimes, can it ever be an acceptable penalty? Does an act
committed by an individual lose its essential character when it is imposed by society?" (p.
A26).

4. "Does fining a criminal show want of respect for property, or imprisoning him, for
personal freedom? Just as unreasonable is it to think that to take the life of a man who has
taken that of another is to show want of regard for human life. We show, on the contrary,
most emphatically our regard for it, by the adoption of a rule that he who violates that right
in another forfeits it for himself. . . ." (John Stuart Mill, "Parliamentary Debate on Capital
Punishment Within Prisons Bill," in *Philosophical Perspectives on Punishment*, ed. Gertrude
Ezorsky [Albany: State University of New York Press, 1972], p. 276; Mill made the speech
in 1868.)

Conrad also makes the familiar appeal to the possibility of executing an innocent person and the impossibility of correcting this tragic mistake. "An act by the state of such monstrous proportions as the execution of a man who is not guilty of the crime for which he was convicted should be avoided at all costs. . . . The abolition of capital punishment is the certain means of preventing the worst injustice" (p. 60). This argument, while not so easily disposed of as the previous one, is, like all claims about what "should be avoided at all costs," neither very persuasive. There is invariably some cost that is prohibitive such that if, for example, capital punishment were necessary to save the lives of potential murder victims, there must be a point at which the number of saved victims would be large enough to justify the risk of executing an innocent—particularly where trial and appellate proceedings are designed to reduce this risk to a minimum by giving the accused every benefit of the doubt.[5] Since we tolerate the death of innocents, in mines or on highways, as a cost of progress, and, in wars, as an inevitable accompaniment to aerial bombardment and the like, it cannot convincingly be contended that, kept to a minimum, the risk of executing an innocent is still so great an evil as to outweigh all other considerations (see pp. 230–31).

Nor will it do to suggest, as Conrad does, that execution implies that offenders are incapable of change and thus presumes the offenders' "total identification with evil," a presumption reserved only to God or, in any case, beyond the province of (mere) men (p. 27; also, pp. 42–43). This is not convincing since no punishment, whether on retributive or deterrent grounds, need imply belief in the total evilness of the punishee—all that need be believed (for retribution) is that what the offender has done is as evil as the punishment is awful, or (for deterrence) that what he has done is awful enough to warrant whatever punishment will discourage others from doing it. "Execution," writes van den Haag, "merely presumes an identification [with evil] sufficient to disregard what good qualities the convict has (he may be nice to animals and love his mother). . . . No total identification with evil—whatever that means—is required; only a sufficiently wicked crime" (p. 35).

Thus far I have tried to indicate how difficult it is to make an argument

5. Mill argues that the possibility of executing an innocent person would be an "invincible" objection "where the mode of criminal procedure is dangerous to the innocent," such as it is "in some parts of the Continent of Europe. . . . But we all know that the defects of our [English] procedure are the very opposite. Our rules of evidence are even too favorable to the prisoner" (ibid., pp. 276–77).

for the abolition of the death penalty against which the death penalty advocate cannot successfully defend himself. But van den Haag's argument is not merely defensive—he poses a positive challenge to anyone who would take up the abolitionist cause. For van den Haag, in order to argue convincingly for abolition, one must prove either that "no [criminal] act, however horrible, justifies [that is, deserves] the death penalty," or that, if capital punishment were found to deter murder more effectively than life imprisonment, we should still "prefer to preserve the life of a convicted murderer rather than the lives of innocent victims, even if it were certain that these victims would be spared if the murderer were executed" (p. 275).

If van den Haag is right and the abolitionist cause depends on proving either or both of these assertions, then it is a lost cause, since I believe they cannot be proven for reasons of the following sort: If people ever deserve anything for their acts, then it seems that what they deserve is something commensurate in cost or in benefit to what they have done. However horrible executions are, there are surely some acts to which they are commensurate in cost. If, as Camus says, the condemned man dies two deaths, one on the scaffold and one anticipating it, then isn't execution justified for one who has murdered two people? if not two, then ten?[6] As for the second assertion, since we take as justified the killing of innocent people (say, homicidal maniacs) in self-defense (that is, when necessary to preserve the lives of their innocent victims), then it seems that we must take as justified the killing of *guilty* people if it is necessary to preserve the lives of innocent victims. Indeed, though punishment is not the same as self-defense, it is, when practiced to deter crimes, arguably a form of social defense—and parity of reason would seem to dictate that if killing is justified when necessary for self-defense, then it is justified when necessary for social defense.

It might be thought that injuring or killing others in self-defense is justifiable in that it aims to stop the threatening individual himself, but that punishing people (even guilty people) to deter others is a violation

6. "As a general rule, a man is undone by waiting for capital punishment well before he dies. Two deaths are inflicted on him, the first being worse than the second, whereas he killed but once" (Albert Camus, "Reflections on the Guillotine," in *Resistance, Rebellion and Death* [New York: Alfred A. Knopf, 1969], p. 205). Based on interviews with the condemned men on Alabama's death row, Robert Johnson presents convincing empirical support for Camus' observation, in *Condemned to Die: Life Under Sentence of Death* (New York: Elsevier, 1981).

of the Kantian prohibition against using people merely as means to the well-being of others.[7] It seems to me that this objection is premised on the belief that what deters potential criminals are the individual acts of punishment. In that case, each person punished is truly being used for the benefit of others. If, however, what deters potential criminals is the existence of a functioning punishment system, then everyone is benefited by that system, including those who end up being punished by it, since they too have received the benefit of enhanced security due to the deterring of some potential criminals. Even criminals benefit from what deters other criminals from preying on them. Then, each act of punishment is done as a necessary condition of the existence of a system that benefits all; and no one is used or sacrificed *merely* for the benefit of others.

If I am correct in believing that the assertions that van den Haag challenges the abolitionist to prove cannot be proven, then the case for the abolition of the death penalty must be made while accepting that some crimes deserve capital punishment, and that evidence that capital punishment was a substantially better deterrent to murder than life imprisonment would justify imposing it. This is what I shall attempt to do. Indeed, I shall begin the case for the abolition of the death penalty by defending the justice of the death penalty as a punishment for murder.

II. Just Deserts and Just Punishments

In my view, the death penalty is a just punishment for murder because the *lex talionis*, an eye for an eye, and so on, is just, although, as I shall suggest at the end of this section, it can only be rightly applied when its implied preconditions are satisfied. The *lex talionis* is a version of retributivism. Retributivism—as the word itself suggests—is the doctrine that the offender should be *paid back* with suffering he deserves because of the evil he has done, and the *lex talionis* asserts that injury equivalent to that he imposed is what the offender deserves.[8] But the *lex talionis* is

7. Jeffrie G. Murphy, "Marxism and Retribution," *Philosophy & Public Affairs* 2, no. 3 (Spring 1973):219.

8. I shall speak throughout of retribution as paying back for "harm caused," but this is shorthand for "harm intentionally attempted or caused"; likewise when I speak of the death penalty as punishment for murder, I have in mind premeditated, first-degree murder. Note also that the harm caused by an offender, for which he is to be paid back, is not necessarily limited to the harm done to his immediate victim. It may include as well the suffering of

not the only version of retributivism. Another, which I shall call "proportional retributivism," holds that what retribution requires is not equality of injury between crimes and punishments, but "fit" or proportionality, such that the worst crime is punished with the society's worst penalty, and so on, though the society's worst punishment need not duplicate the injury of the worst crime.[9] Later, I shall try to show how a form of proportional retributivism is compatible with acknowledging the justice of the *lex talionis*. Indeed, since I shall defend the justice of the *lex talionis*, I take such compatibility as a necessary condition of the validity of any form of retributivism.[10]

---

the victim's relatives or the fear produced in the general populace, and the like. For simplicity's sake, however, I shall continue to speak as if the harm for which retributivism would have us pay the offender back is the harm (intentionally attempted or done) to his immediate victim. Also, retribution is not to be confused with *restitution*. Restitution involves restoring the *status quo ante*, the condition prior to the offense. Since it was in this condition that the criminal's offense was committed, it is this condition that constitutes the baseline against which retribution is exacted. Thus retribution involves imposing a loss on the offender measured from the status quo ante. For example, returning a thief's loot to his victim so that thief and victim now own what they did before the offense is *restitution*. Taking enough from the thief so that what he is left with is less than what he had before the offense is *retribution*, since this is just what he did to his victim.

9. "The most extreme form of retributivism is the law of retaliation: 'an eye for an eye' " (Stanley I. Benn, "Punishment," *The Encyclopedia of Philosophy* 7, ed. Paul Edwards [New York: Macmillan, 1967], p. 32). Hugo Bedau writes: "retributive justice need not be thought to consist of *lex talionis*. One may reject that principle as too crude and still embrace the retributive principle that the severity of punishments should be graded according to the gravity of the offense" (Hugo Bedau, "Capital Punishment," in *Matters of Life and Death*, ed. Tom Regan [New York: Random House, 1980], p. 177). See also, Andrew von Hirsch, "Doing Justice: The Principle of Commensurate Deserts," and Hyman Gross, "Proportional Punishment and Justifiable Sentences," in *Sentencing*, eds. H. Gross and A. von Hirsch (New York: Oxford University Press, 1981), pp. 243–56 and 272–83, respectively.

10. In an article aimed at defending a retributivist theory of punishment, Michael Davis claims that the relevant measure of punishment is not the cost to the offender's victim ("property taken, bones broken, or lives lost"), but the "value of the unfair advantage he [the offender] takes of those who obey the law (even though they are tempted to do otherwise)" (Michael Davis, "How to Make the Punishment Fit the Crime," *Ethics* 93 [July 1983]:744). Though there is much to be said for this view, standing alone it seems quite questionable. For example, it would seem that the value of the unfair advantage taken of law-obeyers by one who robs a great deal of money is greater than the value of the unfair advantage taken by a murderer, since the latter gets only the advantage of ridding his world of a nuisance while the former will be able to make a new life without the nuisance and have money left over for other things. This leads to the counterintuitive conclusion that such robbers should be punished more severely (and regarded as more wicked) than murderers. One might try to get around this by treating the value of the unfair advantage as a function of the cost imposed by the crime. And Davis does this after a fashion. He takes the value of such advantages to be equivalent to the prices that licenses to commit crimes

There is nothing self-evident about the justice of the *lex talionis* nor,
for that matter, of retributivism.[11] The standard problem confronting those
who would justify retributivism is that of overcoming the suspicion that
it does no more than sanctify the victim's desire to hurt the offender back.
Since serving that desire amounts to hurting the offender simply for the
satisfaction that the victim derives from seeing the offender suffer, and
since deriving satisfaction from the suffering of others seems primitive,
the policy of imposing suffering on the offender for no other purpose
than giving satisfaction to his victim seems primitive as well. Consequently, defending retributivism requires showing that the suffering imposed on the wrongdoer has some worthy point beyond the satisfaction
of victims. In what follows, I shall try to identify a proposition—which I
call the *retributivist principle*—that I take to be the nerve of retributivism.
I think this principle accounts for the justice of the *lex talionis* and
indicates the point of the suffering demanded by retributivism. Not to do
too much of the work of the death penalty advocate, I shall make no
extended argument for this principle beyond suggesting the considerations that make it plausible. I shall identify these considerations by drawing, with considerable license, on Hegel and Kant.

I think that we can see the justice of the *lex talionis* by focusing on
the striking affinity between it and the *golden rule*. The *golden rule*
mandates "Do unto others as you would have others do unto you," while
the *lex talionis* counsels "Do unto others as they have done unto you."
It would not be too far-fetched to say that the *lex talionis* is the law
enforcement arm of the golden rule, at least in the sense that if people
were actually treated as they treated others, then everyone would necessarily follow the golden rule because then people could only willingly
act toward others as they were willing to have others act toward them.
This is not to suggest that the *lex talionis* follows from the golden rule,
but rather that the two share a common moral inspiration: the equality

---

would bring if sold on the market, and he claims that these prices would be at least as
much as what non-licenseholders would (for their own protection) pay licensees not to use
their licenses. Now this obviously brings the cost to victims of crime back into the measure
of punishment, though only halfheartedly, since this cost must be added to the value to
the licensee of being able to use his license. And this still leaves open the distinct possibility
that licenses for very lucrative theft opportunities would fetch higher prices on the market
than licenses to kill, with the same counterintuitive result mentioned earlier.

11. Stanley Benn writes: "to say 'it is fitting' or 'justice demands' that the guilty should
suffer is only to affirm that punishment is right, not to give grounds for thinking so" (Benn,
"Punishment," p. 30).

of persons. Treating others as you *would* have them treat you means treating others as equal to you, because adopting the golden rule as one's guiding principle implies that one counts the suffering of others to be as great a calamity as one's own suffering, that one counts one's right to impose suffering on others as no greater than their right to impose suffering on one, and so on. This leads to the *lex talionis* by two approaches that start from different points and converge.

I call the first approach "Hegelian" because Hegel held (roughly) that crime upsets the equality between persons and retributive punishment restores that equality by "annulling" the crime.[12] As we have seen, acting according to the golden rule implies treating others as your equals. Conversely, violating the golden rule implies the reverse: Doing to another what you would *not* have that other do to you violates the equality of persons by asserting a right toward the other that the other does not possess toward you. Doing back to you what you did "annuls" your violation by reasserting that the other has the same right toward you that you assert toward him. Punishment according to the *lex talionis* cannot heal the injury that the other has suffered at your hands, rather it rectifies the indignity he has suffered, by restoring him to equality with you.

"Equality of persons" here does not mean equality of concern for their happiness, as it might for a utilitarian. On such a (roughly) utilitarian understanding of equality, imposing suffering on the wrongdoer equivalent to the suffering he has imposed would have little point. Rather, equality of concern for people's happiness would lead us to impose as little suffering on the wrongdoer as was compatible with maintaining the happiness of others. This is enough to show that retributivism (at least

---

12. Hegel writes that "The sole positive existence which the injury [i.e., the crime] possesses is that it is the particular will of the criminal [i.e., it is the criminal's intention that distinguishes criminal injury from, say, injury due to an accident]. Hence to injure (or penalize) this particular will as a will determinately existent is to annul the crime, which otherwise would have been held valid, and to restore the right" (G.W.F. Hegel, *The Philosophy of Right*, trans. by T. M. Knox [Oxford: Clarendon Press, 1962; originally published in German in 1821], p. 69, see also p. 331n). I take this to mean that the right is a certain equality of sovereignty between the wills of individuals, crime disrupts that equality by placing one will above others, and punishment restores the equality by annulling the illegitimate ascendance. On these grounds, as I shall suggest below, the desire for revenge (strictly limited to the desire "to even the score") is more respectable than philosophers have generally allowed. And so Hegel writes that "The annulling of crime in this sphere where right is immediate [i.e., the condition prior to conscious morality] is principally revenge, which is just in its content in so far as it is retributive" (ibid., p. 73).

in this "Hegelian" form) reflects a conception of morality quite different
from that envisioned by utilitarianism. Instead of seeing morality as ad-
ministering doses of happiness to individual recipients, the retributivist
envisions morality as maintaining the relations appropriate to equally
sovereign individuals. A crime, rather than representing a unit of suffering added to the already considerable suffering in the world, is an
assault on the sovereignty of an individual that temporarily places one
person (the criminal) in a position of illegimate sovereignty over another
(the victim). The victim (or his representative, the state) then has the
right to rectify this loss of standing relative to the criminal by meting out
a punishment that reduces the criminal's sovereignty in the degree to
which he vaunted it above his victim's. It might be thought that this is
a duty, not just a right, but that is surely too much. The victim has the
right to forgive the violator without punishment, which suggests that it
is by virtue of having the right to punish the violator (rather than the
duty), that the victim's equality with the violator is restored.

I call the second approach "Kantian" since Kant held (roughly) that,
since reason (like justice) is no respecter of the sheer difference between
individuals, when a rational being decides to act in a certain way toward
his fellows, he implicitly authorizes similar action by his fellows toward
him.[13] A version of the golden rule, then, is a requirement of reason:
acting rationally, one always acts as he would have others act toward
him. Consequently, to act toward a person as he has acted toward others
is to treat him as a rational being, that is, as if his act were the product
of a rational decision. From this, it may be concluded that we have a duty
to do to offenders what they have done, since this amounts to according
them the respect due rational beings.[14] Here too, however, the assertion

13. Kant writes that "any undeserved evil that you inflict on someone else among the
people is one that you do to yourself. If you vilify him, you vilify yourself; if you steal from
him, you steal from yourself; if you kill him, you kill yourself." Since Kant holds that "If
what happens to someone is also willed by him, it cannot be a punishment," he takes pains
to distance himself from the view that the offender *wills* his punishment. "The chief error
contained in this sophistry," Kant writes, "consists in the confusion of the criminal's [that
is, the murderer's] own judgment (which one must necessarily attribute to his reason) that
he must forfeit his life with a resolution of the will to take his own life" (Immanuel Kant,
The Metaphysical Elements of Justice, Part I of The Metaphysics of Morals, trans. by
J. Ladd [Indianapolis: Bobbs-Merrill, 1965; originally published in 1797], pp. 101, 105–
106). I have tried to capture this notion of attributing a judgment to the offender rather
than a resolution of his will with the term 'authorizes.'

14. "Even if a civil society were to dissolve itself by common agreement of all its members

of a duty to punish seems excessive, since, if this duty arises because doing to people what they have done to others is necessary to accord them the respect due rational beings, then we would have a duty to do to all rational persons *everything*—good, bad, or indifferent—that they do to others. The point rather is that, by his acts, a rational being *authorizes* others to do the same to him, he doesn't *compel* them to. Here too, then, the argument leads to a right, rather than a duty, to exact the *lex talionis*. And this is supported by the fact that we can conclude from Kant's argument that a rational being cannot validly complain of being treated in the way he has treated others, and where there is no valid complaint, there is no injustice, and where there is no injustice, others have acted within their rights.[15] It should be clear that the Kantian argument also rests on the equality of persons, because a rational agent

---

... , the last murderer remaining in prison must first be executed, so that everyone will duly receive what his actions are worth" (Kant, ibid., p. 102). Interestingly, Conrad calls himself a retributivist, but doesn't accept the strict Kantian version of it. In fact, he claims that Kant "did not bother with justifications for his categorical imperative . . . , [but just] insisted that the Roman *jus talionis* was the reference point at which to begin" (p. 22). Van den Haag, by contrast, states specifically that he is "not a retributionist" (p. 32). In fact he claims that "retributionism" is not really a *theory* of punishment at all, just "a feeling articulated through a metaphor presented as though a theory" (p. 28). This is so, he maintains, because a theory "must tell us what the world, or some part thereof, is like or has been or will be like" (ibid.). "In contrast," he goes on, "deterrence theory is, whether right or wrong, a theory: It asks what the effects are of punishment (does it reduce the crime rate?) and makes testable predictions (punishment reduces the crime rate compared to what it would be without the credible threat of punishment)" (p. 29). Now, it should be obvious that van den Haag has narrowed his conception of "theory" so that it only covers the kind of things one finds in the empirical sciences. So narrowed, there is no such thing as a theory about what justifies some action or policy, no such thing as a Kantian theory of punishment, or, for that matter, a Rawlsian theory of jusice—that is to say, no such thing as a *moral* theory. Van den Haag, of course, could use the term 'theory' as he wished, were it not for the fact that he appeals to deterrence theory not merely for predictions about crime rates but also (indeed, in the current context, primarily) as a theory about what justifies punishment—that is, as a *moral* theory. And he must, since the fact that punishment reduces crime does not imply that we should institute punishment unless we *should* do whatever reduces crime. In short, van den Haag is about moral theories the way I am about airplanes: He doesn't quite understand how they work, but he knows how to use them to get where he wants to go.

15. "It may also be pointed out that no one has ever heard of anyone condemned to death on account of murder who complained that he was getting too much [punishment] and therefore was being treated unjustly; everyone would laugh in his face if he were to make such a statement" (Kant, *Metaphysical Elements of Justice*, p. 104; see also p. 133).

only implicitly authorizes having done to him action similar to what he has done to another, if he and the other are similar in the relevant ways.

The "Hegelian" and "Kantian" approaches arrive at the same destination from opposite sides. The "Hegelian" approach starts from the victim's equality with the criminal, and infers from it the victim's right to do to the criminal what the criminal has done to the victim. The "Kantian" approach starts from the criminal's rationality, and infers from it the criminal's authorization of the victim's right to do to the criminal what the criminal has done to the victim. Taken together, these approaches support the following proposition: The equality and rationality of persons implies that an offender deserves and his victim has the right to impose suffering on the offender equal to that which he imposed on the victim. This is the proposition I call the *retributivist principle*, and I shall assume henceforth that it is true. This principle provides that the *lex talionis* is the criminal's just desert and the victim's (or as his representative, the state's) right. Moreover, the principle also indicates the point of retributive punishment, namely, it affirms the equality and rationality of persons, victims and offenders alike.[16] And the point of this affirmation is, like any moral affirmation, to make a statement, to the criminal, to impress upon him his equality with his victim (which earns him a like fate) and his rationality (by which his actions are held to authorize his fate), and to the society, so that recognition of the equality and rationality of persons becomes a visible part of our shared moral environment that none can ignore in justifying their actions to one another.

When I say that with respect to the criminal, the point of retributive punishment is to impress upon him his equality with his victim, I mean to be understood quite literally. If the sentence is just and the criminal rational, then the punishment should normally *force* upon him recognition of his equality with his victim, recognition of their shared vulnerability to suffering and their shared desire to avoid it, as well as recognition of the fact that he counts for no more than his victim in the eyes of their fellows. For this reason, the retributivist requires that the offender be

16. Herbert Morris defends retributivism on parallel grounds. See his "Persons and Punishment," *The Monist* 52, no. 4 (October 1968):475–501. Isn't what Morris calls "the right to be treated as a person" essentially the right of a rational being to be treated only as he has authorized, implicitly or explicitly, by his own free choices?

sane, not only at the moment of his crime, but also at the moment of his punishment—while this latter requirement would seem largely pointless (if not downright malevolent) to a utilitarian. Incidentally, it is, I believe, the desire that the offender be forced by suffering punishment to recognize his equality with his victim, rather than the desire for that suffering itself, that constitutes what is rational in the desire for revenge.

The retributivist principle represents a conception of moral desert whose complete elaboration would take us far beyond the scope of the present essay. In its defense, however, it is worth noting that our common notion of moral desert seems to include (at least) two elements: (1) a conception of individual responsibility for actions that is "contagious," that is, one which confers moral justification on the punishing (or rewarding) re-actions of others; and (2) a measure of the relevant worth of actions that determines the legitimate magnitude of justified reactions. Broadly speaking, the "Kantian" notion of authorization implicit in rational action supplies the first element, and the "Hegelian" notion of upsetting and restoring equality of standing supplies the second. It seems, then, reasonable to take the equality and rationality of persons as implying moral desert in the way asserted in the retributivist principle. I shall assume henceforth that the retributivist principle is true.

The truth of the retributivist principle establishes the justice of the *lex talionis*, but, since it establishes this as a right of the victim rather than a duty, it does not settle the question of whether or to what extent the victim or the state should exercise this right and exact the *lex talionis*. This is a separate moral question because strict adherence to the *lex talionis* amounts to allowing criminals, even the most barbaric of them, to dictate our punishing behavior. It seems certain that there are at least some crimes, such as rape or torture, that we ought not try to match. And this is not merely a matter of imposing an alternative punishment that produces an equivalent amount of suffering, as, say, some number of years in prison that might "add up" to the harm caused by a rapist or a torturer. Even if no amount of time in prison would add up to the harm caused by a torturer, it still seems that we ought not torture him even if this were the only way of making him suffer as much as he has made his victim suffer. Or, consider someone who has committed several murders in cold blood. On the *lex talionis*, it would seem that such a criminal might justly be brought to within an inch of death and then revived (or to within a moment of execution and then reprieved) as many times as he has killed (minus one), and then finally executed. But surely this is a degree of cruelty that would be monstrous.[17]

Since the retributivist principle establishes the *lex talionis* as the victim's right, it might seem that the question of how far this right should be exercised is "up to the victim." And indeed, this would be the case in the state of nature. But once, for all the good reasons familiar to readers of John Locke, the state comes into existence, public punishment replaces private, and the victim's right to punish reposes in the state. With this, the decision as to how far to exercise this right goes to the state as well. To be sure, since (at least with respect to retributive punishment) the victim's right is the source of the state's right to punish, the state must exercise its right in ways that are faithful to the victim's right. Later, when I try to spell out the upper and lower limits of just punishment, these may be taken as indicating the range within which the state can punish and remain faithful to the victim's right.

I suspect that it will be widely agreed that the state ought not administer punishments of the sort described above even if required by the letter of the *lex talionis*, and thus, even granting the justice of *lex talionis*, there are occasions on which it is morally appropriate to diverge from its requirements. We must, of course, distinguish such morally based divergence from that which is based on practicality. Like any moral principle, the *lex talionis* is subject to "ought implies can." It will usually be impossible to do to an offender exactly what he has done—for example, his offense will normally have had an element of surprise that is not possible for a judicially imposed punishment, but this fact can hardly free him from having to bear the suffering he has imposed on another. Thus, for reasons of practicality, the *lex talionis* must necessarily be qualified to call for doing to the offender *as nearly as possible* what he has done to his victim. When, however, we refrain from raping rapists or torturing torturers, we do so for reasons of morality, not of practicality. And, given the justice of the *lex talionis*, these moral reasons cannot amount to claiming that it would be *unjust* to rape rapists or torture torturers. Rather

17. Bedau writes: "Where criminals set the limits of just methods of punishment, as they will do if we attempt to give exact and literal implementation to *lex talionis*, society will find itself descending to the cruelties and savagery that criminals employ. But society would be deliberately authorizing such acts, in the cool light of reason, and not (as is often true of vicious criminals) impulsively or in hatred and anger or with an insane or unbalanced mind. Moral restraints, in short, prohibit us from trying to make executions perfectly retributive" (Bedau, "Capital Punishment," p. 176).

the claim must be that, even though it would be just to rape rapists and torture torturers, other moral considerations weigh against doing so.

On the other hand, when, for moral reasons, we refrain from exacting the *lex talionis*, and impose a less harsh alternative punishment, it may be said that we are not doing full justice to the criminal, but it cannot automatically be the case that we are doing an *injustice* to his victim. Otherwise we would have to say it was unjust to imprison our torturer rather than torturing him or to simply execute our multiple murderer rather than multiply "executing" him. Surely it is counterintuitive (and irrational to boot) to set the demands of justice so high that a society would have to choose between being barbaric or being unjust. This would effectively price justice out of the moral market.

The implication of this is that there is a range of just punishments that includes some that are just though they exact less than the full measure of the *lex talionis*. What are the top and bottom ends of this range? I think that both are indicated by the *retributivist principle*. The principle identifies the *lex talionis* as the offender's desert and since, on retributive grounds, punishment beyond what one deserves is unjust for the same reasons that make punishment of the innocent unjust, the *lex talionis* is the upper limit of the range of just punishments. On the other hand, if the retributivist principle is true, then denying that the offender deserves suffering equal to that which he imposed amounts to denying the equality and rationality of persons. From this it follows that we fall below the bottom end of the range of just punishments when we act in ways that are incompatible with the *lex talionis* at the top end. That is, we fall below the bottom end and commit an injustice to the victim when we treat the offender in a way that is no longer compatible with sincerely believing that he deserves to have done to him what he has done to his victim. Thus, the upper limit of the range of just punishments is the point after which more punishment is unjust to the offender, and the lower limit is the point after which less punishment is unjust to the victim. In this way, the range of just punishments remains faithful to the victim's right which is their source.

This way of understanding just punishment enables us to formulate proportional retributivism so that it is compatible with acknowledging the justice of the *lex talionis*: If we take the *lex talionis* as spelling out the offender's just deserts, and if other moral considerations require us to refrain from matching the injury caused by the offender while still allowing us to punish justly, then surely we impose just punishment if we impose the closest morally acceptable approximation to the *lex talionis*. Proportional retributivism, then, in requiring that the worst crime be punished by the society's worst punishment and so on, could be understood as translating the offender's just desert into its nearest equivalent in the society's table of morally acceptable punishments. Then the two versions of retributivism (*lex talionis* and proportional) are related in that the first states what just punishment would be if nothing but the offender's just desert mattered, and the second locates just punishment at the meeting point of the offender's just deserts and the society's moral scruples. And since this second version only modifies the requirements of the *lex talionis* in light of other moral considerations, it is compatible with believing that the *lex talionis* spells out the offender's just deserts, much in the way that modifying the obligations of promisers in light of other moral considerations is compatible with believing in the binding nature of promises.

Proportional retributivism so formulated preserves the point of retributivism and remains faithful to the victim's right which is its source. Since it punishes with the closest morally acceptable approximation to the *lex talionis*, it effectively says to the offender, you deserve the equivalent of what you did to your victim and you are getting less only to the degree that *our* moral scruples limit us from duplicating what you have done. Such punishment, then, affirms the equality of persons by respecting *as far as is morally permissible* the victim's right to impose suffering on the offender equal to what he received, and it affirms the rationality of the offender by treating him as authorizing others to do to him what he has done though they take him up on it only *as far as is morally permissible*. Needless to say, the alternative punishments must in some convincing way be comparable in gravity to the crimes which they punish, or else they will trivialize the harms those crimes caused and be no longer compatible with sincerely believing that the offender deserves to have done to him what he has done to his victim and no longer capable of impressing upon the criminal his equality with the victim. If we punish rapists with a small fine or a brief prison term, we do an injustice to their victims, because this trivializes the suffering rapists have caused and thus is incompatible with believing that they deserve to have done to them something comparable to what they have done to their victims. If, on the other hand, instead of raping rapists we impose on them some grave penalty, say a substantial term of imprisonment, then we do no injustice even though we refrain from exacting the *lex talionis*.

To sum up, I take the *lex talionis* to be the top end of the range of just punishments. When, because we are simply unable to duplicate the criminal's offense, we modify the *lex talionis* to call for imposing on the offender as nearly as possible what he has done, we are still at this top end, applying the *lex talionis* subject to "ought implies can." When we do less than this, we still act justly as long as we punish in a way that is compatible with sincerely believing that the offender deserves the full measure of the *lex talionis*, but receives less for reasons that do not undermine this belief. If this is true, then it is not unjust to spare murderers as long as they can be punished in some other suitably grave way. I leave open the question of what such an alternative punishment might be, except to say that it need not be limited to such penalties as are currently imposed. For example, though rarely carried out in practice, a life sentence with no chance of parole might be a civilized equivalent of the death penalty—after all, people sentenced to life imprisonment have traditionally been regarded as "civilly dead."[18]

It might be objected that no punishment short of death will serve the point of retributivism with respect to murderers because no punishment short of death is commensurate with the crime of murder since, while some number of years of imprisonment may add up to the amount of harm done by rapists or assaulters or torturers, no number of years will add up to the harm done to the victim of murder. But justified divergence from the *lex talionis* is not limited only to changing the form of punishment while maintaining equivalent severity. Otherwise, we would have to torture torturers rather than imprison them if they tortured more than could be made up for by years in prison (or by the years available to them to spend in prison, which might be few for elderly torturers), and we would have to subject multiple murderers to multiple "executions." If justice allows us to refrain from these penalties, then justice allows punishments that are not equal in suffering to their crimes. It seems to me that if the objector grants this much, then he must show that a punish-

18. I am indebted to my colleague Robert Johnson for this suggestion, which he has attempted to develop in "A Life for a Life?" (unpub. ms.). He writes that prisoners condemned to spend their entire lives in prison "would suffer a civil death, the death of freedom. The prison would be their cemetery, a 6' by 9' cell their tomb. Their freedom would be interred in the name of justice. They would be consigned to mark the passage of their lives in the prison's peculiar dead time, which serves no purpose and confers no rewards. In effect, they would give their civil lives in return for the natural lives they have taken."

ment less than death is not merely incommensurate to the harm caused by murder, but so far out of proportion to that harm that it trivializes it and thus effectively denies the equality and rationality of persons. Now, I am vulnerable to the claim that a sentence of life in prison that allows parole after eight or ten years does indeed trivialize the harm of (premeditated, coldblooded) murder. But I cannot see how a sentence that would require a murderer to spend his full natural life in prison, or even the lion's share of his adult life (say, the thirty years between age twenty and age fifty), can be regarded as anything less than extremely severe and thus no trivialization of the harm he has caused.

I take it then that the justice of the *lex talionis* implies that it is just to execute murderers, but not that it is unjust to spare them as long as they are systematically punished in some other suitably grave way. Before developing the implications of this claim, a word about the implied preconditions of applying the *lex talionis* is in order.

Since this principle calls for imposing on offenders the harms they are responsible for imposing on others, the implied preconditions of applying it to any particular harm include the requirement that the harm be one that the offender is fully responsible for, where responsibility is both psychological, the capacity to tell the difference between right and wrong and control one's actions, and social. If people are subjected to remediable unjust social circumstances beyond their control, and if harmful actions are a predictable response to those conditions, then those who benefit from the unjust conditions and refuse to remedy them share responsibility for the harmful acts—and thus neither their doing nor their cost can be assigned fully to the offenders alone. For example, if a slave kills an innocent person while making his escape, at least part of the blame for the killing must fall on those who have enslaved him. And this is because slavery is unjust, not merely because the desire to escape from slavery is understandable. The desire to escape from prison is understandable as well, but if the imprisonment were a just sentence, then we would hold the prisoner, and not his keepers, responsible if he killed someone while escaping.

Since I believe that the vast majority of murders in America are a predictable response to the frustrations and disabilities of impoverished social circumstances,[19] and since I believe that that impoverishment is

19. "In the case of homicide, the empirical evidence indicates that poverty and poor economic conditions are systematically related to higher levels of homicide" (Richard M. McGahey, "Dr. Ehrlich's Magic Bullet: Economic Theory, Econometrics, and the Death

a remediable injustice from which others in America benefit, I believe
that we have no right to exact the full cost of murders from our murderers
until we have done everything possible to rectify the conditions that
produce their crimes.[20] But these are the "Reagan years," and not many—
who are not already susceptible—will be persuaded by this sort of argument.[21] This does not, in my view, shake its validity; but I want to

---

Penalty," *Crime & Delinquency* 26, no. 4 [October 1980]:502). Some of that evidence can
be found in Peter Passell, "The Deterrent Effect of the Death Penalty: A Statistical Test,"
Stanford Law Review (November 1975):61–80.

20. A similar though not identical point has been made by Jeffrie G. Murphy. He writes
"I believe that retributivism can be formulated in such a way that it is the only morally
defensible theory of punishment. I also believe that arguments, which may be regarded as
Marxist at least in spirit, can be formulated which show that social conditions as they obtain
in most societies make this form of retributivism largely inapplicable within those societies"
(Murphy, "Marxism and Retribution," p. 221). Though my claim here is similar to Murphy's,
the route by which I arrive at it differs from his in several ways. Most important, a key
point of Murphy's argument is that retributivism assumes that the criminal freely chooses
his crime while, according to Murphy, criminals act on the basis of psychological traits
that the society has conditioned them to have: "Is it just to punish people who act out of
those very motives that society encourages and reinforces? If [Willem] Bonger [a Dutch
Marxist criminologist] is correct, much criminality is motivated by greed, selfishness, and
indifference to one's fellows; but does not the whole society encourage motives of greed
and selfishness ('making it,' 'getting ahead'), and does not the competitive nature of the
society alienate men from each other and thereby encourage indifference—even, perhaps,
what psychiatrists call psychopathy?" (ibid., p. 239). This argument assumes that the
criminal is in some sense unable to conform to legal and moral prohibitions against violence,
and thus, like the insane, cannot be thought responsible for his actions. This claim is rather
extreme, and dubious as a result. My argument does not claim that criminals, murderers
in particular, cannot control their actions. I claim rather that, though criminals can control
their actions, when crimes are predictable responses to unjust circumstances, then those
who benefit from and do not remedy those conditions bear some responsibility for the
crimes and thus the criminals cannot be held *wholly* responsible for them in the sense of
being legitimately required to pay their full cost. It should be noted that Murphy's thesis
(quoted at the beginning of this note) is stated in a somewhat confused way. Social conditions that mitigate or eliminate the guilt of offenders do not make retributivism *inapplicable*. Retributivism is applied both when those who are guilty because they freely chose
their crimes are punished *and* when it is held wrong to punish those who are not guilty
because they did not freely choose their crimes. It is precisely by the application of retributivism that the social conditions referred to by Murphy make the punishment of criminals
unjustifiable.

21. Van den Haag notes the connection between crime and poverty, and explains it and
its implications as follows: "Poverty," he holds, "does not compel crime; it only makes it
more tempting" (p. 207). And it is not absolute poverty that does this, only relative deprivation, the fact that some have less than others (p. 115). In support of this, he marshals
data showing that, over the years, crime has risen along with the standard of living at the
bottom of society. Since, unlike absolute deprivation, relative deprivation will be with us

make an argument whose appeal is not limited to those who think that crime is the result of social injustice.[22] I shall proceed then, granting not only the justice of the death penalty, but also, at least temporarily, the assumption that our murderers are wholly deserving of dying for their crimes. If I can show that it would still be wrong to execute murderers,

---

no matter how rich we all become as long as some have more than others, he concludes that this condition which increases the temptation to crime is just an ineradicable fact of social life, best dealt with by giving people strong incentives to resist the temptation. This argument is flawed in several ways. First, the claim that crime is connected with poverty ought not be simplistically interpreted to mean that a low absolute standard of living itself causes crime. Rather, what seems to be linked to crime is the general breakdown of stable communities, institutions and families, such as has occurred in our cities in recent decades as a result of economic and demographic trends largely out of individuals' control. Of this breakdown, poverty is today a sign and a cause, at least in the sense that poverty leaves people with few defenses against it and few avenues of escape from it. This claim is quite compatible with finding that people with lower absolute standards of living, but who dwell in more stable social surroundings with traditional institutions still intact, have lower crime rates than contemporary poor people who have higher absolute standards of living. Second, the implication of this is not simply that it is relative deprivation that tempts to crime, since if that were the case, the middle class would be stealing as much from the rich as the poor do from the middle class. That this is not the case suggests that there is some threshold after which crime is no longer so tempting, and while this threshold changes historically, it is in principle one all could reach. Thus, it is not merely the (supposedly ineradicable) fact of having less than others that tempts to crime. Finally, everything is altered if the temptation to crime is not the result of an ineradicable social fact, but of an injustice that can be remedied or relieved. Obviously, this would require considerable argument, but it seems to me that the current distribution of wealth in America is unjust whether one takes utilitarianism as one's theory of justice (given the relative numbers of rich and poor in America as well as the principle of declining marginal returns, redistribution could make the poor happier without an offsetting loss in happiness among the rich) or Rawls's theory (the worst-off shares in our society could still be increased, so the difference principle is not yet satisfied) or Nozick's theory (since the original acquisition of property in America was marked by the use of force against Indians and blacks, from which both groups still suffer).

22. In arguing that social injustice disqualifies us from applying the death penalty, I am arguing that unjust discrimination in the *recruitment* of murderers undermines the justice of applying the penalty under foreseeable conditions in the United States. This is distinct from the argument that points to the discriminatory way in which it has been *applied* to murderers (generally against blacks, particularly when their victims are white). This latter argument is by no means unimportant, nor do I believe that it has been rendered obsolete by the Supreme Court's 1972 decision in *Furman v. Georgia* that struck down then-existing death penalty statutes because they allowed discriminatory application, or the Court's 1976 decision in *Gregg v. Georgia*, which approved several new statutes because they supposedly remedied this problem. There is considerable empirical evidence that much the same pattern of discrimination that led to *Furman* continues after *Gregg*. See for example, William J. Bowers and Glenn L. Pierce, "Arbitrariness and Discrimination in Post-*Furman* Capital

I believe I shall have made the strongest case for abolishing the death
penalty.

III. Civilization, Pain, and Justice

As I have already suggested, from the fact that something is justly deserved, it does not automatically follow that it should be done, since there
may be other moral reasons for not doing it such that, all told, the weight
of moral reasons swings the balance against proceeding. The same argument that I have given for the justice of the death penalty for murderers
proves the justice of beating assaulters, raping rapists, and torturing
torturers. Nonetheless, I believe, and suspect that most would agree, that
it would not be right for us to beat assaulters, rape rapists, or torture

---

Statutes," *Crime & Delinquency* 26, no. 4 (October 1980):563–635. Moreover, I believe
that continued evidence of such discrimination would constitute a separate and powerful
argument for abolition. Faced with such evidence, van den Haag's strategy is to grant that
discrimination is wrong, but claim that it is not "inherent in the death penalty"; it is a
characteristic of "its distribution" (p. 206). Thus discrimination is not an objection to the
death penalty itself. This rejoinder is unsatisfactory for several reasons. First of all, even if
discrimination is not an objection to the death penalty *per se*, its foreseeable persistence
is—as the Court recognized in *Furman*—an objection to instituting the death penalty *as
a policy*. Moral assessment of the way in which a penalty will be carried out may be distinct
from moral assessment of the penalty itself, but, since the way in which the penalty will
be carried out is part of what we will be bringing about if we institute the penalty, it is a
necessary consideration in any assessment of the morality of instituting the penalty. In
short, van den Haag's strategy saves the death penalty in principle, but fails to save it in
practice. Second, it may well be that discrimination is (as a matter of social and psychological
fact in America) inherent in the penalty of death itself. The evidence of its persistence after
Furman lends substance to the suspicion that something about the death penalty—perhaps
the very terribleness of it that recommends it to van den Haag—strikes at deep-seated racial
prejudices in a way that milder penalties do not. In any event, this is an empirical matter,
not resolved by analytic distinctions between what is distributed and how it is distributed.
Finally, after he mounts his argument against the discrimination objection, van den Haag
usually adds that those who oppose capital punishment "because of discriminatory application are not quite serious . . . , [since] they usually will confess, if pressed, that they
would continue their opposition even if there were no discrimination whatsoever in the
administration of the death penalty" (p. 225). This is preposterous. It assumes that a person
can only have one serious objection to any policy. If he had several, then he would naturally
continue to oppose the policy *quite seriously* even though all his objections but one were
eliminated. In addition to discrimination in the *recruitment* of murderers, and in the *application* of the death penalty among murderers, there is a third sort that affects the justice
of instituting the penalty, namely, discrimination in the *legal definition* of murder. I take
this and related issues up in *The Rich Get Richer and the Poor Get Prison: Ideology, Class,
and Criminal Justice*, 2nd ed. (New York: John Wiley, 1984).

torturers, *even though it were their just deserts*—and even if this were
the only way to make them suffer as much as they had made their victims
suffer. Calling for the abolition of the death penalty, though it be just,
then, amounts to urging that as a society we place execution in the same
category of sanction as beating, raping, and torturing, and treat it as
something it would also not be right for us to do to offenders, *even if it
were their just deserts*.

To argue for placing execution in this category, I must show what
would be gained therefrom; and to show that, I shall indicate what we
gain from placing torture in this category and argue that a similar gain
is to be had from doing the same with execution. I select torture because
I think the reasons for placing it in this category are, due to the extremity
of torture, most easily seen—but what I say here applies with appropriate
modification to other severe physical punishments, such as beating and
raping. First, and most evidently, placing torture in this category broad-
casts the message that we as a society judge torturing so horrible a thing
to do to a person that we refuse to do it even when it is deserved. Note
that such a judgment does not commit us to an absolute prohibition on
torturing. No matter how horrible we judge something to be, we may
still be justified in doing it if it is necessary to prevent something even
worse. Leaving this aside for the moment, what is gained by broadcasting
the public judgment that torture is too horrible to inflict even if deserved?

I think the answer to this lies in what we understand as civilization.
In *The Genealogy of Morals*, Nietzsche says that in early times "pain did
not hurt as much as it does today."[23] The truth in this puzzling remark
is that progress in civilization is characterized by a lower tolerance for
one's own pain and that suffered by others. And this is appropriate, since,
via growth in knowledge, civilization brings increased power to prevent
or reduce pain and, via growth in the ability to communicate and interact
with more and more people, civilization extends the circle of people with
whom we emphathize.[24] If civilization is characterized by lower tolerance

23. Friedrich Nietzsche, *The Birth of Tragedy and The Genealogy of Morals* (New York:
Doubleday, 1956), pp. 199–200.

24. Van den Haag writes that our ancestors "were not as repulsed by physical pain as
we are. The change has to do not with our greater smartness or moral superiority but with
a new outlook pioneered by the French and American revolutions [namely, the assertion
of human equality and with it 'universal identification'], and by such mundane things as
the invention of anesthetics, which make pain much less of an everyday experience" (p.
215; cf. van den Haag's *Punishing Criminals* [New York: Basic Books, 1975], pp. 196–
206).

for our own pain and that of others, then publicly refusing to do horrible things to our fellows both signals the level of our civilization *and, by our example, continues the work of civilizing.* And this gesture is all the more powerful if we refuse to do horrible things to those who deserve them. I contend then that the more things we are able to include in this category, the more civilized we are and the more civili*zing.* Thus we gain from including torture in this category, and if execution is especially horrible, we gain still more by including it.

Needless to say, the content, direction, and even the worth of civilization are hotly contested issues, and I shall not be able to win those contests in this brief space. At a minimum, however, I shall assume that civilization involves the taming of the natural environment and of the human animals in it, and that the overall trend in human history is toward increasing this taming, though the trend is by no means unbroken or without reverses. On these grounds, we can say that growth in civilization generally marks human history, that a reduction in the horrible things we tolerate doing to our fellows (even when they deserve them) is part of this growth, and that once the work of civilization is taken on consciously, it includes carrying forward and expanding this reduction.

This claim broadly corresponds to what Emile Durkheim identified, nearly a century ago, as "two laws which seem ... to prevail in the evolution of the apparatus of punishment." The first, the law of quantitative change, Durkheim formulates as:

> *The intensity of punishment is the greater the more closely societies approximate to a less developed type—and the more the central power assumes an absolute character.*

And the second, which Durkheim refers to as the law of qualitative change, is:

> *Deprivations of liberty, and of liberty alone, varying in time according to the seriousness of the crime, tend to become more and more the normal means of social control.*[25]

Several things should be noted about these laws. First of all, they are not two separate laws. As Durkheim understands them, the second exem-

25. Emile Durkheim, "Two Laws of Penal Evolution," *Economy and Society* 2 (1973):285 and 294; italics in the original. This essay was originally published in French in *Année Sociologique* 4 (1899–1900). Conrad, incidentally, quotes Durkheim's two laws (p. 39), but does not develop their implications for his side in the debate.

plifies the trend toward moderation of punishment referred to in the first.[26] Second, the first law really refers to two distinct trends, which usually coincide but do not always. That is, moderation of punishment accompanies *both* the movement from less to more advanced types of society *and* the movement from more to less absolute rule. Normally these go hand in hand, but where they do not, the effect of one trend may offset the effect of the other. Thus, a primitive society without absolute rule may have milder punishments than an equally primitive but more absolutist society.[27] This complication need not trouble us, since the claim I am making refers to the first trend, namely, that punishments tend to become milder as societies become more advanced; and that this is a trend in history is not refuted by the fact that it is accompanied by other trends and even occasionally offset by them. Moreover, I shall close this article with a suggestion about the relation between the intensity of punishment and the justice of society, which might broadly be thought of as corresponding to the second trend in Durkheim's first law. Finally, and most important for our purposes, is the fact that Durkheim's claim that punishment becomes less intense as societies become more advanced is a generalization that he supports with an impressive array of evidence from historical societies from pre-Christian times to the time in which he wrote—and this in turn supports my claim that the reduction in the horrible things we do to our fellows is in fact part of the advance of civilization.[28]

Against this it might be argued that many things grow in history, some

26. Durkheim writes that "of the two laws which we have established, the first contributes to an explanation of the second" (Durkheim, "Two Laws of Penal Evolution," p. 299).

27. The "two causes of the evolution of punishment—the nature of the social type and of the governmental organ—must be carefully distinguished" (ibid., p. 288). Durkheim cites the ancient Hebrews as an example of a society of the less developed type that had milder punishments than societies of the same social type due to the relative absence of absolutist government among the Hebrews (ibid., p. 290).

28. Durkheim's own explanation of the progressive moderation of punishments is somewhat unclear. He rejects the notion that it is due to the growth in sympathy for one's fellows since this, he maintains, would make us more sympathetic with victims and thus harsher in punishments. He argues instead that the trend is due to the shift from understanding crimes as offenses against God (and thus warranting the most terrible of punishments) to understanding them as offenses against men (thus warranting milder punishments). He then seems to come round nearly full circle by maintaining that this shift works to moderate punishments by weakening the religious sentiments that overwhelmed sympathy for the condemned: "The true reason is that the compassion of which the condemned man is the object is no longer overwhelmed by the contrary sentiments which would not let it make itself felt" (ibid., p. 303).

good, some bad, and some mixed, and thus the fact that there is some
historical trend is not a sufficient reason to continue it. Thus, for example,
history also brings growth in population, but we are not for that reason
called upon to continue the work of civilization by continually increasing
our population. What this suggests is that in order to identify something
as part of the work of civilizing, we must show not only that it generally
grows in history, but that its growth is, on some independent grounds,
clearly an advance for the human species—that is, either an unmitigated
gain or at least consistently a net gain. And this implies that even trends
which we might generally regard as advances may in some cases bring
losses with them, such that when they did it would not be appropriate
for us to lend our efforts to continuing them. Of such trends we can say
that they are advances in civilization except when their gains are outweighed by the losses they bring—and that we are only called upon to
further these trends when their gains are *not* outweighed in this way. It
is clear in this light that increasing population is a mixed blessing at best,
bringing both gains and losses. Consequently, it is not always an advance
in civilization that we should further, though at times it may be.

What can be said of reducing the horrible things that we do to our
fellows even when deserved? First of all, given our vulnerability to pain,
it seems clearly a gain. Is it however an unmitigated gain? That is, would
such a reduction ever amount to a loss? It seems to me that there are
two conditions under which it would be a loss, namely, if the reduction
made our lives more dangerous, or if not doing what is justly deserved
were a loss in itself. Let us leave aside the former, since, as I have already
suggested and as I will soon indicate in greater detail, I accept that if
some horrible punishment is necessary to deter equally or more horrible
acts, then we may have to impose the punishment. Thus my claim is
that reduction in the horrible things we do to our fellows is an advance
in civilization *as long as our lives are not thereby made more dangerous*,
and that it is only then that we are called upon to extend that reduction
as part of the work of civilization. Assuming then, for the moment, that
we suffer no increased danger by refraining from doing horrible things
to our fellows when they justly deserve them, does such refraining to do
what is justly deserved amount to a loss?

It seems to me that the answer to this must be that refraining to do
what is justly deserved is only a loss where it amounts to doing an injustice. But such refraining to do what is just is not doing what is unjust,

unless what we do instead falls below the bottom end of the range of just punishments. Otherwise, it would be unjust to refrain from torturing torturers, raping rapists, or beating assaulters. In short, I take it that if there is no injustice in refraining from torturing torturers, then there is no injustice in refraining to do horrible things to our fellows generally, when they deserve them, as long as what we do instead is compatible with believing that they do deserve them. And thus that if such refraining does not make our lives more dangerous, then it is no loss, and given our vulnerability to pain, it is a gain. Consequently, reduction in the horrible things we do to our fellows, when not necessary to our protection, is an advance in civilization that we are called upon to continue once we consciously take upon ourselves the work of civilization.

To complete the argument, however, I must show that execution is horrible enough to warrant its inclusion alongside torture. Against this it will be said that execution is not especially horrible since it only hastens a fate that is inevitable for us.[29] I think that this view overlooks important differences in the manner in which people reach their inevitable ends. I contend that execution is especially horrible, and it is so in a way similar to (though not identical with) the way in which torture is especially horrible. I believe we view torture as especially awful because of two of its features, which also characterize execution: intense pain and the

29. Van den Haag seems to waffle on the question of the unique awfulness of execution. For instance, he takes it not to be revolting in the way that earcropping is, because "We all must die. But we must not have our ears cropped" (p. 190), and here he cites John Stuart Mill's parliamentary defense of the death penalty in which Mill maintains that execution only *hastens* death. Mill's point was to defend the claim that "There is not . . . any human infliction which makes an impression on the imagination so entirely out of proportion to its real severity as the punishment of death" (Mill, "Parliamentary Debate," p. 273). And van den Haag seems to agree since he maintains that, since "we cannot imagine our own nonexistence . . . , [t]he fear of the death penalty is in part the fear of the unknown. It . . . rests on a confusion" (pp. 258–59). On the other hand, he writes that "Execution sharpens our separation anxiety because death becomes clearly foreseen. . . . Further, and perhaps most important, when one is executed he does not just die, he is put to death, forcibly expelled from life. He is told that he is too depraved, unworthy of living with other humans" (p. 258). I think, incidentally, that it is an overstatement to say that we cannot imagine our own nonexistence. If we can imagine any counterfactual experience, for example, how we might feel if we didn't know something that we do in fact know, then it doesn't seem impossible to imagine what it would "feel like" not to live. I think I can arrive at a pretty good approximation of this by trying to imagine how things "felt" to me in the eighteenth century. And, in fact, the sense of the awful difference between being alive and not that enters my experience when I do this, makes the fear of death—not as a state, but as the absence of life—seem hardly to rest on a confusion.

spectacle of one human being completely subject to the power of another. This latter is separate from the issue of pain since it is something that offends us about unpainful things, such as slavery (even voluntarily entered) and prostitution (even voluntarily chosen as an occupation).[30] Execution shares this separate feature, since killing a bound and defenseless human being enacts the total subjugation of that person to his fellows. I think, incidentally, that this accounts for the general uneasiness with which execution by lethal injection has been greeted. Rather than humanizing the event, it seems only to have purchased a possible reduction in physical pain at the price of increasing the spectacle of subjugation—with no net gain in the attractiveness of the death penalty. Indeed, its net effect may have been the reverse.

In addition to the spectacle of subjugation, execution, even by physically painless means, is also characterized by a special and intense psychological pain that distinguishes it from the loss of life that awaits us all. Interesting in this regard is the fact that although we are not terribly squeamish about the loss of life itself, allowing it in war, self-defense, as a necessary cost of progress, and so on, we are, as the extraordinary hesitance of our courts testifies, quite reluctant to execute. I think this is because execution involves the most psychologically painful features of deaths. We normally regard death from human causes as worse than death from natural causes, since a humanly caused shortening of life lacks the consolation of unavoidability. And we normally regard death whose coming is foreseen by its victim as worse than sudden death, because a foreseen death adds to the loss of life the terrible consciousness of that impending loss.[31] As a humanly caused death whose advent is foreseen by its victim, an execution combines the worst of both.

Thus far, by analogy with torture, I have argued that execution should be avoided because of how horrible it is to the one executed. But there

30. I am not here endorsing this view of voluntarily entered slavery or prostitution. I mean only to suggest that it is *the belief* that these relations involve the extreme subjugation of one person to the power of another that is at the basis of their offensiveness. What I am saying is quite compatible with finding that this belief is false with respect to voluntarily entered slavery or prostitution.

31. This is no doubt partly due to modern skepticism about an afterlife. Earlier peoples regarded a foreseen death as a blessing allowing time to make one's peace with God. Writing of the early Middle Ages, Phillippe Aries says, "In this world that was so familiar with death, sudden death was a vile and ugly death; it was frightening; it seemed a strange and monstrous thing that nobody dared talk about" (Phillippe Aries, *The Hour of Our Death* [New York: Vintage, 1982], p. 11).

are reasons of another sort that follow from the analogy with torture. Torture is to be avoided not only because of what it says about *what* we are willing to do to our fellows, but also because of what it says about *us* who are willing to do it. To torture someone is an awful spectacle not only because of the intensity of pain imposed, but because of what is required to be able to impose such pain on one's fellows. The tortured body cringes, using its full exertion to escape the pain imposed upon it— it literally begs for relief with its muscles as it does with its cries. To torture someone is to demonstrate a capacity to resist this begging, and that in turn demonstrates a kind of hardheartedness that a society ought not parade.

And this is true not only of torture, but of all severe corporal punishment. Indeed, I think this constitutes part of the answer to the puzzling question of why we refrain from punishments like whipping, even when the alternative (some months in jail versus some lashes) seems more costly to the offender. Imprisonment is painful to be sure, but it is a reflective pain, one that comes with comparing what is to what might have been, and that can be temporarily ignored by thinking about other things. But physical pain has an urgency that holds body and mind in a fierce grip. Of physical pain, as Orwell's Winston Smith recognized, "you could only wish one thing: that it should stop."[32] Refraining from torture in particular and corporal punishment in general, we both refuse to put a fellow human being in this grip *and* refuse to show our ability to resist this wish. The death penalty is the last corporal punishment used officially in the modern world. And it is corporal not only because administered via the body, but because the pain of foreseen, humanly administered death strikes us with the urgency that characterizes intense physical pain, causing grown men to cry, faint, and lose control of their bodily functions. There is something to be gained by refusing to endorse the hardness of heart necessary to impose such a fate.

By placing execution alongside torture in the category of things we will not do to our fellow human beings even when they deserve them, we broadcast the message that totally subjugating a person to the power of others *and* confronting him with the advent of his own humanly administered demise is too horrible to be done by civilized human beings to their fellows even when they have earned it: too horrible to do, and

32. George Orwell, *1984* (New York: New American Library, 1983; originally published in 1949), p. 197.

too horrible to be capable of doing. And I contend that broadcasting this message loud and clear would in the long run contribute to the general detestation of murder and be, to the extent to which it worked itself into the hearts and minds of the populace, a deterrent. In short, refusing to execute murderers though they deserve it both reflects and continues the taming of the human species that we call civilization. Thus, I take it that the abolition of the death penalty, though it is a just punishment for murder, is part of the civilizing mission of modern states.

IV. Civilization, Safety, and Deterrence

Earlier I said that judging a practice too horrible to do even to those who deserve it does not exclude the possibility that it could be justified if necessary to avoid even worse consequences. Thus, were the death penalty clearly proven a better deterrent to the murder of innocent people than life in prison, we might have to admit that we had not yet reached a level of civilization at which we could protect ourselves without imposing this horrible fate on murderers, and thus we might have to grant the necessity of instituting the death penalty.[33] But this is far from proven. The available research by no means clearly indicates that the death penalty reduces the incidence of homicide more than life imprisonment does. Even the econometric studies of Isaac Ehrlich, which purport to show that each execution saves seven or eight potential murder victims, have not changed this fact, as is testified to by the controversy and objections from equally respected statisticians that Ehrlich's work has provoked.[34]

33. I say "might" here to avoid the sticky question of just how effective a deterrent the death penalty would have to be to justify overcoming our scruples about executing. It is here that the other considerations often urged against capital punishment—discrimination, irrevocability, the possibility of mistake, and so on—would play a role. Omitting such qualifications, however, my position might crudely be stated as follows: *Just desert limits what a civilized society may do to deter crime, and deterrence limits what a civilized society may do to give criminals their just deserts.*

34. Isaac Ehrlich, "The Deterrent Effect of Capital Punishment: A Question of Life or Death," *American Economic Review* 65 (June 1975):397–417. For reactions to Ehrlich's work, see Alfred Blumstein, Jacqueline Cohen, and Daniel Nagin, eds., *Deterrence and Incapacitation: Estimating the Effects of Criminal Sanctions on Crime Rates* (Washington, D.C.: National Academy of Sciences, 1978), esp. pp. 59–63 and 336–60; Brian E. Forst, "The Deterrent Effect on Capital Punishment: A Cross-State Analysis," *Minnesota Law Review* 61 (May 1977):743–67, Deryck Beyleveld, "Ehrlich's Analysis of Deterrence," *British Journal of Criminology* 22 (April 1982):101–23, and Isaac Ehrlich, "On Positive Methodology, Ethics and Polemics in Deterrence Research," *British Journal of Criminology* 22

Conceding that it has not been proven that the death penalty deters more murders than life imprisonment, van den Haag has argued that neither has it been proven that the death penalty does *not* deter more murders,[35] and thus we must follow common sense which teaches that the higher the cost of something, the fewer people will choose it, and therefore at least some potential murderers who would not be deterred by life imprisonment will be deterred by the death penalty. Van den Haag writes:

. . . our experience shows that the greater the threatened penalty, the more it deters.

. . . Life in prison is still life, however unpleasant. In contrast, the death penalty does not just threaten to make life unpleasant—it threatens to take life altogether. This difference is perceived by those affected. We find that when they have the choice between life in prison and execution, 99% of all prisoners under sentence of death prefer life in prison. . . .

From this unquestioned fact a reasonable conclusion can be drawn in favor of the superior deterrent effect of the death penalty. Those who have the choice in practice . . . fear death more than they fear life in prison. . . . If they do, it follows that the threat of the death penalty, all other things equal, is likely to deter more than the threat of life in prison. One is most deterred by what one fears most. From which it

---

(April 1982):124–39. Much of the criticism of Ehrlich's work focuses on the fact that he found a deterrence impact of executions in the period from 1933–1969, which includes the period of 1963–1969, a time when hardly any executions were carried out and crime rates rose for reasons that are arguably independent of the existence or nonexistence of capital punishment. When the 1963–1969 period is excluded, no significant deterrent effect shows. Prior to Ehrlich's work, research on the comparative deterrent impact of the death penalty versus life imprisonment indicated no increase in the incidence of homicide in states that abolished the death penalty and no greater incidence of homicide in states without the death penalty compared to similar states with the death penalty. See Thorsten Sellin, *The Death Penalty* (Philadelphia: American Law Institute, 1959).

35. Van den Haag writes: "Other studies published since Ehrlich's contend that his results are due to the techniques and periods he selected, and that different techniques and periods yield different results. Despite a great deal of research on all sides, one cannot say that the statistical evidence is conclusive. Nobody has claimed to have *disproved* that the death penalty may deter more than life imprisonment. But one cannot claim, either, that it has been proved statistically in a conclusive manner that the death penalty does deter more than alternative penalties. This lack of proof does not amount to disproof" (p. 65).

follows that whatever statistics fail, or do not fail, to show, the death
penalty is likely to be more deterrent than any other. [Pp. 68–69][36]

Those of us who recognize how common-sensical it was, and still is, to
believe that the sun moves around the earth, will be less willing than
Professor van den Haag to follow common sense here, especially when
it comes to doing something awful to our fellows. Moreover, there are
good reasons for doubting common sense on this matter. Here are four:

1. From the fact that one penalty is more feared than another, it does
not follow that the more feared penalty will deter more than the less
feared, unless we know that the less feared penalty is not fearful enough
to deter everyone who can be deterred—and this is just what we don't
know with regard to the death penalty. Though I fear the death penalty
more than life in prison, I can't think of any act that the death penalty
would deter me from that an equal likelihood of spending my life in prison
wouldn't deter me from as well.[37] Since it seems to me that whoever

36. An alternative formulation of this "common-sense argument" is put forth and defended
by Michael Davis in "Death, Deterrence, and the Method of Common Sense," *Social Theory
and Practice* 7, no. 2 (Summer 1981):145–77. Davis's argument is like van den Haag's
except that, where van den Haag claims that people *do* fear the death penalty more than
lesser penalties and *are* deterred by what they fear most, Davis claims that it is *rational*
to fear the death penalty more than lesser penalties and thus *rational* to be more deterred
by it. Thus, he concludes that the death penalty is the most effective deterrent *for rational
people*. He admits that this argument is "about rational agents, not actual people" (ibid.,
p. 157). To bring it back to the actual criminal justice system that deals with actual people,
Davis claims that the criminal law makes no sense unless we suppose the potential criminal
to be (more or less) rational" (ibid., p. 153). In short, the death penalty is the most effective
deterrent because it would be rational to be most effectively deterred by it, and we are
committed by belief in the criminal law to supposing that people will do what is rational.
The problem with this strategy is that a deterrence justification of a punishment is valid
only if it proves that the punishment actually deters actual people from committing crimes.
If it doesn't prove that, it misses its mark, no matter what we are committed to supposing.
Unless Davis's argument is a way of proving that the actual people governed by the criminal
law will be more effectively deterred by the death penalty than by lesser penalties, it is
irrelevant to the task at hand. And if it is a way of proving that actual people will be better
deterred, then it is indistinguishable from van den Haag's version of the argument and
vulnerable to the criticisms of it which follow.

37. David A. Conway writes: "given the choice, I would strongly prefer one thousand
years in hell to eternity there. Nonetheless, if one thousand years in hell were the penalty
for some action, it would be quite sufficient to deter me from performing that action. The
additional years would do nothing to discourage me further. Similarly, the prospect of the
death penalty, while worse, may not have any greater deterrent effect than does that of life
imprisonment" (David A. Conway, "Capital Punishment and Deterrence: Some Considerations in Dialogue Form," *Philosophy & Public Affairs* 3, no. 4 [Summer 1974]:433).

would be deterred by a given likelihood of death would be deterred by an *equal* likelihood of life behind bars, I suspect that the common-sense argument only seems plausible because we evaluate it unconsciously assuming that potential criminals will face larger likelihoods of death sentences than of life sentences. If the likelihoods were equal, it seems to me that where life imprisonment was improbable enough to make it too distant a possibility to worry much about, a similar low probability of death would have the same effect. After all, we are undeterred by small likelihoods of death every time we walk the streets. And if life imprisonment were sufficiently probable to pose a real deterrent threat, it would pose as much of a deterrent threat as death. And this is just what most of the research we have on the comparative deterrent impact of execution versus life imprisonment suggests.

2. In light of the fact that roughly 500 to 700 suspected felons are killed by the police in the line of duty every year, and the fact that the number of privately owned guns in America is substantially larger than the number of households in America, it must be granted that anyone contemplating committing a crime *already* faces a substantial risk of ending up dead as a result.[38] It's hard to see why anyone *who is not already deterred by this* would be deterred by the addition of the more distant risk of death after apprehension, conviction, and appeal. Indeed, this suggests that people consider risks in a much cruder way than van den Haag's appeal to common sense suggests—which should be evident to anyone who contemplates how few people use seatbelts (14% of drivers, on some estimates), when it is widely known that wearing them can spell the difference between life (outside prison) and death.[39]

3. Van den Haag has maintained that deterrence doesn't work only by means of cost-benefit calculations made by potential criminals. It works also by the lesson about the wrongfulness of murder that is slowly learned in a society that subjects murderers to the ultimate punishment (p. 63). But if I am correct in claiming that the refusal to execute even those who deserve it has a civilizing effect, then the refusal to execute also teaches a lesson about the wrongfulness of murder. My claim here is

38. On the number of people killed by the police, see Lawrence W. Sherman and Robert H. Langworthy, "Measuring Homicide by Police Officers," *Journal of Criminal Law and Criminology* 70, no. 4 (Winter 1979):546–60; on the number of privately owned guns, see Franklin Zimring, *Firearms and Violence in American Life* (Washington, D.C.: U.S. Government Printing Office, 1968), pp. 6–7.

39. *AAA World* (Potomac ed.) 4, no. 3 (May–June 1984), pp. 18c and 18i.

admittedly speculative, but no more so than van den Haag's to the contrary. And my view has the added virtue of accounting for the failure of research to show an increased deterrent effect from executions *without having to deny the plausibility of van den Haag's common-sense argument that at least some additional potential murderers will be deterred by the prospect of the death penalty.* If there is a deterrent effect from *not executing*, then it is understandable that while executions will deter some murderers, this effect will be balanced out by the weakening of the deterrent effect of not executing, such that no net reduction in murders will result.[40] And this, by the way, also disposes of van den Haag's argument that, in the absence of knowledge one way or the other on the deterrent effect of executions, we should execute murderers rather than risk the lives of innocent people whose murders might have been deterred if we had. If there is a deterrent effect of not executing, it follows that we risk innocent lives either way. And if this is so, it seems that the only reasonable course of action is to refrain from imposing what we know is a horrible fate.[41]

40. A related claim has been made by those who defend the so-called brutalization hypothesis by presenting evidence to show that murders *increase* following an execution. See, for example, William J. Bowers and Glenn L. Pierce, "Deterrence or Brutalization: What is the Effect of Executions?" *Crime & Delinquency* 26, no. 4 (October 1980):453–84. They conclude that each execution gives rise to two additional homicides in the month following, and that these are real additions, not just a change in timing of the homicides (ibid., p. 481). My claim, it should be noted, is not identical to this, since, as I indicate in the text, what I call "the deterrence effect of not executing" is not something whose impact is to be seen immediately following executions but over the long haul, and, further, my claim is compatible with finding no net increase in murders due to executions. Nonetheless, should the brutalization hypothesis be borne out by further studies, it would certainly lend support to the notion that there is a deterrent effect of not executing.

41. Van den Haag writes: "If we were quite ignorant about the marginal deterrent effects of execution, we would have to choose—like it or not—between the certainty of the convicted murderer's death by execution and the likelihood of the survival of future victims of other murderers on the one hand, and on the other his certain survival and the likelihood of the death of new victims. I'd rather execute a man convicted of having murdered others than put the lives of innocents at risk. I find it hard to understand the opposite choice" (p. 69). Conway was able to counter this argument earlier by pointing out that the research on the marginal deterrent effects of execution was not *inconclusive* in the sense of *tending to point both ways,* but rather in the sense of *giving us no reason to believe that capital punishment saves more lives than life imprisonment.* He could then answer van den Haag by saying that the choice is not between risking the lives of murderers and risking the lives of innocents, but between killing a murderer with no reason to believe lives will be saved, and sparing a murderer with no reason to believe lives will be lost (Conway, "Capital Punishment and Deterrence," pp. 442–43). This, of course, makes the choice to spare the

4. Those who still think that van den Haag's common-sense argument for executing murderers is valid will find that the argument proves more than they bargained for. Van den Haag maintains that, in the absence of conclusive evidence on the relative deterrent impact of the death penalty versus life imprisonment, we must follow common sense and assume that if one punishment is more fearful than another, it will deter some potential criminals not deterred by the less fearful punishment. Since people sentenced to death will almost universally try to get their sentences changed to life in prison, it follows that death is more fearful than life imprisonment, and thus that it will deter some additional murderers. Consequently, we should institute the death penalty to save the lives these additional murderers would have taken. But, since people sentenced to be tortured to death would surely try to get their sentences changed to simple execution, the same argument proves that death-by-torture will deter still more potential murderers. Consequently, we should institute death-by-torture to save the lives these additional murderers would have taken. Anyone who accepts van den Haag's argument is then confronted with a dilemma: Until we have conclusive evidence that capital punishment is a greater deterrent to murder than life imprisonment, he must grant *either* that we should not follow common sense and not impose the death penalty; *or* we should follow common sense and torture murderers to death. In short, either we must abolish the electric chair or reinstitute the rack. Surely, this is the *reductio ad absurdum* of van den Haag's common-sense argument.

CONCLUSION: HISTORY, FORCE, AND JUSTICE

I believe that, taken together, these arguments prove that we should abolish the death penalty though it is a just punishment for murder. Let me close with an argument of a different sort. When you see the lash fall upon the backs of Roman slaves, or the hideous tortures meted out in the period of the absolute monarchs, you see more than mere cruelty at work. Surely you suspect that there is something about the injustice of imperial slavery and royal tyranny that requires the use of extreme

---

murderer more understandable than van den Haag allows. Events, however, have overtaken Conway's argument. The advent of Ehrlich's research, contested though it may be, leaves us in fact with research that tends to point both ways.

force to keep these institutions in place. That is, for reasons undoubtedly related to those that support the second part of Durkheim's first law of penal evolution, we take the amount of force a society uses against its own people as an inverse measure of its justness. And though no more than a rough measure, it is a revealing one nonetheless, because when a society is limited in the degree of force it can use against its subjects, it is likely to have to be a juster society since it will have to gain its subjects' cooperation by offering them fairer terms than it would have to, if it could use more force. From this we cannot simply conclude that reducing the force used by our society will automatically make our society more just—but I think we can conclude that it will have this tendency, since it will require us to find means other than force for encouraging compliance with our institutions, and this is likely to require us to make those institutions as fair to all as possible. Thus I hope that America will pose itself the challenge of winning its citizens' cooperation by justice rather than force, and that when future historians look back on the twentieth century, they will find us with countries like France and England and Sweden that have abolished the death penalty, rather than with those like South Africa and the Soviet Union and Iran that have retained it— with all that this suggests about the countries involved.

STEPHEN NATHANSON

Does It Matter
If the Death Penalty
Is Arbitrarily Administered?

I

In this article, I will examine the argument that capital punishment ought to be abolished because it has been and will continue to be imposed in an arbitrary manner.

This argument has been central to discussions of capital punishment since the Supreme Court ruling in the 1972 case *Furman v. Georgia*. In a 5-4 decision, the Court ruled that capital punishment as then administered was unconstitutional. Although the Court issued several opinions, the problem of arbitrariness is widely seen as having played a central role in the Court's thinking. As Charles Black, Jr., has put it,

> . . . The decisive ground of the 1972 Furman case anti-capital punishment ruling—the ground persuasive to the marginal justices needed for a majority—was that, out of a large number of persons "eligible" in law for the punishment of death, a few were selected as if at random, by no stated (or perhaps statable) criteria, while all the rest suffered the lesser penalty of imprisonment.[1]

Among those justices moved by the arbitrariness issue, some stressed the discriminatory aspects of capital punishment, the tendency of legally irrelevant factors like race and economic status to determine the severity of sentence, while others emphasized the "freakish" nature of the punishment, the fact that it is imposed on a miniscule percentage of murderers who are not obviously more deserving of death than others.

Although the Supreme Court approved new death penalty laws in *Gregg*

---

1. *Capital Punishment: The Inevitability of Caprice and Mistake*, 2d ed. (New York: W. W. Norton & Co., 1981), p. 20.

v. Georgia (1976), the reasoning of *Furman* was not rejected. Rather, a majority of the Court determined that Georgia's new laws would make arbitrary imposition of the death penalty much less likely. By amending procedures and adding criteria which specify aggravating and mitigating circumstances, Georgia had succeeded in creating a system of "guilded discretion," which the Court accepted in the belief that it was not likely to yield arbitrary results.

The *Gregg* decision has prompted death penalty opponents to attempt to show that "guided discretion" is an illusion. This charge has been supported in various ways. Charles Black has supported it by analyzing both the legal process of decision making in capital cases and the legal criteria for determining who is to be executed. He has argued that, appearances to the contrary, there are no meaningful standards operating in the system. Attacking from an empirical angle, William Bowers and Glenn Pierce have tried to show that even after *Furman* and under new laws, factors like race and geographic location of the trial continue to play a large role and that the criteria which are supposed to guide judgment do not separate those sentenced into meaningfully distinct groups. Perhaps the most shocking conclusion of Bowers and Pierce concerns the large role played by the race of the killer and the victim, as the chances of execution are by far the greatest when blacks kill whites and least when whites kill blacks.[2]

The upshot of both these approaches is that "guided discretion" is not working and, perhaps, cannot work. If this is correct and if the argument from arbitrariness is accepted, then it would appear that a return from *Gregg* to *Furman* is required. That is, the Court should once again condemn capital punishment as unconstitutional.

I have posed these issues in terms of the Supreme Court's deliberations. Nonetheless, for opponents of the death penalty, the freakishness of its imposition and the large role played by race and other irrelevant factors are a moral as well as a legal outrage. For them, there is a fundamental moral injustice in the practice of capital punishment and not just a departure from the highest legal and constitutional standards.

2. Ibid., *passim*; W. Bowers and G. Pierce, "Arbitrariness and Discrimination under Post-*Furman* Capital Statutes," *Crime & Delinquency* 26 (1980): 563–635. Reprinted in *The Death Penalty in America*, 3d ed., ed. Hugo Bedau (New York: Oxford University Press, 1982), pp. 206–24.

II

The argument from arbitrariness has not, however, been universally accepted, either as a moral or a constitutional argument. Ernest van den Haag, an articulate and longtime defender of the death penalty, has claimed that the Supreme Court was wrong to accept this argument in the first place and thus that the evidence of arbitrariness presented by Black, Bowers and Pierce and others is beside the point. In his words:

> ... the abolitionist argument from capriciousness, or discretion, or discrimination, would be more persuasive if it were alleged that those selectively executed are not guilty. But the argument merely maintains that some other guilty but more favored persons, or groups, escape the death penalty. This is hardly sufficient for letting anyone else found guilty escape the penalty. On the contrary, that some guilty persons or groups elude it argues for extending the death penalty to them.[3]

Having attacked the appeal to arbitrariness, van den Haag goes on to spell out his own conception of the requirements of justice. He writes:

> Justice requires punishing the guilty—as many of the guilty as possible, even if only some can be punished—and sparing the innocent—as many of the innocent as possible, even if not all are spared. It would surely be wrong to treat everybody with equal injustice in preference to meting out justice at least to some. ... [I]f the death penalty is morally just, *however discriminatorily applied to only some of the guilty*, it does remain just *in each case* in which it is applied. (emphasis added)[4]

Distinguishing sharply between the demands of justice and the demands of equality, van den Haag claims that the justice of individual punishments depends on individual guilt alone and not on whether punishments are equally distributed among the class of guilty persons.

Van den Haag's distinction between the demands of justice and the demands of equality parallels the distinction drawn by Joel Feinberg

---

3. "The Collapse of the Case Against Capital Punishment," *National Review*, 31 March 1978: 397. A briefer version of this paper appeared in the *Criminal Law Bulletin* 14 (1978): 51–68 and is reprinted in Bedau, pp. 323–33.

4. Ibid.

between "noncomparative" and "comparative" justice.[5] Using Feinberg's terminology, we can express van den Haag's view by saying that he believes that the justice of a particular punishment is a *noncomparative* matter. It depends solely on what a person deserves and not on how others are treated. For van den Haag, then, evidence of arbitrariness and discrimination is irrelevant, so long as those who are executed are indeed guilty and deserve their punishment.

There is no denying the plausibility of van den Haag's case. In many instances, we believe it is legitimate to punish or reward deserving individuals, even though we know that equally deserving persons are unpunished or unrewarded. Consider two cases:

A. A driver is caught speeding, ticketed, and required to pay a fine. We know that the percentage of speeders who are actually punished is extremely small, yet we would probably regard it as a joke if the driver protested that he was being treated unjustly or if someone argued that no one should be fined for speeding unless all speeders were fined.

B. A person performs a heroic act and receives a substantial reward, in addition to the respect and admiration of his fellow citizens. Because he deserves the reward, we think it just that he receive it, even though many equally heroic persons are not treated similarly. That most heroes are unsung is no reason to avoid rewarding this particular heroic individual.

Both of these instances appear to support van den Haag's claim that we should do justice whenever we can in individual cases and that failure to do justice in all cases is no reason to withhold punishment or reward from individuals.

III

Is the argument from arbitrariness completely unfounded then? Should we accept van den Haag's claim that "unequal justice is justice still?"

In response to these questions, I shall argue that van den Haag's case is not as strong as it looks and that the argument from arbitrariness can be vindicated.

5. "Noncomparative Justice," in *Rights, Justice, and the Bounds of Liberty: Essays in Social Philosophy* (Princeton, NJ: Princeton University Press, 1980); originally published in the *Philosophical Review* 83 (1974): 297–338.

As a first step in achieving this, I would like to point out that there are in fact several different arguments from arbitrariness. While some of these arguments appeal to the random and freakish nature of the death penalty, others highlight the discriminatory effects of legally irrelevant factors. Each of these kinds of arbitrariness raises different sorts of moral and legal issues.

For example, though we may acknowledge the impossibility of ticketing all speeding drivers and still favor ticketing some, we will not find every way of determining which speeders are ticketed equally just. Consider the policy of ticketing only those who travel at extremely high speeds, as opposed to that of ticketing every tenth car. Compare these with the policy of giving tickets only to speeders with beards and long hair or to speeders whose cars bear bumper stickers expressing unpopular political views. While I shall not pursue this point in detail, I take it to be obvious that these different selection policies are not all equally just or acceptable.

A second difference between versions of the argument from arbitrariness depends on whether or not it is granted that we can accurately distinguish those who deserve to die from those who do not. As van den Haag presents the argument, it assumes that we are able to make this distinction. Then, the claim is made that from this class of people who deserve to die, only some are selected for execution. The choice of those specific persons from the general class of persons who deserve to die is held to be arbitrary.

Van den Haag neglects a related argument which has been forcefully defended by Charles Black. Black's argument is that the determination of *who* deserves to die—the first step—is itself arbitrary. So his claim is not merely that arbitrary factors determine who among the deserving will be executed. His point is that the determination of who deserves to die is arbitrary. His main argument is that

> the official choices—by prosecutors, judges, juries, and governors—that divide those who are to die from those who are to live are on the whole not made, and cannot be made, under standards that are consistently meaningful and clear, but that they are often made, and in the foreseeable future will continue often to be made, under no standards at all or under pseudo-standards without discoverable meaning.[6]

6. Black, *Capital Punishment*, p. 29.

According to Black, even the most conscientious officials could not make principled judgments about desert in these instances, because our laws do not contain clear principles for differentiating those who deserve to die from those who do not. While I shall not try to summarize Black's analysis of the failures of post-*Furman* capital punishment statutes, it is clear that if van den Haag were to meet this argument, he would have to provide his own analysis of these laws in order to show that they do provide clear and meaningful standards. Or, he would have to examine the actual disposition of cases under these laws to show that the results have not been arbitrary. Van den Haag does not attempt to do either of these things. This seems to result from a failure to distinguish (a) the claim that judgments concerning *who deserves to die* are arbitrarily made, from (b) the claim that judgments concerning *who among the deserving shall be executed* are arbitrarily made.

Van den Haag may simply assume that the system does a decent job of distinguishing those who deserve to die from those who do not, and his assumption gains a surface plausibility because of his tendency to oversimplify the nature of the judgments which need to be made. In contrast to Black, who stresses the complexity of the legal process and the complexity of the judgments facing participants in that process, van den Haag is content to say simply that "justice requires punishing the guilty . . . and sparing the innocent." This maxim makes it look as if officials and jurors need only divide people into two neat categories, and if we think of guilt and innocence as *factual* categories, it makes it look as if the only judgment necessary is whether a person did or did not kill another human being.

In fact, the problems are much more complicated than this. Not every person who kills another human being is guilty of the same crime. Some may have committed no crime at all, if their act is judged to be justifiable homicide. Among others, they may have committed first-degree murder, second-degree murder, or some form of manslaughter. Furthermore, even if we limit our attention to those who are convicted of first-degree murder, juries must consider aggravating and mitigating circumstances in order to judge whether someone is guilty enough to deserve the death penalty. It is clear, then, that simply knowing that someone is factually guilty of killing another person is far from sufficient for determining that he deserves to die, and if prosecutors, juries, and judges do not have criteria which enable them to classify those who are guilty in a just and rational way, then their judgments about who deserves to die will necessarily be arbitrary and unprincipled.

Once we appreciate the difficulty and complexity of the judgments which must be made about guilt and desert, it is easier to see how they might be influenced by racial characteristics and other irrelevant factors. The statistics compiled by Bowers and Pierce show that blacks killing whites have the greatest chance of being executed, while whites killing blacks have the least chance of execution. What these findings strongly suggest is that officials and jurors think that the killing of a white by a black is a more serious crime than the killing of a black by a white. Hence, they judge that blacks killing whites *deserve* a more serious punishment than whites killing blacks. Given the bluntness of our ordinary judgments about desert and the complexity of the choices facing jurors and officials, it may not be surprising either that people find it difficult to make the fine discriminations required by law or that such judgments are influenced by deep-seated racial or social attitudes.

Both legal analysis and empirical studies should undermine our confidence that the legal system sorts out those who deserve to die from those who do not in a nonarbitrary manner. If we cannot be confident that those who are executed in fact deserve to die, then we ought not to allow executions to take place at all.

Because van den Haag does not distinguish this argument from other versions of the argument from arbitrariness, he simply neglects it. His omission is serious because this argument is an independent, substantial argument against the death penalty. It can stand even if other versions of the argument from arbitrariness fall.

IV

I would like now to turn to the form of the argument which van den Haag explicitly deals with and to consider whether it is vulnerable to his criticisms. Let us assume that there is a class of people whom we know to be deserving of death. Let us further assume that only some of these people are executed and that the executions are arbitrary in the sense that those executed have not committed worse crimes than those not executed. This is the situation which Justice Stewart described in *Furman*. He wrote:

These death sentences are cruel and unusual in the same way that being struck by lightning is cruel and unusual. For of all the people convicted of rapes and murders in 1967 and 1968, *many just as reprehensible as these*, the petitioners are among *a capriciously selected random handful* upon whom the sentence of death has in fact been imposed. (emphasis added)[7]

What is crucial here (and different from the argument previously discussed) is the assumption that we can judge the reprehensibility of both the petitioners and others convicted of similar crimes. Stewart does not deny that the petitioners deserve to die, but because other equally deserving people escape the death penalty for no legally respectable reasons, the executions of the petitioners, Stewart thought, would violate the Eighth and Fourteenth Amendments.

This is precisely the argument van den Haag rejected. We can sum up his reasons in the following rhetorical questions: How can it possibly be unjust to punish someone if he deserves the punishment? Why should it matter whether or not others equally deserving are punished?

I have already acknowledged the plausibility of van den Haag's case and offered the examples of the ticketed speeder and the rewarded hero as instances which seem to confirm his view. Nonetheless, I think that van den Haag is profoundly mistaken in thinking that the justice of a reward or punishment depends solely on whether the recipient deserves it.

Consider the following two cases which are structurally similar to A and B (given above) but which elicit different reactions:

C. I tell my class that anyone who plagiarizes will fail the course. Three students plagiarize papers, but only one receives a failing grade. The other two, in describing their motivation, win my sympathy, and I give them passing grades.

D. At my child's birthday party, I offer a prize to the child who can solve a particular puzzle. Three children, including my own, solve the puzzle. I cannot reward them all, so I give the prize to my own child.

In both cases, as in van den Haag's, only some of those deserving a reward or punishment receive it. Unlike cases A and B, however, C and

7. Reprinted in Bedau, pp. 263–64.

D do not appear to be just, in spite of the fact that the persons rewarded or punished deserve what they get. In these cases, the justice of giving them what they deserve appears to be affected by the treatment of others.

About these cases I am inclined to say the following. The people involved have not been treated justly. It was unjust to fail the single plagiarizer and unjust to reward my child. It would have been better—because more just—to have failed no one than to have failed the single student. It would have been better to have given a prize to no one than to give the prize to my child alone.

The unfairness in both cases appears to result from the fact that the reasons for picking out those rewarded or punished are irrelevant and hence that the choice is arbitrary. If I have a stated policy of failing students who plagiarize, then it is unjust for me to pass students with whom I sympathize. Whether I am sympathetic or not is irrelevant, and I am treating the student whom I do fail unjustly because I am not acting simply on the basis of desert. Rather, I am acting on the basis of desert plus degree of sympathy. Likewise, in the case of the prize, it appears that I am preferring my own child in giving out the reward, even though I announced that receipt of the award would depend only on success in solving the puzzle.

This may be made clearer by varying the plagiarism example. Suppose that in spite of my stated policy of failing anyone who plagiarizes, I am regularly lenient toward students who seem sufficiently repentant. Suppose further that I am regularly more lenient with attractive female students than with others. Or suppose that it is only redheads or wealthy students whom I fail. If such patterns develop, we can see that whether a student fails or not does not depend simply on being caught plagiarizing. Rather, part of the explanation of a particular student's being punished is that he or she is (or is not) an attractive female, redheaded or wealthy. In these instances, I think the plagiarizers who are punished have grounds for complaint, even though they were, by the announced standards, clearly guilty and deserving of punishment.

If this conclusion is correct, then doing justice is more complicated than van den Haag realizes. He asserts that it would be "wrong to treat everybody with equal injustice in preference to meting out justice at least to some." If my assessment of cases C and D is correct, however, it is better that everyone in those instances be treated "unjustly" than that only some get what they deserve. Whether one is treated justly or not depends on how others are treated and not solely on what one deserves.[8]

In fact, van den Haag implicitly concedes this point in an interesting footnote to his essay. In considering the question of whether capital punishment is a superior deterrent, van den Haag mentions that one could test the deterrent power of the death penalty by allowing executions for murders committed on Monday, Wednesday, and Friday, while setting life imprisonment as the maximum penalty for murders committed on other days. In noting the obstacles facing such an experiment, he writes:

> . . . it is not acceptable to our sense of justice that *people guilty of the same crime would get different punishments* and that the difference would be made to depend deliberately on *a factor irrelevant to the nature of the crime* or of the criminal. (emphasis added)[9]

Given his earlier remarks about the argument from arbitrariness, this is a rather extraordinary comment, for van den Haag concedes that the justice of a punishment is not solely determined by what an individual deserves but is also a function of how equally deserving persons are treated in general.

In his case, what he finds offensive is that there is no difference between what the Monday, Wednesday, Friday murderers deserve and what the Tuesday, Thursday, Saturday, and Sunday murderers deserve. Yet the morally irrelevant factor of date is decisive in determining the severity of the punishment. Van den Haag (quite rightly) cannot swallow this.

Yet van den Haag's example is exactly parallel to the situation described by opponents of the death penalty. For, surely, the race of the criminal or victim, the economic or social status of the criminal or victim, the location of the crime or trial and other such factors are as irrelevant to the gravity of the crime and the appropriate severity of the punishment as is the day of the week on which the crime is committed. It would be as outrageous for the severity of the punishment to depend on these

---

8. Using Feinberg's terminology, these can be described as cases in which the criteria of comparative and noncomparative justice conflict with one another. I am arguing that in these instances, the criteria of comparative justice take precedence. Although Feinberg does discuss such conflicts, it is unclear to me from his essay whether he would agree with this claim.

9. Van den Haag, "The Collapse of the Case Against Capital Punishment," p. 403, n. 12. (This important footnote does not appear in the shorter version of the paper.)

factors as it would be for it to depend on the day of the week on which the crime was committed.

In fact, it is more outrageous that death sentences depend on the former factors because a person can control the day of the week on which he murders in a way in which he cannot control his race or status. Moreover, we are committed to banishing the disabling effects of race and economic status from the law. Using the day of the week as a critical factor is at least not invidiously discriminatory, as it neither favors nor disfavors previously identifiable or disadvantaged groups.

In reply, one might contend that I have overlooked an important feature of van den Haag's example. He rejected the deterrence experiment not merely because the severity of punishment depended on irrelevant factors but also because the irrelevant factors were *deliberately* chosen as the basis of punishment. Perhaps it is the fact that irrelevant factors are deliberately chosen which makes van den Haag condemn the proposed experiment.

This is an important point. It certainly makes matters worse to decide deliberately to base life and death choices on irrelevant considerations. However, even if the decision is not deliberate, it remains a serious injustice if irrelevant considerations play this crucial role. Individuals might not even be aware of the influence of these factors. They might genuinely believe that their judgments are based entirely on relevant considerations. It might require painstaking research to discover the patterns underlying sentencing, but once they are known, citizens and policymakers must take them into consideration. Either the influence of irrelevant factors must be eradicated or, if we determine that this is impossible, we may have to alter our practices more radically.

This reasoning, of course, is just the reasoning identified with the *Furman* case. As Justice Douglas wrote:

> A law that stated that anyone making more than $50,000 would be exempt from the death penalty would plainly fall, as would a law that in terms said that blacks, those who never went beyond the fifth grade in school, those who make less than $3,000 a year, or those who were unpopular or unstable should be the only people executed. A law which in the overall view reaches the same result in practice has no more sanctity than a law which in terms provides the same.[10]

10. Reprinted in Bedau, pp. 255–56.

Does It Matter
if the Death Penalty
Is Arbitrariliy Administered?

The problem, in Douglas's view, was that the system left life and death decisions to the "uncontrolled discretion of judges or juries," leading to the unintended but nonetheless real result that death sentences were based on factors which had nothing to do with the nature of the crime.

What I want to stress here is that the arbitrariness and discrimination need not be purposeful or deliberate. We might discover, as critics allege, that racial prejudice is so deeply rooted in our society that prosecutors, juries, and judges cannot free themselves from prejudice when determining how severe a punishment for a crime should be. Furthermore, we might conclude that these tendencies cannot be eradicated, especially when juries are called upon to make subtle and complex assessments of cases in the light of confusing, semi-technical criteria. Hence, although no one *decides* that race will be a factor, we may *predict* that it will be a factor, and this knowledge must be considered in evaluating policies and institutions.

If factors *as irrelevant as* the day of the crime determine whether people shall live or die and if the influence of these factors is ineradicable, then we must conclude that we cannot provide a just system of punishment and even those who are guilty and deserving of the most severe punishments (like the Monday killers in van den Haag's experiment) will have a legitimate complaint that they have been treated unjustly.

I conclude, then, that the treatment of *classes* of people is relevant to determining the justice of punishments for *individuals* and van den Haag is wrong to dismiss the second form of the argument from arbitrariness. That argument succeeds in showing that capital punishment is unjust and thus provides a powerful reason for abolishing it.

V

Supporters of the death penalty might concede that serious questions of justice are raised by the influence of arbitrary factors and still deny that this shows that capital punishment ought to be abolished. They could argue that some degree of arbitrariness is present throughout the system of legal punishment, that it is unreasonable to expect our institutions to be perfect, and that acceptance of the argument from arbitrariness would commit us to abolishing all punishment.

In fact, van den Haag makes just these points in his essay. He writes:

The Constitution, though it enjoins us to minimize capriciousness, does not enjoin a standard of unattainable perfection or exclude penalties because that standard has not been attained. . . . I see no more merit in the attempt to persuade the courts to let all capital-crime defendants go free of capital punishment because some have wrongly escaped it than I see in an attempt to persuade the courts to let all burglars go because some have wrongly escaped imprisonment.[11]

It is an important feature of this objection that it could be made even by one who conceded the injustice of arbitrarily administered death sentences. Rather than agreeing that capital punishment should be abolished, however, this objection moves from the premise that the flaws revealed in capital punishment are shared by *all* punishments to the conclusion that we must either (a) reject all punishments (because of the influence of arbitrary factors on them) or (b) reject the idea that arbitrariness provides a sufficient ground for abolishing the death penalty.

Is there a way out of this dilemma for death penalty opponents?

I believe that there is. Opponents of the death penalty may continue to support other punishments, even though their administration also involves arbitrariness. This is not to suggest, of course, that we should be content with arbitrariness or discrimination in the imposition of any punishment.[12] Rather the point is to emphasize that the argument from arbitrariness counts against the death penalty with special force. There are two reasons for this.

First, death is a much more severe punishment than imprisonment. This is universally acknowledged by advocates and opponents of the death penalty alike. It is recognized in the law by the existence of special procedures for capital cases. Death obliterates the person, depriving him or her of life and thereby, among other things, depriving him or her of any further rights of legal appeal, should new facts be discovered or new understandings of the law be reached. In this connection, it is worth recalling that many people were executed and are now dead because they were tried and sentenced under the pre-*Furman* laws which allowed the "uncontrolled discretion of judges and juries."

11. Van den Haag, "The Collapse of the Case Against Capital Punishment," p. 397.

12. For a discussion of the role of discrimination throughout the criminal justice system and recommendations for reform, see American Friends Service Committee, *Struggle for Justice* (New York: Hill and Wang, 1971).

*Does It Matter
if the Death Penalty
Is Arbitrarily Administered?*

Second, though death is the most severe punishment in our legal system, it appears to be unnecessary for protecting citizens, while punishments generally are thought to promote our safety and well-being. The contrast between death and other punishments can be brought out by asking two questions. What would happen if we abolished all punishments? And, what would happen if we abolished the death penalty?

Most of us believe that if all punishments were abolished, there would be social chaos, a Hobbesian war of all against all. To do away with punishment entirely would be to do away with the criminal law and the system of constraints which it supports. Hence, even though the system is not a just one, we believe that we must live with it and strive to make it as fair as possible. On the other hand, if we abolish capital punishment, there is reason to believe that nothing will happen. There is simply no compelling evidence that capital punishment prevents murders better than long-term prison sentences. Indeed, some evidence even suggests that capital punishment increases the number of murders. While I cannot review the various empirical studies of these questions here, I think it can plausibly be asserted that the results of abolishing punishment generally would be disastrous, while the results of abolishing capital punishment are likely to be insignificant.[13]

I conclude then that the argument from arbitrariness has special force against the death penalty because of its extreme severity and its likely uselessness. The arbitrariness of other punishments may be outweighed by their necessity, but the same cannot be said for capital punishment.

VI

In closing, I would like to comment briefly on one other charge made by van den Haag, the charge that the argument from arbitrariness is a

13. In support of the superior deterrent power of the death penalty, van den Haag cites I. Ehrlich, "The Deterrent Effect of Capital Punishment: A Question of Life and Death," *American Economic Review* 65 (1975): 397–417. Two reviews of the evidence on deterrence, both of which criticize Ehrlich at length, are Hans Zeisel, "The Deterrent Effect of the Death Penalty: Facts v. Faith," and Lawrence Klein et al., "The Deterrent Effect of Capital Punishment: An Assessment of the Evidence." (Both of these articles appear in Bedau.) The thesis that executions increase the number of homicides is defended by W. Bowers and G. Pierce in "Deterrence or Brutalization: What is the Effect of Executions?," *Crime & Delinquency* 26 (1980): 453–84.

My thanks are due to Hugo Bedau, William Bowers, Richard Daynard, and Ernest van den Haag for reactions to my thinking about the death penalty. I would especially like to "sham" argument because it is not the real reason why people oppose the death penalty. Those who use this argument, van den Haag claims, would oppose capital punishment even if it were not arbitrarily imposed.

At one level, this charge is doubly fallacious. The suggestion of dishonesty introduced by the word "sham" makes the argument into an *ad hominem*. In addition, the charge suggests that there cannot be more than one reason in support of a view. There are many situations in which we offer arguments and yet would not change our view if the argument were refuted, not because the argument is a sham, but because we have additional grounds for what we believe.

Nonetheless, van den Haag's charge may indicate a special difficulty for the argument from arbitrariness, for the argument may well strike people as artificial and legalistic. Somehow, one may feel that it does not deal with the real issues—the wrongness of killing, deterrence, and whether murderers deserve to die.

Part of the problem, I think, is that our ordinary moral thinking involves specific forms of conduct or general rules of personal behavior. The argument from arbitrariness deals with a feature of an *institution*, and thinking about institutions seems to raise difficulties for many people. Believing that an individual murderer deserves to die for a terrible crime, they infer that there ought to be capital punishment, without attending to all of the implications for other individuals which will follow from setting up this practice.

The problem is similar to one that John Stuart Mill highlighted in *On Liberty*. For many people, the fact that an act is wrong is taken to be sufficient ground for its being made illegal. Mill argued against the institutionalization of all moral judgments, and his argument still strikes many people as odd. If the act is wrong, they ask, shouldn't we do everything in our power to stop it? What they fail to appreciate, however, are all of the implications of institutionalizing such judgments.

Likewise, people ask, If so and so deserves to die, shouldn't we empower the state to execute him? The problem, however—or one of many problems—is that institutionalizing this judgment about desert yields a system which makes neither moral nor legal sense. Moreover, it perpetuates and exacerbates the liabilities and disadvantages which unjustly befall many

thank Ursula Bentele for helpful discussions and access to unpublished research, Nelson Lande for spirited comments (both philosophical and grammatical), and John Troyer, whose keen and persistent criticisms of my views forced me to write this article.

of our fellow citizens. These are genuine and serious problems, and those who have raised them in the context of the capital punishment debate have both exposed troubling facts about the actual workings of the criminal law and illuminated the difficulties of acting justly. Most importantly, they have produced a powerful argument against authorizing the state to use death as a punishment for crime.

ERNEST VAN DEN HAAG   Refuting Reiman and
                          Nathanson

I shall consider Jeffrey Reiman's view of the punishment offenders deserve before turning to his moral scruples, alleged to justify lesser punishments, and to the discriminatory distribution of the death penalty which Stephen Nathanson stresses.

Reiman believes the death penalty is deserved by some murderers, but should never be imposed. Moral scruples should preclude it. If the punishment deserved according to the *lex talionis* is morally repugnant, we may impose less, provided the suffering imposed *in lieu* of what is deserved is proportional to the suffering inflicted on the crime victim. However, suffering exceeding that of his victim can never be deserved by the offender; to impose it would be "unjust for the same reasons that make punishment of the innocent unjust."[1]

MEASUREMENT

How do we know whether the punitive suffering to be imposed on the offender is less or "equal to that which he imposed on the victim" so as not to exceed what he deserves?[2] Cardinal and interpersonal measurement of suffering would be required to find out. Although ordinal measurement is possible in some cases, the cardinal and interpersonal meas-

1. See Jeffrey H. Reiman, "Justice, Civilization, and the Death Penalty: Answering van den Haag," *Philosophy & Public Affairs* 14, no. 2: 128. Unless otherwise noted, all my quotations are taken from Reiman's article.

2. This question arises only when the literal *lex talionis* is abandoned—as Reiman proposes to do, for good reason—in favor of the proportional retribution he suggests. How, by the way, would we punish a skyjacker? Summing up the suffering of all the skyjacked passengers? What about the damage to air traffic?

urement required by Reiman's scheme is not.[3] How many days must the kidnapper be confined, to suffer as much, but no more, than his victim? If he kept his victim three days, are three days of confinement correct? Or three hundred? Or one thousand? If he half-starved his victim, should we do as much to him, or, how do we commute starvation into additional time?

Punishment for kidnapping can be, within limits, of the same kind as the crime, although all we can actually do to conform to Reiman's prescription even here is to confine for a longer time the kidnapper who kept his victim for a longer time. We have no way of comparing the victim's suffering with the victimizer's, and to limit the latter accordingly. Execution too bears some similarity to the murderer's crime. But confinement? How do we make it commensurate with murder? What about the punishment for assault, burglary, or rape? How do we compare the pain suffered by the victims with the pain to be imposed on the offender by confinement, to make sure that the latter not exceed the former? There is no way of applying Reiman's criterion of desert. Fortunately, we don't need to.

ACTUAL DESERT

Even if, somehow, we knew that three days' confinement inflicts as much pain as his victim suffered on the kidnapper who kept his victim three days, we would feel that the kidnapper deserves much more punishment. That feeling would be appropriate. The offender imposed undeserved suffering on his victim. Why should society not impose undeserved (in Reiman's terminology) suffering on the offender? It would be undeserved only if one accepts Reiman's flawed view of retribution, for, in addition to whatever he deserves for what his victim suffered, the offender also deserves punishment for breaking the law, for imposing undeserved, unlawful suffering on someone. Retributionism of any kind cannot authorize less, despite Reiman's view that suffering imposed on the criminal is unjust when it exceeds the suffering of his victim.

Although occasionally he indicates awareness of the social harm caused by crime and even of the social function of punishment, Reiman treats crimes as though involving but a relationship between victim and offender

3. The order of punishments is notoriously hard to coordinate with the order of crimes: even when punishments are homogenous, crimes are not.

implemented by judicial authorities.[4] From this faulty premise he infers
that retribution should not exceed the harm done to the victim, an idea
derived from the *lex talionis*. But that primitive rule was meant to limit
the revenge private parties could exact for what was regarded as private
harm. The function of the rule was to guard against social disruption by
unlimited and indefinitely extended vengeance.

Crimes are no longer regarded merely as private harms. Retribution
for the suffering of the individual victims, however much deserved, is
not punishment any more than restitution is. Punishment must vindicate
the disrupted public order, the violated law, must punish for the social
harm done. If my neighbor is burglarized or robbed, he is harmed. But
we all must take costly precautions, and we all feel and are threatened:
crime harms society as it harms victims. Hence, punishment must, whenever possible, impose pain believed to exceed the pain suffered by the
individual victim of crime. No less is deserved. Punishment must be
determined by the total gravity of the crime, the social as well as the
individual harm, and by the need to deter from the harmful crime. There
are ordinal limits to deserved punishments, but cardinal upper limits are
set only by harm, habit and sentiment—not by victim suffering.

Let me now turn to the moral scruples which should lead us to reduce
punishment to less than what is deserved in some cases. I share some
of Reiman's scruples: although he deserves it, I do not want to see the
torturer tortured. Other scruples strike me as unjustified.

POVERTY AND CULPABILITY

Reiman believes "that the vast majority of murders in America are a
predictable response to the frustrations and disabilities of impoverished
social circumstances" which could be, but are not remedied because
"others in America benefit," wherefore we have "no right to exact the
full cost . . . from our murderers until we have done everything possible
to rectify the conditions that produce their crimes."[5] Murder here seems
to become the punishment for the sins of the wealthy. According to

4. Perhaps Reiman's excessive reliance on the Hegelian justification of retribution (to
vindicate the equality of victim and offender) or on the Kantian version (to vindicate the
rationality of both) is to blame.

5. Reiman does not say here that murder deserves less than the death penalty, but only
that "the vast majority of murderers" deserve less because impoverished. However, wealthy
murderers can be fully culpable, so that we may "exact the full cost" from them.

Reiman, "the vast majority" of current murderers are not fully culpable, since part of the blame for their crimes must be placed on those who fail to "rectify the conditions that produce their crimes."

I grant that certain social conditions predictably produce crime more readily than others. Does it follow that those who commit crimes in criminogenic conditions are less responsible, or blameworthy, than they would be if they did not live in these conditions? Certainly not. Predictability does not reduce responsibility. Reiman remains responsible for his predictable argument. Culpability is reduced only when the criminal's ability to control his actions, or to realize that they are wrong, is abnormally impaired. If not, the social conditions in which the criminal lives have no bearing on his responsibility for his acts. Conditions, such as poverty, just or unjust, may increase the temptation to commit crimes. But poverty is neither a necessary nor a sufficient condition for crime, and thus certainly not a coercive one. If there is no compulsion, temptation is no excuse. The law is meant to restrain, and to hold responsible, those tempted to break it. It need not restrain those not tempted, and it cannot restrain those who are unable to control their actions.

Reiman's claim, that even "though criminals can control their actions, when crimes are predictable responses to unjust circumstances, then those who benefit from and do not remedy those conditions bear some responsibility for the crimes and thus the criminals cannot be held *wholly* responsible for them . . ." seems quite unjustified. Those responsible for unjust conditions must be blamed for them,[6] but not for crimes that are "predictable responses to unjust circumstances," if the respondents could have avoided these crimes, as most people living in unjust conditions do.

If crimes are political, that is, address not otherwise remediable "unjust circumstances," they may be held to be morally, if not legally, excusable, on some occasions.[7] But the criminal's moral, let alone legal, responsibility for a crime which he committed for personal gain and could have avoided, is not diminished merely because he lives in unjust circumstances, and his crime was a predictable response to them. Suppose the predictable

6. Who are they? They are not necessarily the beneficiaries, as Reiman appears to believe. I benefit from rent control, which I think unjust to my landlord, but I'm not responsible for it. I may benefit from low prices for services or goods, without being responsible for them, or for predictable criminal responses to them. Criminals benefit from the unjust exclusionary rules of our courts. Are they to blame for these rules?

7. See my *Political Violence & Civil Disobedience, passim* (New York: Harper & Row, 1972) for a more detailed argument.

response to unjust wealth were drunken driving, or rape. Would his wealth excuse the driver or the rapist? Why should poverty, if wealth would not?[8]

Crime is produced by many circumstances, "just" and "unjust." The most just society may have no less crime than the least just (unless "just" is defined circularly as the absence of crime). Tracing crime to causal circumstances is useful and may help us to control it. Suggesting that they *eo ipso* are excuses confuses causality with nonresponsibility. *Tout comprendre ce n'est pas tout pardonner*, Mme. de Staël's followers to the contrary notwithstanding. Excuses require specific circumstances that diminish the actor's control over his actions.

Since "unjust circumstances" do not reduce the responsibility of criminals for their acts, I shall refrain from discussing whether Reiman's circumstances really are unjust, or merely unequal, and whether they do exist because someone benefits from them and could be eliminated if the alleged beneficiaries wished to eliminate them. I am not sure that unjust circumstances always can be remedied, without causing worse injustices. Nor do I share Reiman's confidence that we know what social justice is, or how to produce it.

CIVILIZATION

Reiman thinks that the death penalty is not civilized, because it involves the total subjugation of one person to others, as does slavery, or prostitution.[9]

Whereas slavery usually is not voluntary, the murderer runs the risk of execution voluntarily: he could avoid it by not murdering. I find nothing uncivilized in imposing the risk of subjugation and death on those who decide to murder.

Nota bene: Persons who act with diminished capacity, during moments of passion, are usually convicted of manslaughter rather than murder.

---

8. Suppose unjust wealth tends to corrupt, and unjust poverty does not. Would the wealthy be less to blame for their crimes?

9. Prostitution does not involve total subjugation and is voluntary. In an ambiguous footnote Reiman asserts that it is the perception of prostitution as subjugation that makes it offensive. But this perception, derived from pulp novels more than from reality, is not what makes the voluntary act offensive. Rather, it is the sale of sex as a fungible service, divorced from affection and depersonalized that is offensive. Anyway, when something is offensive because misperceived it is not the thing that is offensive.

Even if convicted of murder, they are not sentenced to death; only if the court believes that the murderer did have a choice, and intended to murder, can he receive the death sentence.

Reiman refers to research finding a brutalization effect, such that executions lead to more homicides. The data are unpersuasive. Some researchers find an increase, some a decrease, of homicides immediately after an execution.[10] Either effect seem ephemeral, involving bunching, rather than changes in the annual homicide rate.

To argue more generally, as Reiman also does, that capital punishment is inconsistent with the advancement of civilization, is to rely on arbitrary definitions of "advancement" and "civilization" for a circular argument. If civilization actually had "advanced" in the direction Reiman, quoting Durkheim, thinks it has, why is that a reason for not preferring "advancement" in some other, perhaps opposite, direction? I cannot find the *moral* (normative) argument in Reiman's description.

DETERRENCE

The death penalty should be retained if abolition would endanger us, Reiman believes. But he does not believe that abolition would. He may be right. However, some of his arguments seem doubtful.

He thinks that whatever marginal deterrent effect capital punishment has, if it has any, is not needed, since life imprisonment provides all the deterrence needed. How can it be ascertained that punishment x deters "everyone who can be deterred" so that punishment x-plus would not deter additional persons? I can see no way to determine this, short of experiments we are unlikely to undertake. Reiman may fear life imprisonment as much, or more, than death. Couldn't someone else fear death more and be insufficiently deterred by life imprisonment?

I cannot prove conclusively that the death penalty deters more than life imprisonment, or that the added deterrence is needed. Reiman cannot prove conclusively that the added deterrence is not needed, or produced. I value the life of innocents more than the life of murderers. Indeed, I value the life of murderers negatively. Wherefore I prefer over- to under-protection. I grant this is a preference.

10. David P. Phillips, "The Deterrent Effect of Capital Punishment: New Evidence on an Old Controversy," *The American Journal of Sociology* (July 1980). For further discussion see loc. cit., July 1982. See also Lester, *Executions as a Deterrent to Homicides* 44 *Psychological Rep.* 562 (1979).

Self-Defense

Reiman also believes that murderers who are not deterred by the risk
they run because their victims may defend themselves with guns will
not be deterred by the risk of execution. This seems unrealistic. Murderers rarely run much risk from self-defense since they usually ambush
unsuspecting victims.

Torture

On my reasoning, Reiman contends, torture should be used, since it may
deter more than execution; or else, even if more deterrent than alternatives, the death penalty should be abolished as torture was: "either we
must abolish the electric chair or reinstitute the rack," is his colorful
phrase. But there is a difference. I do not oppose torture as undeserved
or nondeterrent (although I doubt that the threat of the rack, or of anything adds deterrence to the threat of execution), but simply as repulsive.
Death is not; nor is the death penalty. Perhaps repulsiveness is not enough
to exclude the rack. If Reiman should convince me that the threat of the
rack adds a great deal of deterrence to the threat of execution he might
persuade me to overcome my revulsion and to favor the rack as well. It
certainly can be deserved.

Moral Theory

In *The Death Penalty: A Debate*[11] I noted that only when punishments
are based not on retribution alone, but also on deterrence, they rest on
a theory, that is, on a correlation of recurrent facts to a prediction: punishment x will, *ceteris paribus*, reduce the rate of crime y by 10%, and
x-plus will bring a reduction of 20%. Reiman censures me for using
"theory" when I should have written "empirical theory." He is right.
Further, deterrence does not morally justify any punishment, unless one
has first accepted the moral desirability of reducing crime, and the tol-
erability of the costs. I should have pointed that out. Finally, I did not
mean to deny that there are moral theories to justify retribution. They
strike me as more dependent on feeling than empirical theories are. More
to the point, unlike deterrence theory, justice theories are not meant to
predict the effect of various punishments, and are not capable of deter-

11. Ernest van den Haag and John P. Conrad (New York: Plenum Press, 1983).

mining, except ordinally, what these punishments should be, although they can help to justify the distribution of punishments.[12]

MODES OF EXECUTION

As Reiman stresses, the spectacle of execution is not pretty. Nor is surgery. Wherefore both should be attended only by the necessary personnel.[13] I do not find Reiman's aesthetic or moral scruples sufficient to preclude execution or surgery. However, I share his view that lethal injections are particularly unpleasant, not so much because of the subjugation which disturbs him, but because of the veterinary air. (We put animals "to sleep" when sick or inconvenient.) In contrast, shooting strikes me as dignified; it is painless too and probably the best way of doing what is necessary.

LIFE IMPRISONMENT

Reiman proposes life imprisonment without parole instead of execution. Although less feared, and therefore likely to be less deterrent, actual lifelong imprisonment strikes me as more cruel than execution even if perceived as less harsh. Its comparative cruelty was stressed already by Cesare Bonesana, Marchese di Beccaria, and by many others since.

Life imprisonment also becomes undeserved over time. A person who committed a murder when twenty years old and is executed within five years—far too long and cruel a delay in my opinion—is, when executed, still the person who committed the murder for which he is punished. His identity changes little in five years. However, a person who committed a murder when he was twenty years old and is kept in prison when sixty years old, is no longer the same person who committed the crime for which he is still being punished. The sexagenarian is unlikely to have much in common with the twenty-year-old for whose act he is being punished; his legal identity no longer reflects reality. Personality and actual identity are not that continuous. In effect, we punish an innocent

---

12. See my *Punishing Criminals* (New York: Basic Books, 1975) which is superseded to some extent by the views expressed in my "Criminal Law as a Threat System 73, *Journal of Criminal Law and Criminology* 2 (1982).

13. Both spectacles when graphically shown may also give rise to undesirable imitations or inspirations.

sexagenarian who does not deserve punishment, instead of a guilty twenty-year-old who did. This spectacle should offend our moral sensibilities more than the deserved execution of the twenty-year-old. Those who deserve the death penalty should be executed while they deserve it, not kept in prison when they no longer deserve any punishment.

DISCRIMINATION

Disagreeing with the Supreme Court, Stephen Nathanson believes that the death penalty still is distributed in an excessively capricious and discriminatory manner. He thinks capital punishment is "unjust" because poor blacks are more likely to be sentenced to death than wealthy whites. Further, blacks who murdered whites are more likely to be executed than those who murdered blacks.[14] This last discrimination has been thrown into relief recently by authors who seem to be under the impression that they have revealed a new form of discrimination against black murderers. They have not. The practice invidiously discriminates against black victims of murder, who are not as fully, or as often, vindicated as white victims are. However, discrimination against a class of victims, although invidious enough, does not amount to discrimination against their victimizers. The discrimination against black victims, the lesser punishment given their murderers, actually favors black murderers, since most black victims are killed by black murderers. Stephen Nathanson and Jeffrey Reiman appear to think that they have captured additional discrimination against black defendants. They are wrong.

Neither the argument from discrimination against black victims, nor the argument from discrimination against black murderers, has any bearing on the guilt of black murderers, or on the punishment they deserve.

Invidious discrimination is never defensible. Yet I do not see wherein it, in Reiman's words, "would constitute a separate and powerful argument for abolition," or does make the death penalty "unjust" for those discriminatorily selected to suffer it, as Stephen Nathanson believes.[15] If we grant that some (even all) murderers of blacks, or, some (even all) white and rich murderers, escape the death penalty, how does that reduce

14. Despite some doubts, I am here granting the truth of both hypotheses.

15. Stephen Nathanson, "Does It Matter if the Death Penalty Is Arbitrarily Administered?" *Philosophy & Public Affairs* 14, no. 2 (this issue). Unless otherwise noted, all further quotations are taken from Nathanson's article.

the guilt of murderers of whites, or of black and poor murderers, so that they should be spared execution too? Guilt is personal. No murderer becomes less guilty, or less deserving of punishment, because another murderer was punished leniently, or escaped punishment altogether. We should try our best to bring every murderer to justice. But if one got away with murder wherein is that a reason to let anyone else get away? A group of murderers does not become less deserving of punishment because another equally guilty group is not punished, or punished less. We can punish only a very small proportion of all criminals. Unavoidably they are selected accidentally. We should reduce this accidentality as much as possible but we cannot eliminate it.[16]

EQUAL INJUSTICE AND UNEQUAL JUSTICE

Reiman and Nathanson appear to prefer equal injustice—letting all get away with murder if some do—to unequal justice: punishing some guilty offenders according to desert, even if others get away. Equal justice is best, but unattainable. Unequal justice is our lot in this world. It is the only justice we can ever have, for not all murderers can be apprehended or convicted, or sentenced equally in different courts. We should constantly try to bring every offender to justice. But meanwhile unequal justice is the only justice we have, and certainly better than equal injustice—giving no murderer the punishment his crime deserves.

MORE DISCRIMINATION

Nathanson insists that some arbitrary selections among those equally guilty are not "just." He thinks that selecting only bearded speeders for ticketing, allowing the cleanshaven to escape, is unjust. Yet the punishment of the bearded speeders is not unjust. The escape of the cleanshaven ones is. I never maintained that a discriminatory distribution is just—only that it is irrelevant to the guilt and deserved punishment of those actually guilty.

16. Discrimination or capriciousness is (when thought to be avoidable and excessive) sometimes allowed by the courts as a defense. Apparently this legal device is meant to reduce discrimination and capriciousness. But those spared because selected discriminatorily for punishment do not become any less deserving of it as both Reiman and Nathanson think, although not punishing them is used as a means to foster the desired equality in the distributions of punishments.